Michael Brenner is Professor of International Affairs at the University of Pittsburgh, USA. His writings on US foreign policy and European–American relations include recent articles in *Foreign Policy, International Affairs, Politique Etrangère, International Politik, Survival*, and a monograph, *Europa und de vereinigten Staaten: Amerikanische Sicherheitspolitik in den neuziger Jahren*, with Phil Williams, for the Konrad Adenauer Stiftung. He is author of *Nuclear Energy and Non-Proliferation, The Political Economy of International Monetary Reform, The Functionalist Theory of European Integration* and editor of *Multilateralism and Western Strategy*. Professor Brenner has held teaching and research positions at the Brookings Institution, Cornell University, Harvard University, and MIT. He has been a consultant to the US Department of Defense and the Foreign Service Institute.

NATO AND COLLECTIVE SECURITY

Also by Michael Brenner

MULTILATERALISM AND WESTERN STRATEGY (*editor*)

NUCLEAR ENERGY AND NON-PROLIFERATION

THE FUNCTIONALIST THEORY OF EUROPEAN INTEGRATION

THE POLITICAL ECONOMY OF INTERNATIONAL MONETARY REFORM

NATO and Collective Security

Edited by

Michael Brenner
Professor of International Affairs
University of Pittsburgh
USA

First published in Great Britain 1998 by
MACMILLAN PRESS LTD
Houndmills, Basingstoke, Hampshire RG21 6XS and London
Companies and representatives throughout the world

A catalogue record for this book is available from the British Library.

ISBN 0–333–71113–0

First published in the United States of America 1998 by
ST. MARTIN'S PRESS, INC.,
Scholarly and Reference Division,
175 Fifth Avenue, New York, N.Y. 10010

ISBN 0–312–21007–8

Library of Congress Cataloging-in-Publication Data
NATO and collective security / edited by Michael Brenner.
  p. cm.
Includes bibliographical references and index.
ISBN 0–312–21007–8 (cloth)
1. North Atlantic Treaty Organization. 2. Security,
International. I. Brenner, Michael J.
JZ5930.N38 1997
355'.031'091821—dc21   97-28033
                                                     CIP

Selection and editorial matter © Michael Brenner 1998
Text © Macmillan Press Ltd 1998

All rights reserved. No reproduction, copy or transmission of this publication may be made without written permission.

No paragraph of this publication may be reproduced, copied or transmitted save with written permission or in accordance with the provisions of the Copyright, Designs and Patents Act 1988, or under the terms of any licence permitting limited copying issued by the Copyright Licensing Agency, 90 Tottenham Court Road, London W1P 9HE.

Any person who does any unauthorised act in relation to this publication may be liable to criminal prosecution and civil claims for damages.

The authors have asserted their rights to be identified as the authors of this work in accordance with the Copyright, Designs and Patents Act 1988.

This book is printed on paper suitable for recycling and made from fully managed and sustained forest sources.

10 9   8   7   6   5   4   3   2   1
07 06 05 04 03 02 01 00 99 98

Printed in Great Britain by
The Ipswich Book Company Ltd
Ipswich, Suffolk

Contents

Acknowledgements		vi
Notes on the Contributors		vii
Glossary		ix
1	Introduction *Michael Brenner*	1
2	Britain *Michael Clarke*	6
3	France *Frédéric Bozo*	39
4	Germany *Michael Meimeth*	81
5	Italy *Mario Zucconi*	116
6	The United States *Michael Brenner*	139
7	Strategic Outlook: Compatibilities and Incompatibilities *Hanns W. Maull*	222
8	Interface between NATO/WEU and UN/OSCE *Jean Klein*	249
9	Reconciliation of Western Security Institutions *Mario Zucconi*	278
	Conclusion *Michael Brenner*	288
Index		307

Acknowledgements

This study was financed with a grant from the Ford Foundation's Program on Peace and Security. There, Geoffrey Wiseman gave the project his critical, sympathetic attention. Supplementary assistance was provided by NATO's Office of Press and Information. In particular, Ms Karen Aguilar, the US liaison officer, offered the encouragement and support that enabled the research team to expand its working meetings. We wish to thank the Institut Français des Relations Internationales (IFRI) for its hospitality in hosting two of the meetings. A special word of appreciation goes to Mme Cécille Hua-Lafèvre who handled the practical arrangements.

Mr T. M. Farmiloe and his staff at Macmillan were both responsive to the idea of publishing the project's results and the model of professionalism in bringing to fruition this transatlantic enterprise. A special word of appreciation goes to John M. Smith, Senior Book Editor, and Annabelle Buckley, Commissioning Editor. Burkart Holzner, Director of the University Center for International Studies at the University of Pittsburgh, helped expedite that process. My friend and colleague, Phil Williams, Director of the Ridgway Center for International Security Studies, was a source of valuable counsel and moral support throughout.

The burden of preparing the manuscript for publication was handled with skill and unflagging patience by Ms Kendall Stanley, and most especially Ms Kathy Rud.

The editor also had the dedicated help of two exceptionally able students at the Graduate School of Public and International Affairs: Matthew Dixon and Susan Masse.

Notes on the Contributors

Frédéric Bozo is associate professor at the Université Marne-la-Vallée where he teaches contemporary history and international relations. He is a senior research fellow at the Institut Français des Relations Internationales (IFRI) where his work focuses on European security issues and transatlantic relations. He is the author of *La France et l'OTAN: De la Guerre Froide au Nouvel Ordre Européen* (1991); *Deux Stratégies pour l'Europe: De Gaulle, les Etats-Unis et l'Alliance Atlantique 1958–1969* (1996); and *La Politique Etrangère de la France depuis 1945* (1997).

Michael Brenner is Professor of International Affairs at the University of Pittsburgh. His writings on US foreign policy and European–American relations include recent articles in *Foreign Policy, International Affairs, Politique Étrangère, International Politik* and *Survival*; and a monograph, *Europa und de vereinigten Staaten: Amerikanische Sicherheitspolitik in den neuziger Jahren*, with Phil Williams, for the Konrad Adenauer Stiftung. He is author of *Nuclear Energy and Non-Proliferation* (1981), *The Political Economy of International Monetary Reform* (1976), *The Functionalist Theory of European Integration* (1970), and editor of *Multilateralism and Western Strategy* (1994). Professor Brenner has held teaching and research positions at the Brookings Institution, Cornell University, Harvard University, and MIT. He has been a consultant to the US Department of Defense and the Foreign Service Institute.

Michael Clarke is Professor of Defence Studies and Director of the Centre for Defence Studies at King's College in London. He is the author of *British External Policy-making in the 1990s* (1992), the editor of the *Brassey's Defence Yearbook* (1995), and writes numerous articles on British defence and security policy.

Jean Klein is Professor of International Relations at the University of Paris–Sorbonne and Senior Fellow at the Institut Français des Relations Internationales. From 1968 until 1979 he was a Research Fellow of the Centre National des Recherches Scientifiques (CNRS). He also has taught at l'Ecole Militaire (Saint Cyr) and l'Ecole Polytechnique. He is the author of *l'Enterprise du Désarmement en Europe* (1986), and *Maitrise des Armements et Désarmement: Les Accords Conclus depuis 1945* (1991).

Hanns W. Maull holds the Chair for Foreign Policy and International Relations at the University of Trier in Germany. He has taught at the Universities of Munich and Eichstaett in Germany, and as Visiting Professor of International Relations at the Johns Hopkins School of Advanced International Studies Bologna Center. Hanns W. Maull has authored and edited more than a dozen books, and has contributed widely to journals in German, English, French, Italian and Japanese, including *Foreign Affairs, International Affairs, Politique Etrangère, Europa Archiv* and *Chuo Koron.*

Michael Meimeth is a member of the Department of Political Science at the Universitat des Saarlandes, Germany. He had held previous positions at the Universities of Cologne and Trier. He is a Fellow at the Stiftung Wissenschaft und Politik, Ebenhausen and the Research Institute of the Konrad-Adenauer-Foundation. He is author of *Frankreichs Entspannungspolitik der 70er Jahre: Zwischen Status quo Sicherheitspolitik nach dem Ende des Ost-West-Konflikts* (1996).

Mario Zucconi is Professor at the University of Urbino and Visiting Professor at the Johns Hopkins Bologna Center. He is founder and former director of the Centro Studi di Politica Internazionale (Rome). He is the editor of *The International Response to the Conflict in the Former Yugoslavia: Reorganizing Multilateralism after the Cold War* (1997).

Glossary

ACE	Allied Command Europe
AFSOUTH	Allied Forces Southern Europe
APC	Atlantic Partnership Council
ARRC	ACE Rapid Reaction Corps
CD	Christian Democratic Party (Italy)
CFE	Conventional Forces in Europe (Treaty 1990)
CFSP	Common Foreign and Security Policy (European Union)
CIS	Commonwealth of Independent States
CJTF	Combined Joint Task Force
CPC	Conflict Prevention Center (OSCE)
CSCM	Conference for Security and Cooperation in the Mediterranean
CSU	Christian Social Union (Germany)
EMU	Economic and Monetary Union
ESDI	European Security and Defence Identity
EU	European Union
FDP	Free Democratic Party (Germany)
HQBHC	Headquarters Bosnia-Herzegovina Command (NATO)
IFOR	NATO Implementation Force (Bosnia)
IGC	Inter-Governmental Conference (Europe)
NAC	North Atlantic Council
NACC	North Atlantic Cooperation Council
NATO	North Atlantic Treaty Organization
NORTHAG	NATO's Northern Army Group
OSCE	Organization for Security and Cooperation in Europe
PCI	Italian Communist Party
PDS	Democratic Party of the Left (Italy)
PfP	Partnership for Peace (NATO)
SACEUR	Supreme Allied Commander Europe (NATO)
SACLANT	Supreme Allied Commander Atlantic
SFOR	Stabilization Force (Bosnia)
SPD	Social Democratic Party (Germany)
UN	United Nations
UNPROFOR	UN Protection Force (Bosnia)

UNSC	UN Security Council
UNSCR	UN Security Council Resolution
WEU	Western European Union

1 Introduction
Michael Brenner

The post-Cold War project of revamping the Atlantic Alliance is more than an exercise in structural engineering. Reform of NATO's military organization, force deployments, contingency plans and command arrangements has been extensive. Expansion of membership, too, is now underway. Those steps, taken together, significantly affect the Alliance's readiness for undertaking missions different from those that had shaped it during the era of East–West confrontation. To evaluate fully their value and consequence, internal reform must be placed in the wider strategic context created by the political upheavals since 1989. It is the West as a political community that is challenged by the opportunities created in the wake of Communism's demise – not just NATO the alliance.

A new chapter has been opened in the political history of Europe and of the transatlantic community. The West's stunning triumph in the Cold War was remarkable for its erstwhile enemy's voluntary retirement from the field of combat. Just as striking, and potentially more significant, was the Soviet Union's shedding of an antithetical ideology, along with the autocratic system it sustained – yielding Moscow's empire in the process.

The successor regimes throughout Eastern Europe and the former USSR now profess the doctrines of democracy and free enterprise. Liberalism's ascendancy across the continent is accompanied by the rejection of *realpolitik* as the standard of state behaviour – the former Yugoslavia being the glaring exception. Near-universal espousal of these enlightened creeds carries the possibility that habits of cooperation, institutionalized and buttressed by emergent civil societies, could lead to an extension of the West's own Kantian law community. The West's unprecedented achievement in constituting that community is a landmark that figures all the more prominently on the landscape of global politics now that it stands without serious challenge. The success of the liberal democracies in subordinating conflict to constructive engagement is as important, and distinguishing, a feature of the postwar world as the Cold War – and a more enduring one. An historic opportunity seemingly exists to build a pan-continental security community on the same principles.

Formalizing the appropriate codes of conduct and inculcating the values that justify them is a formidable project. Its implications extend even beyond Europe. For it is there that the reconciliation of the former antagonists in common adhesion to tolerant liberal beliefs will or will not occur; and there that a crucial test is taking place of the proposition that the concept of reciprocated good intentions among countries has general applicability. If post-Cold War security conditions encourage us to visualize a lasting break from the logic of power politics, then we must contemplate a revision of existing security structures. Collective self-defence, embodied in NATO, logically should be complemented (if not superseded) by some form of collective security. That proposition provides the basis for this study.

Its twin premises are: (1) the effectiveness of any type of collective security system in Europe requires that the North Atlantic Alliance retain its integrity and remain competent to act either in concert with the United Nations (and the Organization for Security and Cooperation in Europe), or under their aegis; and (2) ensuring the Alliance's capacity for action depends on maintaining a unity of agreed purpose while developing methods of decision and operation suited to a more egalitarian partnership. The contributors set out to analyse how the dual processes of devising viable mechanisms for operationalizing collective security on an undivided continent, and – at the same time – of reconstituting while reorientating Western defence bodies, intersect. Perfecting multilateralism among the Atlantic partners is a companion enterprise to enhancing the effectiveness and authority of the United Nations' (and OSCE's) multilateral security missions. With the demise of the bipolar system, Europe's security depends on making both forms of multilateralism work, and work together. This is the one undisputable moral to be drawn from the experience of Yugoslavia.

The record since 1989 shows, however, that the political evolution of post-Cold War Europe – and all that depends upon it – is problematic. The first years of the new era have made it abundantly clear that a common Western strategy and a concerted diplomacy are imperative to secure the West's and the world's stake in Europe's concord and stability. But they are not to be taken for granted. Yugoslavia in particular brought home the lessons that order in a reunited Europe is not wholly divisible, and that Western incoherence belies its implicit claim to be mentor and monitor of the new Europe. The Western powers' collective shortcomings there carried a heavy cost in the ineffectiveness of multilateral diplomacy, lost respect for collective security bodies, and lost control over a potentially turbulent continent.

Another feature of the experience in Yugoslavia stands out: the mutual dependency of NATO's politico-military capabilities, on the one hand, and the United Nations' 'authoritativeness' on the other. The world organization has the unique authority to mandate collective security operations that carry international legitimacy. It is deficient, though, in two attributes essential to their success: a competent military organization, and the ability to generate popular approval for the activation of nationally controlled armed forces. This complementarity in the deployment of military force is paralleled by the mutual reinforcement of diplomatic initiative. The Western allies are in a position to exercise direct influence on parties to a regional conflict situation that can bolster and focus the United Nations' efforts to resolve disputes in accordance with its own methods for conflict prevention and peacekeeping. The most successful formulas are ones where the Western powers are able to act in unison within a collective security framework.

When this project was first conceived in early 1994, peacekeeping broadly defined was the most prominent expression of collective security. The United Nations seemingly had regained its vocation once freed from the paralysis of the Cold War. The world supposedly had been made safe for multilateral intervention. In Yugoslavia, both NATO and then the European Union ceded authority for mediating Europe's first post-Cold War security conflict to the world body in part on the basis of that belief. Only the UN could act for the international community. In addition, it had the experience and practised methods for performing the classic roles of mediating disputes, monitoring ceasefires, and deploying interpositional forces.

The picture changed markedly as the UN mission in Yugoslavia faltered. The Balkan conflict punctured illusions: as to the UN's aptitude for conflict management; as to expectations that common norms would rule a Europe free, whole and at peace; as to the Western Europeans' ability to muster the political will to act together effectively through the EU, the UN or otherwise; and as to a smooth transition in the transatlantic division of labour. Consequently NATO could not stand aloof from a European security crisis. Nor could the United States confidently (and conveniently) let its allies take custody of Western interests. The challenge of Europe's collective security is now more finely etched for all parties: national governments, Alliance institutions, and collective security organizations.

This study has four mutually supporting purposes:

1. To identify the practical requirements for operationalizing norms of consensual decision-making and concerted action within the Atlantic Alliance that do not depend on directive American leadership, and to propose strategies for their implementation with specific reference to peacemaking, peace-enforcing, and peacekeeping missions in conjunction with collective security bodies.
2. To consider what terms of cooperation between NATO and the European Union/Western European Union would augment and extend their joint capacity for performing the range of functions that fall under the headings of preventive diplomacy and crisis management.
3. To examine how Alliance assets (military, political and diplomatic) can be composed so as to dovetail with United Nations' mandated collective security activities – with particular attention paid to the reconciliation of diplomatic styles and operational methods.
4. To assess the implications for a reformed Alliance and for collective security in Europe of the moves to enlarge NATO's membership and to grant Russia, by way of compensation, a permanent mechanism chartered to institutionalize consultation and promote collaboration.

Chapters 2 to 6 present fine-grain portraits of security perspectives and policies in Britain, France, Germany, Italy and the United States. The manifold issues of European collective security we examine in this book can best be illuminated by viewing them from the vantage-point of the major Alliance capitals. Those governments' judgements and conduct will largely determine how the Atlantic partners respond to the opportunities and dangers that history presents them. Consensus, the *sine qua non* for mastering the future, will be hard won.

Prevailing perspectives in leading Western capitals on the shape of a new European system are not identical. So, too, preferences vary as to where to draw the jurisdictional boundaries among security organizations, how to distribute responsibilities, and the precise terms of their collaboration. Even on the crucial question of opening Western organizations to new members there is not complete unanimity. Pulling into focus these various national viewpoints is the key to meeting Alliance commitments. To do so, there must be a candid recognition of the attitudes and sentiments, anxieties and aspirations, that lie behind policy differences. Only then can a collective effort at composing them succeed. The superimposition of abstract security designs and architectural plans, however ingeniously drawn, will not work.

The authors of this book aim to contribute to a frank process of self-examination by shedding light on how each government views itself *and* views its allies. It is an 'inside-out' approach that provides insight into the requirements for winning the accord of governments on a common strategy, or for anticipating the consequences if that cannot be achieved. Smothering national differences under weighty generalities or compromise formulations is of no intellectual value (and a dubious diplomatic practice). Similarly, a set of admonitions, in and of itself, is of limited use. Better that any prescriptions for what should be done emerge from a searching look at the outlook, proclivities and preferences of the main parties. Elucidating them is the most useful contribution this study can make to the Alliance policy debate.

The book's second section considers the implications of the national portraits drawn for fashioning an Alliance strategy for collective security in Europe. Chapters 7 to 9 consider the policy consequences of the political and diplomatic field depicted in the country studies, concentrating on an appraisal of what Western governments must do individually and together in order to act effectively.

A concluding chapter returns to the themes stated at the outset. It reconceptualizes the West's dilemma and presents a set of guidelines for reconciling the goals of preserving the Atlantic Alliance's institutional integrity while shaping a pan-continental system.

2 Britain
Michael Clarke

BRITAIN'S STRATEGIC VISION OF ITS SECURITY ENVIRONMENT

Successive generations of British ministers, officials, and for that matter the general public, have felt uncomfortable when confronted with the need to express a strategic vision of Britain's security environment.[1] Partly, this arose out of the Cold War, where the strategic objective was simple, namely to persevere in the struggle as a contribution toward the time – in the distant future – when the confrontation might come to an end. Indeed, the ending of the Cold War on terms more favourable to the West than could ever have realistically been imagined has visited on Britain more than most powers the curse of having its wishes granted. The Cold War was good for Britain. It played to the country's strengths as a major military power at a time when it was no longer a major economic power on a global scale, it provided Britain with disproportionate influence within the Western alliance, it prolonged the status of Britain as a victorious power of 1945; and it restricted Britain's European concerns to those parts of the Continent – Scandinavia, Northern Europe and the Mediterranean – with which Britain was familiar and had some tradition of diplomatic leverage. It is noticeable for example that British influence within the Western alliance was at its greatest in those periods when the Cold War was at its most intense. During periods of détente the British influence declined, since it was a less central player in *ostpolitik*, economic cooperation or the normalization of disputed borders. Though its diplomatic skills were generally well regarded in détente it had less to gain and to lose from the process. When tension was higher, however, the United States was proportionately more grateful for so loyal an ally and the diverse contributions which Britain made to the Atlantic Alliance and a tradition of diplomatic resolve tempered by experience made Britain a more central player during the darker days of the Cold War.[2] None of this required a very elaborate 'strategic vision'. The Cold War was a long-term – apparently inescapable – reality and the fighting of it was an essentially short-term tactical process.

Then, too, the British aversion to strategic visions is also partly explained within the national political culture. Britain has been a *status quo* power in world politics since the end of the period of imperial expansion, having no overriding motives to overturn the existing order. British ministers and officials are frankly nervous at the prospect of articulating major blueprints for future security structures. Though Britain was undoubtedly one of the architects of the post-1945 restructuring of world security – which may be regarded as both visionary and successful – there can be no doubt that the vision was provided mainly by the United States and that Britain concurred with the concepts, sometimes against its better judgement, for the sake of solidarity and rapid reconstruction.[3]

For British foreign and defence planners, the policy is in essence the *process*. As the process goes forward, core and secondary interests are recognized and safeguarded, but the characteristic British response to grand visions of a European future is to worry about the details, the financing, the staffing implications, and to insist that the participants address the practical issues before signing up to more ambitious schemes. British policymakers, for example, were traditionally sceptical at successive suggestions in the 1960s and 1970s that the Western European Union could perform a more substantive role in European defence than it was bequeathed in 1955. In June 1984 when President Mitterrand used the Fontainebleau Summit to try to revitalize the WEU, it provoked a British paper, *Europe – The Future*, which expressed exactly all the practical reservations the British felt to an explicitly political initiative.[4] For Britain, a revitalized WEU in this period seemed only to represent a challenge to the unity of NATO, the political and economic costs of which would far outweigh the benefits, and officials in Whitehall during these years were frankly derisive of what they saw as political initiatives towards greater European unity that were dressed up as military reorganizations. That remains the essence of British thinking about the WEU post-Berlin accords on Combined Joint Task Forces. As the institutional expression of the idea of a European pillar within NATO, WEU has symbolic value and some small utility. As the embodiment of a European Security Identity within the EU, it would undercut NATO's integrity and contribute to an unwelcome and delusory federal European state. In a period when the *status quo* was in the interests of most – as it was during the Cold War years – this conservative approach could be regarded as pragmatic and helpful; it is useful to have at least one ally who keeps others' feet on the ground. In a period of rapid change, however – such as that which was clearly emerging in Europe from late 1984 – it is frequently regarded as pedantic obstructionism by those who worry that the Western world may be missing the tide of history and Western Europeans in particular missing an historic occasion to consolidate their unity.

From the early 1990s, therefore, it has been normal to hear British ministers and officials rehearse the daunting uncertainties which European leaders now face. NATO is poised on the brink of an expansion which would change its character more radically than at any time since its foundation; the European Union is similarly set to expand and is in the process of major institutional reform in giving political and organizational substance to the Maastricht vision (and if reform is thwarted it faces economic stagnation and political regression); the fulcrum of immediate security threats to Europe is switching from an East/West axis to a North/South axis as Mediterranean issues preoccupy some of the major European powers; and there is a significant danger of the development of a 'new Cold War' with a more nationalistic Russia which will take very different forms to the old Cold War with the Soviet Union, ones involving widespread instability within and between the peripheral states of the Russian Federation.

In such circumstances, the British, unlike the French, are inherently sceptical over the viability of pan-European approaches to security. The CSCE, in the British view, was always a useful forum, as the OSCE continues to be, and there are a number of roles it might play: but the maintenance and enforcement of collective security is not among them.[5] During 1990 and 1991, one reason British policymakers were keen to move quickly to reform the force structure and the strategic concept of NATO, was to forestall any initiatives to try to invest the CSCE with NATO's traditional importance as the keystone European security organization.

British officials characteristically point out that all we have is diplomatic process and that it is far too early in the transition to the twenty-first century to pursue a single strategic vision of a European future. When optimistic ministers from partner countries articulate security constructs which could be achievable in the short term – pan-European, EU-centric, or regional collective security systems – if only several elements can be successfully juggled, the British normally point out with an almost perverse pleasure that there are far more balls in the air than the juggler seems to be aware of, most of which are already perilously close to the floor.

Nevertheless, the British attachment to process over strategic vision is not devoid of core values or long-term thinking; rather, as a *status quo* power, Britain is more acutely aware of that which should be preserved as the process goes forward rather than that which might be constructed. And if the British are generally vague over what might be constructed, they are very clear on what must be preserved in any future European security arrangements.

The first element to be preserved is the interest and involvement of the United States in European security matters.[6] For the British, US involvement in European security is a simple necessity which it would be both dangerous and impractical to forgo. The US provides a fund of tangible economic and military resources for which the Europeans cannot realistically substitute; it also brings to the Alliance the intangible but enormous value of its interest in European security; US political involvement in an issue normally brings about diplomatic movement for good or ill.[7] This was demonstrated anew over the Bosnian crisis where three years of US vacillation gave way, in summer 1995, to a series of US-led initiatives that had the effect of driving a peace deal along which, 'for good or ill', did bring an end to the fighting and changed the political context of the conflict in former Yugoslavia. Above all, the US brings to European security the prospect – however distantly – of the employment of huge physical resources *in extremis*. Neither of the two world wars or the Cold War could have been won by the West without the employment of the resources of a superpower. Although contemporary American involvement in European security may appear sometimes quixotic, the British view of Europe is based on a bedrock belief that, if necessary, at some time in the future the United States would again be prepared to commit itself fully to the defence of the Western powers should the need ever arise. The institutionalization through NATO and close bilateral relations of this enormous US potential in European security provides considerable reassurance that it will not be called upon.

The British fully accept that the relationship between the United States and Europe is in the process of rapid evolution and that US involvement in the particulars of European security has changed greatly over recent years.[8] There is a vigorous debate among the interested public over whether America has now in effect become a 'Pacific first' as opposed to an 'Atlantic first' power, but few disagree with the perception that the intensity of US interests in European security is now less and that the degree of US involvement in

European crises will vary considerably on a case-by-case basis.[9] The British approach, therefore, to the development of a European security and defence identity is balanced between the rationale that an ESDI will be necessary to compensate for the lack of American interest in certain crises and the realization that it is an essential pillar in creating a reformed transatlantic relationship precisely to maintain the institutionalization of American involvement in European security. British ministers and officials have moved a long way in their view of the future of a European security and defence identity since the debates of 1991 before the Maastricht summit on the reformed NATO force structure (June 1991) and the New Strategic Concept (November 1991), and the commitment to implementing CJTF. But all subsequent authoritative statements have nevertheless been preceded by the assertion that the continued involvement of the United States in European security is a *sine qua non* of the process.[10]

A second core element in the British approach is the preservation, as far as possible, of the relationship between London and Washington. The so-called 'special relationship' between Britain and the United States certainly still preoccupies many British defence planners, and a majority of British politicians. Its existence is extremely difficult to verify in the 1990s, yet it is capable of making foreseen and sudden reappearances. It was a relationship uniquely appropriate to the circumstances of the Cold War. At the apex, it consisted of a genuine friendship between certain leaders – Churchill and Roosevelt, Macmillan and Kennedy, Callaghan and Carter, Thatcher and Reagan – which on occasion had discernible impacts on British policy and its standing in the world. At the practical base, it consisted of intelligence cooperation at a high level of detail, nuclear cooperation in both the deployment and testing of weapons, and the habits of cooperation and natural closeness born of experience between the three armed services – particularly the respective navies and air forces. In between the base and the apex of the relationship, however, it is impossible to discern any real substance to the 'special relationship' and the vast majority of normal peacetime relations occur somewhere in this space.[11]

For that reason, the special relationship is very difficult to spot on any given day. On the other hand, it has made surprising reappearances in time of armed conflict such as during the Falklands War, the Gulf War and in some of the operational details of the UNPROFOR and IFOR deployments in former Yugoslavia. It is reasonable to suppose, though it is by no means inevitable,[12] that the substantive elements in the special relationship will decline in importance in the post-Cold War environment, even as it remains a major tenet of British security thinking that there is a national interest in preserving as much substance in the relationship as possible.

The third core interest with which Britain approaches the future in European security matters is in the need to maintain room for political and military manoeuvre. In a changing European environment it has become abundantly clear since 1990 that only Britain and France presently possess the physical and political resources to engage in major external security operations. They are the only two European countries who can project significant amounts of military power and sustain them. The British Ministry of Defence, for example, normally aims to keep four battalions available at any given time for contingency operations, over and above other 'normal' commitments.[13] In a political sense, too, Britain has some natural room for manoeuvre, being apart from the geographical centre of Europe, suffering no extensive uncontrolled immigration pressures as a result of European crises, and having a domestic cultural diversity that reflects the new Commonwealth rather than Europe and the Mediterranean.[14] Very few events that take place in the new Commonwealth have any domestic resonance within British society; British racial problems are created from within, not imported from the outside world, as is the case for some of Britain's European partners. Whether or not this leads Britain (and for different reasons, France) into a greater leadership role in European security questions, it is clear that British policymakers feel they have both the opportunity and the desire to retain some real flexibility in the way they may deploy their forces. Like France, Britain has a permanent seat on the UN Security Council, extant overseas dependent territories – some 14 at present – and a number of important foreign policy commitments which demand freedom of action.

This core interest appeared in very tangible form in Britain's approach to the Inter-Governmental Conference of 1996. As the process of building European security goes forward to its unknowable destination, the British approach all defence and security questions on the basis of strict inter-governmentalism: only this can guarantee sufficient freedom of manoeuvre to serve both external interests and the requirements of domestic unity, where both main political parties are neuralgic at the implications of increased federalism. As the Government's memorandum of March 1995 on European defence questions stated, 'The Government believes that the nation state should be the basic building block in constructing the kind of international order we wish to see; and that the nation state remains in particular the fundamental entity for cooperation in the field of defence... so the unshakable conviction on which our approach to the development of a European defence policy will be based will be that the basis for European action in the defence and security field should be inter-governmental, based on cooperation between nation states.'[15]

These core interests form a reasonably coherent whole and are mutually reinforcing. They are easier to safeguard in institutional debates, such as over the security architecture which Europe should adopt, than over policy debates in the face of real crises. They were strongly defended, for example, in the Government's positions in the approach to the Turin Inter-Governmental Conference beginning in March 1996 which in its consideration of steps to implement Maastricht and *inter alia* dealt with some of the major architectural questions of the EU/WEU's place in European security. On the other hand, all three interests have arguably been damaged by the course of the Bosnian crisis. Certainly, British policymakers would have been appalled in 1991 had they appreciated the level of British military involvement in the conflict, the limited scope for diplomatic or military manoeuvre, the damage the conflict has done to the Anglo-American relationship and the damage it may yet do to the reputation of NATO – not least in Washington. For this, if no other reason, the British may be more wary of engaging in similar operations in the future, even though other pressures may lead them towards interventionism in regional and factional conflicts. In this respect, much will depend on the fate of the IFOR in Bosnia. If it is generally successful, at least in the narrow military sense of ending the fighting, then Whitehall may conclude that – after a shaky start – the transatlantic relationship proved its worth in the former Yugoslavia and that those ties will emerge somewhat strengthened. If, on the other hand, IFOR had become a victim of entanglement, rather as UNPROFOR did, then there was a serious risk that US forces planned withdrawal in early 1997 could provoke either a corresponding withdrawal by other contingents, or else a crisis in relations as the major European powers attempt to fill the gap left by the US while condemning American irresponsibility. In the event, the Alliance scraped through, while exposing its fault-lines.

It is generally accepted in Britain that future crises will not concern wars of survival but rather 'wars of discretion'.[16] Britain will have the choice of the degree and level of involvement that is deemed appropriate though there is no shortage of potential crises over which discretion will have to be exercised. Wars in Europe are certainly possible, not least on the periphery of the Russian Federation, but they will not necessarily involve Britain and the degree and type of engagement in such crises will be up to the Government on a case-by-case basis. Britain can bring few economic or politically heavyweight resources to bear on crises in Central, Eastern or Southern Europe. Its strength lies in its military instrument and the military specialisms it can employ. Since the end of the Cold War, Britain has engaged, at its discretion, in high-intensity wars, as in the Gulf in 1990 to 1991, in civil conflicts, as presently over northern and southern Iraq, and in peacekeeping and peace support operations, as in Cyprus, Former Yugoslavia, Angola, Rwanda, Mozambique, Cambodia, Western Sahara, Somalia and Haiti.[17] In a sense, the British are not frightened of the prospects of European crises: they tend to take a neo-realist view that the present relaxation will prove an all-too-brief holiday since such crises will always be with us. The European crises that British ministers and officials tend to foresee include further crises in the Balkans, a Russian–Baltic crisis, particularly over Estonia and Latvia, smaller crises involving groups of the 3.8m Hungarian minorities in Europe, and persistent instability around the southern periphery of the Russian Federation – in particular in relation to Ukraine. Structural instability in the Mediterranean is also a likely contingency. Some of these crises are closer to home for Britain than others, and all of them, it could be argued, have a relevance to British security in Europe. But the outbreak of crises as such is not the prime worry of British ministers and officials who, after all, perceive that the country is fundamentally safe. Rather, the dangers and threats which British planners see arise from a collapse in the collective Western approach to security issues and in respect of the longer-term relationship between the West and Russia. The lack of a shared strategy for dealing with the renascence of Russia as a great power – or, even more, competing strategies – would both lessen the effectiveness of Western diplomacy and lay the basis for intra-Alliance conflicts.[18]

Britain has benefited more than most from multilateral security approaches in Western Europe. Its diplomacy was critical in founding the NATO organization and it can be argued that Britain has benefited disproportionately from collective defence in Western Europe, paying a relatively modest military and economic price for a very robust allied defensive organization in the integrated military structure. This is not merely a security interest but an intensely felt foreign policy interest too, since Britain has gained in several ways from the intense economic interdependence of Western Europe, particularly over the last 30 years. For Britain, therefore, we may say that no European crises are uncontainable if the Western allies deal with them through a genuinely collective approach. But a comparatively minor and distant crisis could be debilitating for British interests if it sows disunity within the Western camp – as the Bosnian crisis has so nearly done. Indeed, such a crisis would undermine a principle which the British have nurtured for exactly half a century.

The second real danger which the British foresee in European security is that relations with the Russian Federation might enter a long-term spiral of decline. No less than Churchill in the 1940s or the Liberal leadership in 1907, the present British Government regards business-like and workable relations with Russia as the essential linchpin of a constructive European policy. This is a key reason why Britain worked hard to accommodate Russian demands on the revision of the CFE Treaty, and was so muted in its reactions to Russian suppression of the guerrilla campaign in Chechnya. Relations with Russia may not be genuinely cordial; Britain, though, has always been relaxed at the idea that they can be no more than cool and correct. The pattern of bilateral relations with Russia has never been very intense (though on particular issues they have often been very delicate), trade relations are thin by comparison with Russian trade relations with other major European countries, and the British have been generally less affected by periods of poor East–West relations than many other countries (or, at least, have experienced them with less *angst*).

British governments have never minded, particularly, that Russia was undemocratic, nor do they feel that the economic reform process in Russia is vital in itself, except in so far as it is a key element in Russia's external behaviour. The view, rather, is that a good working relationship with Russia must be established in order to facilitate diplomacy in Central and Eastern Europe (C & EE). This will be as much a requirement in the post-Cold War world as it was during the Cold War itself. If the West fails to establish such a relationship then little else in Central and Eastern Europe will succeed or, if it does, will be insecure. In this circumstance, the West would need to fall back again on its collective defence assets, the United States and the centrality of NATO as an institutional linking mechanism. This, clearly, serves to reinforce the importance of NATO, the American connection and the Anglo-American relationship in British thinking, since the possibility of poor relations with Russia, coupled with unstable economic and political conditions in C & EE, for perhaps a considerable period, must now be considered a serious prospect. Such a consideration also reinforces Britain's attachment to policy process rather than policy blueprints. The onset of a new Cold War is possible and only a concentration on process – preserving NATO, continuing to institutionalize the American commitment, fostering the Anglo-American relationship and maintaining diplomatic room for manoeuvre – will allow the West to find a sensible way forward with appropriate reassurance that we are not throwing out the baby with the bathwater.

THE INTERNAL SETTING

The Underlying Consensus

British ministers are fortunate in labouring under few constitutional or political constraints on their employment of armed forces. Parliament has no formal role to play in the employment of armed forces beyond that of providing general political consent to the Government. Indeed, apart from certain specific matters concerning European Union legislation, Parliament has no constitutional role beyond the conventional one of ratifying treaties. The 'Ponsonby Rule' of 1924 merely advises that treaties be made available to be consulted by both Houses of Parliament for 21 days, after which time they are deemed to be ratified in the absence of any convincing objections.

Public opinion in Britain is uniquely supportive of the employment of armed forces, as successive opinion polls over some 30 years have demonstrated. Though there has been notable public dissent in Britain over the war in Korea, the Suez crisis of 1956, and in the emergence of the anti-nuclear peace campaign in the 1960s and then the 1980s, these controversies were almost exclusively over the political stance of the Government rather than the employment of the armed forces as such.[19] Though the tolerance of the British public for casualties has not been severely tested since the Korean War, circumstantial evidence from a succession of post-colonial operations, from the Falklands War and from opinion poll data on the present crisis in former Yugoslavia, indicates that the British public do not object to casualties providing that they are not due to avoidable accidents or pointless.[20]

The party-political impact on British security thinking has traditionally shown more fluctuations than trends in public opinion though since the end of the Cold War it has been, of necessity, bipartisan. There have been times in British political history when security questions have been matters of intense political bitterness, most notably in the late 1940s over the onset of the Cold War and the question of American leadership, and then again in the early 1960s and early 1980s on nuclear issues. A great deal of parliamentary heat has been generated over attitudes to the Russians, nuclear deterrence, and the perceived over-assertiveness of American leadership on all sides of the House of Commons. But with the exception of a relatively brief period from 1981 to 1985, when the Labour Party adopted an outright policy of nuclear disarmament, such debates, heated as they were, have been within rather than between the main political parties. Since 1945, the front benches have been at one in their adherence to NATO, the importance of the American connection, and their general attitude of wary scepticism toward the prospects of reform in the Soviet Union. Nor is there a discernible party-political pattern in attitudes among the party leaders to the relationship with the United States. Leaders of the Labour Party are not generally less committed to the relationship with Washington than those in the Conservative Party. Rather, it has been a matter of circumstance and friendship at the apex of the 'Special Relationship' described above. Harold Wilson as Labour leader was caught up in the period of the Vietnam War and clearly did not enjoy good personal relations with Lyndon Johnson. It seemed at the time – particularly in the light of Britain's withdrawal from East of Suez in 1967 – that the relationship with the United States was in decline. This impression may have been reinforced by the succeeding, Conservative, premiership of Edward Heath, who similarly did not enjoy good relations with President Nixon, and was also in office not only during the most delicate period of the Vietnam withdrawal but also in the post de-Gaulle era when he was able to achieve one of his major political ambitions in negotiating British entry into the European Community in 1973. But this apparent trend was quite reversed by the Labour premiership of James Callaghan, who struck up a close friendship with President Carter at a time when 'interdependence' G7 summits had become fashionable in the mid-1970s. It reached new heights of cooperation under his (Conservative) successor in the Thatcher/Reagan–Bush relationship of the 1980s, which spanned for Britain the fighting of two important wars. Though the party political scene has fluctuated greatly since the 1940s, the underlying bipartisan consistency is undeniable. It is, however, true that there is greater volatility underlying now than was the case some twenty years ago.

Attitudes to European Security

Faced by the ambiguities and uncertainties of the post-Cold War era in European security, there is little party-political debate on European security structures as such. It is an arcane and confusing subject which most politicians assume is best left to officials who, in the British case, have developed the process with some consistency. On the other hand, both main political parties have major problems in their attitudes to European integration. It was apparent, with the onset of the Inter-Governmental Conference of March 1996 that addressed the question of institutional reform in the three pillars of the European Union that defence and security questions can easily be caught up in a vociferous debate between 'Eurosceptics' and 'Europhiles' within each of the two main political parties. Only the third party, the Liberal Democrats, have no ideological problems on European issues, though they too, have some disagreements over policy and tactics.

The British Conservative Government has become far more sceptical about the future of European integration since the Inter-Governmental Conference of 1991. In her famous speech in Bruges in 1987, Mrs Thatcher set out an approach to the European Community which stressed a particularly British interpretation of national sovereignty, and that won increasing acceptance among Tory MPs during the Major years. The European ideal, in this version, was best envisaged through the centrality of the nation-state and via intense cooperation between states; not through integration that undermines them. This expression of the European ideal also appealed to the emerging leaderships in a democratizing Eastern Europe since they saw in this conception a way of being more politically integrated with Western Europe at a time when they also needed to build (or in some cases to cope with) a post-communist national consensus within their own countries. Moreover, they were anyway unprepared for full functional economic integration with their Western neighbours. The 'Bruges vision' of Europe, it was thought, resolved their dilemma. But subsequent Conservative administrations have also been politically much weaker than that of 1987. The Major Government, with its shrinking, barely workable parliamentary majority, was deeply split between a predominance of Europhiles – though many are only tepid – and a minority – albeit vociferous – of Eurosceptics. In those circumstances, the core of Conservative Eurosceptics, perhaps no more than 30 strong at most, saw the constitutional issue as more important than the survival of the Conservative Government. They thus were prepared to risk the government's demise to maintain their position. The Government, which in cabinet numbers at least was predominantly pro-European, fell hostage to these votes. It felt constrained to move a good way to embrace the Eurosceptic Right, trying all the time not to alienate the Centre-Left of the party. At least on European defence issues, the Government could exploit some sense of party consensus, where movement towards a common defence policy and 'eventually a common defence' as envisaged in the Maastricht wording is not favoured by anyone. The Government can also take some comfort from the fact that Britain cannot be so easily by-passed by the more *communautaire* members of the European Union (EU) on defence issues as it can on economic integration, monetary policy and social provision.

In the run-up to the 1997 general election, the Labour Party was able to paper over its cracks on European Union issues – which in the past have been debilitating – in its determination to regain power. It is impossible to judge, therefore, how deep are the ideological splits on European issues, though circumstantial evidence indicates that they are significant.

Where European security issues touch on the European Union – such as in questions over the most appropriate security architecture, the role of the Western European Union, or any prospect of 'European only' defence cooperation, it becomes difficult to disentangle security questions from the intra-party debates over European integration. The Eurosceptics argue that British sovereignty is at stake; the Europhiles that British influence in the tide of history is the real issue. The result is that, at the political level, the rhetorical stakes are higher and a weakened Government – particularly weakened on European issues – has little room for detailed manoeuvre, as was evident in the process of the IGC when British officials had to operate within a highly constraining political context.[21] The Government found itself having to speak on European issues simultaneously to four distinct audiences: the Conservative party, domestic public opinion, official opinion in the United States, and other European governments. In the last two years, the demands of the latter audience have been accorded probably the lowest priority, with the result that Britain is generally perceived at home and abroad to be increasingly detached from West

European mainstream debates. Eurosceptics and Europhiles generally agree that this is the case, but draw from it different conclusions.

WESTERN COOPERATION

If British planners have no clear sense of what the future of European security will be, and have to operate within a domestic political framework that gives them so little political leadership, they nevertheless have a consistent view over how the process of decisionmaking among the Western allies should be structured. NATO remains the cornerstone of all allied military cooperation embodying the political and military virtues and having demonstrated in war, peace, and now 'peace support', the invaluable habits of cooperation. The British do not feel that any further case need be made for NATO: its centrality to the picture is demonstrated by the history of European security since 1991 and the fact that it is presently the almost exclusive focus for security thinking among the non-member states who wish to join it through the Partnership for Peace (PfP) programme or outright membership.

The British are, however, determinedly conservative on PfP and expansion issues. The were keen on the establishment of the North Atlantic Cooperation Council (NACC) as a way of forestalling East European demands for NATO membership, and took very much the same view of the PfP process. When it was first announced, at the Brussels Summit of January 1994, it was welcomed in London as a way of reconciling a difference within NATO over expansion and serving the same function as the NACC – to forestall precipitate membership. But within the year, the process had followed the logic and momentum of events: PfP had become the mechanism by which NATO *would* eventually expand to embrace new members, perhaps around the year 2000. London has gone along with this evolution somewhat reluctantly. Unlike Germany, Britain stands to lose more tangible advantages than it will gain intangible ones by such a process. An expanded NATO may be a more diluted NATO: harder to manage internally, more difficult to maintain the transatlantic commitment to, less of a vehicle for British diplomacy and politically dominated (as opposed merely to influenced) by Germany; it would probably be a NATO less 'north-European' in its orientation if the expansion were only realistically to involve the Visegrad 4 and, later, possibly Romania and Bulgaria; above all, it would risk alienating

Russia in a way that might be irredeemable. That, for the British, would be a general price higher than any localized benefits in Central and Eastern Europe, where British interests are comparatively slight.

Within two years, therefore, Britain's position on expanded membership of NATO has been reversed. Up to 1993, British officials argued forcefully that expansion was not possible. By 1995, they accepted that it was part of NATO policy. For the sake of collective solidarity in the alliance, therefore, Britain goes along with the PfP process and states, logically enough, that all applications for membership will be judged on their merits and that Moscow will never be given the right of veto over NATO decisionmaking. Nevertheless, the 1995 Defence White Paper went out of its way to establish the fact that PfP was a general partnership arrangement and should not be seen only as a mechanism to facilitate membership. We should not lose sight, in the current obsession with the membership issue, of the central purposes of PfP which are to improve relations between NATO and all other European states. As the Defence White Paper pointed out in uncharacteristically direct terms: 'We place great value on the concept of partnership, for we seek a balance between partnership and membership in the development of the wider Europe we wish to see. But there is an unhelpful preoccupation with the latter, and in particular with membership of NATO and the European Union. Playing down the value of cooperation and playing up the significance of decisions on membership will risk re-creating the type of divide in Europe which we wish to avoid.'[22] This sentiment is echoed very faithfully in states such as Ukraine, Moldova or Belarus where it is understood quite clearly that membership for them is a very distant prospect indeed.[23]

Britain is also more conservative than some of its European partners regarding the future of the WEU, for reasons not dissimilar to those behind British attitudes to PfP. Britain sees the WEU in strictly functional terms and resists moves to elevate it – for essentially political reasons – to a position that would undermine the cohesion that underpins NATO. Again, however, British planners are more relaxed on WEU questions than they appeared to be prior to 1992 since they consider that events have confirmed NATO's practical competence and emphasized the WEU's limitations by comparison.

For these reasons the British Government is opposed to any suggestion that the WEU should be formally merged into the European Union as a fourth pillar. Rather, the WEU should concentrate on the further elaboration of the Petersberg missions articulated in 1992.

The Maastricht Treaty left the WEU finely balanced between NATO and the EU. The British Government accepts the logic that the WEU should be more explicitly adjacent to the EU, but regards as impractical the possibility of an integration between the two. Instead, it argues for a greater specification of the distinctive tasks which the WEU should be capable of performing, and officials looked towards the British presidency of the WEU during 1996 as an opportunity to make real progress in upgrading its operational capability (which is presently very small) to the level where it may be capable of running perhaps one or, at most, two full divisions with attendant air and maritime assets, in operational circumstances.[24] Beyond that, the British approach to Western cooperation lies in two particular practical directions.

The first is to address the question of a more effective European military contribution to Western security by making the best of those European-only military assets which presently exist. British policy-makers begin from the assumption that all effective defence planning must be task-based. It is pointless to define forces and political structures unless there is some clear exposition of the military tasks to be fulfilled. For the British, this helps to define the difference between the rationales of NATO and the WEU. NATO, say British officials, must still be capable of fighting a major strategic war as envisaged in the original Washington Treaty. In real terms, this requires NATO to have an ability to engage in high-tempo operations on more than one main front simultaneously for a prolonged length of time. Though it is extremely unlikely that NATO will be called upon to fulfil such a mission in the foreseeable future, the alliance must nevertheless be maintained and sized upon this continuing requirement.

In the British view, any lesser operations which NATO forces engage in cannot be allowed to detract from the need to maintain such an overall capability. The WEU, on the other hand, is not required to fulfil such a collective defence mission (at least as long as the full membership of the WEU remains coincidental with that of NATO), even though the revised Brussels Treaty is written in somewhat stronger terms than that of the Washington Treaty. Nevertheless, the WEU is regarded by British officials as having more potential flexibility in its command and control arrangements and the missions for which it can be adapted. This dichotomy does not presuppose that NATO should be preserved for war and the WEU for operations short of war; no such simple distinctions will be possible, and the eventualities in which European military forces may be deployed will be so contingent on particular circumstances that judgements will have to be made on a case-by-case basis.

Though NATO may find itself performing nothing more than crisis management roles for the next two decades, London believes that it is important that NATO's collective defence function is not compromised. For the British, therefore, the task is not to devise a new organization for the defence of Western Europe, but rather to develop arrangements whereby the growing multinationality of European forces can be most efficiently used and interoperability encouraged. A number of potentially important European multinational forces already exist, such as the ACE Rapid Reaction Corps (ARRC) and within that the Multinational Division (Central), the UK/Netherlands Amphibious Task Force, the Eurocorps, EUROFOR and EUROMARFOR, the German/Dutch Corps, the French–British Air Group agreed in November 1994, and the Franco-British Rapid Reaction Force founded in early 1995 for operations in support of UNPROFOR in Bosnia. More such initiatives are likely in the future, and may be further extended as joint multinational exercises involving Partnership for Peace countries and WEU members and observers are developed. By the end of 1995 there were over a dozen major PfP joint military exercises. In these circumstances, the British argue, it is vital to develop some command coherence among formations which, after all, are so far generally composed of the same physical assets available to NATO.

British defence officials also are generally relaxed about this proliferation of multinational European forces, e.g. the Eurocorps, since greater interoperability in these formations will increase the interoperability among all NATO forces, including those of the US. Then, too, officials stress that they see British self-defence almost entirely in a collective framework, pointing out that Britain devotes very few resources to the defence of the homeland itself. Rather, the British see the need for Europeans to be capable of projecting significant military power quickly to particular areas to engage, if necessary, in high-intensity operations, and then withdraw. The chances that this can be achieved neatly by the members of only one European security arrangement are remote and *ad hoc* coalitions of the willing are almost certain to be required if European military assets are to be used at all.

The second thrust in the British approach is to move forward as far as practicable on the concept of Combined Joint Task Forces (CJTF), announced at the Brussels NATO Summit in January 1994, and codified by the Berlin ministerial meeting in June 1996. The CJTF idea was stalled for two years in intra-alliance debate, chiefly between French and American views of the way the concept should be operationalized. At the end of the year, it still awaited specific implementation. But the principle of CJTFs appeals to the British sense of practicality and offers a framework that should be flexible enough to meet various needs.[25] On the other hand, there is evidence that in the light of the Berlin compromise there is a danger that the concept will come to mean whatever individual states want it to mean.[26] In this sense, the British still have reservations over the way that officials have sought to develop the concept.

For Britain, CJTFs provide 'separable but not separate elements of NATO's command structure for European-led missions', and, on this interpretation, represent a way of using NATO assets more efficiently for 'European only' operations.[27] Though NATO's authorities have validated the concept, from a practical point of view it remains to be seen to what extent the devil will lie in the detail. In particular, British military planners have generally taken the view that the first proper attempt to specify the concept was too much driven by SHAPE planning processes. The report 'A Concept for a CJTF Headquarters' drawn up at SHAPE in March 1994 implied an extensive staff requirement of several thousand people. For the British, this was simply too big and implied a corps-level deployment that would probably be responsible to SACEUR. Apart from the fact that this was regarded as too big to be either efficient or appropriate to the likely circumstances of its employment, it would probably exclude a role for British command. Nor should CJTF HQs require new personnel: they should be drawn from existing HQs and it is by no means clear that such a major headquarters could be extracted from existing structures without damaging them. The most detailed planning presently undertaken within the Ministry of Defence is to work on the devolution of resources to a CJTF from within existing HQ resources.

Nevertheless, in the absence of authoritative guidelines until the Berlin accords were reached, the SHAPE concept was the point of departure. British officials argued for the specification of a CJTF structure that would allow for smaller operations at Brigade or Task Group Level, run from the most appropriate HQ according to its size and purpose. The British also argue for a smaller structure for political reasons, precisely so that it would not exclude a role for the WEU and in order to agree with French reservations which – for different reasons – also attach to the SHAPE-based approach. The

Royal Navy, in particular, did some specific planning for smaller CJTFs, envisaging three types of HQ that would be most useful: a large HQ ashore; a small naval HQ; and an HQ afloat that is capable of moving ashore. Though the Royal Navy has no vessel on the scale of the USS *Mount Witney*, the *Invincible* class aircraft carrier is earmarked for this role and now carries a communications suite for command of joint operations.

Despite the fact that the outgoing SACLANT spoke warmly about the potential for CJTFs,[28] other major NATO commanders – including Americans – expressed their doubts about the practicality of pre-established HQs for operations that will involve a number and combination of partners that is unknown in advance.[29] The Select Committee on Defence considered this to be a soluble technical problem, however. Post-Berlin, they hoped that the Pentagon would not drag its heels. More troublesome have been the political issues such as the form of a SACEUR presence in any NATO-based CJTF where the US may not be a direct participant; winning Washington's approval for the transfer of its logistical assets where the US may not otherwise be engaged; or the question of payment for the use of collective NATO military facilities by nations within a CJTF who are not members of NATO's Integrated Military Structure. Then, too, the most likely Partnership for Peace participants in a future CJTF would much prefer that it be a NATO-based operation – linking them to the United States – than a WEU-based operation that would not. For Britain, CJTFs must be operated pragmatically and in that respect the compromise of June 1996 in Berlin – though still leaving a number of important issues to be resolved – was regarded as satisfactory. It ensured that CJTFs could not be undertaken without the consensual agreement of NATO through the North Atlantic Council; thus CJTFs could not be used as a device to develop a European Security and Defence Identity in opposition to NATO, still less to drive a wedge between the Europeans and the United States. Moreover, the active link with NATO would ensure the logistical practicality of any CJTF that could be deployed.

The fact remains, however, that CJTFs are not merely an initiative that NATO could usefully pursue, but rather an acid-test of the alliance's operational ability in the new European order. British officials point out that the next NATO operation is likely to be in effect a CJTF in any case – as its involvement in Bosnia has turned out to be in the event. There is no problem, they claim, in putting together either CJTF forces or even HQ assets once the specific context is known. NATO does this all the time both in exercises and in real operations. The problem lies in the *pre-designation of command* in situations which are hypothetical at the time of planning. This, it must be admitted, is essentially a political problem, one that is presently slowing progress on the whole CJTF initiative and divided the US from France within the Alliance. For the British, this posed a dilemma: agreeing with Paris on a tactical level that smaller CJTFs would be more appropriate, but agreeing with the US on a political level that CJTFs are best conceived as a NATO-based concept to guarantee resources and efficiency. A failure to agree on CJTFs for political reasons might have forced us simply to conclude that NATO is incapable of mounting appropriate military operations.

COMPARATIVE ESTIMATION OF MUTUAL DEFENCE IN COLLECTIVE SECURITY ORGANIZATIONS

Britain has traditionally upheld a distinction between 'defence' and 'security'; a distinction which served it well in early debates on European political cooperation, the military restructuring of NATO and the articulation of the new strategic concept in 1991. 'Security' was a wider concept than defence, and implied the application of broad political, diplomatic and economic techniques to address major strategic or structural issues. British officials claimed that they took the lead in the late 1980s in specifying the enhanced security role which the European Community should then play in matters such as arms control, non-proliferation, the Middle East peace process, the greater regulation of the arms trade, and the outreach to the European members of the Warsaw Pact. 'Defence', on the other hand, was defined as that which concerned the application of military forces and this should be exclusively the preserve of NATO, since only the integrated military structure of the alliance was capable of deploying multinational forces effectively. Though this distinction cannot now be upheld so easily, it is still the derivative from which present British ideas stem. It follows, therefore, that in British eyes while security questions are capable of being seen in a more integrationist framework, defence issues *per se* are strictly inter-governmental.

The range of organizations with a European security role are multiple: the United Nations, the OSCE, NATO, the WEU and the EU. In 1990–92 it would be fair to say that the British were tempted to make clearer distinctions between the competence of these organizations for the different purposes of crisis management, crisis prevention, peace-making or peace support operations, than would now be the case. In the immediate aftermath of the Cold War, it seemed that only NATO and the WEU could have a practical role in the employment of forces for peacekeeping or peace enforcement, while the CSCE, as it then was, the UN and the EU would provide legitimacy, political backing, and possibly early warning of future crises. The course of the crisis in former Yugoslavia, however, has made such relatively simple distinctions impossible.

It is apparent now that 'crisis management' (as in the case of Macedonia) may require the deployment of armed forces no less than 'peace enforcement' and that it is, in reality, difficult to uphold the distinctions between peace support, peacemaking and peace enforcement, however distinct they are in theory. All three armed services in Britain have wrestled with these definitions as they have tried to articulate doctrines for peace-support operations. All three are still some way from finalized versions of a doctrine and the armed forces in general are a long way away from a joint and agreed doctrinal statement.[30] For the British, therefore, both the political and the operational definitions of crisis management activities are in a continual process of evolution. To cope with this uncertainty there is a general acceptance that Europe's future security structure will be one of 'variable geometry' where a different combination of organizations will be required according to the differential intensity of interests and level of engagement that each ally shows. This will be particularly the case for the US, and it may become normal to expect American involvement to wax and wane over time in the event of a protracted crisis. Whereas this would have been anathema to British officials even five years ago they now approach the prospect with unaccustomed equanimity:[31] partly because it is a simple statement of the inevitable, but also because they feel the events of the last five years have demonstrated the continuing relevance of NATO to any variation in the geometry which requires the deployment of armed forces.

The key problem in the British view is not, therefore, the relationship between NATO and the WEU. This can be worked out both in theory and practice if the WEU sticks to the Petersberg tasks and the IGC settles on an appropriate political relationship – excluding complete integration – between the EU and the WEU. After a shaky start in the Adriatic, NATO and the WEU defined workable arrangements and the WEU was wholly responsible for the riverine operation on the

Danube. The problems arise rather in relation to two weak points in the organizational geometry.

The first and most important weak spot arises in the relationship between the WEU and NATO on the one hand and the UN on the other. In principle, the British are in favour of the UN's use of regional organizations. In its July 1993 response to *The Agenda for Peace* the British Government supported the view that regional organizations enjoyed unique advantages: 'they have an intimate knowledge of local conditions and can provide expert knowledge on background.... We support the concept of a division of labour, with regional organizations taking a greater role in their own areas, particularly as regards peacemaking, while recognizing at all times the primacy of the UN in situations relating to international peace and security.'[32] In practice, however, this is not so easy. While NATO and the WEU have both learned from the Bosnian crisis, it appears that NATO/WEU and the UN have failed to improve their relationship as a result of the lamentable record in the crisis. The virtually complete exclusion of the UN from the IFOR operation is driven by a deep distrust of UN operating procedures within the US military establishment, and not a little by personal differences between the US negotiators of the Dayton Accords and the UN Secretary-General. The broad institutional interface is clearly unsatisfactory, and this has translated to grave deficiencies in the civil/military interface in general. Though British, French, Netherlands, Nordic and Canadian troops in particular performed with some distinction in the UNPROFOR operation their commanders ran up against UN restrictions which they found barely tolerable. The UN, NATO and the WEU are likely to be much more wary of entering into a symbiotic relationship in future crises as a result of the disagreements and confusion caused by this one. This will remain the case despite the relatively smooth IFOR operation, since Operation Joint Endeavour was a NATO enterprise requiring only a UN mandate.[33] Though many can see what needs to be addressed to refine the relationship of the UN to regional organizations under Chapter 8 of the Charter, it is quite likely that appropriate action in this regard will not follow, leaving this part of the security arrangement fundamentally – and perennially – weak.

The second weak point in the variable geometry of European security concerns the relation between NATO and the WEU, on the one hand, and the EU, on the other. The problem here is not that relations are demonstrably bad but that they are so far in a melting-pot while EU institutional reform and possible expansion move at a deliberate pace toward an uncertain outcome. Though the WEU is presently equidistant between NATO and the EU and though it is likely to be brought much closer to the EU over the next two to three years, the fact remains that its relationship with NATO is easier to specify than that with the EU. It is not clear quite how EU political authority will be translated into military tasks that the WEU might be asked to perform; not because such specification is in itself difficult, but because the already expanded membership of the EU includes countries which will probably not be full members of the WEU and therefore would not take part in a pre-organized military structure. For ambitious security architects in the new Europe, this is a genuine problem; for British officials it provides yet another pragmatic comfort. For it reinforces what the British believe to be the simple reality that only NATO will continue to provide an all-purpose integrated military structure. That which can be derived for the WEU will be essentially complementary and should, in any case, draw upon NATO assets in a dual-hatting arrangement as outlined in the Berlin accords. The British proposal for the future of the WEU, presented at the Inter-Governmental Conference, had been that a Head of State and Head of Government summit of the WEU should meet back-to-back with the European Council, supported by the relevant staff work and greater liaison between the relative secretariats. This, it is said, would provide greater coherence between the EU and the WEU, and invest WEU implementation with greater political authority. While undoubtedly a practical proposal, the reaction among Britain's European partners is that this does not go far enough and that a more explicit integration between the WEU and the EU should be attempted. This, however, is as far as the British are so far prepared to go and they point out that in operational terms it will be far more important to refine the relationship with the UN than with the EU for the purposes of military deployments in crisis prevention, crisis management and peace support roles.

MULTILATERAL PEACE SUPPORT OPERATIONS

British attitudes to multilateral peace support operations are presently surrounded by a high degree of ambiguity as the apparent lessons of the crisis in the former Yugoslavia are absorbed into security thinking. On the one hand, there is no question about the relative willingness of Britain to engage in multinational peace support operations, both in the wider world and in particular in Europe. The political will to be engaged in multilateral operations is clearly present, driven both by a residual sense of Great Power status among politicians and the more particular concerns of the Foreign and Commonwealth Office that British influence should be exerted through the most appropriate instruments. Nor is the marginal cost of PSO operations prohibitively expensive. In 1993 the cash cost to the government of military contributions to the UN over and above the normal assessed British contribution to the peacekeeping budget (which is in addition to the normal assessed contribution for UN activities in general) was just under $218 million. This was not set against the defence budget, but rather that of the FCO which was able to lay it against the central contingency reserve.[34] The FCO has been constantly more enthusiastic than some other areas of government that British forces should be involved, where appropriate, in peace support operations; indeed, in 1994 the FCO received 22 separate requests from the United Nations for troop contributions to multinational operations. The military, though more wary about the problems of overstretch and the degradation of war-fighting training that PSOs involve, are also willing to demonstrate their usefulness and relevance by deploying forces in multinational operations. The broad consensus is that Britain's comparative advantage lies in the deployment of specialist forces, and throughout the 1990s the Ministry of Defence has been able to record that some 25–30 operational deployments are normally undertaken in different parts of the world every year. Public opinion, too, is very supportive of multilateral peace support activity. In opinion polls on the Bosnian crisis, the most consistent trend of support (above 75 per cent) is demonstrated in answer to questions concerning the appropriateness of a British involvement in the event that multinational forces 'are sent' to Bosnia for some purpose or other. Opinions were more variable regarding what the outside world can do about Bosnia, the tolerance of the British public for casualties and the confidence the public feels in present policies towards Bosnia; but there was no doubt in the mind of the majority of the public that if a multinational force were engaged in Bosnia – for whatever purpose – then Britain should be a part of it.

This general trend of support, however, does not transfer to a similar certainty over either doctrine or operational deployments. Since 1992, all three armed services in Britain have written, or rewritten, their keynote doctrinal statements with more than half an eye on peacekeeping and peace support operations. The most advanced expression in doctrinal terms is presently the army's *Wider Peacekeeping* document, which was launched in 1994 and has been widely circulated, forming the basis for some of the doctrinal thinking on maritime and air operations. *Wider Peacekeeping* maintains that there is a clear line between peacekeeping and peace enforcement: that line represents a Rubicon which, once crossed, cannot easily be recrossed. The key virtue in avoiding the crossing of such a Rubicon is the maintenance of impartiality. Where external forces are perceived not to be impartial then there will be no choice but to engage in peace enforcement rather than peacekeeping, and the nature of the operation necessarily changes. The doctrine makes no recommendations as to the relative moral or political merits of peacemaking as opposed to peace enforcement; it simply points out that they are two distinct military functions for which forces must be appropriately sized and equipped. The writing of this doctrine in 1993–94 inevitably owed a great deal to the evolving tactics of the British in Bosnia and indeed was drawn up in close consultation with force commanders on the ground. Nevertheless, the experience of peace support operations in Bosnia has already cast some doubt on the doctrine, particularly in relation to the irrevocable character of the 'Rubicon' between peacemaking and peace enforcement, and the centrality which the doctrine accords to impartiality.[35] The Rubicon appears to be fordable in both directions at a number of places and impartiality, it seems, can be broken and re-established. In particular, most recent doctrinal thinking inclines to the view that it may well be possible to cross the Rubicon at a tactical level – becoming highly partial – and recross the line back again to impartiality, as long as the line is not crossed at the strategic level. Operations as a whole may have to remain impartial, but there may be scope for more tactical flexibility to 'police' a local situation. The dynamic nature of the crisis in which peace support operations may take place creates a grey area on the ground which is not so amenable as a war-fighting situation to the precepts of military doctrine.

It should also be observed that the general British willingness to be involved in multilateral operations, coupled with the expertise of professional and specialized forces in such a situation, has resulted in a considerable degree of 'mission creep'. An operation which began on strictly humanitarian grounds developed into a containment and peacemaking operation and during 1995 verged on peace enforcement with the concomitant necessity of deploying more troops differently and more appropriately equipped. Bosnia, of course, is the outstanding example. Given a willingness to be involved, and the inherent nature of crises in which PSOs are deemed appropriate, it is not obvious how such 'mission creep' can be avoided in the future, even if the lessons of Bosnia are well drawn.[36]

Finally, Britain possess comparatively rich resources with which to engage in multilateral peace support operations. British military thinking is still vehement and unanimous that it is necessary to prepare for war in order to have the capabilities to engage in operations short of war. In the words of General Sir Michael Rose, 'the best war fighters turn out to be the best peacekeepers'. This view is consistent with a long tradition in the post-colonial world where British forces were structured to fight a third world war but found themselves, in practice, doing everything but that. It is a moot point whether this assertion can be sustained when the demands of modern peace support operations are so much greater than the demands made by either post-colonial operations or UN operations in the pre-1989 period, and where involvement in European crises necessarily suggests deeper commitments to peace support as an act of enlightened self-interest for the European powers. Nevertheless, on a conservative estimate, Britain can almost certainly field at one month's notice a high-intensity intervention capability that could consist of one corps HQ, one armoured division consisting of two brigades, one air mobile brigade, two MLRS regiments, two fighter and three fighter ground-attack squadrons, and one naval carrier task group, which could be deployed almost anywhere in the world, and certainly in or around the fringes of the European continent. For lesser operations, such as a major peacekeeping operation, Britain is capable of deploying at one month's notice a minimum of one brigade HQ plus signal squadron, one to two infantry battalions, one engineering regiment, one logistic battalion, transport helicopter support, two fighter and two fighter ground-attack squadrons, plus a small naval task force. In the case of either contingency, specialist troops are also potentially available, up to one brigade each of airborne troops and marines.[37] For operations that require a bigger build-up, of course, then much greater resources are potentially available, depending on the political will to incur the costs of deployment and the use of regular or territorial reserves. In 1993–94 the legislation concerning the call-up of reserves was altered to provide a more flexible structure and territorial army elements were better integrated with regular regiments in order to bring their numbers up to strength in case of further deployments in Bosnia.

In sum, therefore, it is clear that Britain has both the will and the capacity to engage in multilateral peace support operations. There is every expectation that Bosnia will not be the last, however messily the final political outcome of the effort to implement the Dayton Accords. The problems, rather, involve broader political questions concerning the appropriate command structures and lines of political authority that multilateral operations will require. Unlike the United States and possibly France, the British – after 45 years' experience in NATO – have no trouble either operationally or psychologically with the concept of multilateral operations either in war or in situations short of war. Nor do they have particular problems with the idea of being commanded at the top level by a non-British commander. It passed almost without comment in Britain in the Bosnia case from 1992. British concerns centre rather on the subordinate command structures and the civil–military interface and any possibilities that may raise for the degradation of the military effectiveness of national force operations. The military building blocks in the British Army are battalion task groups and as long as they are allowed to function in their own way and respond flexibly to the situation with which they are confronted on the ground, then it is generally felt that the operation can be effective.

CONCLUSION

In looking at national approaches to European security after the Cold War it is difficult to resist the conclusion that Britain is a *status quo* power in a situation where the *status quo* is rapidly changing. This does not make it irrelevant to the issue: indeed, on defence questions Britain cannot be effectively sidelined by its European partners as it could be over questions of monetary integration. But it does mean that Britain's approach to the future of European security has some very singular characteristics and that it remains an open question how much the emerging situation in Europe will play to Britain's relative weaknesses rather than its strengths.

To summarize the analysis presented in this chapter, it is clear that British attitudes carry a large historical legacy with them: a traditional influence within NATO; a strong relationship with the United States which has facilitated a great deal of diplomatic influence at certain periods during the Cold War; a traditional dualism toward Europe, whereby collective approaches to defence are a *sine qua non* of British interests whereas collective approaches to social and economic development in Europe are not; and, not least, a residual world role – backed by the United States – which lasted longer and declined more gradually than it might otherwise have done in the absence of the pressures of the Cold War.

Secondly, Britain views the future of European security as a process more than an exercise in architectural engineering. The pieces of the security jigsaw are too numerous, and the picture we are aiming to construct too vague, for the British to depart from their concentration on process. This faith in the efficacy of process stems partly from a relative satisfaction with previous security arrangements. The Cold War provided some predictability in international behaviour and the Western Alliance functioned as a most effective institution of collective defence. For the British, therefore, it would be most unwise to undermine institutions which have proved themselves, in favour of more vague institutional arrangements which are as yet quite unproven, or worse, have performed badly so far in post-Cold War crises. Hence, a step-by-step process of change will allow us to evaluate the costs of what we may be giving up as against the gains of any new security structure.

Thirdly, the British are entirely pragmatic in their view of any given change to European security structures. Political structures such as the EU must recognize the importance of inter-governmentalism which, together with the natural differences of interest that are bound to arise among a community of 15 nations, will make an EU security role more palatable. Military organizations such as NATO and the WEU must remain firmly task-based in their approach so that military forces can be sized, equipped, and commanded in such a way that they perform specified roles which are themselves regarded as useful and not duplicative of military tasks already assigned somewhere else. The British are naturally sceptical of the use of military organizations to make purely political gestures. Though NATO was used many times throughout the Cold War to make expansive political gestures it never lost its essential military rationale, whereas organizations which now may claim a significant defence role, such as the WEU and the EU, have yet to establish an essential military rationale that would give real point to any political messages they intended to send.

This summary indicates that, in practical terms, British attitudes to European security over the next two to three years are fairly easy to predict. The British believe that NATO has proved itself as an integrated military structure, that the WEU has a useful subsidiary role to play but yet has a very long way to go before it can be a competent and self-sustaining military structure capable of commanding significant military forces. Even if this were a desirable outcome, it is not likely to be achieved in the short or even the medium term. The result for the British, therefore, is that they feel a general European consensus has been arrived at whereby NATO remains the keystone organization and allows its assets to be used by other organizations or command structures as required in a flexible way to respond to current and future crises, as now being developed in accordance with the concept of CJTFs. For the British, the war in the former Yugoslavia has reawakened an awareness that British forces can have a valuable role to play in European peace support operations and that they will have to be at least partially restructured in order to play it efficiently. But if the Bosnia crisis has taught the British the importance of multinational peace support operations in Europe, it has also demonstrated for them the value of traditional coordination between national forces rather than the need for more integrated defence structures as such. This is the lesson of the trilateral Rapid Reaction Force (UK, France and the Netherlands) and of Operation Joint Endeavour. The costs, the dangers, the professionalism and the political will which are all part of deploying major forces in peace support operations, indicate for the British that they have an influential role to play at an inter-governmental level rather than a destiny to help create politically integrated defence structures where such elements would be diluted and possibly ineffective in future crises. If Bosnia has indicated that the Europeans have an important military job to do in Europe, then it has also demonstrated that they should do it inter-governmentally.

For similar reasons, the British are extremely sceptical at the prospect that the European Union should move toward the eventual framing of a common defence policy. Any move toward the introduction of Qualified Majority Voting is regarded by the British as a side issue. Where the European Council has been deadlocked on a particular issue, officials argue, it has almost always been for a very good reason. When countries stand up for their national interests as Greece did in the European Council over the recognition of Macedonia, or Germany did over the recognition of Croatia, it would have been unwise to have overridden them since in Athens and Bonn such issues were critically important politically. Just as the UN Security Council would be fatally weakened by majority voting so, the British argue, would the European Council. Indeed, there is a neat irony in the position for Britain and France since on the issue of peace support operations and related measures of crisis management, a qualified majority vote against one of these two countries could be overturned by their veto within the United Nations Security Council.

At root, British officials point to the logical consequences of a common European defence policy. Defence entails the symbolism of sovereignty and the British ask the rhetorical question, 'which European countries are prepared to give up their national control over defence and foreign policy?' In truth, countries such as Belgium and Luxembourg and perhaps even Italy would be prepared to do so. But it is inconceivable to officialdom in London that France, Germany or Spain would do so. The British themselves certainly have no expectation of doing so in the foreseeable future.

This attitude leaves the British increasingly unsympathetic to any prospects of deepening European integration in the defence field. Instead, it leaves them suggesting or supporting a number of sensible and limited initiatives: the creation of a European centre for security analysis within the EU; an increase in the directive powers of the Secretary-General of the European Council; an improvement across the board in the staff work prior to European Council and WEU summit meetings; a back-to-back summit of the European Council with Heads of State and Heads of Government of the WEU countries; and a determined attempt to coordinate more efficiently the command arrangements between the growing number of European military structures. This approach is entirely sensible and difficult to criticize either on ideological or practical grounds. It enjoys overwhelming backing within the country. It seems unlikely, however, that such gradualism will be enough to satisfy Britain's European partners whose views are frequently more expansive.

NOTES

1. See, for example the conclusions of over twenty years ago in the seminal work by W. Wallace, *The Foreign Policy Process in Britain* (London: Royal Institute of International Affairs, 1975).
2. M. Clarke, 'A British View', in R. Davy, ed., *European Detente: A Reappraisal* (London: Sage, 1992), pp. 90–7.
3. D. Sanders, *Losing an Empire, Finding a Role: British Foreign Policy since 1945* (London: Macmillan, 1990).

4. *Financial Times* (2 July 1984). See also, Ad Hoc Committee for Institutional Affairs, *Report to the European Council* (SN/1187/85 (SPAAK 11) (Brussels: 29–30 March 1985).
5. See the speech of the Defence Secretary on 'NATO' of 16 December 1993, in Centre for Defence Studies, *The Framework of United Kingdom Defence Policy* (London Defence Studies: 30/31 December 1995), pp. 51–2.
6. J. Baylis, *Anglo-American Defence Relations 1939–1980* (London: Macmillan, 1984).
7. See, for example, D. Hurd (writing as Foreign Secretary), 'No European Defence Identity Without NATO', *Financial Times* (15 April 1991), p. 15.
8. See, for example, British views as expressed in J. M. O. Sharp, ed., *Europe after an American Withdrawal* (Oxford: Oxford University Press/SIPRI), 1990.
9. See B. Heuser, *The Transatlantic Relationship*, Chatham House Paper (London: RIIA), 1996.
10. See M. Rifkind, 'The Future of European Security', Centre for Defence Studies, *op. cit.*, p. 175.
11. M. Clarke, 'The Europeanisation of NATO and the Problem of Anglo-American Relations', in M. Clarke and R. Hague, eds, *European Defence Cooperation* (Manchester: Manchester University Press, 1990), pp. 29–33.
12. It is possible that if Western nations engage in a great deal more 'constabulary' action, then the military basis to the special relationship could be revitalized, since there are few Western nations, other than the US itself, capable of projecting and maintaining specialist military forces in an expeditionary capacity.
13. Information from a personal interview, 2 March 1995. It was also observed that this guideline is now more honoured in the breach than the observance, but it still remains an aspiration of defence planners, which indicates a certain sense of Britain's self-image.
14. On patterns of foreign immigration into Britain, see M. Clarke, *British External Policymaking in the 1990s* (London: Macmillan/RIIA, 1992), pp. 183–4.
15. Unpublished Memorandum, 1 March 1995, *Memorandum on the United Kingdom Government's Approach to the Treatment of European Defence Issues at the 1996 Inter-Governmental Conference.*
16. L. Freedman, 'Wars of Necessity and Wars of Choice', in *Brassey's Defence Yearbook 1996* (London: Brassey's/Centre for Defence Studies, 1996), pp. 1–12.
17. Britain has made contributions to all these operations, though in some cases, such as Somalia and Haiti, token ones, mainly as an expression of Anglo-American solidarity.
18. See the prospective assessment of possible points of divergence among the Western allies as they contend with a more self-assertive and less cooperative Russia by M. Brenner: 'The United States Perspective', in *Reshaping the Transatlantic Partnership*, ed. J. Weiler (New York: John Wiley and Sons, 1997).

19. See M. Clarke, 'British External Policymaking in the 1990s', *op. cit.*, pp. 188–94.
20. See I. Crewe, 'Britain: Two and a Half Cheers for the Atlantic Alliance', in G. Flynn and H. Rattinger, eds, *The Public and Atlantic Defence* (London: Croom Helm, 1985), pp. 26–9.
21. See Centre for Defence Studies, *A Common Foreign and Security Policy for Europe: The Inter-Governmental Conference of 1996* (London: Centre for Defence Studies, 1995), pp. 38–9.
22. *Statement on the Defence Estimates 1995: Stable Forces in a Strong Britain*, Cm 2800 (London: HMSO, 1995), p. 22, para. 234.
23. See, for example, Gen. Maj. I. P. Smeshko, 'Partnership for Peace from a Ukrainian Perspective', Paper to the 11th USNATO Annual Strategic Studies Conference, September 1995.
24. Personal interviews.
25. See C. M. Kelleher, *The Future of European Security: An Interim Assessment* (Washington, DC: The Brookings Institution, 1995), pp. 67–73.
26. At the Berlin ministerial meeting, the compromise was that the US agreed to the creation of a NATO capability for WEU-controlled military operations, but only with the agreement of the North Atlantic Council. Thus even WEU-led CJTFs would be created within NATO, using the Alliance's procedures and perhaps its command assets.
27. Memorandum *op. cit.*, para. 30.
28. Adm. Paul David Miller USN, 'Adapting National Forces and Alliances to a New Security Environment', *Brassey's Defence Yearbook 1995* (London: Brassey's 1995), pp. 86–8.
29. House of Commons Defence Committee, *op. cit.*, p. xix.
30. The Army's doctrinal statement is *Wider Peacekeeping*, presently being incorporated into a doctrine that will include peacekeeping and peace enforcement. The Royal Navy and the Royal Air Force deal with such questions in their general doctrinal publications, *The Fundamentals of British Maritime Doctrine*, BR 1806 (London: HMSO, 1995); and, *Airpower Doctrine, AP 3000*, 2nd edn (London: HMSO, 1993).
31. See for example, the Statement by the then Foreign Secretary, Douglas Hurd, on 28 February 1995, when he said in a speech to the Deutsche Gesellschaft für Assenpolitik that we must be intensely practical about making the best use of WEU assets since we in Europe cannot 'expect direct American involvement in every crisis or operation in Europe or on the periphery'.
32. Quoted in B. White-Spunner, 'The Thin Blue Line: Britain's Military Contribution to the United Nations', *Brassey's Defence Yearbook 1995* (London: Brassey's for the Centre for Defence Studies, 1995), p. 37.
33. This possibility was first openly acknowledged at the end of January 1996. See S. Erlanger, 'Making the Bosnia Deal Work: US Carrots and Sticks', *International Herald Tribune* (5 Feb. 1996).
34. B. White-Spunner, *op. cit.*, pp. 38–9.

35. This analysis is based on personal interviews and participation in certain service working groups.
36. See M. Clarke, 'The Lessons of Bosnia for the British Military', *Brassey's Defence Yearbook 1995*, pp. 51–2.
37. A. Duncan, M. Clarke, and D. Stevens, *Contingency Forces Available Among WEU Member, Associate and Observer States* (London: Centre for Defence Studies, 1995).

3 France
Frédéric Bozo

Thirty years after General de Gaulle's decision to withdraw France from NATO's military integration, Jacques Chirac, his neogaullist successor, has embarked on a far-reaching transformation of the France–NATO relationship. This 'revolution' in French strategic policy, which takes place in the context of a far-reaching NATO reform, marks the end of a long period of French caution and scepticism on the possibility, after the end of the Cold War, of a profound transformation of the Alliance of the kind Paris has always called for. In French eyes, this holds true in particular with regard to two key, interrelated issues: NATO's role in collective security and Europe's identity in NATO. This chapter first looks at the persistence of the traditional framework of France–NATO relations in the period 1989–92; it then moves on to analyse the next phase, between 1992 and 1995, in which Paris started to selectively adapt that relationship to the new strategic context; next, it tries to offer an interpretation of the new concept of France–NATO relations which Jacques Chirac has developed since his election in 1995; finally, it examines the outlook for the Alliance reform process and for French policy in the light of the results of the accords reached at the historic June 1996 Berlin ministerial meeting and of its aftermath.

THE PERSISTENCE OF THE TRADITIONAL FRAMEWORK (1989–92)

In the immediate aftermath of the Cold War, France's policies towards NATO were mainly determined by the country's attempt to promote an autonomous European defence identity and by its reluctance to accept NATO's assumption of collective security missions. Both these orientations had been at the basis of France–Alliance disagreements dating from the late 1960s. In order to analyse France–NATO relations after 1989,[1] it is thus essential to keep in mind the durable framework within which the country's Alliance policy has evolved since 1966.

The Weight of the Past

Beyond the obvious goal of restoring French political independence and military autonomy, the long-term, and often overlooked rationale of de Gaulle's decision to withdraw France from the NATO integrated military structure was two-fold, with ramifications both at the West–West and at the East–West levels.[2] At the West–West level, it aimed at preserving the option of an autonomous European strategic entity which France alone, after the failure of the Fouchet plan and the semi-failure of the Elysée treaty, could anticipate. In other words, an independent France in the Alliance was a prefiguration of an independent Europe in the Alliance. At the East–West level, it was meant to foster a general evolution towards the overcoming of the bipolar bloc system which France, by loosening its ties with the NATO military structure, could precipitate. In that sense, the rupture between France and NATO in 1966 already reflected a fundamental disagreement on the articulation between NATO and collective security. For Gaullist diplomacy, the Atlantic Alliance was indeed an obstacle to the ending of the bipolar system, as long as it remained faithful to its Cold War model. In essence, NATO was seen as prolonging the Cold War by fostering the logic of bloc confrontation and by preventing the establishment of a pan-European security system from the Atlantic to the Urals which would serve as the framework for overcoming the division of Europe. For the other allies, by contrast, a NATO that would retain its Cold War characteristics of military integration, strategic unity and political cohesion would be in a better position to meet the challenge of detente as it emerged in the mid-sixties. Their thinking is expressed in the Harmel Report of December 1967 (which France had only reluctantly accepted). It stressed that the combination of a closely integrated defence and of a strictly bipolar management of East–West relations provided the best hope of ending the confrontation.

The 1966 French decision, far from being reducible to a sheer manifestation of national interest or ambition, was thus very much the reflection of a specific perspective on the long-term evolution of the European system. As a result, with the fall of the Berlin Wall and the passing of the 'Yalta' order, the opposition between the Gaullist vision and the Atlanticist vision of the European system was bound to appear in full light. From the traditional French point of view, the events of 1989 were naturally seen as a vindication of de Gaulle's prophesies. They called for an adaptation of the European security framework of the type that the General had anticipated: i.e. one that placed more emphasis on West European and pan-European institutions (the EC/WEU and the CSCE respectively), and less on NATO. As seen from Paris, the fading away of bipolar confrontation was finally making it possible to build an autonomous European strategic entity while the disappearance of the Cold War system called for a strengthening of cooperative or collective security in Europe.[3]

For France's allies, on the contrary, those same events demonstrated the validity of the Harmel approach: the West had won the Cold War thanks to the solidity and solidarity of the Alliance as well as to US leadership. Hence, NATO should remain the hard core of European security, not only by maintaining itself as a closely integrated military alliance, but also by developing its political role. It followed that Western European institutions should not be transformed into entities able to compete with NATO. As seen from France, the 'politicization' of NATO was in fact the key element in the strategy followed by the Bush Administration in 1989–90, designed to keep NATO both the centrepiece of European security and the primary framework for American involvement in Europe, in spite of the fading away of the Soviet threat. Logically, for Washington, NATO would survive as an effective military alliance, and become an effective instrument for a concerted Western diplomacy as well, if and only if it were allowed to bypass the narrow limits of its Article 5 defensive missions and encouraged to assume new security functions whose geographic scope would extend beyond its Article 6 boundaries. Such a strategy was implicit in Secretary James Baker's declarations in the fall of 1989 and soon spelled out by the Secretary-General of NATO, Manfred Wörner.[4]

In that context, the military aspects of the NATO reform, which was launched at the July 1990 London summit, were inevitably seen in Paris as an attempt to put the Alliance in a position to actually implement those new missions before they were even formally agreed to by the allies. The emphasis put on mobility and projection capabilities, thanks notably to the creation of a Rapid Reaction Corps in Allied Command Europe, was indeed interpreted by the French as a preparation for potential out-of-area operations rather than as a way to reinforce the defence of NATO's flanks. When viewed in relation to other developments in 1990–91 (the Gulf War and the Inter-Governmental Conference on the European Union in the background), these orientations were naturally equated with an attempt to make NATO into a vehicle for future Western operations out of area, and to preempt the role of the soon-to-be European Union in peacekeeping contingencies in Europe or at its periphery.[5]

This reading of US and allied attempts to transform NATO after 1989 and, more specifically, to give it a more encompassing function, explains much of France's Alliance policies in the initial post-Cold War period. Until 1992–93, French attitudes towards NATO (in spite of rare episodes like the Bush–Mitterrand Key Largo meeting in early 1990 which seemed to open the possibility of a rapprochement) were characterized by the traditional policy of military non-participation and political aloofness.[6] On the military level, the French attitude towards the NATO reform, most of all in the period between the London summit and the Rome summit of November 1991, was one of criticism towards what was dismissed as an attempt to put the cart before the horse, namely to embark on military changes before agreeing on future political tasks.

On the political level, Mitterrand in fact opposed the 'politicization' of the Alliance. He made it clear that in his mind NATO should remain primarily a defence organization, and he criticized decisions which tended to turn NATO into a forum for the management of East–West relations after the Cold War.[7] Hence, France did not favour the creation of the North Atlantic Cooperation Council (an idea first broached in late 1991), mostly on the ground that the CSCE was best suited to provide a framework for cooperative security at the pan-European level and, eventually, to serve as a full-blown collective security institution.

Paris thus staunchly opposed the increasing pressure on the part of its partners, and the US above all, to give NATO the capability for playing a collective security role as opposed to a strictly collective defence one. This opposition was all the more fierce because, in the context of the Inter-Governmental Conference, the French were emphasizing their traditional policy of favouring the build-up of West European institutions in the sphere of defence and security, a policy highlighted by the Mitterrand–Kohl October 1991 initiative on Common Foreign and Security Policy and the decision to create a Franco-German Corps.[8] Simultaneously the French were doing their best, albeit unsuccessfully, to promote European institutions (the EC and/or the WEU) with respect to crisis management and peacekeeping, as was particularly clear in the early months of the war in the Balkans, notably in the fall of 1991. Thus, it was not until the Oslo NATO ministerial in June 1992 and the Brussels ministerial in December 1992 that France finally agreed to subscribe formally to the notion that NATO could be asked by the CSCE and/or the UN to perform collective security tasks under their auspices. It was a decision which, as argued below, marked a turning point both for the Alliance in general and for France in particular.

The Strategic Vision

Beyond the legacy of past policies, and in spite of the persistence of analytical frameworks inherited from the Gaullist period, France's aloofness from, if not opposition to, the post-1989 NATO reform was also a function of a specific vision of the post-Cold War European order, in terms of both the institutional setting and the management of actual crises. France's conception of European security architecture in the early post-Cold War period was indeed, to a large extent, in contradiction with her allies' view of NATO and of its prospective role after the disappearance of the bloc system.[9]

As hinted above, the main focus of French diplomacy in 1989–92, in a context dominated by the Maastricht process, was first and foremost directed toward endowing the West Europeans with an autonomous strategic entity, capable of a common foreign and security policy (CFSP) and, later on, a common defence policy, with a view to building a common defence, eventually. This sequence, as it is actually formulated in the text of the Maastricht treaty, was not decided randomly: it was a reflection of a deliberate approach for achieving European strategic autonomy. It was indeed clear, in Paris as in other capitals, that the only way for title V of Maastricht not to antagonize Atlanticists on both sides of the Atlantic was deliberately to draw a distinction between the building of a projected defence arm for the European Union (which was deemed unrealistic) and developing a European Security Identity (ESI). As Mitterrand himself recognized, defence should remain a NATO function for the foreseeable future.[10] This division of labour between the EU/WEU and NATO, in which the Europeanists accepted that the former would be confined to non-Article 5 missions, made it obviously difficult for them to accept NATO's post-Cold War tendency to infringe upon what amounted, at least on paper, to Europe's virtual strategic *domaine réservé*, i.e. security functions.

This was all the more so because another emphasis of French diplomacy was on the need to strengthen the CSCE, as highlighted at the Paris summit of November 1990. In spite of second thoughts in Paris on the appropriateness of building up the Helsinki process into an actual security organization (which, in the context of 1990, was briefly seen as too 'loose' to effectively 'contain' a unified Germany), French diplomacy quickly returned to its traditional interest in pan-European security schemes. The CSCE, indeed, was the framework in which (notably through the CFE treaty) the reunification of Germany, and of all of Europe, had been achieved. It also presented the advantage of including the then Soviet Union as a full partner in the European security system while lowering the risk of an artificial maintenance of the bloc-to-bloc logic that the superpowers seemed tempted to cling to in spite of the sea-change in the politico-strategic environment, as made clear at the Bush–Gorbachev meeting at Malta in December 1989. Finally, as implicitly confirmed by Mitterrand's aborted plan for a European Confederation – a process designed to offer Central/East European countries practical ties with Western Europe or, in other words, to throw bridges between 'Petite Europe' and 'Grande Europe' – France was not eager to let the United States interfere with the former's role in securing the latter. Needless to say, all these considerations on the need to strengthen the pan-European level of security left little room for France's acceptance of NATO's role in that dimension, be it through the workings of NACC, let alone by contemplating either admitting new members into the Alliance, as some already were advocating, or by allowing NATO to go out of area. In other words, France, because of its specific conception of the post-Cold War pan-European security setting, was not inclined to accept an enlarged NATO role either in terms of membership or function.

Finally, the French view of the role of nation-states in the post-Cold War strategic architecture played a role in France's reluctance to accept NATO's expanded security role beyond its classical mission. France, in that period, clung to its traditional posture of non-integration in NATO military structures because integration *à la* NATO was incompatible both with the Gaullist vision of a European system that transcended the logics of blocs and the goal of a truly autonomous European entity. In addition, integration was still seen as a threat to the country's political and military independence.[11] In turn, the persistence of France's special position in the Alliance was a clear factor in the French reluctance to accept NATO's new security role. Indeed, accepting a central role for the Alliance in collective security while keeping NATO's Cold War military mechanisms unchanged would have meant taking the risk of France's isolation from preventive diplomacy and crisis management.

The Security Environment

In France, as elsewhere, national policies towards defence and security organizations in the post-Cold War context have been shaped both by the country's conception of European architecture and by the actuality of international crises in Europe and at its periphery. Starting in 1990–91, against the backdrop of the Gulf and Yugoslav crises, the realities of crisis management were arguably the strongest influences shaping France's attitudes *vis-à-vis* NATO and its evolution.

To be sure, the Gulf crisis of 1990–91 was not, at least formally, a NATO contingency. The notion of 'out of area' was then still a clear-cut concept and at no time was the possibility of a direct NATO intervention considered, even though its three major members and other allies were involved in Desert Shield/Desert Storm. Yet it was bound to have an impact on the debate over NATO's collective security role; indeed, in the aftermath of the operations against Iraq, supporters of a NATO out-of-area role naturally used the events in the Middle East in support of their thesis. For France, however, the lessons of the Gulf War were exactly the opposite ones. At the military level, they had shown (notably as far as the operational relations between France and her key allies were concerned) that NATO procedures and assets could easily be used in such contingencies without any serious need for NATO commands and the rest of the NATO machinery. At the political level, the French view was that NATO's formal involvement in future similar contingencies was unthinkable, both because major allies such as Germany likely could or would not take part in such operations and because the support of non-NATO members such as the Soviet Union or the involvement of moderate Arab countries would be impossible if the NATO flag was visible. If anything, the Gulf War, in French eyes, in fact underlined the need for a stronger Western Europe in the defence dimension and crisis management as a counterweight to the US predominance – not the need for NATO to go out of area.[12]

The Yugoslav crisis, coming almost immediately after the Gulf War, was, at least until early 1993, another and perhaps even more important factor in France's reluctance to accept NATO's new collective security role which others were actively trying to push in reference to Yugoslavia.[13] France's reading of the nature and origins of the Yugoslav crisis in its early phase left little, if any room for a NATO role. For Paris, the problem was, from the very outset, one that should be dealt with primarily in political, not military terms. Even though

France quickly became the first contributor to UN operations in Croatia and Bosnia, the belief was firmly held in Paris that the peace could only stem from an agreement on both borders and minority rights among the successor states of the ex-Yugoslavia rather than from recognizing the *fait accompli* of individual declarations of independence on the part of its former Republics. The latter approach, as seen from Paris, could only make things worse – hence the serious tensions between France and Germany over the recognition of Slovenia and Croatia in early 1992. This reading of the crisis was, initially at least, obviously more geared towards conflict-prevention than towards peace enforcement, therefore leaving little room for an active NATO role. This was all the more so because, as a logical consequence of this reading of the crisis, French diplomacy insisted on the need for military neutrality on the part of the international community. In such an analytical and political framework, NATO's involvement was clearly seen as entailing the risk of transforming a mission of humanitarian support or interposition into a confrontation with one of the parties, i.e. the Serbs, and, therefore, that of an escalation of the crisis. Moreover, in French eyes, NATO's direct implication in Yugoslavia would at best complicate relations with Russia and, at worse, antagonize Moscow with equal risks of escalation, if not spill-over. On the opposite, a EU/WEU role in the crisis was not seen as entailing similar risks.

Another way in which the Yugoslav crisis had an impact on the French view of NATO's potential role in collective security was, obviously, through the twofold issue of the United States' involvement and Europe's assertion as a strategic player. Right from the beginning events in the Balkans were seen on both sides of the Atlantic as potentially decisive with regard to the evolution of the US presence in Europe and of European autonomy in the Alliance. There is no denying that, on the French side, there was at least initially, and in some quarters, a tendency to read ulterior motives into US attitudes: the Americans were suspected either of deliberately letting the Europeans on their own in the management of the crisis with the hope that their likely failure would make the US active involvement seem desirable, and/or of preparing themselves to take the lead in the crisis with a view to excluding the Europeans from its settlement.[14] Hence, France's strong insistence on a European role in the crisis (notably, the Summer 1991 suggestion of a EU/WEU peacekeeping intervention in Yugoslavia) and its staunch opposition to a NATO involvement in the first phase of the crisis.

Finally, NATO's intervention in the crisis was not seen as a desirable option because Paris clearly saw events in the Balkans as a major stake for France's status as a great power. There is no denying that, for French diplomacy, French leadership in the Yugoslav crisis was needed if France was to justify its permanent seat in the UN Security Council at a time when post-Cold War redistribution of power and European integration could threaten it. Decisionmakers fully understood that France could not act on its own in Yugoslavia and that she had to use multilateral institutions; yet the CSCE, the UN and the EU were clearly seen, in the early stage of the crisis, as preferable to NATO as frameworks for multilateral action. There, France would have been both overshadowed by the United States and disconnected from the integrated machinery in which she did not participate. Thus, for reasons of national prestige and a desired extension of France's international influence, NATO was rejected as a suitable framework for crisis management and collective security.

Underlying Assumptions of the Policy and Its Limits

The French reluctance to accept a NATO role in collective security and, as a result, to normalize France's role in the Alliance in the early post-Cold War period thus stemmed from the country's specific status in the Alliance, from its vision of post-Cold War architecture and from its approach to actual crises such as those in the Gulf and, most of all, in Yugoslavia. With hindsight, this attitude also rested on a series of assumptions having to do respectively with the nature of the international system, with the dynamics of US–Europe relations and with France's own capabilities.[15] It is because those assumptions turned out to be at least partially wrong that this attitude, as seen below, began to change, starting in late 1992.

The first series of assumptions were those bearing on the European system after the end of the Cold War. As explained above, there was, in French minds, a natural tendency rooted in the Gaullist vision of the overcoming of blocs to believe that the end of bipolar confrontation would make possible the advent of a European system based on cooperative or collective security with the CSCE as its main framework. To be sure, the thinking of decisionmakers and politicians was not a rerun of the naïve idealism of the interwar period. But there may well have been in the French strategic community, if only for the brief period in which the Soviet threat had vanished and the 'new risks' had not yet materialized, a sincere confidence that the system would work and preserve security and stability. In that somewhat optimistic vision of the European system, the peace would be guaranteed by a combination of political factors (conflict-prevention at the CSCE level, economic integration at the EU level and, in between, the CIS itself) and last-resort military tools (NATO in its traditional Article 5 incarnation, and nuclear deterrence). While there was room in that picture for the actual use of military force in support of conflict-prevention or peacekeeping processes, it can be argued that few analysts and decisionmakers in that period believed in the likelihood that eventualities would arise that actually required using military force in the large scale, integrated way of NATO. In short, the underlying threat or rather risk assessment in France's European security policy in the early 1990s simply did not call for a NATO geared towards an active role in collective security enforcement.

The second series of assumptions bore on US–Europe relations. In that same time-frame, which was dominated by the Maastricht agenda, there was arguably, in the French strategic community, whether among policymakers, analysts or politicians, a sincere European faith which, until late 1992 not many challenged. The 'spirit' of Maastricht then clearly dominated French thinking on security. It grew out of a sincere confidence in the ability of the Twelve to organize themselves into a coherent diplomatic and military grouping of a *sui generis* nature (maybe less than a federation, but more than a classical alliance) and to actually become the main player in the European strategic game. Such confidence pushed the French to make the kind of proposal Mitterrand made in September 1991, even before the Treaty was signed, to send troops to Yugoslavia under the aegis of the Twelve in order to try to stem the conflict between Croatia and Serbia. Such hopes for a major European role were shattered when the divisive issue of the recognition of Slovenia and Croatia revealed the depth of misunderstanding between the two main protagonists of European construction, i.e. France and Germany. It nearly led to a split between them just weeks after signing the Maastricht Treaty. The recognition episode was bound to gravely call into question the viability of a European strategic actor which had been for the previous few years the keystone of France's post-Cold War strategy.

Finally, there was an assumption about French capabilities and power, and about the country's degree of strategic independence from the United States. The long tradition of perceived national independence and strategic autonomy inaugurated by de Gaulle was indeed bound to have a bearing on the French perception of the country's strategic margin of manoeuvre after the Cold War. If France had been able to adopt an independent stance in the context of the Soviet threat and, above all, to keep a measure of autonomy *vis-à-vis* the United States – thanks notably to her independent nuclear deterrent – then why could she not do the same in the absence of that threat, in face of much less serious risks, especially if she pooled her resources with other European countries? To a large extent, France's initial post-Cold War European activism and aversion to an expanded NATO role thus rested on an optimistic evaluation of the conditions and requirements of strategic autonomy after the fading away of what was perceived as the only justification of four decades of West European military reliance on the United States, i.e. the Soviet threat.

It is, as we shall see, the calling into question of all three foregoing sets of assumptions that explains what can be described as a new phase in France–NATO relations which started in late 1992.

THE NEW SETTING OF FRANCE–NATO RELATIONS (1993–95)

By 1993, a new framework of France–NATO relations was slowly emerging. The turn was in fact taken before the coming to power of Balladur's conservative government and the inauguration of a new phase of *cohabitation*. France's new policy, rather than merely a change in domestic politics, reflected a deep-rooted evolution in strategic perceptions derived from a realization of the limits of Europe's strategic autonomy and of the need for an Alliance role beyond its narrow Article 5 mission. In the light of developments in the Yugoslav crisis, the French had to scale down their European ambitions and to reconsider their refusal of any collective security role for the Alliance. With NATO's actual, if at first marginal, involvement in the crisis, starting in 1993, France no longer tried to block the transformation of NATO into an organization performing collective security functions. At the same time, it *de facto* gave up attempts to use the crisis in order to build up the EU/WEU as a major strategic actor. As a result, France was coming closer than ever since 1966 to a fundamental revision of its ties with the Alliance. The Brussels NATO summit of

January 1994, and the French–American sponsored ultimatum on Sarajevo of February 1994, made that evolution quite clear. By autumn of 1995, France announced a major revision in its policy regarding participation in NATO's politico-military bodies. In the meantime, Jacques Chirac had been elected Mitterrand's successor as President of the Republic, and the Yugoslav crisis, after reaching its climax in July 1995, had entered a new phase as a result of US military involvement and diplomatic leadership.[16]

Yugoslavia: Test Case

The change in French attitudes towards NATO's collective security role was first and foremost a reflection of changing conditions in the evolution of the crisis in the former Yugoslavia. By the Spring of 1993, all major international institutions, whether collective security organizations (the CSCE, the UN) or defence alliances (NATO, the WEU) were or had been involved in the crisis. But the logic of institutional competition which had to a large extent conditioned national policies, including France's own, had demonstrated the limits of the concept of 'interlocking institutions' and was, in fact, leading to a deadlock. Moreover, the failed mission of Warren Christopher in May 1993, in which the French and the British rejected the air strikes which the incoming Clinton Administration strongly advocated, revealed the sharp divisions within the Alliance over what strategy should be implemented in Bosnia. It is in that context that positions started to change on both sides of the Atlantic as the need for a clarification of the respective roles of security organizations was now patently clear.[17]

With the involvement of NATO in the surveillance and implementation of the 'no fly' zone over Bosnia starting in April 1993, which France had reluctantly accepted, the Alliance was for the first time operating out of area.[18] The following summer, the coordination of NATO and WEU naval operations in the Adriatic – with NATO as the key player – confirmed the Alliance's increasing role in the crisis. France's participation in NATO operations 'Sharp Guard' and 'Deny Flight' were significant steps. But the evolving situation on the ground was arguably fraught with greater consequences for France–NATO relations and for the evolution of the Alliance as a whole. The chief of staff of the French armed forces, Admiral Jacques Lanxade, and the chairman of the US Joint Chiefs of Staff, General John Shalikasvili, had undertaken a negotiation on the planning for the deployment of a large, NATO-led peacekeeping force in Bosnia in case a peace agreement was reached in the framework of the Vance–Owen plan of early 1993. Even though this French–US led contingency planning exercise (which resulted in NATO plan MC 40103 for operation 'Disciplined Guard') was never implemented, and some unresolved issues notwithstanding (MC 40103 was, in fact, not approved by the NAC), it marked a turning-point in the politics of NATO's collective security role and of France's attitude toward it. Paris, in fact, for the first time, accepted at least in principle a meaningful out-of-area ground intervention by NATO in what had become the most important post-Cold War crisis in Europe. Meanwhile, Washington seemed ready to recognize the need for such an operation to be led in a UN framework.

In the next few months, this French–American convergence became both more dramatic and more concrete. In the wake of the NATO Brussels summit in January 1994, Paris and Washington played a decisive role in the issuing of NATO ultimatums intended to protect the safe areas of Sarajevo (February) and Gorazde (April). The clear success of this policy, particularly in the case of Sarajevo, was an important event in three ways, even though it turned out to be of short duration. First, for the first time in the unfolding of the crisis, the West succeeded at least for some time in thwarting aggression; second, the Alliance was effectively used as a credible military instrument at the service of the international community; third, the French–American rapprochement proved to be a key to the effectiveness of the Alliance in that particular context. If only for that reason, it was perceived by many as a historic moment in French–American and France–NATO relations.

The developments throughout 1994 and 1995 only confirmed this trend. France's full participation to the discussion in NATO of plan MC 40104 ('Determined Effort') for the extraction of UNPROFOR – should the steady degradation of the situation on the ground make it necessary – was another sign of the Alliance's pivotal role in crisis management and of France's readiness to acknowledge it. In Spring 1995, the UNPROFOR hostage crisis, which Chirac had to manage shortly after taking over at the Elysée, came as a demonstration *par l'absurde* of the political and military limits of the UN peacekeeping posture. The subsequent decision to set up a Franco-British led rapid reaction force in Bosnia only reinforced the growing tendency to resort to coercion rather than interposition to deal with the crisis. With the deployment of the FRR in July 1995, and the changing rules of engagement that accompanied it, the international community was edging closer to a direct NATO intervention on the ground than at any time since 1991. The Croat offensive in Krajina, followed by the Croat-Muslim offensive in Bosnia, finally confirmed NATO's military intervention: the air campaign dubbed 'Deliberate Force'. The military setbacks suffered by the Bosnian Serbs, and the all-out US involvement in the crisis, opened the way to the peace agreement reached in Dayton. IFOR was to be its military instrument, thus leading to the first NATO ground operation ever – with France fully participating.

NATO's progressive involvement in the Yugoslav crisis was both the background and the motor of the changes that have occurred in the past three years in the framework of France-NATO relations. The turning-point in those relations was thus, as hinted above, in 1992, when Paris accepted, in principle, NATO's role as a military instrument performing collective security tasks on behalf of the UN or the CSCE. Indeed, France was now routinely involved in actual NATO military operations, a fact which, in turn, required an adaptation of its institutional and operational participation in the Alliance. For France's non-participation in NATO decisionmaking bodies was becoming unsustainable as her involvement in actual NATO operations was increasing.

Starting in the Spring of 1993, France began to qualify, at first selectively, its traditional aloofness from the NATO politico-military apparatus from which Paris was cut off since 1966.[19] It was decided in April that the Chief of the French Military Mission to the NATO Military Committee would from then on fully participate in the deliberations of that body for non-Article 5 operations in which the country would be involved. Another step was taken under the phase of 'cohabitation' when the government decided to allow (for the first time since 1966) the Minister of Defence, François Léotard, to participate in an 'informal' meeting with his NATO colleagues in Seville in September 1994. Meanwhile, the new defence White Paper, issued in 1994 (the first such exercise since 1972), marked an evolution of the declaratory policy on France-NATO relations. While acknowledging NATO's 'new missions' and the 'evolutions which have taken place since 1991 in the organization and activities of the Alliance' as well as France's 'participation in this renovation', the White Paper stressed the fact that, without 'changing [her] specific military situation vis-à-vis NATO', France intended to participate in the 'decisionmaking bodies of the organization' as her interests may require. This included the participation of the Minister of Defence in the Atlantic

Council and that of the Chief of Staff in the Military Committee 'as may be decided on a case by case basis by the President of the Republic and the Prime Minister'.[20]

In the Spring of 1995, the presidential campaign made it clear that Jacques Chirac, if elected, would likely continue this trend.[21] Indeed, starting in the summer, the government of now Prime Minister Juppé embarked on a wide-ranging overhaul of the France–NATO relationship. It was coordinated by the interministerial Secrétariat Général de la Défense Nationale (SGDN) with the Elysée closely monitoring the exercise. Logically, it was decided and announced in December 1995 that France was now ready to normalize its participation in NATO non-integrated bodies.[22] From then on, the French representative in the Military Committee would fully participate in the deliberations of that body and the Defence Minister would participate in NATO defence meetings (while not in the DPC itself). In addition, France would return to NATO institutions – such as the Defence College in Rome – which she had left in 1966. The decisions of December 1995, which France's allies and NATO officials warmly welcomed, were thus the logical outcome of three years of progressive change in the France–NATO relationship which, by then, was comparable to the 'Spanish model' of full political-military participation with no military integration, a model which many had advocated since the late 1980s.

While not leading to France's return to NATO integration for the time being, the events of 1992–95, however, also had an impact on the question of its relationship with the integrated military structure itself. In December 1992, the arrangement reached by Admiral Lanxade, General Naumann and General Shalikasvili on procedures for the command of Eurocorps in a NATO contingency marked a welcome milestone in the two years' Franco-American feud over its NATO status. Meanwhile, growing NATO involvement in Yugoslavia, combined with disillusion as to the WEU's effective role in the crisis, was forcing the French to reconsider their conception of European military autonomy *vis-à-vis* NATO. With UNPROFOR, the French accepted a routine dependence on NATO infrastructure and logistics and were progressively accepting the notion that a European defence pillar would somehow have to rely on NATO assets and capabilities. French acceptance of the concept of Combined Joint Task Forces (CJTF) in the Fall of 1993, and the formal agreement reached at the January 1994 Brussels summit, were thus a clear if implicit recognition on the part of France of the need for closer ties with the NATO integrated military structures, provided they are adapted to collective security missions and to the need for a stronger European defence and security identity.

The Reasons: An Analytical Framework

Beyond the pragmatic adaptation of the Gaullist model to the new military realities of the post-Cold War world in the context of the Yugoslav crisis, the evolution of the France–NATO relationship between 1992 and 1995 also, and more importantly, reflects deep changes in the strategic vision which had pervaded the country's position in the Alliance for thirty years.[23] With the expectations of the immediate post-Wall period crumbling, new assumptions have come to underlie France's NATO policy as it evolved in the critical period of 1992–93 and then following Chirac's coming to power.[24]

There is little doubt that the main catalyst of that evolution has been the realization of the limits of France's European strategic design. The maximalist vision of an integrated, strategically autonomous Europe, which was seemingly that of France's leaders in the years 1990–92, when they advocated the build-up to the WEU into the EU's military arm, soon fell victim to its own excess and to the test-case of Yugoslavia. The Maastricht ratification processes (and, to begin with, France's referendum in September 1992) did a lot of damage to France's European ambition by showing the gap between elite thinking and the expectations of public opinion. Meanwhile, as noted above, the near-split of the soon-to-be European Union and, most of all, of the Franco-German partnership, over the recognition of Croatia, i.e. over a fundamental issue of the post-Cold War era, had led Mitterrand himself to recognize the limits of his European design as early as 1992 (when, for example, he decided to fly on his own from a European Council meeting in Lisbon to Sarajevo without consulting with his European counterparts or even informing them). The coming to power of neo-Gaullist Prime Minister Edouard Balladur in March 1993 later confirmed the shift in France's European policies, particularly in the field of foreign and security policy, toward a more pragmatic low-key approach. Because European autonomy had been, since the 1960s, the main source of France–NATO antagonism, the revision of French European goals after 1992, however implicit, was bound to have an impact on France's view of NATO. At a time when the incoming Clinton Administration was giving strong signs of a new US readiness to accept the emergence of an ESDI in the Alliance, this evolution was naturally leading to a *de facto* French acceptance of the notion of a European pillar in NATO, which Paris had fought fiercely in 1990–92.

The US policy was indeed another essential catalyst of France's changing NATO policy starting in 1992, one that reversed a key assumption of the Gaullist approach to the Alliance. The main rationale of that approach was the anticipation of an unavoidable US disengagement in the long term. Yet at the same time, the key assumption in the French–NATO calculus was that France's NATO policy and the build-up of a West European strategic entity would not, contrary to American caveats, seriously increase the risk of a US withdrawal from Europe (at least as long as the Soviet threat continued). Furthermore, even if it did, the Europeans would have reached strategic self-sufficiency by the time it happened. With the end of the Cold War, this assumption was bound to be revised sooner or later: without a Soviet threat, the United States could but redefine the rationale of its strategic involvement in Europe and lower the level of its military presence – if not, in the longer run, cease to be a key player in European security. What the French policymakers then may have started to realize in 1992–93 was that this was perhaps becoming a reality, and one which was not in the French interest.

The first few months of the Clinton Administration indeed showed that the United States was simply not interested in what the French and other Europeans saw as the major challenge to security and stability in Europe, i.e. the Yugoslav conflict. This American attitude, combined as it was with the clear shift of US national priorities away from international issues to domestic ones, was certainly a catalyst in changing French perceptions of the American presence in Europe. What had been taken for granted for the past 40 years or so, i.e. the permanence and viability of that involvement, was now very much called into question at a time when the deterioration of the strategic context in Central and South Eastern Europe, the poor showing of Western Europe after the Maastricht backlash, and the risks of a return to old patterns of balances of power in Europe made the importance of a US active role arguably greater than before. Keeping the United States as a major player in European security was in fact becoming a key French objective, both in the context of the Yugoslav crisis where Paris was clearly trying to implicate the United States, and in the reform of NATO whose essential, core function of collective defence under Article 5 of the Washington Treaty was seen as increasingly linked to its showing in the new, non-Article 5 tasks.

In fact, France's new-found interest in NATO's role in collective security may also be attributed to the disillusions with the post-Cold War European system. 1992–93 may in fact have been the turning-point between the period of early post-Cold War euphoria and the realization, in Paris as elsewhere, of the darkening outlook for European security. With the situation in Bosnia deteriorating into what after all was the first military conflict in Europe since 1945, mainstream security thinking in France, by then the most active country in trying to solve the crisis on the ground, was bound to abandon the rosy and idealistic scenarios *à la* Charter of Paris for a new European security order. They shifted to a bleaker, more realistic appraisal of European security and its problems. It is also noteworthy that events in the same period showed the limits of the much celebrated notion of the Western 'security community' (i.e. the supposed blurring of classical disputes between Western nations who for half a century had developed multilateral institutions in the face of the Soviet threat). The seriously deteriorated relations between France and Germany over the recognition of Slovenia and Croatia in 1991–92 were taken as an ominous sign of the risk of a return to old-style geopolitics and of the possibility that crisis could degenerate into larger confrontations. The failure of international organizations to solve the Yugoslav crisis, and to maintain a minimal level of understanding among major players in the European security game, due in good part to the institutional competition and 'interblocking' described above, called for a rethinking of the interaction among those organizations and, most importantly, a clarification of the articulation between organizations of collective security and organizations of collective defence.

The evolving French perspective on the Alliance's role in collective security also reflected a change in the perception of France's international and strategic autonomy in security policy *vis-à-vis* NATO. As noted earlier, France's participation in NATO operations was still seen in the early post-Cold War period as threatening the country's international ranking and independent role in crisis management as a result of US predominance in the Alliance. By 1993, this perception was changing, mostly as a result of the redefinition of the requirements of strategic autonomy in the post-Yalta context. While France may have enjoyed a status of relative strategic self-sufficiency within the Alliance in front of a massive Soviet threat, thanks to nuclear deterrence, this was no longer the case after the Cold War in the face of the new strategic challenges. For another lesson of the Gulf and Yugoslav crises was that France, as indeed her European partners with the relative exception of Britain, lacked the military assets that make for strategic self-sufficiency in out-of-area contingencies, such as command, control, communications and intelligence (C^3I) as well as logistics and lift capabilities. The realization of France's actual level of strategic dependence on the United States was thus bound to relativize the perception of NATO as a danger to a French strategic autonomy which was itself relative. Moreover, at the political level, the Sarajevo ultimatum demonstrated that far from sidelining France, NATO's involvement, the result of French initiative – if not leadership – rather than being imposed on a reluctant French diplomacy, could in fact give considerable weight to the country's actions. When Paris proved able, as was done in February 1994, to draw Washington into joint actions, the Alliance framework did not diminish French influence and status but, on the contrary, could function as a multiplier of French initiatives. The realization that NATO could be used by France as the primary framework of its policy without running the risk of absorption by the 'Anglo-Saxons' came as a happy surprise to most policymakers. It was bound to change substantially the traditional French perception of NATO. As Foreign Minister Alain Juppé put it in the aftermath of the ultimatum, the Franco-American entente has become 'the most visible factor of dynamism in the Alliance'.[25] In many ways, this unprecedented situation of French–American collusion in NATO, far from being a betrayal of the Gaullist vision, appeared to many as a confirmation of its very relevance: because France had an active, independent security policy, it was in a better position to influence American policies and secure an active US involvement in European security.

Finally, bureaucratic politics also played a role in reducing traditional French apprehensions *vis-à-vis* NATO and thus in making policymakers less reluctant to accept an increased Alliance role in collective security.[26] Since the Gaullist period, the politics of French–NATO relations were characterized by a split between the diplomats and the military. While the former traditionally acted as the guardians of what they perceived to be Gaullist orthodoxy, the latter on the contrary were eager to step up the quality and importance of operational links between France and NATO at the expense of 'doctrinal' considerations. With the end of the Cold War, this gap between the diplomats and the military was bound to be bridged. For one thing, the political dimension of France's specific posture within the Alliance, linked as it was to the East–West order, was losing its systemic logic. As a result, conditions no longer justified the kind of monopoly enjoyed by the Quai d'Orsay in the management of NATO ties since 1966. Furthermore, the operational dimension of French NATO relations which, as was now clear to the public, had never ceased to evolve since 1966, was a far less sensitive issue and, therefore, one that could be openly dealt with by the Ministry of Defence – all the more so because of the country's growing participation in actual NATO operations requiring an effective politico-military coordination. With a new 'cohabitation' starting in Spring 1993 and Mitterrand's presidential prerogatives reduced, this evolution, already under way, was accelerated. Most key positions in both ministries, and in the staffs of both ministers as well as of the Prime Minister, were now held by individuals sharing a pragmatic view of France–NATO relations. They were ready to adjust France's Alliance policy to the pragmatic requirements of crisis management rather than to follow doctrinal considerations.

CHIRAC AND NATO: COMING FULL CIRCLE? (1995–96)

While France's NATO policy between 1989 and 1995 can be described as mainly reactive – whether in 1989–92 when it opposed almost any major change in the France–NATO relationship and in the Alliance at large, or in 1992–95 when it started to adapt selectively to strategic evolutions – it is clear that Jacques Chirac's approach, as it developed in the first year of his presidency, was both a more ambitious and proactive one. When decisions in various domains (such as the resumption of nuclear testing, the suppression of conscription, the restructuring of military industry) are analysed as a whole, they indeed amount to no less than a 'strategic revolution' of which the new French NATO policy is a key element.[27] Instead of responding to external factors, the new President is determined to exploit ongoing European and transatlantic evolutions in order to restore France as a major player in the Alliance and to change and, most of all, to Europeanize NATO from within – a major departure from past policies of estrangement from the Alliance and from past attempts to promote alternative European strategic structures. While some critics might argue that Chirac is simply trying to make a virtue out of necessity, his policy of seeking a sufficiently thorough restructuring of NATO for a full French participation to become possible is clearly the most ambitious and extensive adaptation of the country's defence and security policy since de Gaulle.

Restoring France's Influence and Status

Chirac's policy and its objectives may be analysed on three separate yet closely interdependent levels.[28] While this may not be the most explicit motivation of the new approach, the restoration of the country's influence and status in the Western Alliance and beyond – an utterly Gaullist objective – is clearly a major, if not the main goal of the new French NATO policy. This, to a large extent, is an old problem. Paradoxically, the 1966 decision, because it marginalized France in the integrated military structure but also in the Alliance's non-integrated bodies, became progressively detrimental to the country's interest as, during the 1970s and 1980s, the French contribution in the NATO collective defence, which was steadily growing in spite of France's non-integrated status, could not be matched by an equally growing French influence in the Alliance. By the end of the 1980s, many analysts and decisionmakers already believed that the gap between France's military importance for NATO, which in some respects was now second to none, and her lack of leverage over the evolution of the Alliance had become unmanageable and that a normalization was needed, at least with regard to relations with non-integrated bodies. The Yugoslav crisis, as seen above, only confirmed this and, after the turn of events in Summer 1995, made the *status quo* unacceptable. France, by then a major military contributor to NATO-led operations in Bosnia, could not continue to be cut off from the NATO decisionmaking process. The country's position of independence in NATO, originally seen as strengthening its strategic ranking in the West and beyond, was now seen as generating negative returns. A rapprochement with NATO's non-integrated bodies was therefore needed in order to reverse the phenomenon. While independence was a relevant objective in 1966, influence was now becoming to be seen as more important. In that sense, Chirac's policy can thus be seen as the outcome of a long maturation.

Yet the scope of France's new NATO policy goes far beyond settling the independence *vs* influence dilemma within NATO. It can also, and more importantly, be analysed as an attempt to change the balance of power among the main NATO powers to France's advantage. Normalizing the France–NATO relationship is, clearly, a means of increasing France's role in the Western alliance by restoring close links with the 'Anglo-Saxons'. In many ways, this dimension of Chirac's policy recalls the first phase of de Gaulle's NATO policy which started with his September 1958 memorandum in which the General sought the creation of a US–UK–French 'directorate' of the Alliance. While this attempt failed (thus leading down the road to the 1966 decision), the present strategic context can indeed be seen as favourable to a formalization of France's status as a 'great' Alliance power. Events in the former Yugoslavia have demonstrated that France, Britain and the US have a leadership role that others cannot pretend to have to the same degree as far as the use of force in such contingencies is concerned, and the new French policy clearly aims at some sort of a recognition of that situation.

Admittedly, unlike in 1958, Germany is seen by the French as one among the leading Western powers, and France is obviously keen on the FRG's participation in what would then be a 'quadripartite' leadership of the Western Alliance. Yet those same events have also shown the limits of Germany's role, as a result of German reluctance to play an active military role in non-Article 5 crises. In fact, the new French NATO policy must also be analysed in the context of a profoundly changing Franco-German relationship. While not explicitly acknowledged by decisionmakers, balancing the Franco-German *face-à-face* with an intensified dialogue with the UK and above all the US in the Alliance framework may be one of the key (and perhaps not wholly conscious) objectives of Chirac's new NATO policy. The normalization of France's relations with NATO, and the establishment of a Franco-American partnership of a kind within the Alliance, also means that Germany will no longer play the role of a go-between in France–NATO relations, something she benefited from so long as France refused to entertain an active American connection. In a way – *mutatis mutandis* of course – France's return after more than three decades to NATO activism is comparable, in terms of a potential strengthening of the country's status, to Germany's engaging in *Ostpolitik* three decades ago.

A New Vision of European Strategic Integration

The most explicit objective of the new approach to NATO, however, is to restore the credibility and viability of France's policy in the realm of European defence.[29] Beyond the Yugoslav experience which, as discussed above, demonstrated in real time the limits of European ambitions and capabilities, most French decisionmakers, by 1995, had concluded that the goal of a European strategic entity outside NATO, which had shaped France's security policy since the 1960s, was not – at least in the short or mid term – a realistic objective, because her

European partners were unwilling to accept what Atlanticists on both sides of the ocean have always characterized as a useless 'duplication' of existing NATO structures.[30] Once elected, Jacques Chirac was ready to face the fact that a European strategic entity would only be able to emerge within the Alliance framework and that in order to restore a European strategic dynamic, France had to explicitly rally to the concept of a European pillar in NATO, as opposed to that of a separate defence pillar subordinate to the EU/WEU. Moreover, since France's NATO posture since 1966 represented, in the eyes of her European partners, the very model of European autonomy which they did not accept, this posture had to change in order to remove what was now seen in Paris as the real obstacle on the path to European defence. By clarifying France's relationship with NATO and dropping the objective of a strictly independent European defence pillar, it is thus hoped that her main European allies will be more forthcoming to her European strategic designs; i.e. France's NATO policy will no longer be a pretext for European strategic immobility.

France's new policy does not mean that the objective of developing a European strategic identity is no longer a key dimension in the country's strategic concept. Whatever doubts there may have been during the initial months of Chirac's presidency as to the firmness of his European convictions and commitments were dispelled by a series of gestures made in the Fall of 1995. They included a strong reaffirmation of the goal of a common European currency and the elaboration of a joint French-German position on the future of CFSP and the prospects for a common European defence policy. To be sure, Chirac's approach to European defence and security policy is influenced by his Gaullism; hence his emphasis on intergovernmental procedures and national sovereignty in any future European strategic decision-making process. As 'smaller' powers in the EU bitterly remark, Chirac's vision of a European strategic entity has a flavour of 'directorates', which France's rapprochement with NATO naturally emphasizes.[31] Yet, at the same time and somewhat paradoxically, it is also marked by the realization of the limits of European strategic autonomy *vis-à-vis* the United States – at least for the time being; hence France's less insistent call for the build-up of specific WEU operational capabilities and admission of the need for Europe's future defence pillar to rely on NATO assets.

In spite of their apparent contradiction, each of these two main characteristics of Chirac's concept of the European strategic construction, i.e. his insistence on the primary role of national governments in strategic affairs and his realistic, not to say modest approach to European autonomy, are arguably pivotal in the country's new defence and security policy. For they allow for heretofore impossible synergies between NATO reform and European defence integration. In fact, the key assumption behind France's new policy may be that after having diverged for three decades, the European and Atlantic agendas can again converge. It is at long last possible to make both dynamics interact. Ever since de Gaulle, such an interaction had proved impossible. On the one hand, France would not fully participate in a reform of NATO in the absence of a clear commitment to build a strategically autonomous Europe on the part of its partners. On the other hand, the Europeans would only consider building such a strategic entity within a Europeanized NATO in which France was expected to participate fully. With the notion of a European pillar in NATO and that of a military arm of a European Union now compatible, it becomes possible to undertake both tasks simultaneously. Decisionmakers in Paris accordingly clearly saw the 1996-97 intergovernmental conference on the future of the European Union, and the NATO reform, as two interdependent and mutually reinforcing processes. This, at any rate, is a key assumption behind the current policy.

Towards a Major NATO Reform

The third level of analysis is that of the Alliance as a whole. The last objective of the new French policy is indeed no less than to change NATO itself in order to adapt it, at long last, to post-Cold War realities. Whereas France since de Gaulle has always denounced the NATO structure as both unadapted and unadaptable to strategic realities – this was indeed the very basis for the 1966 decision – Chirac's new approach clearly assumes that NATO can now be thoroughly transformed and that France should be an active participant – and perhaps a catalyst – in that process. That ended a thirty years' dialogue of the deaf which, as seen above, continued well into the post-Cold War era. In the French view – which mixes long-time grievances over the organization and workings of the Alliance with new thinking on the essentials of a drastic NATO reform, the Alliance's adaptation to new realities means both making a European autonomy within NATO possible and adjusting the NATO structure to the requirements of collective security. Both objectives are seen as intertwined, because the French believe ESDI to be mostly relevant in non-Article 5 contingencies and because they anticipate future collective security missions to be carried out mostly by Europeans. To reach them, longstanding French objections to NATO structures need to be met. These objections have mainly focused on: first, the question of military integration; and second, that of political control. Both questions are seen to be even more relevant since the fall of the Berlin Wall which has turned the Gaullist prophecies into strategic realities.

The first question addresses the perceptual need for more flexibility and greater effectiveness. French criticism of NATO's integrated military structure (IMS), which has been denounced since the 1960s as too rigid in spite of a still-tangible Soviet threat, is obviously thought to gain validity with the end of that threat. First, an excessively tight integrated structure in peacetime is seen as clearly unsuited to contingencies that, unlike Cold War ones, cannot be foreseen. Most scenarios for peacekeeping and peace enforcement in Europe or at its periphery are unlikely to involve all NATO members, while most are likely to involve non-NATO countries. Also, most such scenarios would require a much more decentralized command structure than the present SACEUR-dominated one, in order to better contend with the particular characteristics of the theatre and to avoid giving a strategic (if not 'East–West' dimension) to NATO involvement. That is to say, they should be treated, by definition, as local contingencies. Second, the American predominance in the military structure is no longer justified by the need for the US to keep control of military operations as was the case previously. Moreover, it does not accord with the likelihood of US non-participation in crisis management when vital US interests are not at stake. NATO must therefore be transformed to allow for greater European freedom of action and for a greater availability of NATO assets for European forces, as was decided in principle at the Brussels summit of January 1994.

These changes, in concrete terms, would amount to a radical overhaul of the present integrated military structure, which is a direct legacy of Cold War NATO. For a brief period (roughly during the 1993–95 preliminary phase of the France–NATO rapprochement), the French pressed for a two-pronged NATO military structure. While the 'old' IMS would remain largely unchanged and be kept as an insurance policy against the resurgence of Article 5-type threats, a 'new' (and distinct) military structure would emerge in order to deal with non-Article 5 missions and permit the assertion of a European identity. France would remain absent from 'NATO 1', but she would participate fully in 'NATO 2'.[32] Yet because of opposition to such a scheme on the part of her partners on the grounds that this would, again, lead to 'duplication' of present structures, the French, as made clear by Chirac himself, came around to the position of accepting the concept of a simple military structure in which France would fully participate. While precise descriptions of such a structure have not been publicly offered, changes in the present IMS would clearly need to be of a great magnitude in order to fit the requirements of a 'normal' French participation. The most important of these requirements is for the NATO chain of command to be able to function in a European mode in order for Europeans to be in a position, when the time comes, to use elements that are necessary to command an operation undertaken by Europeans.[33] This 'politically visible' and 'militarily effective' European capability to lead operations in the NATO framework entails the identification of European elements in the NATO chain of command, thanks to a peacetime WEU–NATO double-hatting system, including the 'strategic' level, where a European Deputy SACEUR with effective European command capabilities should be designated. Beyond a thorough rethinking of the NATO command system – in which arrangements would have to be made to give France its share of responsibilities – the transformation of the military structure should also, in the French view, bear on the workings of the structure above the command level, i.e. at the planning and politico-military control levels. Institutional arrangements there should also be adapted to permit its Europeanization and functional adaptation to sub-strategic collective security tasks.[34]

The second question is indeed that of political control. Ever since the 1950s, at a time when the requirements of nuclear strategy and the overwhelming US military predominance left little room for a collective direction of the Alliance, France has emphasized the need for stronger political control over military structures and operations in NATO.[35] It is therefore not surprising that this requirement is seen as even more urgent after the Cold War and, most of all, in non-Article 5 contingencies. Indeed, the French have come to accept an active NATO role in collective security, but this, almost by definition, requires a radical change in the Alliance's internal decisionmaking process in order for peacekeeping or peacemaking operations to be decided and conducted on a truly collective basis. Furthermore, they by no means see NATO itself as having the authority to make decisions on its own to undertake such operations. That is to say, the Atlantic Alliance should not presume to act on behalf of the international community. In the French view, the political and legal primacy of collective security organizations with a universal (the UN) or pan-European (the OSCE) status must be clearly preserved if NATO (or for that matter WEU) actions are to be acceptable for the entire international community. As the Yugoslav case has demonstrated, this concern is essentially about keeping Russia involved in – or not letting her obstruct – the process. Moreover, a NATO both Europeanized and adapted to the new requirements for peacemaking/keeping, and thus built on a loose conception of integration, would make it easier for Russia to accept the Alliance's expansion to former Warsaw Pact countries of East/Central Europe and for her to establish stable ties with the Alliance – whether through a 'charter' or less formal arrangements.

This requirement for political control has a two-fold set of implications. First, it points to the need for a clearer definition of UN–NATO relations, both in political and operational terms. On the political level, French insistence on the need for NATO's role to be mandated and clearly defined by UN Security Council resolutions is likely to remain unchanged, both because it is key to preserving the legitimacy of NATO actions and because it puts France on an equal footing with the US, something unlikely to happen at the Alliance level whatever its future evolution. On the operational level however, the once-strong French insistence on a tight control on NATO operations exercised by the UN is not likely to loom very large in the future. The experience in Yugoslavia, until Summer 1995, of 'dual key' arrangements, has indeed proved both inefficacious (the international community has arguably been paralysed because of obstruction on the part of UN bureaucrats) and dangerous (the complexity of decision-making arrangements might have been one of the reasons for the hostage crisis in May 1995). As a result, direct coordination between UN military commanders and NATO commanders is likely to be favoured in the future in situations combining a UN peacekeeping force on the ground and NATO operations at sea or in the air, while in the more likely case of a NATO-only, IFOR-type peacekeeping/making configuration, no UN control over operations is likely to be required.

Second, as a result of this shift away from tight UN operational control over NATO actions, the French are likely to ask more insistently for increased political control over military actions within the NATO framework itself. This, in fact, is an old French criticism of NATO mechanisms which dates back to the origins of the Alliance. In the early 1950s, integrated commands and SHAPE *de facto* absorbed most of the politico-military functions nominally attributed to the non-integrated Military Committee. Indeed, in the original conceptions, the latter was endowed with two key functions: that of developing operational planning in peacetime and of serving as the interface between the North Atlantic Council and the integrated commands in times of crisis or war. With non-Article 5 missions acquiring more strategic importance than during the Cold War, greater political control over military operations as well as a more satisfactory politico-military coordination is desirable and possible and could be met by strengthening the strategic role of the Military Committee. Paris, therefore, is obviously eager to return to what should have been the normal functioning of the Alliance in order to avoid NATO-led operations being simply US-led operations, even though it is recognized that, in cases of a sizeable US troop contribution on the ground, the operational command should clearly remain in US hands.

Thirty years after de Gaulle's decision to withdraw his country from NATO's integrated structure, a revolution in France–NATO relations is clearly underway as a result of the coming to power of the first Gaullist president in over twenty years. While his socialist predecessor ironically appeared committed to defending a conservative vision of the Gaullist model, Jacques Chirac is ready to challenge the inherited dogmas of the General's legacies. Yet it would be wrong to interpret the new French NATO policy as a sheer surrender of the country's traditional objectives in the Alliance, let alone as a 'reintegration' in NATO. While the new approach is undoubtedly more pragmatic and open to compromise on means than in the past, it has arguably not abandoned its long-term goals. France's new NATO policy is new because NATO is now seen as reformable and therefore compatible with a European strategic identity, not because France is ready to abandon its European vision, let alone to return to the present NATO fold.

WHERE DO WE GO FROM HERE?

Whether the ongoing NATO reform will, in the months and years to come, actually lead to such a thorough transformation of the Alliance is therefore the critical question for the future of France–NATO relations. In the French view, success depends ultimately on the allies' ability to carry the process of Alliance adaptation to its completion. Because the Yugoslav crisis has been a key factor in recent developments, to try and answer this question requires a serious analysis of its long-term consequences on the future of the transatlantic relations and of NATO. To what extent should the intervention in Yugoslavia be taken as a precedent for future NATO operations and therefore as a model for France–NATO relations? For many in NATO circles, in Allied capitals and for that matter in France, the answer is clearly 'yes'; in fact, the NATO reform process and, as argued above, France's new policy are essentially premised on that positive answer. Admittedly, France, as a key player in the management of the crisis, must inevitably draw the lessons of Bosnia for the Alliance and for its own specific position. Yet at the same time the very ambiguities of the Yugoslav experience make it difficult to use that crisis as a case-study for how the Alliance will operate in the future.[36]

The Ambiguous Lessons of Yugoslavia

As seen from Paris as well as from other European capitals, it cannot – or should not – be forgotten that, in the three years or so before the turning-point of Summer 1995, the Alliance came closer than ever since 1956 to a major crisis. For three years, transatlantic relations have been characterized by two sets of ambiguities, both of them closely linked to US policies. On the political level, those uncertainties stemmed from the existence of severe divergences across the Atlantic among allies (for the most part, pitting the US against Britain and France) over the Yugoslav conflict. Those divergences (e.g. 'lift and strike' *vs* maintaining the UNPROFOR and the embargo) bore on the reading of the crisis as well as on the terms of an eventual settlement (and, as a consequence, on the military means to implement it). Moreover, there was another set of uncertainties, at the military level. For American policy had been marked, until Summer 1995, by a major unknown in the eyes of many Europeans: how willing was the US actually to commit troops on the ground – whether to implement a peace settlement (in 1993 and, again, in the Fall of 1995) or to rescue UNPROFOR soldiers in case of a failure of the UN mission?

To be sure, developments beginning in Summer 1995 have reconciled heretofore conflicting US national objectives (to avoid a defeat of the Croatian–Muslim federation, a commitment of US troops in the fighting and a rupture in the Alliance) and resulted in a more coherent US policy, which opened the way to Dayton and IFOR. As a result, they bridged the gap between the European and American strategies in the crisis. It remains to be seen, however, whether the process can remain on track in spite of the pitfalls of what, until the last moment (including that of IFOR's withdrawal), will remain a highly risky operation and whether it can bring about a durable settlement in Bosnia. Even a successful outcome of the one-year NATO involvement on the ground in Bosnia will not erase events of the previous three years and European anxieties stemming from them. Those anxieties will have a lasting meaning for the future of the Alliance in terms of both its cohesion and effectiveness. They raise two major questions: first, how can one be sure that NATO will avoid severe transatlantic turbulence in dealing with future non-Article 5 crises? Second, how can one rely on NATO as a military tool for collective security without a clear commitment on the part of its leader to participate actively in such operations?

The Yugoslav experience has confirmed the validity of the strategy of expanding NATO's missions beyond its original function of common defence, a development actively encouraged by the US after the collapse of the Soviet Union in order to reaffirm NATO's legitimacy and *raison d'être* and to maintain the framework for America's presence and leadership in Europe. At the same time, Yugoslavia has also shown the limits of that strategy. Indeed, the Alliance's credibility as an instrument for performing collective security functions, as was evident during the Yugoslav conflict, will depend ultimately on the nature of US policy and the level of US involvement in future crises. The reverse, however, is probably less true. The structural adaptation of NATO to its new security tasks will have a limited influence over the ability of the Americans and the Europeans to agree on common approaches in future crises and on the US readiness to play an active military role on the ground. Both issues are more influenced by strategic interests and perceptions than by the workings of institutions.

This uncertainty as to NATO's future collective security role obviously is bound to have an impact on the other big issue in NATO reform, i.e. the question of European autonomy. How one assesses prospects for European autonomy in the Alliance vary a great deal depending on whether one believes or not in the ability of the Europeans and the Americans to act in concert in future crises, and on whether one believes or not in the likelihood of US military involvement on the ground in those crises. Yet in either eventuality, although for opposite reasons, European autonomy within NATO remains an objective whose relevance and feasibility seem questionable. Consider first a scenario in which the United States decides not to act while the Europeans are involved in what they believe is a significant crisis: how could the latter be sure that NATO assets necessary to carry out their mission effectively will be made available given the fact that most of them are in fact American assets? The precedent of 'Sharp Guard' (the unilateral US decision to withdraw partially from the operation of surveillance of the embargo and indeed to withold relevant satellite information) is a case in point. While this move had little operational impact and its political consequences were muted on both sides, the incident clearly illustrates the potential danger of Europe's excessive dependence on the United States in situations of Euro-American strategic divergences or simply of US abstention. However tolerable this danger when limited interests are at stake, it would be unacceptable in situations in which vital interests may be involved as would have been the case, for instance, in a NATO-led operation to withdraw the UNPROFOR.

Consider now the opposite scenario, one in which the United States decides to participate actively in a NATO peacemaking or peacekeeping operation. How, in such a contingency, could the Europeans maintain a significant degree of military autonomy? Indeed, discussions on the setting-up of IFOR as well as on MC 40104 or MC 40103, have clearly displayed an American propensity to keep an exclusive direction of operations. Washington, in both instances, asked for a maximum NATO integration while trying to hold levels of US troop participation on the ground to a minimum. Not only does this not bode well for the European defence and security identity within NATO, but it could raise serious questions of acceptability for the Europeans. How could they accept to participate with significant troop contributions to a NATO-led (and as a result a US-led) operation, when US participation would be piecemeal if not symbolic in their judgement, without *ipso facto* transforming themselves into support forces of a tightly US-controlled Atlantic Alliance – a new version of the risk/responsibility sharing debate of the nuclear era?

The Europeans, in the post-Cold War context, indeed face a dilemma not unlike the nuclear dilemma of the Cold War period. If, on the one hand, they cannot count with confidence on US military commitment, then it is perilous for them overly to depend on American goodwill and means within NATO. If, on the other hand, US involvement is to be taken for granted, then it becomes vain to seek greater European autonomy within NATO. Because of this dilemma, it is therefore not surprising that the decisions of the Brussels summit of January 1994 took so long before they were given concrete expression in the Berlin and Brussels ministerial meetings of Summer 1996. This holds true notably of the Combined Joint Task Forces (CJTF) which were meant to be a pragmatic answer to the twin challenges of 'Europeanization' and collective security. And beyond CJTF, this same dilemma will obviously make it difficult to define the terms of a 'definitive' NATO reform which would permanently adapt the Alliance to its new collective security tasks while at the same time allowing for more European autonomy.

This is all the more so because NATO's post-Cold War identity is still blurred, as the articulation between the 'old' function of the Alliance and the 'new' one remains to be clearly defined. How can the latter be expanded without deriving it from the former? Conversely, how can one maintain the positive legacy of the former without atrophying the latter? In other words, will not collective defence be diluted as preparation is made to assume collective security? Or will not collective security requirements suffer from the unsuitable inheritance of collective defence? Answers to these questions will be all the more difficult to give as a result of the process of Alliance enlargement that regained acceleration with the conclusion of Presidential elections in the United States and Russia. The enlargement process indeed makes the NATO identity problem even more acute as a result of the gap between the demands of potential new members – mostly geared towards the 'old' NATO – and the offer of present members – essentially interested in shaping a 'new' NATO. In addition, there is the potential for a crisis over the meaning of Article 5, which inevitably will be discussed – for the first time since 1949 – as the accession treaties for new members are presented for ratification in the Congress and in other allied capitals.[37]

Berlin and Beyond

Even though it arguably avoided an open crisis in the context of the Yugoslav conflict until the summer of 1995 and in spite of converging trends on NATO reform since then, the Alliance thus still confronts decisive choices. It is in that context that France's sustained willingness to carry the rapprochement with NATO to its logical term, that of a full French participation in military structures, must be assessed. To be sure, as mentioned above, Paris has welcomed the results of the Berlin and Brussels ministerials as validating the new French NATO policy. Most allies, too, have seen them as the fulfilment of the objectives of the 1994 Brussels summit. Whether Foreign Minister Hervé de Charette was right when he commented that 'for the first time [in Alliance history] we have gone from words to deeds'[38] on the issue of NATO reform and Europeanization is, however, not yet quite clear. It remains to be seen how far the process can effectively go when it comes to the implementation phase and, above all, whether the new course of France–NATO relations will remain unchallenged by future events.

Many French commentators stress the fact that Berlin is only the beginning of the process of NATO's restructuring and that it will take many months before it translates into an actual transformation of the integrated structure. Judging from the comments made by US Secretary of State Warren Christopher, who was eager to downplay the significance of the Berlin language, a cautious attitude is in order.[39] While official discourse on both sides stresses the fact that definitive NATO reform and the normalization of French participation is a question of 'when', the clear fact that it is also still a question of 'how' means that, until it is actually achieved, it will remain a question of 'if'.

To be sure, the Berlin meeting has resulted in a compromise on reifying the concept of CJTFs which, since the Brussels summit, have become the touchstone of NATO reform. France has obtained the recognition of the possibility for European forces to use 'separable but not separate [NATO] military capabilities in operations led by the WEU' and of the need for such forces to be 'capable of operating under the political control and strategic direction of the WEU'. That is a fairly satisfactory formula given US resistance to such language during most of 1994–95. Other significant results, in the French point of view, include the decision to establish a Policy Coordination Group (PCG) for increased politico-military concertation; the objective of an 'effective exercise of political control' by the NAC through the MC; and the meeting of the North Atlantic Council of 16 at the defence ministers level, a formula allowing France's participation to defence ministers' meetings without returning to the DPC.[40]

Yet this compromise was hard to reach. It is no secret that, until the last moment, the possibility of a failure was there. This gives an indication of the difficulty that will remain before the Alliance moves from the concept to the reality of CJTF. To be sure, the French can satisfy themselves that politically unacceptable notions, such as that of a NAC 'overseeing' of a WEU-led CJTF, do not appear in the

Berlin language. Yet, because major conceptual differences were papered over in the search of a compromise, that language remains essentially ambiguous, making further quarreling over its interpretation and implementation a near certainty. Beyond that ambiguity, the limits of the CJTF concept are clear. The NAC 'will approve the release of NATO assets and capabilities for WEU-led operations, keep itself informed on their use through monitoring with the advice of the NATO Military Authorities and through regular consultations with the WEU Council, and keep their use under review'.[41] As if things were not sufficiently clear, American diplomats in Berlin were prone to emphasize that, in any case, they could hardly see scenarios in which the US would not participate in such operations in future European crises.[42]

This obviously brings us to the heart of the problem of European autonomy in NATO, which the CJTF concept may have obscured in the eyes of many: whatever arrangement is reached on CJTF, the ability of the Europeans to act will remain dependent on the US, as the vast majority of 'NATO' assets, most of all in the critical area of command and control, are US assets. And in spite of whatever illusions some may have had on that score, the US is most unlikely to sign blank cheques to the Europeans for them to draw on their strategic capabilities without keeping a *droit de regard* on their use, whether directly or through the NAC, and whether it is called 'monitoring' or 'overseeing'. Some might even argue that the moment is particularly ill-chosen for the Europeans to try to exact concessions from the United States. The post-Dayton climate as well as the ongoing IFOR operation, in their view, can only revalidate the present US-dominated NATO structure and leave little room for a profound change in NATO. Moreover, the present mood in US public opinion and Congress seems to be in contradiction with notions of increased European autonomy if they mean a decreasing US control over American military assets.[43]

Beyond the specific – and in fact marginal – issue of CJTF, this kind of scepticism was confirmed by the outcome of the Berlin meeting on the subject of future NATO reform. Whereas the French were hoping for some sort of a commitment to a radical transformation of NATO integration on the part of the United States, the result is a rather meagre one. The French requirement of a permanent European pillar which would be both politically visible and militarily effective even though it would remain part of the US-led NATO integrated structure, has not been met in the Berlin language. The vision of a

WEU chain of command, not separate from the NATO chain of command, but visible in peacetime, separable from it in times of crisis and capable of using NATO assets, which describes the kind of transformation in NATO necessary for France to return to a full status of integration, is therefore still elusive. To be sure, the French government, after Berlin, remains committed to its policy of gradual but complete normalization of France's participation in a completely transformed NATO. Hence the expressions of satisfaction heard in the aftermath of the meeting, including on the part of President Chirac himself.[44] The intense and at times bitter discussions leading up to the Berlin accords made the difficulty and the length of the process increasingly apparent. Few believed that the big NATO reform would be wrapped up by the December 1996 target date agreed at Berlin, let alone that the France–NATO normalization would be carried out within that time frame. Indeed the divisive issue of whether the position of CINCSOUTH should (as the French claim) be devolved to a European officer has shown how delicate the reform of NATO's military structures and the adjustment of the French posture are likely to be.

What Future Options?

As the feasibility of France's ambitions in and for NATO is likely to remain unclear for some time, questions are likely to arise as to the appropriateness of Chirac's policy. To be sure, one of the most striking features of recent adjustments in France–NATO relations is that they so far have stirred almost no domestic opposition. The most obvious explanation for this is the fact that, since 1993, they have been conducted by Gaullist governments, with a strong conservative majority and, at least since 1995, under a Gaullist president. Thus the voices of orthodox Gaullists have been barely heard, and former Prime Minister Pierre Messmer's contention that France's return into NATO integration under US command would amount to a 'betrayal' has had little if any echo.[45] As to the opposition, it has shown little interest in making Chirac's NATO policy and, in general, his foreign and security policy, a major issue. Of course the communists have voiced their criticism of a policy described as one of France's return to US domination. But the Socialists have hesitated to denounce a policy which they realize is not likely to stir much discontent in a public opinion whose primary concern is not international affairs.[46]

It remains unclear whether this relatively serene climate in the political class and in public opinion might deteriorate if further Alliance reform were to prove more difficult (and French-NATO rapprochement less harmless) in the future. Yet even if it will not necessarily degenerate into a political liability for the pursuit of the present policy, questioning of that policy is likely to intensify as difficulties materialize. As a result, the debate is likely to move from the issue of feasibility to that of desirability, at least within the strategic community. Indeed serious arguments can be made against carrying the present policy to its logical conclusion, that of France's full participation into a fully revamped NATO military apparatus.

These arguments bear, respectively, on the European and the transatlantic dimensions of the present French NATO policy. The key question is, obviously, that of European autonomy. It is both a technical and a political question. In technical terms, even if France and her European partners were to obtain a profound recasting of NATO's integrated military structures, the problem of European autonomy would in essence remain unresolved. Because the vast majority of 'NATO' assets, most of all in the critical area of command and control, would remain US assets – a fact of life that no reshuffling of the Alliance command structure would change – European autonomy in NATO would be as illusory in the new structure as it is in the present one. Supporters of such an option would respond that this may be the case today, but that it would change as the Europeans develop military capabilities of their own, whether in NATO or not, and thus acquire a substantial level of strategic autonomy. Yet there is a considerable risk that a 'Europeanized' NATO, precisely because it would entertain the illusion of European autonomy within the Alliance framework, would in fact reduce incentives for the build-up of truly European strategic capabilities. Hence the political question: would not the further pursuit of the objective of the WEU as the European pillar in NATO amount to restricting the scope of Europe's strategic identity and ambition to one delimited by the NATO framework, especially if the notion that the WEU should be at the same time the military arm of the EU is tacitly abandoned? If yes, then Henry Kissinger was right in 1973 when, in order to 'sell' the 'year of Europe' to the Europeans, he remarked that Europe was but a regional power, while the US was a world one.

This leads to questions as to the appropriateness of France's present NATO policy in the light of how the future of transatlantic relations may evolve. They are both short- and long-term questions. In the short term, the issue of the relationship between NATO reform and actual NATO operations was bound to resurface. As the IFOR mandate expired in December 1996, with the US unwilling to consider its extension, the question of a successor, European-only peacekeeping force was raised. While France and her main European partners rejected such a prospect for a number of reasons, opponents to a further Europeanization of NATO pointed to the Europeans' unwillingness to take over the burden of peacekeeping in Bosnia as an illustration of the uselessness of profound changes in the present NATO structure.

In the long term, the pursuit of present trends in NATO and France–NATO relations raises geopolitical questions of considerable magnitude which mostly revolve around the issue of the future of the Franco–German relationship. Germany has always insisted on the need for a clarification of France's NATO posture as a prerequisite for the build-up of a European defence identity and the intensification of the Franco-German relationship. But Bonn, among France's European and Atlantic partners, is arguably and paradoxically the most ill-at-ease with the new policy.[47] As hinted above, there are reasons to believe that, consciously or not, France's new NATO approach is indeed part of a policy of balancing Germany. Yet its consequences on Franco-German relations might in fact go further than that; for many Germans, France's NATO rapprochement, together with the new defence policy (most of all the abolition of conscription and the emphasis on projection capabilities) means that France, is more interested in military ventures with her Anglo-Saxon allies in 'out of area' intervention scenarios than in building, together with the FRG, a European defence, in the full meaning of the term. Not only does this reading of the French strategic design have, for many Germans, a flavour of 'great power' behaviour (which the resumption of nuclear tests in 1995 has strengthened), it does not bode well for the future of French-German relations: even though both countries are committed to making their strategic conceptions and perceptions converge, the trend seems to be one of increasing divergence between Germany's 'Kultur der Zurückhaltung' and France's taste for intervention.[48] This impression, however, has been partially corrected by the Franco-German 'Strategic Concept' adopted in Nuremberg in December 1996. Even though it contains no major breakthrough in terms of substance, its very existence seems reassuring with regard to relations between Paris and Bonn in the field of security and defence.

Unsurprisingly, all these questions lead some segments of the political spectrum to a questioning of the new French policy. Guardians of national independence and defenders of the Gaullist orthodoxy warn against the risk to France of abandoning her status as an autonomous ally in exchange for little more than the illusion of influence within the Alliance. In spite of official discourse on the 'new NATO', they see the continuation of the present policy as leading to a sheer French reintegration in the old NATO. Advocates of the European construction denounce what they see as France's giving up Europe's strategic autonomy and putting at risk political unity between its members and, most of all, between France and Germany. While seeking a Europeanized NATO, France, they argue, would only obtain a 'NATOized' Europe with a dismantled Franco-German tandem. Even Atlanticists can make the point that the solidity of the transatlantic partnership and the durability of the US involvement in Europe would not necessarily profit from a complete French 'normalization' in NATO and/or a weak if not non-existent European defence pillar in the Alliance.

While such analyses may prove valid, their operational relevance remains doubtful as a result of the lack of credible alternatives to the present policy. Hence, while some could be tempted to return to a more intransigent approach of European strategic independence and to reverse the recent trend of French policy of accommodation with NATO, such an option would not be realistic in the present context. Even were there a breakdown of the peace process in the former Yugoslavia and/or of US failure to remain militarily committed to its implementation, France's European partners are unlikely to draw definitive lessons on the future US presence in Europe. Moreover, such an acceleration of the European strategic construction is hard to imagine in the present situation marked by the uncertainty as the outcome of the IGC. France, once again, might find herself isolated in calling for a Europe independent from the United States. The European Union, already made fragile as a result of profound internal divergences, would be damaged by such an upsurge of strategic Gaullism. As for the transatlantic relationship, it would obviously suffer from such a policy. Whereas de Gaulle's decisions thirty years ago could be justified as anticipating a US withdrawal from Europe, a similar policy today would inevitably be seen as precipitating such a withdrawal. Again, France would be accused of trying to exclude the United States from the Old Continent without actually being ready, or able to build Europe. And while de Gaulle's France could accept a measure of isolation as the price to be paid for its long-term vision, the same is probably not true of Chirac's France.

Analysts and future historians are likely to discuss for some time whether the new French policy towards the Alliance amounts to the liquidation of the Gaullist legacy or whether, on the contrary, it marks its logical, post-Cold War transubstantiation. This, however, may be but a sterile academic question. The real issue is: how far will the Alliance reform process go, and how far will the redefinition of France–NATO ties proceed? It is too early to answer this question. On the one hand, the present trend seems irreversible; on the other, many uncertainties remain and are likely to remain, at least in the mid-term. One thing is likely however: whatever future evolutions there are in the Alliance and in relations between France and NATO, France, between European ambitions and Atlantic realities, will remain one of a kind in the Western Alliance: the odd one in – or the odd one out.

NOTES

1. The first three sections of this chapter are based on open sources as well as on interviews with high-ranking diplomats and officers in Paris. The author wishes to express his appreciation to those concerned. Published sources on French foreign policy under François Mitterrand are considerable. They include, for this period: J. Attali, *Verbatim* III (Paris: Fayard, 1995); R. Dumas, *La Fil et la pelote. Mémoires* (Paris: Plon, 1996); P. Favier and M. Martin-Roland, *La Décennie Mitterrand*, III '*Les Défis*' (Paris: Seuil, 1996); and H. Védrine, *Les Mondes de François Mitterrand and À l'Élysée 1981–1995* (Paris: Fayard, 1996).
2. For an analysis of General de Gaulle's policy towards the Atlantic Alliance, see F. Bozo, *Deux stratégies pour l'Europe. De Gaulle, les Etats-Unis et l'Alliance atlantique (1958–1969)* (Paris: Plon, 1996); see also M. Vaïsse, P. Mélandri, F. Bozo (ed.), *La France et l'OTAN 1949–1996* (Bruxelles: Complexe, 1996).
3. The influence of the Gaullist vision on immediate post-Cold War French policy is discussed in Philip H. Gordon, *A Certain Idea of France: French Security Policy and the Gaullist Legacy* (Princeton: Princeton University Press, 1993); see also Frédéric Bozo, 'France' in Richard Davy (ed.), *European Détente: A Reappraisal* (London: Sage/RIIA, 1992), and 'France and Security in the New Europe: Between the Gaullist Legacy and the Search for a New Model', in Gregory Flynn (ed.), *Remaking the Hexagon: the New France in the New Europe*, (Boulder, CO: Westview Press, 1995).

4. See for example Secretary of State James Baker's speech at the Berlin Press Club, 12 December 1989.
5. For an analysis of France's initial attitude in the early phase of NATO reform, see F. Bozo, *La France et l'OTAN. De la guerre froide au nouvel ordre européen* (Paris: Masson, 1991), pp. 181 ff. See also Favier and Martin-Roland, pp. 248, 224 ff and Védrine, *op. cit.*, pp. 729 ff.
6. On this aborted rapprochement between France and NATO, see Ambassador Gabriel Robin's letter to the Editor, *Survival*, 38 (Summer 1996), and the analysis in C. Tréan, 'La France et le nouvel ordre européen', *Politique étrangère*, no. 1/91, 81–90.
7. 'M. Mitterrand et le <<prêchi-prêcha>> de l'OTAN', *Le Monde* (November 10–11, 1991).
8. See P. H. Gordon, *France, Germany and the Western Alliance* (Boulder: Westview, 1995).
9. On French strategic options in this period, see P. H. Gordon, *French Security Policy after the Cold War: Continuity, Change and Implications for the United States* (Rand, 1992); R. Tiersky, 'France in the New Europe', *Foreign Affairs* (Spring 1992), 131–46; and S. Hoffmann, Dilemmes et stratégies de la France dans la nouvelle Europe', *Politique étrangère*, no. 4/92, 879–92.
10. See his speech at the Ecole Militaire, 11 April 1991, in *Quelle sécurité en Europe à l'aube du XXIe siècle?* (Ecole Supérieure de Guerre, 1991).
11. See Favier and Martin-Roland, *loc. cit.*, and Védrine, *loc. cit.*
12. See the discussion of this question in F. Heisbourg, 'Quelles leçons stratégiques?', and F. Prater (pseud.), 'La France et la crise du Golfe', *Politique étrangère*, no. 2/91, 411–22 and 441–53.
13. Analyses of France's policy in Yugoslavia are scarce. See N. Gnesotto, 'Leçons de la Yougoslavie', *Cahiers de Chaillot*, no. 14 (mars 1994); A. Macleod, 'La France: à la recherche du leadership international', *Relations internationales et stratégiques*, No. 19 (Fall 1995), 69–80; and C. Guicherd, 'L'heure de l'Europe: premières leçons du conflit yougoslave', *Cahier du Crest*, no. 10 (mars 1993).
14. This may not have been a sheer French fantasy. See M. Ignatieff, 'The Missed Chance in Bosnia', *New York Review of Books* (29 February 1996), 8–10.
15. These assumptions, as they have pervaded the decisionmaking process in Paris in those years, appear, for example, in an article by two close associates of F. Mitterrand, H. Védrine and J. Musitelli, 'Les changements des années 1989–1990 et l'Europe de la prochaine décennie', *Politique étrangère*, no. 1/91, 165–77. See also Védrine, *Les Mondes de François Mitterrand, op. cit.*
16. For a much detailed and reliable analysis of France's evolving NATO policy after 1992, see R. P. Grant, 'France's New Relationship with NATO', *Survival*, 38 (Spring 1996).
17. See J. Paolini, 'A French Perspective', in M. Brenner (ed.), *Multilateralism and Western Strategy* (London: Macmillan, 1995), and F. Bozo, 'Organisation de sécurité et insécurité en Europe', *Politique étrangère*, no. 2/93, 447–58.

18. For a description of NATO's steady involvement in the Bosnian crisis, see D. A. Leurdijk, *The United Nations and NATO in Former Yugoslavia* (Netherlands Atlantic Commission, 1994).
19. See R. P. Grant, *op. cit.*
20. *Livre blanc sur la Défense* (Paris: Documentation française, 1994).
21. See his speech on 16 March 1995 at the Hôtel Méridien, Paris. See also A. Juppé's interview in *Le Monde* (24 mars 1995).
22. See Foreign Minister Hervé de Charette's remarks during the Brussels Ministerial, on 5 December 1995.
23. The best description of the conceptual framework of France's evolving security perceptions and threat assessment in that period is arguably that in the *Livre blanc sur la Défense, op. cit.*
24. For an analysis of French policy in that period, see R. Tiersky, 'The Mitterrand Legacy and the Future of French Security Policy', McNair Paper no. 43 (August 1995).
25. A. Juppé, 'Quel horizon pour la politique étrangère de la France?', *Politique étrangère*, 60 (printemps 1995), 245–59.
26. See W. T. Johnson and T. D. Young, *French Policy towards NATO: Enhanced Selectivity, Vice Rapprochement* (US Army War College, 9 September 1994).
27. D. Vernet, 'La révolution stratégique de Jacques Chirac', *Le Monde* (8 June 1996).
28. There have been few analyses of Jacques Chirac's strategic policy so far. See D. Vernet, *art. cit.*; and D. Moïsi, 'Chirac of France: A New Leader of the West?', *Foreign Affairs*, 74 (November/December 1995), 8–13.
29. On Chirac's approach to European defence, see the book by his strategic adviser, P. Lellouche, *Légitime défense. Vers une Europe en sécurité au XXIe siècle* (Paris: Editions Patrick Banon, 1996), with a forward by Minister of Defence Charles Millon. See also D. Vernet's comments, 'Onze idées pour l'Europe', *Le Monde* (7 June 1996).
30. For a historical analysis of France's approach of European defence construction, see N. Gnesotto, 'L'Alliance et l'Union: Les Dilemmes de la Défense Européenne', *Notes de l'IFRI*, no. 2 (1996).
31. See the comments by the Belgian Minister of Foreign Affairs, on 11 June 1996, warning against the set-up of a 'great powers directorate', quoted in *Le Monde* (16 June 1996).
32. See for example G. Robin, 'OTAN: un sommet instructif', *Le Figaro* (31 January 1994); and 'A quoi sert l'OTAN?', *Politique étrangère*, no. 1/95 (Spring 1995), 171–80.
33. C. Millon, 'La France et la rénovation de l'Alliance atlantique', *Revue de l'OTAN* (May 1996), 13–16.
34. *Ibid.*
35. See F. Bozo, *La France et l'OTAN, op. cit.*, p. 57.
36. See a discussion of this in F. Bozo, 'La France et l'Alliance: les limites du rapprochement', *Politique étrangère*, no. 4/95 (Winter 1995), 865–77.
37. See a discussion on the US dimension of this problem in J. D. Rosner, 'NATO Enlargement's American Hurdle', *Foreign Affairs*, 75 (July/August 1996), 9–16.
38. Quoted in *Nouvelles Atlantiques*, no. 97 (5 juin 1996).

39. *Libération* (4 June 1996); *Le Monde* (5 June 1996); *Financial Times* (4 June 1996).
40. Text of Berlin Communiqué in *Documents Atlantiques*, no. 97 (5 juin 1996).
41. *Ibid.*
42. *Libération* (4 June 1996).
43. See P. H. Gordon, '"Europeanization" of NATO: A Convenient Myth', *International Herald Tribune* (7 June 1996).
44. See his speech at the Institut des Hautes Etudes de Défense Nationale (IHEDN), 8 June 1996.
45. 'L'histoire en direct', *France Culture* (7 March 1996). See also P. Maillard, 'La France et l'OTAN', *Le Figaro* (4 June 1996).
46. See, for example, Paul Quilès, 'Défense Européenne et OTAN: la dérive', *Le Monde* (11 June 1996); P. Delmas, 'Quatre questions sur un gambit', *ibid.*; and P. Boniface, 'OTAN: une autonomie européenne sous contrôle', *La Tribune Desfossés* (10 June 1996).
47. See A.-M. Le Gloannec, *Défense Nationale* (July 1996), 37–42. On the evolving Franco-German strategic partnership, see G.-H. Soutou, *L'Alliance Incertaine. Les Rapports Politico-stratégiques Franco-Allemands 1954–1996* (Paris: Fayard, 1996).
48. Le Gloannec, *op. cit.*

4 Germany
Michael Meimeth

INTRODUCTION

The end of the Cold War has left German foreign policy with the formidable task of meeting the expectations of its partners that Germany assume a greater responsibility in the management of international affairs. This view is almost universally shared within the German strategic community.[1] There also is a widespread consensus within this community that assuming a greater international responsibility requires Germany's willingness to participate in military actions of a collective security type. However, the political debate in Germany for the most part centred on the legal question of whether or not the German constitution allowed the participation of the Bundeswehr in such international military operations other than for self-defence.[2] In its decision of 12 July 1994 the Bundesverfassungsgericht, the German Supreme Court, has rejected the position of those who claimed that the German Constitution did not allow the out-of-area deployment of the German Bundeswehr, i.e. its use for a purpose other than meeting the mutual defence obligations stipulated in the Washington Treaty and the WEU. According to the Bundesverfassungsgericht, article 24, section 2 provides a clear justification for the participation of German armed forces in multilateral peacekeeping as well as in peace-enforcement actions, whether under the auspices of the United Nations or within the framework of NATO or the WEU.[3]

While it has now been made clear by the Court that there are no constitutional obstacles for such missions, it still remains to be seen whether German governments would overcome their own inhibitions and the public's widespread aversion to military action to engage the Bundeswehr for these various and wide-ranging purposes. The political constraints that in most democratic states are limiting the use of military force only to such cases where their own security is vitally threatened are especially strong in Germany.[4] The readiness to act will be greater if the proposed use of force is represented as conforming to principles of multilateralism and bears the imprimatur of the international community. Germany's willingness to participate in collective security operations, therefore, will critically depend not only on an assessment of its own military-strategic interests but also on a parallel assessment of its partners with whom it wished to act in concert. During the Cold War, due to a permanent, long-term uniform Soviet threat, this condition was institutionalized. Today, by contrast, external security risks are more diffuse and ambiguous, while responsibilities are blurry. Since the Atlantic Alliance's overall strategic purpose corresponded largely with Germany's own security aims, there was no need for German policy to develop any distinctive national strategy beyond that relating to the protection of its own territory and that of Western Europe from military threat.[5] The fact that Germany's security policy was synonymous with Alliance policy also meant that if deterrence should fail, for Germany the option of non-participation in collective defence of Alliance territory simply was non-existent.[6] Germany was in no position even to contemplate a facsimile of France's avowedly independent defence strategy.

The end of the Cold War has brought more varied and less direct threats for Western Europe's and Germany's security. Instead of having an integrating effect, this changed nature of security risks fosters the differentiation of approaches to security matters among member states of the Atlantic Alliance and allows for divergent assessments of individual problem situations (e.g. Yugoslavia). As Uwe Nerlich has suggested, it will become more and more difficult for German security policy in the foreseeable future either to accept uncritically security concepts and strategies already preformulated by multilateral security organizations to which a still reticent Germany has contributed little. Consequently, Germany is confronted with the urgent task of reviewing its traditional policy of 'instinctive multilateralism', both in the sense that it must contribute to the formulation of a common Western security perspective and in the process consider developing its own, distinctive national aims and approaches.

Set in this context, the analysis first examines the security interests of a united Germany and the potential threats perceived by the political and military decisionmakers in Bonn. The second part then examines the conceptional and operational consequences drawn from this assessment by German policymakers with regard to multilateral military operations. A concluding section discusses the role military power should play in the security policy of Germany and assesses the current operational capabilities of the German Bundeswehr to participate in collective peacekeeping and peace-enforcement operations.

GERMAN SECURITY OBJECTIVES AFTER THE COLD WAR: INTERESTS AND POTENTIAL RISKS

In a neorealist perspective, basic foreign policy goals of states after the end of the Cold War remained unchanged. These goals are to maintain their sovereignty and to secure the welfare of their citizens. In the abstract, this truism was incorporated in the formulation of united Germany's vital security interest principle by the so-called Naumann report, issued in January 1992.[7] It defined basic German security interests: the continuation of a collective, alliance-bound security and defence policy within the framework of NATO; and the preservation of a strong transatlantic tie with the United States, while at the same time furthering the process of European integration – including the development of a Common Foreign and Security Policy. Beyond those core interests, the Naumann report declared Germany's further important security interests as including the promotion of democracy and economic growth in Central and Eastern Europe; the promotion and protection of international political, economic, military and ecological stability; the preservation of free trade as well the protection of free access to strategic raw materials; and, finally, the continuation of a stability-orientated arms control process in and around Europe.

This catalogue of German security interests was adopted, with only slight modifications, in the 'Verteidigungspolitischen Richtlinien' (VPR), the Defence Policy Guidelines, a document prepared by the planning staff of the German Defence Ministry and endorsed by Defence Minister Volker Rühe in November 1992.[8] These guidelines were highly influential in providing intellectual and policy guidance for a Germany that, theoretically at least, had recovered strategic self-will. They provided a definitive restatement of German national security interests as well as outlining the basic posture of German security policy and spelling out the future tasks of the German armed forces for the post-Cold War world. Moreover, in the German defence planning system, the Defence Policy Guidelines constitute the primary document for all subsequent planning. As such, the VPR establish a binding basis for future Bundeswehr planning and force development.[9] It is not surprising that the German White Paper on Defence, published in April 1994, broadly echoes the views expressed in the VPR. However, there is one important difference. While in the VPR the German security interests mentioned above are all treated equally, the White Paper formulates clear priorities that rank individual items on the German security agenda. This clear statement of priorities was dictated by the Bundeskanzleramt, the Federal Chancellory. Chancellor Kohl, who had his own definite ideas concerning the definition of Germany's security interests, placed the 'advancement of European integration around the Franco-German axis' at the top of the foreign policy agenda of the united Germany. In second place, clearly subordinated to EU development, comes the preservation of the transatlantic relationship with the United States. Commenting on the corresponding paragraphs of the White Paper, Defence Minister Rühe declared that after the end of the Cold War the alliance with the United States, although still necessary, is automatically, i.e. in accordance with the logic of new circumstances, ranked behind European integration.[10] And within this context the stabilization of Eastern Europe and Russia was third on the priority listing.[11]

Despite their relative obscurity, the Naumann report and the Defence Policy Guidelines did not completely escape public criticism. For instance, some critics have argued that these two documents would prepare the ground for a militarization of German foreign policy.[12] However, as Thomas-Durell Young has pointed out, this criticism has been largely misplaced, based on an inaccurate reading of the documents' intent. The concepts articulated in the VPR and the Naumann report mirror the Alliance's New Strategic Concept, which of course, the German government has approved.[13] Moreover, the definition of German security interests formulated in these two documents closely matched preoccupations in the ongoing German debate on Germany's new role in the post-Cold War international system.[14] Thus, the notion that the preservation of a strong transatlantic relationship with the United States as well as the deepening and widening of European integration constitute core security interests of the united Germany is not controversial. It is shared by the Federal government and the opposition Social Democratic Party (SPD).[15] There is also a broad consensus in favor of Germany's dedicating itself to the task of promoting democracy and economic welfare in Europe. Since Germany is highly dependent on a stable external environment, for subjective as well as objective reasons, it is generally recognized by the German political elite and German foreign policy experts that an extension of the Western zone of political stability and economic prosperity toward the eastern part of the European continent could be of crucial importance for Germany's future security. Profound disagreement between the German government and the SPD does exist, however, with regard to the Defence Policy Guideline's claim that the free access to strategic raw materials should constitute a vital security interest for Germany. As a prominent member of the SPD-Bundestagsfraktion put it at the time, this goal could only be realized with the support of ultra-modern German gunboats which the German Navy does not have at its disposal at the present time. The SPD opposes both the aim of preparing German armed forces to be deployed 'out of area' and the allocation of financial resources for building the capability for doing so.

Overall, Germany's security environment is seen by most as extraordinarily favourable. As defence expert Lothar Rühl has put it: 'For the first time since the eighteenth century, Germany is no longer exposed to a direct military threat involving the potential risk of an offensive war in Europe.'[16] The threat assessment made by the Defence Policy Guidelines is similar: 'Today, Germany is surrounded only by friendly partners.... For Germany, the existential threat of the Cold War is irreversibly overcome.'[17] Despite this optimistic assessment, German military planners are fully aware of the potential risks resulting from reshaping the political and strategic landscape in Europe. They are sensitive to new sources of conflict (exemplified by Yugoslavia), and less than sanguine that Eastern Europe's liberal revolution will take root everywhere (or even every place that counts).

German military risk analysis centred on Russia and the geographical region of the former Soviet Union. Although there are no indications that Russia will have either the intention or the means to pose a military threat at any time in the foreseeable future, German defence planners argue that the very existence of Russia's huge arsenal of conventional and nuclear weapons needs to be balanced by a symmetrical force posture in the West. As the former head of the planning staff in the German Defence Ministry, Hans Rühle, wrote, Russia remains the only power in Europe which is in a position to change the present European power-configuration by military means. Therefore, according to the former Generalinspekteur Klaus Naumann, special attention has to be paid to the reconstitution capabilities of the Russian armed forces as well as to the so-called 'mobile-forces command'. It is assumed that this unit will have at its disposal up to 100 000 combat-ready troops within seven days. In this perspective, priority in future military peacekeeping in Europe should be given to the balancing of Russia's military power through joint efforts within the institutional framework of NATO in order to prevent this arsenal being used one day by Russian leaders as an instrument of political blackmail.[18]

There are additional reasons for a policy of conservatism and caution. For one thing, there are the still unresolved disputes over security issues between Russia and its CIS partners; second, the Russian military doctrine first promulgated in November 1993 that looks beyond defence alone. Third, there is the turn to a more forceful, self-interested foreign policy against a backdrop of mounting nationalist rhetoric, and a leadership struggle in the Kremlin. Taken together, these internal developments are a matter of growing concern among the German foreign policy establishment. As early as December 1993, the former German Minister of Defence, Rupert Scholz, pointed out that Russia's new military doctrine, although primarily designed for the defence of the Russian homeland, would not exclude the out-of-area deployment of Russian troops. According to this assessment, Russia was not prepared for a complete withdrawal of its troops from foreign territories, such as Tajikistan, Kazakhstan, Georgia, Belarus, or Moldova. Moreover, for the Russian military planners, nuclear weapons were designed not only for strategic and political purposes, but also for concrete military options. Scholz came to the conclusion that, especially with regard to Central and Eastern Europe, the orientation of Russian military policy is in many ways far from certain. A similar assessment was made in a position paper published by the foreign-policy working-group of the CDU/CSU-Bundestagsfraktion in January 1994. Citing the strong Russian military presence around Kaliningrad, the paper stated that the maintenance of military forces in this region at present levels, let alone a further military build-up, could threaten the evolving post-Cold War European security structure.[19] A later risk assessment by a Defence ministry analyst came to the conclusion that Russian foreign policy is more and more determined by hegemonic aspirations as Russia actively enhances its sphere of influence by stationing its troops in several former Soviet Republics. Legally backed by the treaty of Tashkent (15 May 1992) a deployment of Russian troops at the north-eastern border of Turkey could also become possible. In this case the strategic interests of NATO would be directly affected.[20]

The German Foreign Ministry does not fully share those concerns.[21] It makes a more optimistic assessment of the developments in Russian foreign and security policy. Although made uneasy by Russian attempts to amend the CFE Treaty in order to improve its military capabilities to police the Caucasian republics,[22] German diplomats for the most part contend that there are no indicators which could be interpreted as signs of a resumption of an imperialistic Russian foreign policy. Russia's participation in IFOR is cited as proof of this. Therefore, they argue, there is no reason to panic.[23]

With regard to the new security challenges, concerns over instability in Eastern Europe, the Balkans and the former Soviet Union receive closest attention in German risk assessment. Instability in those regions could affect Germany's own security and prosperity in several ways. First, if instability results in armed conflict, there would be no guarantee that it could be kept isolated. Any spread in turn would 'put at risk the current process of a peaceful and stable merging of post-Cold War Europe'.[24] Thus, with regard to the war in former Yugoslavia, the German foreign establishment was not only dismayed by the atrocities of the war but also by the fact that the blatant violation of international rules, norms and agreements there could set precedents and produce imitation leading to similar developments elsewhere in Eastern Europe.[25]

Moreover, as a result of a breakdown of political order, as happened in former Yugoslavia, there is the perceived danger of mass migration and waves of refugees arriving at Germany's borders from the East. Although Chancellor Kohl and Foreign Minister Genscher, in dealing with the early recognition of Slovenia and Croatia, did not make reference to the problem of refugees in public statements, German concerns about a large influx of refugees coming from Yugoslavia coloured thinking about the war in Croatia.[26] The Chairman of the Foreign Relations Committee of the Bundestag, Hans Stercken, declared the recognition of Croatia and Slovenia as necessary in order to produce stability in this region and to contain the potential risk of mass migration from those former Yugoslav republics.[27] The refugee problem for Germany transcends the specific security effects of the war in former Yugoslavia. In 1992 alone, 438 191 people sought political asylum in Germany, compared to 256 000 in 1991. This number, combined with a rise in xenophobic violence in Germany, prompted Foreign Minister Klaus Kinkel to warn that Germany's political stability was at stake if Germany's partners in the EU did not help share this burden.[28]

Finally, the third group of risks German military planners foresee having to deal with, comprises the so-called extra-European threats, especially threats coming from North Africa and the Middle East. These regions are described as zones of high instability with a permanent risk of armed conflicts and violence with a good possibility of spreading to the territories of Germany's southern NATO allies.[29] Moreover, the fact that some states in this region are striving to build nuclear, biological or chemical weapons adds to the danger for European and German security. According to a report of the Bundesnachrichtendienst (BND), the German Intelligence Agency, a reasonable working assumption is that the states concerned will have at their disposal delivery systems with a range of 1000 kilometres within eight to ten years. While the vulnerability of West European territory to threats from abroad is an obvious matter of worry for German defence planners, a direct large-scale military attack from the south is not seen as a realistic option. However, as far as the Middle East is concerned, the very development of weapons of mass destruction poses a significant risk for European security, not least by making it more difficult to deal with actions that could disrupt oil supplies from the region.[30]

Given the nature and variety of those threats, there is widespread consensus among German political and military decisionmakers that the new security challenges for post-Cold War Europe can only be met by a combination of measures including preventive crisis-management and the will to use military means in order to enforce peace and to observe collective defence commitments. Therefore, most German foreign policy and defence experts agree that German security policy in a post-Cold War world has to be extended beyond simple protection against a military threat from outside.[31] Since a direct military threat has disappeared – while political, economic and ecological problems have become more and more important for German security – priority has to be given to non-military means in the prevention and the management of international crisis.[32] Military power, though, remains important in the sense that it has to play a supporting role in lending credibility to political measures of preventive diplomacy and crisis management. In case the escalation of a crisis could not be prevented by diplomatic means, early use of military power is aimed at reestablishing a situation in which the political control of the crisis would again become possible.[33]

There is also a widespread consensus in the current German debate that these measures to stabilize European security can and should only be performed in a multilateral framework. However, as we examine in this chapter, the formula for melding into an embracing German security strategy the institutional pieces represented by NATO, the CSCE, the WEU, the EU and the UN is an elusive one.

THE INSTITUTIONAL FRAMEWORK FOR POST-COLD WAR GERMAN SECURITY POLICY

In the early days of German unification, a broad policy consensus agreed that the Conference on Security and Cooperation in Europe (CSCE), now the Organization for Security and Cooperation in Europe (OSCE), would provide the most appropriate framework for Europe to tackle its post-Cold War security problems. During the Cold War, the CSCE was seen as not only softening the rivalry between the blocs but also as preparing the ground for the evolution of a new, more constructive relationship between East and West. Thus, from a German perspective, it seemed to be logical to entrust this well-tried institution with the task of shaping and stabilizing the emerging pan-European order. By integrating the Soviet Union as well as its successor states into the CSCE, security risks stemming from the breakdown of the Warsaw Pact and the Soviet Union could be kept manageable. In a long-term perspective, it was even envisaged that the CSCE evolve into a regional collective security community grounded on shared norms and common rules of behaviour.[34]

German foreign policy under the direction of Hans-Dietrich Genscher not surprisingly gave priority to the institutional strengthening of the CSCE. Even after the CSCE's failure in preventing the outbreak of war in former Yugoslavia or in stopping the fighting, Germany continued to press for an institutional strengthening of this multilateral body. Defending the CSCE against its critics, Foreign Minister Genscher pointed out that Germany 'must and will continue to further develop the CSCE process with new impulses.... I think that Yugoslavia is not an argument against the CSCE process – on the contrary it is an argument to strengthen it and to continue this activity.' In this perspective, German diplomacy actively pressed for creation of mechanisms to protect minority rights and initiated the creation of a conflict prevention centre. Furthermore, in order to improve the CSCE's crisis management capabilities, Foreign Minister Genscher called for the establishment of a 'steering committee' (a CSCE version of the UN Security Council) that would enable the CSCE to undertake peacekeeping operations.[35] His project was finally defeated by the strong opposition of the United States and Great Britain. At the Helsinki summit in July 1992, the CSCE did declare itself a regional body in accordance with chapter VIII of the UN Charter, thereby qualified to organize peacekeeping operations under the auspices of the United Nations Security Council. However, since the CSCE lacked the appropriate infrastructure, it would remain heavily dependent on NATO and WEU assets to mount any such operations.[36] From a German perspective, this rather looked like a makeshift arrangement than a real breakthrough towards empowering the CSCE to play a role in European conflict prevention and crisis management.[37] The high expectations German foreign policy placed in the CSCE have been largely disappointed. Consequently, diplomatic attention shifted to the functional and geographical enlargement of the Atlantic Alliance. This was not a completely new departure. It followed from an initiative taken in May 1991 by a Common Declaration of Foreign Minister Hans-Dietrich Genscher and his American counterpart, James Baker.[38] The so-called Baker–Genscher initiative prepared the ground for the creation of the North Atlantic Council for Cooperation (NACC) in November 1991. The establishment of NACC was generally seen as a first, although very modest, move towards a more active role for NATO in building a post-Cold War European security structure embracing former Communist states.

Actually, NATO proved a contentious issue. There were serious disagreements within the German government concerning the nature and speed of NATO's geographical enlargement – if not on the principle. In the view of Defence Minister Volker Rühe, a formless NACC was inadequate to provide the Central and Eastern European states with the firm organizational links that both protect against threat and encourage internal democratization. Consequently, he supported actively the geographical extension of NATO notably to those states which comprise the so-called Visegrad Group, in order to avoid their occupying an ambiguous security zone between the West and the East. As he put it, 'The opening of the Alliance to the East is a vital German interest. One does not have to be a strategic genius to understand this. You only have to look at the map. A situation in which Germany's eastern border is the border between stability and instability in Europe is not sustainable in the long run. Germany's eastern border cannot be the eastern border of the European Union and NATO. Either we export stability or we import instability.'[39] Growing concerns about the uncertain prospects of Russian foreign policy made NATO's eastward enlargement for him a matter of top priority.[40] Rühe did strike a cautionary note in emphasizing the necessity that NATO's enlargement be complemented by a close strategic partnership between Russia and the Western Alliance. In a speech before the Committee of Foreign Affairs of the German Parliament on 15

February 1995, Defense Minister Rühe proposed the conclusion of a formal treaty between Russia and NATO.[41] Aside from the institutionalization of regular consultations, the substance of such a treaty remains still unclear. Legal codification of a strategic partnership between Russia and NATO, however, could not prevent Russia's alienation, were enlargement to become an open-ended process offering NATO membership eventually to all of the Eastern Europeans. A step-by-step move of NATO up to the western borders of Russia could only be seen as a menace by Moscow.[42]

Minister Rühe's proposal of a treaty on a strategic partnership between Russia and NATO presumes that – even in a long-term perspective – Germany has a strong interest in limiting NATO's eastern enlargement to only a few Eastern European countries. It is an approach that seeks to balance and contain Russia's potential hegemonic aspirations in Eastern Europe without unduly antagonizing it and, thereby, acting so as to bring about a self-confirming prophecy. Within this strategic context, Poland is seen as the primary candidate to profit by this transfer of stability by joining the Atlantic Alliance.[43] In this vein, Defence Minister Rühe repeatedly pointed out that Poland should and could become a member of NATO before the year 2000.[44] Poland's privileged status in terms of NATO's eastern enlargement is clearly demonstrated by the fact that it has benefited from 82 out of 450 military cooperation and training programmes signed between Germany and 11 Eastern European countries during recent years. By comparison, there exist only 10 such programmes between Latvia and Germany and not more than seven with Belarus.[45]

Foreign Minister Klaus Kinkel, in contrast, repeatedly declared that he had strong reservations about NATO's eastward enlargement in the immediate future.[46] He was especially concerned by the fact that the discriminating geographical extension of the Atlantic Alliance could alienate Russia from the merging pan-European security structure. That outcome 'could call into question any prospect of a positive international development that has been made possible by the end of the East–West conflict'.[47] With this in mind, the Foreign Ministry's planners argued for a more prudent approach, recommending that a network of multiple cooperative security arrangements be developed within the framework of NACC, thereby including Russia and the former Soviet republics as well as the Eastern Europeans. Kinkel so publicly proposed that NACC become a more formal institution 'within whose framework armed forces in East and West could plan and train for joint peacekeeping operations'.[48] However, in a long-term perspective, even Kinkel foresaw the geographical enlargement of NATO as a logical and necessary consequence of growing ties between the Eastern Europeans and the West. In the end, he bowed to Chancellor Kohl's judgement that enlargement would be in Germany's interest. NATO's conclusive action to enlarge ended the internal German debate as far as the principle was concerned. Modalities of timing and the ranking of prospective new members in a priority list of candidates remained open, though. While there was no dispute over the precedence that should be given the Visegrad 3 or 4 (Poland above all), the issue of the Baltic's possible membership has been a prickly one for Germany. Geography, historical ties, and a sense of justice argued in favour of keeping open the prospect of their eventually joining the Alliance. Geo-political considerations, i.e. sensitivity to adamant Russian objections, argued for foreclosing a place in the Alliance for the Baltics. In this sense, the implication of the NATO decision on enlargement encapsulated Bonn's quandary in trying to reconcile its desire to project stability to the east with the conviction that cordial Russo-German relations was a foundation stone for a stable and peaceful European security structure. NATO's enlargement should also include the three Baltic states.[49]

Russia's membership in the Western Alliance was not seen as a realistic option. The official view was that NATO's approach towards Russia had to be guided by two principles: loose connection instead of incorporation; and cooperation rather than integration. As a practical matter, the Kohl government proposed three steps: (1) NATO should strive for the conclusion of a treaty on strategic partnership with Russia. It should precede any further negotiations about NATO membership of East European States. (2) NATO should explicitly renounce the deployment of nuclear weapons and foreign troops on the soil of new member states and (3) NATO should widen the scope of its security cooperation with Russia to embrace non-military issues.[50]

On these issues, there were some points of disagreement between the Defence and Foreign ministries. The Foreign Ministry assigned the OSCE a crucial role in binding Russia into the emerging European security structure. It deemed the OSCE the most appropriate framework to cooperate with a reforming Russia on the one hand, and, on the other hand, to deal with the potential challenges created by a more anti-Western Russian foreign policy by codifying a set of binding principles and common rules of behaviour.[51]

On this enduring intra-governmental dispute on the 'how' and 'when' of NATO's enlargement, Chancellor Kohl held his own counsel. On balance, though, he supported the rather cautious approach of Foreign Minister Kinkel. For example, Kohl repeatedly pleaded for a simultaneous enlargement of NATO and the European Union. Since there is widespread consensus that the eastward enlargement of the EU will not take place in the near future, one could infer that for the German Chancellor NATO's enlargement was not an immediate priority.[52] On a visit in Poland in July 1995, Kohl declared that he would not accept the German–Polish border as the Eastern border of the European Union in the long run.[53] Yet, in a speech before the Polish Parliament, he explicitly held out the prospect of a Polish membership in NATO as well as in the European Union before the year 2000.[54]

Chancellor Kohl has sought to fashion a unified policy that bridged the divergent positions of Rühe and Kinkel. In November 1994, the policy statement of the governing coalition stated that Germany supports 'the step-by-step enlargement of NATO which should develop in close relationship with widening of the European Union and the WEU'.[55] This means that German government will accept only those states as new NATO members who will become members of the European Union at the same time.[56] Moreover, NATO's opening to the East has to be an integrated part of an overall European security structure. 'In order to prevent a new split, integration has to be supplemented by cooperation, notably by a strong and close partnership with Russia. In this context, the strengthening of the OSCE is important.'[57] This represents an important shift in Germany's OSCE policy away from the approach followed by Hans-Dietrich Genscher during the early days of German unification. Today, from a German perspective, the OSCE, although still important with regard to its role in crisis prevention, has primarily a compensating function. That is to say, it has specific, concrete value as a vehicle for binding those states which cannot become members of NATO to a common code of conduct and to its collective enforcement.[58] With regard to OSCE's crisis-management capabilities, German foreign policymakers are nonetheless cautious and sceptical, especially as regards Rumanian conduct. Foreign Minister Kinkel rejected the demand of various members of the German Bundestag to activate OSCE's mechanisms to settle the conflict in Chechnya on the grounds that the OSCE lacked appropriate instruments and authority.[59] Chechnya was technically an internal Russian problem, inviting criticism and raising doubts as to the OSCE's jurisdiction. A restricted view of its sensitivity role, though, stems from a more general assessment.

The attitude of the opposition SPD is also ambivalent. While he was party leader, Rudolf Scharping supported a careful redefinition of NATO's future tasks.[60] Other influential party members, though, in an article in *Der Spiegel* concerning the future role of the OSCE and NATO, argue strongly against any functional enlargement of the Alliance. Scharping's successor Oskar Lafontaine pointed out that, in view of the prohibitive costs connected with the new tasks assumed by NATO, the Alliance should only concentrate on its original task, i.e. common defence.[61] Likewise, the SPD's foreign policy expert, Egon Bahr, strongly argued against any eastward enlargement of NATO since this would antagonize Russia instead of producing stability all over Europe. He argued that for the German government the institutional development of the OSCE should be of prime concern.[62] This view was rejected by Karsten Voigt, foreign policy spokesman of the SPD's parliamentary group in the Bundestag. For him, only NATO could produce stability all over Europe. Moreover, only an enlarged NATO would provide the appropriate institutional framework for a definitive multilateral binding (and controlling) of the power of a unified Germany.[63] The Voigt view is regarded within the SPD as a rather 'extreme' position, and is supported only by a small minority.

German policy toward NATO's eastward expansion is constrained by cost-cutting pressures and inner contradictions. The key players agree in principle on the necessity of NATO's enlargement, since this would be the only way to satisfy the security needs of East European states. Yet, there is widespread consensus within the German government that pan-continental stability can only be achieved if Russian security interests and concerns are taken seriously into account. Neither the Rühe concept of a transfer of stability to Eastern Europe by a limited eastward enlargement of NATO nor the project of a treaty on strategic partnership between Russia and NATO show the way out of this dilemma. While the latter carries the risk of giving Russia a *de facto* role in Alliance deliberations on the enlargement issue (and on whatever continental security problems as might arise), the former cannot easily be brought into harmony with the basic challenge to avoid differentiated zones of security in the emerging pan-European security order. Moreover, this *de facto* acceptance of new spheres of influence in Europe could evoke latent fears about the rise of a German–Russian dominance in Europe.[64] At least up until now, the proponents of a discriminating geographical enlargement of NATO[65] have not been able to offer a clear and convincing solution for this problem.

Crisis-Management

In the light of the recent experiences in former Yugoslavia and Somalia, there is growing consensus among the German foreign policy and military elites that military crisis-management can only be done effectively within the framework of NATO. As Defence Minister Rühe declared in a 1993 speech in Prague: 'In the future, we have to be prepared to defuse potential risks, to smother emerging conflicts or to settle them by military means. It makes no sense to be prepared only for a large-scale attack on NATO which has become most unlikely today.... Collective crisis-management is now as important as collective defense.'[66] This view of NATO's new tasks was fully supported by Foreign Minister Kinkel: 'NATO, too, will have to play a new role, looking beyond its own area and addressing new challenges. NATO has to become capable of dealing with the full spectrum of tasks, from collective defence to crisis-management and peacekeeping.'[67] Both also agreed that NATO's new tasks have to be carried out within the legal framework of the United Nations, i.e., with regard to its new tasks of peace-keeping and international crisis-management NATO should not act on its own but needs a clear mandate of the UN Security Council.[68] However, unlike Kinkel, Rühe strongly rejects the idea that such operations should be exclusively carried out under the auspices of the UN, i.e. that NATO – as is the case in former Yugoslavia – should only act on the explicit request of the UN.

The keen interest shown by the German government in expanding NATO's role in the process of building a new, pan-European security structure contradicts, to a certain extent, its continuing efforts to establish a functioning Common Foreign and Security Policy (CFSP) for the European Union.[69] That ambitious goal was set in the anxious period ushered in by Germany's sudden unification. In February 1991, German Foreign Minister Hans-Dietrich Genscher and his French counterpart, Roland Dumas, published a joint position paper that foresaw a CFSP leading to a full-blown European Defence Community. At the centre of this proposal was the WEU which, it was stated, should be developed in such a way 'that an organic relationship between the Political Union and the WEU should be made possible in order to enable the WEU to work out a CFSP for the Political

Union with the aim finally becoming part of it'.[70] The first concrete steps in this direction were taken with the Franco-German decision of May 1992 to set up the so-called Eurocorps, a project to which Bonn has been steadfastly supportive – even if it differs somewhat with Paris as to its possible 'out-of-area' deployment.

For the German government, this policy conformed to the logic of the European integration process. Chancellor Kohl stated in an address to the Bundestag in late 1991 that the idea of a unified Europe is inexorably linked to a common European defence. At a more practical level, the strengthening of the operational role of the WEU could provide the European Union with the appropriate instruments to act in those cases in which common military actions within the framework of NATO might not be possible.[71] This was the position of Generalinspekteur Naumann. It was, though, somewhat misleading. As Dr Dieter Mahncke, then a member of the Defence planning staff put it: 'there is in fact no conceivable instance where NATO could not act but Europeans could. NATO capabilities are by definition superior to those of the Europeans alone, and this will remain so even if and when the Europeans will develop their own capabilities. So it comes down to cases where NATO will not act: either because the United States is against such action or because it is not against such action but prefers to let the Europeans act without American participation.'[72]

Since the former possibility is hard to envisage, the most likely case would then be the one in which Europe could act alone but with American political backing and the logistical support of NATO. From this point of view, the strengthening of the WEU should not aim at replacing but rather supplementing NATO, a means to establish a more symmetrical relationship between the United States and Western Europe.[73] Nevertheless, by signing the Petersberg Declaration of June 1992, the German government has contributed to a certain extent to bolstering the WEU as a potential rival institution to NATO. The Declaration stated that 'Military units of the WEU may be employed in conjunction with their contribution to common defence in accordance with Article 5 of the Washington Treaty and Article V of the modified Brussels treaty.'[74] NATO and WEU were thus formally placed on the same level with regard to the mission of collective defence of Western Europe. Moreover, at French urging, WEU member states agreed to a regional delimitation of military activities of the WEU. These activities include the full spectrum of military crisis-management up to combat missions. This purely European approach to the security problems of post-Cold War Europe ran the risk of becoming incompatible with NATO's long-term existence by opening rifts between Western Europe and the United States. In this perspective, even strong supporters of a common European security and defence policy, such as the influential leader of the CDU/CSU parliamentary group in the Bundestag, Wolfgang Schäuble, expressed strong reservations on the compatibility of NATO and WEU in the long run were Germany to press too strongly for a European Defence Identity largely independent from NATO.[75]

Until now, Germany has been relatively successful in reconciling European and transatlantic institutions as instruments of Germany's core security interests. The way in which the Franco-German Eurocorps was integrated into NATO with the agreements signed in January 1993 is testimony to Bonn's ability to manage the development of both. France's willingness to make available to SACEUR active troops, i.e. troops with a high degree of readiness, has significantly widened France's former cooperation agreements with NATO. Previously, France only provided troops as operational reserves and refused to participate on a regular basis in NATO defence planning. On the basis of the 1993 accord, French units of the Eurocorps have become part of the integrated defence planning of the Alliance.[76]

As the recent Franco-American dispute over the Combined Joined Task Forces (CJTF) showed, even in the near future it will become more and more difficult for the German foreign policymakers to harmonize these two perspectives. The core problem of this new transatlantic dispute was the French claim to establish an independent command structure outside of NATO for those military missions not being part of Alliance collective defence obligations. France demonstrates a strong tendency to use NATO solely as a 'military toolbox', a policy which – if followed by France's European partners – would undermine NATO's institutional integrity.[77] Not surprisingly, the United States has rejected the French conception of CJTF.

This transatlantic dispute has been settled – in principle. On 3 June 1996, NATO member states approved the CJTF concept of 'separable but not separate' military capabilities allowing Europe to act where the United States does not want to or cannot act. The terms of the Berlin accords became possible only after France had shelved its demand to create an independent command structure outside NATO for those missions in which WEU would use NATO's intelligence as well as its command and control facilities.[78] Moreover, France agreed that the use of these facilities will depend on a unanimous consent of the North Atlantic Council.

In the official German view, the positive outcome at Berlin does not mean that, as Frédéric Bozo explains, it will attempt to change the NATO system from within. Thus, commenting on NATO's decision, French Foreign Minister de Charette declared that for France the primary task of NATO's internal reform has to be to provide Western Europe with a far-reaching independence in military and security affairs.[79] Up until now, the German government has not taken an official stance on this issue. Nevertheless, it is evident that the German government is far more inclined to the American than to the French position. In particular, it has strong reservations about French plans for a more thorough-going reform of NATO. So long as the Franco-German differences on the future institutional reform of NATO cannot be resolved, divergent perspectives on a division of labour between Western security organizations too will prevent a complete meeting of the minds between Bonn and Paris.

That said, Germany's strategic perspective is being modified in ways that narrow differences with France. There is a growing recognition that it no longer is reasonable to rely exclusively on American leadership to meet the European allies' security needs. Volker Rühe has been most forthright in expressing a growing belief that '[it] has become obvious that the traditional willingness of the US to get involved in European security is increasingly being called into question in the US Congress and throughout the country. I very much admire the courageous decision taken by President Clinton to make 20 000 troops available for the former Yugoslavia to implement the Dayton peace agreement. But I am well aware that this decision was not easy and that it would be even more difficult to make a similar one in the future.'[80]

Among the implications, he noted, was the point that '[the] new NATO has to be used in a flexible way. We have to utilize NATO's structures for different purposes. In the future, the Alliance must reflect a transatlantic partnership based on the understanding that the US remains committed to Europe's security but takes advantage of organized European solidarity. The new NATO must cope with a broad spectrum of missions and it must provide the basis for European-led operations. The European dimension of the Alliance's structural reform must be designed both to permit and support the emerging European capability to act strategically.'[81]

Logically, this line of thinking leads to the further conclusion that developing the European Union's proclaimed Foreign and Security Policy is a project to be pursued with renewed energy. That objective indeed figured on Bonn's agenda for the Intergovernmental Conference (IGC) launched in 1996.[82] By contrast, though, it was of diminishing importance for Jacque Chirac's government in Paris which was casting a jaundiced eye on federalizing elements of the Maastricht Treaty. The Berlin accords notwithstanding, therefore, German foreign policy will have to deal with a more fundamental institutional problem. The proclaimed common security interests of Western Europe, which serve as the prime rationale for Germany's demands for the establishment of a CFSP guided by decisions taken on a weighted majority basis, are not yet a reality. At least, the consensus is not strong enough to allow for the actual formulation and implementation of common policies. In this sphere of European integration, the Franco-German axis – the necessary condition for any progress in this field – does not really function. Franco-German differences over how to deal with the war in former Yugoslavia were evident from 1991. While the German government pressed for an early international recognition of Slovenia and Croatia by the European Community, France, for a long time, argued for the maintenance of an integral Yugoslav state. Former French foreign minister Roland Dumas went so far as to accuse Germany of being responsible for the escalation of the conflict by pressing for the early recognition.[83] Though these particular differences were settled, frictions over how to handle the protracted Yugoslav conflict persisted. One should not expect solutions given growing divergence in assessment of individual problem situations. The frustrating EU experience in dealing with the war in former Yugoslavia supports the conclusion that probably leadership by the United States (or certainly its active participation) will remain an important condition for effective crisis-management in Europe. It will therefore be no easy task for German diplomacy to reconcile this obvious need for a major United States role with its ambitious project to establish an effective and more independent European Security Identity. That task is exacerbated by the cooling of French interest in giving body and substance to a CFSP for the EU.

THE ROLE OF MILITARY POWER IN POST-COLD WAR GERMAN SECURITY POLICY: OPERATIONAL AND POLITICAL ASPECTS

Germany's conception of NATO's and the WEU's new tasks is reinforced by its own military planning. The decision to divide the

German armed forces into Main Defence Forces and Crisis Reaction Forces – and to give priority to the latter with regard to training, equipment and personnel – indicates the growing importance given the ability of the Bundeswehr to react rapidly to international crises.[84] In addition to the possession of highly mobile and combat-ready forces of the three services, German defence planning aims at the development of national command and control capabilities which are judged necessary in order to engage the Bundeswehr to participate in collective military operations outside the NATO framework. As a result, the three services of the Bundeswehr have been provided with their own operational headquarters during the last few years. Both the Luftwaffe and the Bundesmarine have long possessed service operational headquarters of varying degrees of independence. They are currently being modestly expanded: Luftwaffenführungskommando in Köln-Wahn and Flottenkommando in Glücksburg. In contrast, there has been no army operational command headquarters above corps level since the creation of the Bundeswehr. It was necessary to establish the Heeresführungskommando in March 1994 in Koblenz.[85] As stated by its commanding general, the Heeresführungskommando has three important tasks: first, it exercises command and control over the three Army Corps, on behalf of the Chief of Staff of the Army; second, it ensures the operational readiness of the major combined arms units of the Army; and finally, it plans for and controls the employment of army forces in national and multinational formations.[86]

Since 1 January 1995, the Bundeswehr for the first time in its history has at its disposal a 'nationales Führungszentrum', a national command centre which is able to coordinate and to command military operations including all three services. Admittedly, the Führungszentrum is not an independent agency and is not conceived as the nucleus of a future German Generalstaff. As a practical matter, it cannot conduct large-scale military operations. But the periodic, intensive reviews which it undergoes are designed to keep under review evolving operational requirements.[87]

According to the German Defence Ministry it will take up to ten years to put the German crisis-reaction forces in full operational service. Then, as stated in the 'Konzeptionellen Leitlinien', they could participate in the full spectrum of international crisis-management and collective security operations foreseen in the United Nations Charter. In the presentation of his Bundeswehrplan (Armed Forces Plan) for 1997, Volker Rühe laid out the steps to be taken for preparing the army for its new missions. He optimistically predicted that by the year 2000, the German military will have fulfilled the primary prerequisites for adequate international crisis management; by 2009, he expects the crisis reaction forces to be completely outfitted with modern equipment.

To do so, though, would require some extensive equipment purchases. In the light of the budgetary austerity necessitated to meet the strict Maastricht criteria for European monetary union, the outlook for obtaining the requisite finding was dark. In an era of heavy cutbacks in Germany's politically sensitive social programmes, the military budget would come under intense, sceptical scrutiny.

Even before this fiscal squeeze, there was reason to question whether those ambitious targets could be met. The lead times cited were viewed as unrealistic by some German defence experts. They point out that the Bundeswehr has serious deficiencies in the areas of reconnaissance, logistics and transport capacities. To put those crisis-reaction forces in full operational service, costly projects (such as the establishment of an satellite-borne communication and control structure as well as the procurement of new armoured troop-carriers) would have to be realized within the next few years. The German Defence Ministry is fully aware of these problems.[88] However, it is questionable whether these deficiencies can be overcome in the short term in the light of the strained German defence budget.[89] The total budget of the German Defence Ministry in 1994 was 47.5 billion Deutschmarks. Of this, only 21.4 per cent were spent for modernization investments and this share will only be slightly raised to 22.1 per cent or 23.3 per cent within the next years, while the budget as a whole will remain constant until 1997.[90] Based on the coalition agreement of November 1994, a slight increase up to 48.4 billion Deutschmarks was planned for 1998.[91] However, with the tightening of budgetary pressures against the backdrop of economic recession and political strife over Kohl's intention to reduce social programmes, it was not surprising that the defence budget instead was threatened by cuts of up to 2 billion Deutschmarks.[92] This amount is too small to establish effective crisis-reaction forces of nearly 50 000 troops. Thus, Defence Minister Rühe contends that Germany will only be able to contribute 10 000 to 12 000 troops in collective security operations.[93] More pessimistic assessments came to the conclusion that, if trends continue, the Bundeswehr will be able to provide no more than 2000 to 3000 soldiers (notably paratroopers) for collective security-type operations within NATO or within the WEU.[94] These lightly armoured troops, however, can be deployed over long distances and quickly activated. But without the support of heavily armoured forces, these troops could only be engaged in a very limited spectrum of collective peace-keeping operations – as is the case for SFOR in Bosnia.[95]

As the German engagement in Somalia clearly demonstrated, the Bundeswehr also has also serious deficits to overcome in order to deploy even rather small-sized military units over long distances. A study initiated by Generalinspekteur Klaus Naumann in 1994 came to the conclusion that a stronger maritime support would be absolutely necessary for future overseas deployment of German armed forces. Therefore, this report proposed the construction of a Mehrzweckschiff (MZS), a multipurpose ship which should provide the Bundeswehr with the capacity to carry out UN-authorized missions all over the world.[96] The MZS would be able to fulfil three main tasks. First, it would be able to project military units with a size of 1200 troops over long distances, 270 armoured vehicles included. Second, it would serve as a hospital ship. And finally, it would provide appropriate national command and control capabilities.[97] In May 1995, though, the German Defence Ministry abruptly cancelled this ambitious project.[98] Rühe argued that the size and the scope of Germany's contribution to collective military crisis management should be limited to Europe and its periphery. Therefore, he believed there was no longer a need for such a costly project which would burden the German defence budget by 600 million Deutschmarks.[99]

Operational shortcomings notwithstanding, the Kohl government showed a growing willingness to engage German armed forces in international peacekeeping and peace-enforcement operations. A more pressing element of uncertainty is the continuing lack of consensus among the German political elite on the operational need and the political legitimation for the use of military power beyond the defence of German territory. The issue of German participation in military intervention in so-called out-of-area conflicts is highly controversial.[100] As the hesitant German military support for Turkey during the Gulf war has shown, this seems to be true even with regard to actions undertaken to meet existing Alliance commitments. Although German debate at that time largely centred on concerns relating to international law, Germany's behaviour could also be interpreted as evidence that attitudes toward military security are in flux and that no consensus on the aims and conditions for deploying military forces existed. After the end of the Cold War, Turkey's role in containing the Soviet Union was perceived by the German foreign policy elite as less important than in the past. Therefore a military attack on Turkey was no longer presumed to constitute a threat to Germany's own security.[101]

In this setting, it is not surprising that, according to opinion polls, only 25 per cent of the German public would support the extension of NATO's security guarantees to new members. The same is true with regard to a German participation in collective peace-enforcement operations: while a large part of the German population expresses clear consent to a participation of the Bundeswehr in humanitarian interventions (92 per cent) and traditional peacekeeping operations (57 per cent), only a slight majority of Germans (51 per cent) would support the participation of the Bundeswehr in collective peace-enforcement operations.[102] German public opinion seems to support 'engagement in principle but seems to shy away when it entails involvement in specific scenarios'.[103] This view is largely confirmed by a survey done by the Allensbach Institute in January 1995. It showed that 51 per cent of Germans would be against the participation of German ECR-Tornados if NATO should intervene in Bosnia. With regard to the Tornado issue, there is a significant cleavage between East and West Germany. While only 48 per cent of West Germans had strong reservations on this topic, up to 62 per cent of the East German population opposed a Tornado mission over Bosnia.[104] The creation and deployment of IFOR by NATO posed the issue concretely. Promulgation of the Dayton accords had a positive effect on German opinion, the percentage of those supporting German participation in IFOR rose to 59.4 per cent.[105] Many Germans, though, still had strong reservations about engagement of the Bundeswehr in large-scale collective security operations. To avoid a breakdown of the internal consensus on Germany's participation in peacekeeping operations, any German government would have to take into account those reservations. Its own scope of action with regard to multilateral security operations would be commensurately constrained. IFOR set a precedent and Germany crossed a threshold. But any further deployments, especially where combat threatens, will have to surmount a serious political obstacle.[106]

Given official declarations in the White Paper on Defence that German security is no longer threatened,[107] and that the new security risks cannot effectively be met by military means or 'cannot be balanced by military capabilities',[108] even strong supporters of a German participation in collective military interventions are struggling to find a consistent, persuasive argument to justify future out-of-area deployments of the Bundeswehr. The need for a German participation is therefore explained by the fact that Germany has to remain a reliable partner in European and Atlantic Alliance affairs. As the foreign policy spokesman of the CDU/CSU parliamentary group in the Bundestag, Karl Lamers, has put it: 'Since Germany is highly integrated with its European partners, since it is an important and irreplaceable member of the international community, its attitude towards basic problems of international life should not be different from those of its partners.' By staying aloof Germany would seriously damage the idea of a unified Europe because 'without Germany there will not be a common European defence and without this, there will be no common Foreign and Security policy and, as result, there will be no Political Union'.[109] Thus, Germany's participation in the full spectrum of international crisis-management within NATO and the WEU is seen from this perspective as a fundamental requirement with regard to Germany's dependence on the multilateral Alliance rather than in terms of the intrinsic importance of conjectured missions. In short, German armed forces serve primarily as an instrument to anchor united Germany within a transatlantic and European frame work. This is one of the main reasons why the German government has pushed for a multinational integration of the Bundeswehr since the early days of unification. Consequently, today the greater part of the German ground forces are integrated in multinational army-corps under one institutional arrangement or another.

The rationale given by governmental forces for a full participation of the Bundeswehr in collective security actions cannot rest solely on assertions that Germany's reputation as a reliable partner within the Atlantic Alliance and the European framework is at stake. A supplementary argument is that out-of-area deployment of German armed forces is a potential instrument to enhance Germany's international status and influence. Klaus Naumann pointed out as early as 1989 that the persistent reluctance of a great part of the German political elite to consider the armed forces as an instrument of legitimate national policy makes Germany's position within the Atlantic Alliance extremely difficult. Since military power will remain important in international life, the continuing rejection of its use in addressing international crises will end up in a loss of international influence and will limit Germany to the status of second-rank power, not only worldwide but also within Europe. This view prevailed in the Defence Policy Guidelines published in 1992. There, German influence on international institutions based on 'our military contribution' is defined as a vital German security interest. For his part, Rühe proclaimed with characteristic assurance that 'German forces are now able to perform the same tasks and face the same risks as their fellow soldiers in NATO and the WEU. For many years our allies provided us with security in our own country. Today, we are preparing to help our allies in order to contain conflicts where and when they arise and to stop them spreading like wildfire. The Bundeswehr is being developed into an instrument commensurate with the conditions of our day and age – capable of defending our country, of reacting to crises throughout the Alliance territory and of serving in and beyond Europe under a mandate of the United Nations if needed.'[110]

It is widely recognized among German foreign policymakers that these abstract considerations alone cannot serve as sufficient justification for a specific out-of-area deployment of German troops.[111] Klaus Kinkel has repeatedly pointed out that the government's decision to engage the Bundeswehr in international peacekeeping and peace-enforcement operations has to be made in accordance with the German national interests being at stake in the specific situation.[112] This view is strongly held by Defense Minister Rühe.[113] The Defence Policy Guidelines recognize that the variety and the multiplicity of external threats of Germany's post-Cold War security interests means that German perceptions – although concurrent in principle – could not always be brought into congruence with the perceived security interests of its partners.[114] As a result, German foreign policy could find itself in the awkward situation where its considered interpretation of a security problem points away from the application of military force even though German participation in collective military action is accepted as desirable in principle.

As the German government's diplomatic shilly-shallying about the participation of the Bundeswehr in protecting a possible disengagement of UN-peacekeeping troops from Bosnia in 1994–95 showed, there is a serious risk of being entrapped by this dilemma. At that time, Supreme Allied Commander Europe, General Joulwan, approached the German government in November 1994 to provide military support to cover a possible withdrawal of UNPROFOR from the former Yugoslavia. Since this NATO request was graded as an informal inquiry, the German government saw no need for an immediate decision. Its delayed response, almost two weeks after a second NATO request had been made, did pronounce a readiness to support NATO with logistical assistance and combat air-cover in the event of a NATO-led extraction mission in the Balkans. However, the government's decision was largely based on the assumption that, at least in the near future, this option would not materialize and therefore a German military engagement in former Yugoslavia would not become necessary.[115] As the situation in Bosnia underwent a dramatic deterioration in early summer 1995, the Kohl government was forced to commit itself to providing active military assistance far earlier than envisaged. On 26 June 1995, the Kohl government agreed to expand the German contribution to the multinational Rapid Intervention Force in Bosnia. The government's decision was approved with a large majority by the Bundestag on 30 June 1995. Since the role of the ECR-Tornado was exclusively limited to the protection of the Intervention Force, the German contribution to NATO's military operations in Bosnia would be marginal. Indeed, in accordance with the Bundestag's decision, German aircraft were not allowed to participate in NATO's 'deny-flight' operation or to provide direct military support to UNPROFOR in case it should be under attack.[116] As one commentator rightly pointed out, the German Tornados over Bosnia would be seen as more or less redundant than as a substantial contribution to the military side of NATO's efforts at conflict resolution in the Bosnian civil war. In this perspective, the government's later decision on IFOR participation (which was approved with a large majority by the Bundestag on 6 December 1995) to contribute 4000 troops to Operation Joint Endeavour in Bosnia can be seen as an important change in German foreign and security policy. It is noteworthy, though, that the German contribution was limited to logistical support of its allies and the permanent deployment of German military units in Bosnia is explicitly ruled out. German troops, therefore, would not bear the same risks as its NATO allies. Germany's qualified participation in IFOR left open the question of whether Germany was prepared to meet the fundamental requirement for being a major player in European and Atlantic security affairs.[117]

The issue took on immediacy as IFOR's self-imposed one-year mandate approached its end while conditions in Bosnia clearly indicated the need for a continued outside military presence. American reluctance to prolong the participation of US troops increased the pressure on all the European allies. Anticipating a September meeting of the NATO defence ministers, the Kohl government began to prepare public opinion to expect that German troops would remain in Bosnia after the initial mandate expired in December. It was encouraged by indications of growing cross-party support for continued involvement by the Bundeswehr. The prevailing sentiment combined a humanitarian concern for the future of the war-wracked Bosnians with a sense of European responsibility for dealing with a European problem in the wake of repeated declarations that the days of sheltering behind a protective US were over. For officials, Germany's multiple interests in Balkan stability and in encouraging a competent Europe overcame qualms about an open-ended commitment to a still dangerous mission. It is noteworthy that Rühe was the first senior minister to break the informal understanding that Western leaders would avoid broaching the issue in public before the Bosnian elections in September.[118] Germany crossed a threshold in committing itself to a substantial Bundeswehr presence in the Bosnian follow-on-force (SFOR) that succeeded IFOR in early 1997. The 3000-man German contingent was composed of combat troops operating on an equal footing with those of its allies.

The future role of German armed forces in collective security operations is not preordained. But a strong diplomatic and institutional logic is developing that points to involvement.

Since German ground forces are highly integrated in multinational army corps, German diplomacy will have reduced room for equivocation. The issue of German participation will entail more than the need for symbolic demonstration of Germany's reliability as an ally; it will help to determine the success of any postulated operation. At the organization level, this issue already has arisen for the Multinational Division Central put into service in summer 1994. This unit is primarily designed for military crisis-management under the command of NATO's Rapid Reaction Corps. Germany's contribution for the MND-Central includes a brigade of paratroopers and military personnel for logistics and command and control. In the event of Germany's non-participation in an out-of-area deployment of this military unit, the MND-Central would, as a result, be rendered ineffective. With regard to the Eurocorps this danger is already real. A primary task of this multinational military unit is to contribute to sub-strategic collective security challenges.[119] In this perspective, France already has developed concrete scenarios for future missions of the Eurocorps. At the time of the civil war in Rwanda, former French Defence Minister Léotard pleaded in Summer 1994 for the creation of an international intervention force with participation of the Eurocorps for the pacification of the civil war.[120] More recently, Foreign Minister Hervé de Charette proposed to engage the Eurocorps in a future peace-implementation force in Bosnia. On both proposals, the German government showed strong reservations. In the light of the enduring German reluctance to engage German armed forces in such operations, there is a growing concern among the French *classe politique* that this military unit could remain functionally inoperative and degenerate into a meaningless symbol of Europe's unrealized aspirations to act as a great power. Logically, it follows that this ambitious Franco-German project will not fulfil one of its main political functions, i.e. instead of stimulating the process of European integration as intended by Chancellor Kohl and President Mitterrand, it could become a serious obstacle to achieving a true European common security and defence policy.

CONCLUSIONS

As our analysis has shown, Germany's policy with regard to participation in collective security operations is – at best – ambivalent. On the one hand, German foreign and defence policy planners are fully aware that after the end of the Cold War, Germany still is vulnerable and exposed to external risks and threats, albeit on a diminished scale. To cope with them, Germany needs to be engaged in functioning multilateral security organizations. Hence its strong interest in the institutional strengthening and the functional enlargement of all those organizations – NATO, the WEU, and the OSCE. The other side of the coin, Germany's approach to the security problems of post-Cold War Europe and its surroundings, is closely focused on conflict prevention while remaining chary about military action. The participation of the Bundeswehr in IFOR has not solved that fundamental ambivalence. For the foreseeable future, Germany will remain a reluctant power with regard to peacemaking and peace-enforcing. As a consequence, German policy may diminish the effectiveness and authority of the very multilateral security structures it urgently needs, both to cope with the post-Cold War security environment and to establish an accepted place for itself in Europe's new order.

Germany's approach to multilateral security and defence cooperation has been largely symbolic. Bonn's policy aimed at promoting the political integration of the West rather than being oriented towards concrete military necessities. It was in this perspective that the Eurocorps was set up by Chancellor Kohl and President Mitterrand. As Germany's reaction to recent developments in French security policy has shown, a compelling political purpose could not avoid differences over operational needs and missions. Reacting to French plans to abolish conscription, Defence Minister Rühe averred that German defence planning gives a clear priority to the defence of German and Alliance territory; all other military missions, including collective security ones, are of minor importance. German and French strategic conceptions, and defence philosophy, diverge. Future conflict between Bonn and Paris on missions for the Eurocorps seems to be unavoidable. The problematic situation reflects the larger dilemma of German foreign policymakers as they strive to reconcile the opposing logics. They have yet to formulate a satisfactory set of unambiguous guidelines for the diverse forms of allied cooperation, under diverse institutional arrangements, such as current circumstances call for. Today nothing of that kind is in sight.

NOTES

1. H. Haftendorn, 'Gulliver in der Mittel Europas. Internationale Verflechtung und nationale Handlungsmöglichkeiten', in K. Kaiser and H. W. Maull (eds), *Deutschlands neue Außenpolitik*. Band 1 (Grundlagen: München, 1994), 129–52, 149.
2. See on the current German debate i.a. K.-H. Kamp, 'Die Debatte um den Einsatz deutscher Streitkräfte außerhalb des Bündnisgebietes, Forschungsinstitut der Konrad-Adenauer-Stiftung', *Interne Studie*, Nr. 22 (St. Augustin, März 1991); O. Diel, 'UN-Einsätze der Bundeswehr. Außenpolitische Handlungszwänge und innenpolitischer Konsensbedarf', in *Europa-Archiv*, 8 (1993), 2129–227; and J. Shea and M. de Weger, 'Ein europäischer Pfeiler in der NATO?, Konrad-Adenauer-Stiftung', *Interne Studie*, Nr. 90 (St. Augustin, November 1994). See also the pathbreaking analysis made by N. Phillippi, *Bundeswehr-Auslandseinsätze als außen- und sicherheitspolitisches Problem des geeinten Deutschland* (Trier, 1996).
3. See on the decision of the Bundesverfassungsgericht the interesting interpretations by U. Fastenrath, 'Was ist der Bundeswehr nach dem Karlsruher Spruch erlaubt?', *FAZ* (22 July 1994); and D. Blumenwitz, 'Ende einer verfassungsrechtlichen Begriffsakrobatik', *FAZ* (5 August 1994).
4. This argument is put forward by the former deputy head of the German Defence Ministry planning staff, D. Mahncke, *Parameters of European Security*, Chaillot Paper 10 (Paris: Institute for Security Studies Western European Union, September 1993), p. 8.
5. See W. F. Schlör, *German Security Policy*, Adelphi Paper 277 (London: IISS, 1993), S. 6.

6. U. Nerlich, 'Sicherheitspolitik und nationale Verteidigungsfähigkeit', in *Soldat und Technik*, 1 (1994), 9–12, 11.
7. 'Militärpolitische und militärstrategische Grundlagen und konzeptionelle Grundrichtung der Neugestaltung der Bundeswehr. Vorlage des Bundesverteidigungsministeriums der Verteidigung an den Verteidigungsausschuβ des Bundestages' vom 20. printed in *Blätter für Deutsche und internationale Politik*, 4 (Januar 1992), 506–10.
8. 'Verteidigungspolitische Richtlinien für den Geschäftsbereich des Bundesministers der Verteidigung' vom 26. printed in *Blätter für Deutsche und Internationale Politik*, 12 (November 1992), 1138–51.
9. For the importance of the Defence Policy Guidelines see D. Mahncke, 'Wandel im Wandel Bundeswehr und europäische Sicherheit', in *APuZ*, 15–16 (1993), 40–6; and T.-D. Young, 'Trends in German Defense Policy', *The Defense Policy Guidelines and the Centralization of Operational Control* (US Army War College, 14 June 1994).
10. Quoted in *FAZ* (16 March 1994). See also the interpretation of the White Paper by the Parlamentarische Staatssekretärin im Verteidigungsministerium, M. Geiger, 'Die Analyse und die Konsequenzen. Zur Lage und Zukunft der Bundeswehr', *Bayernkurier* (25 March 1994).
11. See C. Gennrich, 'Kohl will Züge auf das passende Gleis setzen, Kinkel soll sie dann in Fahrt bringen', *FAZ* (28 July 1993).
12. See for this argument K. Fuchs, 'Mit deutschen Soldaten eine neue Weltordnung schaffen', in *Sicherheit und Frieden*, 1 (1993), 36–42. Katrin Fuchs is member of the SPD-Bundestagsfraktion. See also M. Martin and P. Schäfer, 'Militärische Dimensionen der neuen deutschen Auβenpolitik', in *Blätter für Deutsche und Internationale Politik*, 10 (1993), 1185–98.
13. T.-D. Young, *Trends in German Defense Policy*, p. 10.
14. See on this R. D. Asmus, *German Strategy and Opinion after the Wall* (Santa Monica, CA: RAND Corporation, 1994), p. 15.
15. For the Social Democratic Party see F. Gerster, 'Deutschland auf dem Weg zur internationalen Normalität', in *Der Mittler-Brief*, 1 (1994), pp. 1–4.
16. Quoted in *Die Welt* (6 February 1993).
17. *Verteidigungspolitische Richtlinien*, points 9 and 18.
18. See General Naumann's speech at the 34. Kommandeurstagung der Bundeswehr in Mainz, 5 October 1993.
19. W. Böhm, H. Koschyk, F. Pflüger, and C. Schmidt, *Kaliningrad/Königsberg – Risiken und Chancen seiner Entwicklung, Standortpaiere der Arbeitsgruppe Auβenpolitik der CDU/CSU-Fraktion im Deutschen Bundestag* (Bonn, 1994), p. 2.
20. M. Zepperitz, 'Lagebeurteilung aus deutscher Sichet', in *Europäische Sicherheit*, 1 (1995), 26–8, 27.
21. See C. Gennrich, 'Deutschland, die Balten und der Schirinowskij-Faktor', *FAZ* (9 March 1994).
22. See H. Bacia, 'Über den KSE-Vertrag ist das letzte Wort noch nicht gesprochen', *FAZ* (28 April 1995).

23. See H. Vogel, 'Rußland als Partner der europäischen Politik', *FAZ* (29 February 1996). Professor Vogel is director of the Bundesinstitut für ostwissenschaftliche und internationale Studien which is closely connected to the German Foreign Ministry.
24. *Veerteidigungspolitische Richtlinien*, point 20.
25. For a comprehensive analysis of Germany's policy towards the conflict in Yugoslavia see H. W. Maull, 'Germany in the Yugoslav Crisis', in *Survival*, Nr. 4 (Winter 1995/96), 99–130.
26. See H.-J. Axt, 'Hat Genscher Jugoslawien entzweit? Mythen und Fakten zur Außenpolitik des vereinten Deutschlands', in *Europa-Archiv*, 12 (1993), 351–60, 353. See also M. Rosefeldt, 'Deutschlands und Frankreichs Jugoslawienpolitik im Rahmen der Europäischen Gemeinschaft (1991–1993)', in *Südosteuropa*, 11–12 (1993), 621–53, 623.
27. Fernseh- und Hörfunkspiegel, Presse-und Informationsamt der Bundesregierung, 16 January 1992.
28. W. F. Schlör, *German Security Policy*, p. 28.
29. See K. Naumann, 'Sicherheitspolitik in Zeiten globalen Umbruchs', *Frankfurter Rundschau* (9 December 1992).
30. D. Mahncke, *Parameters of European Security*, p. 11.
31. In contrast, Dieter Mahncke has cogently argued that 'it does not seem helpful to include everything under the term security as having to be ensured by a "security policy", for if a term means everything it no longer means anything', D. Mahncke, *Parameters of European Security*, p. 9.
32. See the report of the Unabhängige Kommission für die zukünftigen Aufgaben der Bundeswehr (Bonn, 24 September 1991).
33. See V. Rühe's statement made at the Kommandeurstagung der Bundeswehr in Leipzig, 14 May 1992; see also K. Kinkel, 'Das Konzept der "Erweiterten Sicherheit"' *Frankfurter Rundschau* (16 December 1993); and H. H. von Sandrart, 'Konsequenzen der neuen sicherheitspolitischen Situation', in *Europäische Sicherheit*, 7 (1993), 333–6.
34. See on the German CSCE conception the pathbreaking analysis made by R. Roloff, 'Auf dem Weg zur Neuordnung Europas. Die Regierungen Kohl/Genscher und die KSZE-Politik der Bundesrepublik Deutschland 1986–1992', *Vierow bei Greifswald 1995* (Kölner Arbeiten zur Internationalen Politik, Band 1).
35. See the speech by H.-D. Genscher made at the CSCE Foreign Ministers meeting in Prague on 30 January 1992, printed in *Bulletin der Bundesregierung* Nr. 12 (4 February 1992).
36. See the so-called Helsinki Document of July 1992, printed in *Europa-Archiv*, 18 (1992), D539-D576, D552.
37. R. Roloff, *Auf dem Weg zur Neuordnung Europas*, p. 419.
38. See on this *FAZ* (13 May 1991), 'Baker und Genscher wollen für die NATO eine stärkere politische Rolle'.
39. V. Rühe, Address on 'The New NATO', Washington, DC, 30 April 1996.
40. See L. Rühl, Anstoß und Begrenzung der NATO-Erweiterung. 'Kein zweites Jalta im Osten' als Parole der Allianz, *Neue Zürcher Zeitung* (25 April 1995).

41. See *FAZ* (16 February 1995).
42. K.-H. Kamp, 'Zwischen Friedenspartnerschaft und Vollmitgliedschaft – Die NATO und die Erweiterungsfrage, Konrad-Adenauer-Stiftung, Bereich Forschung und Beratung', *Interne Studien*, Nr 102 (St. Augustin, Juni 1995), S. 30.
43. On this interpretation of Defence Minister Rühe's attitude see K. Feldmeyer, 'Die NATO spielt auf Zeit. Den Balten fällt das Warten auf einen möglichen Beitritt besonders schwer', *FAZ* (29 August 1995).
44. See 'Rühe raises Polish hopes over NATO', *Financial Times* (19 July 1994) and *FAZ* (23 August 1995).
45. See R. Clement, 'Ende der goldenen Zeiten', in *Loyal* (April 1995).
46. See e.g. Foreign Minister Kinkel's programmatic speech before the Heeresführungskommando at Koblenz on 6 October 1994, quoted in *FAZ* (7 October 1994).
47. Foreign Minister Kinkel in a speech at the Führungsakademie der Bundeswehr on 9 November 1993, quoted in *Süddeutsche Zeitung* (10 November 1993).
48. K. Kinkel, 'Das Konzept der "Erweiterten Sicherheit"', *Frankfurter Rundschau* (16 December 1993).
49. '"Das darf Herr Rühe nicht tun" Kritik an den Äußerungen des Verteidigungsministers zum Baltikum', *FAZ* (24 August 1995).
50. *FAZ* (29 February 1996).
51. See C. Gennrich, 'Vom Verhalten Moskaus soll es abhängen, ob und wie weit es sich selbst isoliert', *FAZ* (9 July 1994). Obviously, Gennrich reports an analysis made by the Foreign Ministry's planning staff.
52. See K.-H. Kamp, 'Zwischen Friedenspartnerschaft und Vollmitgliedschaft', p. 15. On 10 February 1995, in a speech before members of the American Congress, Chancellor Kohl warned about a hasty accession of the East European States to NATO and the EU, see *FAZ* (11 February 1995).
53. See N. Grunenberg, 'Das Tor ist offen', *Die Zeit*, Nr. 29 (14 July 1995).
54. See *FAZ* (23 August 1995).
55. Quoted in *FAZ* (25 November 1994).
56. It was at Germany's urging that the NATO report on enlargement has explicitly acknowledged the close relationship between NATO's eastward enlargement and the widening of the European Union. See *FAZ* (29 September 1995).
57. Qoted by K. Feldmeyer, 'Europa mit Rußland, Europea gegen Rußland. Eine Frage für alle und deshalb für keinen', *FAZ* (7 December 1994).
58. See W. Ischinger and R. Adam, 'Alte Bekenntnisse verlangen nach neuer Begründung. Die deutschen Interessen nach der Wiedervereinigung und ihre außenpolitische Verwirklichung in Europa und der Welt', *FAZ* (17 March 1995); and H. W. Ganser, 'Die OSZE nach dem Gipfel von Budapest', in *Europäische Sicherheit*, 4 (1995), 22–4, 24.
59. See *FAZ* (4 January 1995) and R. Seiters, 'Bald sind Entscheidungen fällig, Wie können Frieden, Stabilität und Sicherheit in Europa organisiert werden?', *FAZ* (9 May 1996).

60. See R. Scharping, 'Deutsche Außenpolitik muß berechenbar sein', in *Internationale Politik* (August 1995), 38–45, 42.
61. Quoted in *Der Spiegel* (2 January 1995), 21–2.
62. E. Bahr, 'Die Gefahr liegt im Nichtstun', *Die Zeit*, Nr. 13 (23 March 1995).
63. Karsten Voigt in a speech given at the Deutsch-Atlantische Gesellschaft in Lebach, 23 March 1995.
64. This argument is put forward by Chancellor Kohl in his speech given at the Wehrkundetagung in Munich in February 1996, quoted in C. Bertram, 'Um Moskau werben...', *Die Zeit*, Nr. 7 (9 February 1996).
65. Thus, Minister Rühe's position is supported by the former Staatssekretär in the German Defence Ministry, Lothar Rühl. See L. Rühl, 'Erweiterung und Abgrenzung', *Die Welt* (27 March 1995).
66. V. Rühe, 'Europäische Einigung und transatlantische Partnerschaft', speech given at the Karls University in Prague, 8 October 1993.
67. K. Kinkel, 'NATO requires a bold but balanced response to the East', *International Herald Tribune* (21 October 1993).
68. See the speeches of Defence Minister Rühe and Foreign Minister Kinkel, held at the Wehrkundetagung in Munich on 4 and 5 February 1995, printed in *Internationale Politik*, 4 (1995), 88–96.
69. On these contradictions, see especially P. Schmidt, 'Partners and Rivals: NATO, WEU, EC and the Reorganization of European Security Policy: Taking Stock', in Peter Schmidt, ed., *In the Midst of Change: On the Development of West European Security and Defence Cooperation* (Baden-Baden, 1992), pp. 187–228.
70. *Gemeinsames Deutsch-Französisches Papier zur sicherheitspolitischen Zusammenarbeit im Rahmen der Gemeinsamen Außen- und Sicherheitspolitik der Politischen Union* (Bonn, 6 February 1991).
71. Generalinspekteur Klaus Naumann in a speech given at the Kommandeurstagung in Leipzig on 12 May 1992, printed in *Europa-Archiv*, 13 (1992), D448-D454, D452.
72. D. Mahncke, *Parameters of European Security*, p. 34.
73. See especially Volker Rühe's comments on the results of the Franco-German summit in December 1995, quoted in *FAZ* (13 December 1995).
74. Text of the Declaration reprinted in *Europa-Archiv*, 14 (1992), D469–D489.
75. Quoted in K. Feldmeyer, 'Noch lange nicht perfekt. Wie Schäuble die Europapolitik im Zeichen des Bosnienkrieges und der Atomversuche Frankreichs sieht', *FAZ* (24 July 1995).
76. See M. Meimeth, 'France Gets Closer to NATO', in *The World Today* (May 1994), 84–6.
77. See P. Schmidt, 'Germany, France and NATO, US Army and War College', Strategic Outreach Paper and Conference Report, 17 October 1994, p. 19.
78. P. Schmidt, 'Frankreichs neues Verhältnis zur NATO: Preisgabe oder Verwirklichung gaullistischer Prinzipien?', *SWP-AP 2957* (May 1996). See also D. Cycon, 'Frankreichs Doppespiel', in *Saarbrücker Zeitung* (23 May 1996).
79. H. de Charette quoted in *FAZ* (4 June 1996).

80. V. Rühe, 'The New NATO', *op. cit.*
81. *Ibid.*
82. See K. Feldmeyer, 'Bei der Suche nach einer neuen Struktur des NATO-Bündnisses geht es vor allem um Einflu?', *FAZ* (5 August 1996).
83. Quoted in H. Stark, 'France-Allemagne: entente et mésententes', *Politique Etrangère* (Winter 1993/94), 989–99, 994. For a detailed discussion of the Franco-German differences on the war in former Yugoslavia, see P. H. Gordon, 'Die Deutsch-Französische Partnerschaft und die Atlantische Allianz, Arbeitspapiere zur Internationalen Politik 82', *Forschungsinstitut der Deutschen Gesellschaft für Auswärtige Polik* (Bonn, April 1994), 43–66.
84. See the corresponding paragraphs of the White Paper on Defence.
85. See T.-D. Young, *Trends in German Defense Policy*, p. 17.
86. See K. Reinhardt, 'Das Heeresführungskommando. Auftrag und Organisation', in *Wehrtechnik*, 1 (1994), 68–9.
87. K. Feldmeyer, 'Bundeswehr erhält Führungszentrum. Einen Generalstabschef gibt es weiter nicht', *FAZ* (12 January 1995).
88. See M. Inacker, 'Besser gerüstet für Kriseneinsätze', *Die Welt am Sonntag* (12 November 1995).
89. See H. Rühle, 'Bedingt einsatzbereit. Die deutsche Bundeswehr vor neuen Aufgaben', *Neue Zürcher Zeitung* (6 July 1992); and H. H. Mey, Director of the Institute for Strategic Analyses in Bonn, quoted by Q. Peel and G. Graham, 'Germans Step Warily Into the Front Line', *Financial Times* (13 July 1994).
90. See *Neue Zürcher Zeitung* (16 July 1993) and *FAZ* (2 April 1994).
91. *FAZ* (11 May 1995).
92. *Ibid.*
93. See M. Inacker, 'Bundeswehr vor Kürzungen – bis zu 2 Milliarden Mark?', *Welt am Sonntag* (23 March 1996).
94. *Süddeutsche Zeitung* (2/3 March 1996).
95. See H. Rühle, 'Welche Armee für Deutschland?', p. 147. This is even true with regard to future out-of-area combat missions of the Eurocorps. As a well-informed report of the *FAZ* has indicated, Germany's contributions to those missions will probably be limited to 3000 troops. See K. Feldmeyer, 'Einsatzbereit. Das Euro-Korps ist nun in der Lage, die ihm zugewiesenen Aufgaben zu übernehmen', *FAZ* (28 November 1995).
96. See G. Koch, 'Krisenreaktionskräfte des Heeres. Forderungen an Kampf- und Kampfunterstützungstruppen', in *Soldat und Technik*, 7 (1993), 401–9.
97. See K. Feldmeyer, 'Ein Merhzweckschiff muβ her', *FAZ* (14 January 1995).
98. See *FAZ* (4 May 1995).
99. K. Feldmeyer, 'Folgen der Friedensdividende', *FAZ* (11 May 1995).
100. See H. Müller, 'Military Intervention for European Security: The German Debate', in Lawrence Freedman, ed., *Military Intervention in European Conflicts* (Oxford, 1994), pp. 125–41; and N. Philippi, 'Bundeswehrauslandseinsätze als auβen -und sicherheitspolitisches Problem des geeinten Deutschlands', pp. 30–178.

101. On this interpretation see R. Wolf, 'Opfer des eigenen Erfolgs?. Perspektiven der NATO nach dem Kalten Krieg, in Aus Politik und Zeitgeschichte', *Beilage zur Wochenzeitung Das Parlament*, 13 (1992), 3–16, 12.
102. Survey conducted by Infratest Burke Berlin for RAND and the Friedrich-Naumann-Foundation after the October 1994 elections, quoted in *FAZ* (8 March 1995).
103. R. D. Asmus, *Germany's Geopolitical Maturation: Public Opinion and Security Policy in 1994* (Santa Monica, CA: RAND, January 1995), p. 32.
104. Numbers quoted in E. Noelle-Neumann, 'Öffentliche Meinung and Außenpolitik. Die fehlende Debatte in Deutschland', in *Internationale Politik* (August 1995), 3–12, 6.
105. Numbers quoted in N. Philippi, 'Bundeswehreinsätze als außen -und sicherheitspolitisches Problem des geeinten Deutschlands', p. 171.
106. See R. D. Asmus, 'Keine Zurückhaltung mehr. Das Meinungsbild der deutschen Elite zur Außen- und Sicherheitspolitik', *FAZ* (11 April 1996).
107. *Weißbuch zur Sicherheit der Bundesrepublik Deutschland und zur Lage und Zukunft der Bundeswehr* (Bonn, 5 April 1994), p. 23.
108. *Verteidigungspolitische Richtlinien*, point 18; 'The New NATO', ibid.
109. K. Lamers, 'Zum Einsatzzweck deutscher Streitkräfte' (Bonn, 11 January 1993), unpublished manuscript.
110. Quoted in *Der Mittler-Brief*, 3 (1989), p. 3. At the time of writing, Klaus Naumann was the head of the department of military planning in the Führungsstab der Streitkräfte.
111. *Verteidigungspolitische Richtlinien*, point 8.
112. Quoted in *FAZ* (12 July 1994) and *FAZ* (14 July 1994).
113. See Rühe's interview with the Süddeutsche Zeitung, where he said that there must be a compelling reason for any mission beyond territorial or Alliance defence. A threat to Germany's security, to stability in Europe or to international peace must be evident. However, in contrast to Minister Kinkel, Volker Rühe is strongly against any engagement of the Bundeswehr beyond Europe and its periphery. See *Süddeutsche Zeitung* (25 November 1994).
114. See e.g. *Verteidigungspolitische Richtlinien*, point 7.
115. On this see F.-J. Meiers, 'Germany: The Reluctant Power', in *Survival* (Autumn 1995), 82–103, 87.
116. See *FAZ* (1 July 1995). Text 'des Bundestagsbeschlusses abgedruckt in Blätter für Deutsche und Internationale Politik', 8 (1995), 1015–17.
117. On this interpretation of the Bundestagsbeschluß see M. Weller, 'In Bosnien ein diffuser Auftrag für Blauhelme und NATO. Die widersprüchlichen Mandate der Vereinten Nationen machen auch deutsches Mitwirken zu einem brisanten Unterfangen', *FAZ* (12 July 1995).
118. Quoted in *FAZ* (11 August 1995).
119. See G. Gillessen, 'Die erste multinationale NATO-Division wird in Dienst gestellt. Mehr Integration verlangt stille Souveränitätsverzichte', *FAZ* (22 June 1994).
120. See F. Léotard, 'Pour une force d'action africaine', *Le Monde* (6 July 1994).

5 Italy
Mario Zucconi

INTRODUCTION

As during the Cold War decades, today Italy can be counted upon to be an important contributor to collective security initiatives. Italy's participation in multilateral interventions, within different frameworks, in recent years has been substantial. Following up on decisions taken within NATO, Rome has begun adapting the force structure, training and equipment of its armed forces to new requirements, and in particular to the need of collective peace-supporting operations.

As with other industrialized countries, the motives of Italy's readiness to participate in multilateral efforts are complex and changeable – reflecting, besides specific domestic political factors, the changing character of today's multilateralism and the evolving role and often broadened competences of the different international organizations, such as the roles and competences which have grown out of the relationship between NATO (the premier military alliance) and the United Nations (the world community's collective security body) in the former Yugoslavia.

Rome's preference for – or special influence over – specific international forums is much less pronounced than for other influential Western capitals. Italian officials univocally state that their selection of possible options for multilateral action is based above all on a realistic assessment of the capabilities of the different institutions for dealing with a particular security problem. Other considerations, such as Italy's relative influence in one or another body, are secondary. However, officials frequently cite the impulse given a particular institution by Italian leadership (e.g. when holding the rotating EU presidency), to support the contention that Italy can make a positive contribution to collective efforts when presented with an opportunity.

Italy's strong multilateralist disposition derives increasingly from a genuine desire to shoulder a share of the collective burden in dealing with the challenges of post-Cold War instability. As experience has shown, it is impossible to separate such a desire from a companion interest in being recognized as a leading member of elite clubs. The country's participation in multilateral initiatives has become a central element of Italy's foreign policy and of Italy's strategy to raise its international profile. Yet it is difficult to identify a planned, consistent national political strategy for realizing its ambition.[1] Italian participation in the international intervention in Somalia is a case in point. It may have been exceptional to the extent to which it reflected clearly identifiable and long-established political interests and the desire to remain an influential player in the region. It expressed a more general disposition as well. As the Italian Minister of Foreign Affairs stressed, reacting to being denied admission to the Contact Group for Bosnia constituted in 1994, if anything, that Italy's availability for participating in multilateral operations which it neither helps initiate or direct tends to be taken too much for granted.[2]

Thus, while Italy's approach to multilateralism is deficient in design and orchestration, the willingness to shoulder burdens is not in doubt. Rather, the problem lies in Italy's failure to generate a sustained diplomacy. Ironically, it cannot do so if the country is reticent about affirming distinctly Italian positions within a multinational context. There is growing awareness of this failing. As former Minister of Foreign Affairs, Susanna Agnelli, explained the offer to participate in the ground operation in Bosnia, 'to be there means to be important'. Yet, the same Minister's request for admission into the Contact Group for Bosnia was criticized as being in the Italian tradition of 'the policy of the seat' – indifferent, that is, to the merit of such foreign policy initiatives.[3]

BACKGROUND: ITALY'S MULTILATERAL DISPOSITION

For a number of reasons, Italy's readiness to pursue its national interests largely through various international institutions has grown in recent years. The profound political and institutional crisis the country has gone through since early 1992 is one of those reasons. While a strong multilateralist inclination was present throughout the post-war period, Italian foreign policy in the 1980s had taken a somewhat higher and more distinctive national profile.

Italy's strong multilateralist attitude is rooted in its history – the history of a country that never fully developed the political culture and confidence of an independent great power, the Mussolini years notwithstanding. To the extent that it tried to do so (establishing a colonial empire, carving out spheres of influence, etc.), pre-Fascist and Fascist Italy managed only to collect the residues of European colonialism, remaining politically subordinate to other European powers, and did not succeed in solidifying Italy's position among the ranks of leading powers.

After World War II, Italy, like the then West Germany, because of fascism and defeat, found in its integration into international organizations and in its incorporation into multilateral structures a way of restoring political respectability and regaining an international legitimacy. As for West Germany, the division of Europe and the strong bloc discipline of the Cold War was seen as expedient for consolidating Italy's new status. Able Italian politicians of the early postwar years were in the forefront in building the early European institutions. In contrast with its participation in the Atlantic Pact (Italy was invited to join, and was not a negotiator of the Treaty), Italy was among the architects of the European Coal and Steel Community, and the European Economic Community. Via those bodies, Italy succeeded in establishing a place for itself at the heart of the emerging community of Western democracies.[4]

Moreover, the conditioning effect of active involvement in those institutions contributed strongly to structuring the domestic politics of the country. The important Atlantic and Western European ties established the boundaries of what constituted legitimate political discourse and methods. In particular, it offered a strong rationale for keeping the powerful Italian Communist Party (PCI) out of power. In turn, the PCI's electoral strength created further incentives to keep Italy tightly, and uncritically, integrated into Western multilateral organizations. In contrast with France, where the Communists reached their apex immediately after the war and then were replaced as the main opposition force by the Socialists, in Italy the PCI grew steadily and peaked in the mid-1970s, when, for a while, it matched the strength of the ever-ruling Christian Democratic Party (DC). It is possible, as some have maintained, that the antipodal character of the internal party alignment also inhibited the emergence of more pronounced elements of foreign policy. That political situation contributed, through the 1960s and 1970s, to the Italian foreign policy's low-profile and *routine* character, to its passivity and its willing subordination toward Italy's main allies, the United States above all.[5]

However, those inhibitions had largely disappeared in the late 1970s when the PCI abandoned its challenge (at the PCI XIVth Congress, in

1975) to Italy's Western allegiances. At that time its Secretary-General, Enrico Berlinguer, went as far as to qualify the Atlantic Alliance as a protective 'shield' for the construction of 'socialism in freedom'.[6] Two years later, the PCI joined the governing parties in supporting two parliamentary resolutions which identified 'the Atlantic Alliance and the European commitments' as 'the basic point of reference of the Italian foreign policy'.[7] They thereby completed what has been defined as the 'constitutionalization' of Atlanticism and Europeanism in Italian politics.

Italian foreign policy acquired a greater international visibility during the 1980s. Italy's profile within the Atlantic Alliance rose when it decided (with the PCI offering mild resistance to the move) to accept a substantial fraction of the new intermediate-range nuclear missiles the Alliance decided to deploy in December 1979. Rome's decision helped shift the terms of the critical debate in Germany in favour of the missile deployment to counter the Soviet SS-20 buildup. Those decisions cleared the way for NATO's 'dual track' strategy (deployment and negotiation of an intermediate nuclear missile limitation accord) that resolved a potentially grave Alliance crisis. Soon thereafter, Italy offered the Crotone base for the US F-16 fighter planes Spain was no longer prepared to accept on its territory. Within the EC, too, Italy showed considerable initiative in jointly sponsoring the Genscher–Colombo Plan for speeding European integration (1981) and then with an active presidency in two important phases of that process (1985 and 1990).

The Sigonella incident in 1985 (US special forces were not permitted to seize the *Achille Lauro*'s terrorists, whose plane the Americans had forced to land at the Sicilian air base) was a sign of an increasing assertiveness of Rome and reflected Italy's fast emerging Mediterranean policy of its own. Besides a more active diplomacy, Rome's policy toward the southern shore of the Mediterranean and the Red Sea area was supported by growing and very substantial programmes of economic aid (in particular for the Horn of Africa). The guarantee offered to Malta's neutrality (1980), and the participation in the multinational forces in Sinai (starting in 1982) and in Lebanon (1982–83), came in the same context of that fast-emerging Mediterranean and African policy. Finally, as the proponent of the 'Pentagonal initiative', in the late 1980s Italy volunteered itself to fashion cooperative ties among the countries of the Danubian–Balkan area in an effort to bring order to one region of post-Cold War Europe. The potential relevance of that initiative grew at the end of the decade as Germany was seen as acquiring a dominant position in Southeastern Europe.

However, in the early 1990s most of those initiatives ran into difficulties or were overtaken by events – with the consequence of once again confining Italy's foreign policy to that elaborated collectively within the international institutions to which the country belongs. Beginning in 1993, the Palestinian–Israeli peace process radically changed the premises of any Mediterranean policy. The political crises in Somalia and Yugoslavia became quickly militarized – making Italy a non-player with regard to such issues and causing it to lose much of its influence both in the Balkans and in the Horn of Africa. Concomitantly, the country's mounting political and institutional crisis sapped its energies and undermined its ability to seize the opportunities for diplomatic initiative offered by the end of the Cold War and the division of Europe. The sizeable Italian programme of cooperation (foreign aid) was stalled by a wide-ranging judicial inquiry and bureaucratic reorganization even before the financial squeeze imposed by the most recent governments began to be felt. (In the most recent budgets presented to Parliament, the allocation for the cooperation programme was a fraction of what it had been until 1992).[8] Above all, the rapid succession of governments (there was a quick turn-over of three 'governments of experts', plus the Berlusconi government, in a six-year period) made it difficult to devise a coherent foreign policy strategy or to take an action that carried political risk. An Italian foreign policy ever more devoid of strong national positions, and reduced to following standard formulas, was increasingly left in the hands of the bureaucracy.

Shortly before that political crisis, the Gulf war opened a debate – new to Italy – about whether and how to participate in similar or related collective security missions. Despite important differences between Prime Minister Giulio Andreotti, concerned about the future of Italian ties with the Arab world, and Foreign Minister Gianni De Michelis, strongly in favour of intervening on the side of the US, the UK and France, the cabinet decided to send combat aircraft and a naval contingent. The debate about the Gulf war, and shortly afterward that concerning the international intervention in Somalia, helped to bring forth and to deepen an Italian desire to participate in those kinds of multilateral initiatives. However, Rome's decision to join the Gulf and the Somali operations was based more on political-diplomatic considerations than on a realistic assessment of the

country's technical-military capabilities and of the character and feasibility of the operations themselves.
European Community allegiances also were a factor. Being part of the accelerating ambition, the European integration process acquired mounting importance in the Italian foreign policy debate. With the quickening pace of integration embodied in the Maastricht Treaty, meeting the conditions and standards set for integration became the line of separation between virtue and vice – between a mature, respected Italy and a marginal Italy. The discrediting of a political system overly controlled by party apparatuses ('partitocrazia'), indicated to many Italians the importance of European integration as a way of keeping the country on the track of a rigorous fiscal policy. 'We are lucky to be tied to Europe', is a common expression of pessimism among the public about the Italian ruling class.

A similar logic shaped thinking about NATO. In addition to conferring equal status with other more influential countries, while finding today very broad support among the public, Italy's membership in the Alliance (as is the case with the United Nations peacekeeping operations) has been consistently presented, in recent years, as one of the main motivations for maintaining the level of military expenditure. External obligations were being called upon to justify Italy's doing the necessary called for by prudent stewardship of the country's affairs.

In conclusion, Italy's foreign and security policy has been increasingly centred, in recent years, on contributing to the collective working of international institutions. That trend builds on Italy's broad and traditional multilateral inclination of the past half-century. Continuity along these lines also owes much to the progressive bureaucratization of Italian foreign policy, most apparent in periods of weak political leadership. The growing reliance on the collective judgement and joint strategy of NATO on security affairs is a feature of Rome's policy environment. In 1996, senior civilian Defence Ministry officials proposed that a preamble assessing Italy's present strategic situation be added to the request for the annual military budget allocation being prepared. It was rejected and overridden by the military who declared it unnecessary in the light of clear strategic guidelines promulgated by Brussels with Italy's backing. Similarly, officials responding to queries about possible threats to Italian security and other external interests characteristically refer to analyses elaborated collectively at NATO and the EU.[9]

ITALY'S PERCEPTION OF ITS SECURITY ENVIRONMENT

A diminishing visibility and a narrowing strategic scope of Rome's foreign policy should not be taken as evidence of an absence of debate in the country on Italy's changing security environment. As already mentioned above, events since 1990 – especially the Gulf war – caused policymakers to reassess the country's security situation and opened the way to Italy's participation in other multilateral military operations, such as Somalia. While the Gulf crisis was unfolding, the House of Deputies' Defense Committee held hearings and debated the guidelines for a post-Cold War national security strategy.[10] The first version of the resulting 'New Defence Model' (NDM) was presented by the Minister of Defence, Virgilio Rognoni, to Parliament on 26 November 1991.[11]

The triggering events were the Gulf crisis, the end of the division of the continent, the dissolution of the Warsaw Pact, and the breakup of the Soviet Union. Cumulatively, they radically changed the political and strategic situation in Europe. As in other major Western countries, the issues they posed engendered a reappraisal involving experts, political leaders and the public at large as to: (a) changing perceptions of Italy's security environment, and (b) the evolution of Italy's position with regard to participation in multilateral military operations abroad. The end of the division of Europe largely eliminated the preoccupation that had existed earlier with possible Soviet/Russian menace. Needless to say, Italy is not Poland – both geographically and historically. Possible interests related to and threats deriving from the difficult transition in the Eastern part of Europe and in the former Soviet state were defined in largely theoretical terms. Moreover, the sudden disappearance of the Soviet/Russian factor allowed other concerns that motivated Italy's participation in the Western alliance to surface.

With the end of the Cold War, the attention rapidly switched – to quote one expert – to 'the possible reawakening of bitter regional and sub-regional disputes, in the European area and especially in the Balkans, with deep historical roots'.[12] Besides the simmering civil war in Yugoslavia, in the early 1990s the Mediterranean's southern and eastern shores revealed multiple unresolved or emerging crises: *inter alia* the Arab–Israeli disputes, Lebanon, the pressure from Islamic fundamentalism, Iraq's aggressive policies. Italy could not avoid being concerned about such sources of instability. Indeed, some analysts attempted – somewhat arbitrarily – to connect the Middle East and the Balkans in identifying an 'arc of instability' around the Southern edge of the European Community.[13]

A 1993 survey of policymakers' opinions (based on interviews with members of the House and Senate Defence Committees) largely matches the experts' assessment.[14] Asked to identify the most important threats to Italian security, over 50 per cent indicated 'Islamic fundamentalism', 36 per cent 'the instability in the Mediterranean', 32 per cent referred to 'North–South economic disparities', and 20 per cent to 'the Balkans'. Another 20 per cent of interviewees pointed to other Eastern countries or even – interestingly – the political–organizational shortcomings of the international institutions. In a 1995 assessment by the members of the Defence Committees, even more emphasis grew on Islamic fundamentalism (almost 60 per cent) and on the North–South divide (over 40 per cent), while the preoccupation with instability in the Mediterranean dropped to less than 10 per cent of respondents.[15] In the 1993 survey, representatives of the leftist parties tended to emphasize the non-military sources of instability (the North–South divide, etc.), while centrist parties were more concerned with the behaviour of states as a cause of instability and accordingly focused on the political-military aspects of security. In contrast, concern about the Islamic fundamentalist threat cut across the full spectrum of Italian parliamentary forces.[16]

Military experts reacted uneasily to the drawing of strategic implications from such analyses (a large number of senior Italian officers participated in the debate). 'The reduction of the threat-perception from the East', wrote General Goffredo Canino, 'has produced an excessive emphasis on the so-called threat from the South, which, in fact... is not very substantial....The movement South of the main focus of security is anything but certain.' Based on the same threat-assessment, General Luigi Salatiello pointed out that 'no one of the states of the [Southern shore of the] Mediterranean is capable, with the exception of Israel, of launching substantial [military] operations against Italy'.[17] In fact, as another participant in the debate noticed, 'the pre-existing threat from the South appears rather to have decreased, because the main supporting factor to it – the East–West tension – has come to an end'.[18]

The deepening conflict in the former Yugoslavia confirmed the view that Italy's most serious challenges were associated with the transition from the Cold War system in Europe. Among the Italian political parties, the Democratic Party of the Left (PDS in the Italian acronym: the PDS is the main successor party of the Italian Communist Party) most clearly articulated its assessment of the present security environment. As its 'Government Programme' presented before the March 1994 elections stated, after the fall of the Berlin Wall, the main challenges to the security of Europe are nationalism, racism, xenophobia and religious fundamentalism. It follows that 'ethnic, political, cultural, social, and supranational integration is the inevitable framework that all countries that want to build a world order with justice and democracy need to accept for themselves'.[19]

THE INTERNAL SETTING

As noted, several specific issues evoked a broad debate about security policy in the Italian Parliament and among the public. Those issues were given point and dimension by the Gulf crisis of 1990–91, the intervention in Somalia, and the presentation to Parliament of the New Defence Model (NDM). What was novel, and quite contentious, in that debate was conjectured participation in military operations outside of national territory and beyond the area specified by the North Atlantic Treaty. In particular, the NDM was the first major effort to redefine the mission, format and structure of the Italian armed forces and to adjust them to the new, post-Cold War security environment, to the early reforms established collectively at NATO, and to the issues and necessities brought to the fore by the recent experience in the Gulf. For the first time, the NDM indicated that, in addition to the traditional functions of national defence, there was a need to develop capabilities to intervene in areas of crisis with the goal of (a) defending national interests, and (b) contributing to the management of international stability.[20]

The debate – parallel to that then being conducted in Germany – dealt with the legality of the use of the armed forces outside the national territory, and for those who accept such a possibility, the modalities of any such intervention – that is to say, the institutional framework within which those interventions can take place. The starting-point of the debate was Article 11 of the Italian Constitution: 'Italy rejects war as an instrument of attack against the freedom of other peoples and as an instrument for settling international disputes; it accepts, in conditions of parity with the other states, limitations of sovereignty that may be necessary to arrangements that secure peace and justice among the nations; it promotes and favours the international organizations which aim at such goals.'

In the 1993 opinion surveys carried out among members of Parliament, a total of 65 per cent of the interviewees judged the proposal contained in the NDM perfectly in line with Article 11 of the Constitution. However, strong reservations in that regard were expressed by roughly three-quarters of the members of parties of the left (from the far left to the moderate left). Declared a deputy of Riforndazione Comunista (the neo-communist party with 6 per cent of the popular vote in the 1994 elections): 'Modifying the role [of the armed forces] from "defence of the Fatherland" to "defence of the national interests wherever they may be challenged" means to violate in practice Article 11 of the Constitution and to create in effect a sort of neocolonial army.... NATO and the WEU are not legitimated to act on behalf of the UN.... The United Nations should have its own troops under its direct command.'[21]

A different position was offered by deputies of the Democratic Party of the Left (PDS, former PCI). Beyond the legality of sending Italian troops abroad, they saw a need for a source of legitimation for operations in support of international stability. They maintained that any intervention should take place only when requested by and under control of the United Nations, and not of military alliances.[22] In the case of the Gulf war, the ruling majority had bypassed the constitutional limitation on the use of Italian armed force abroad by dubbing it an 'operation of international policing'. The PDS had opposed the decisions taken by the government.

Among those who found that the NDM did not violate the Constitution, many emphasized how the proposal to create capabilities for peace support operations was a natural adaptation of the country's capabilities to a changed international environment. In the opinion of this latter group – made up mostly of members of centrist parties – the need for Italy to share the burden collectively shouldered by international institutions was of paramount importance. One of the interviewees stressed the last clause of Article 11 of the Constitution: 'Italy is inserted in a system of international cooperation and therefore, by fulfilling the obligations taken up in support of its interests it contributes to international stability.'[23] Most recently, criticism of this section of the NDM has decreased. That probably reflects the broadening international experience with multilateral peacekeeping. Whereas in 1993, 30 per cent of the members of the two Defence Committees were critical of the NDM on constitutional grounds, that percentage was down to a mere 15 per cent in 1995. Moreover, four out of five deputies and senators of the PDS were now finding the document conforming perfectly with the Italian Constitution.[24]

ITALY AND WESTERN COOPERATION

The 1993 survey of policymakers' opinions indicates that, after the Gulf war, a majority of them concerned themselves more with the proper institutional framework for carrying out peace support operations than with the legality of the Italian participation in those operations. Differences with regard to the institutional framework, which were quite discernible a few years back, later seemed to become less relevant. Both the most recent experiences of international operations (Somalia and Bosnia) and the institutional and political crisis in Italy (producing a more inward-looking political debate) contributed to such a development. Indeed, especially the most recent phase of the international intervention in Bosnia, the deployment of IFOR, went a long way to bringing about a convergence in the positions of most political parties in Parliament and among the bureaucracy.

Policymakers and Public

Analyses of Italian public opinion made in 1995 and 1996 concluded that, with the disappearance of the Cold War dichotomy between the neutralism of the left and the interventionist and mostly pro-NATO position of the centre and right, discernible differences among the public with regard to foreign and security policies have tended to narrow. Moreover, where differences persisted among policymakers, they were differences in relative emphasis – not of real substance. While maintaining its support for the Atlantic alliance, a majority of the representatives of the moderate left (the PDS) favoured the development of a European pillar within it (70 per cent of them in the 1995 survey).[25] The main right-wing party (National Alliance, or AN, successor party to the openly neo-fascist Movimento Sociale Italiano) meanwhile has abandoned its reservations against complete integration of the national forces into NATO and most strongly supports the same position as the PDS (80 per cent of AN representatives).[26]

Among policymakers, in 1993 a large majority accepted the need for Italy to shoulder part of the responsibility for international stability – both in Europe and outside the Treaty area. 'The disappearance of the USSR brings to the fore issues that demand a conscious participation to international security', said one senior official. 'Therefore, from being a consumer, Italy must become a provider of security.'[27] The need for a more active policy was stressed by the then Minister of Foreign Affairs Nino Andreatta: '[I]t is no longer enough to belong: we need to work, demonstrate, qualify ourselves with our presence and our weight.'[28] However, as already noted, considerable differences persisted with regard to the preferred and most appropriate institutional framework for carrying out those operations.

In the opinion survey conducted among policymakers in 1993, three-quarters (75.8 per cent) of the respondents identified NATO as the most important framework for future Italian security policy. However, a slight majority of those NATO supporters also favoured the development within the Atlantic Alliance of a Western European force under European command. That position was taken then by two-thirds of the deputies and senators of the PDS, and a somewhat smaller majority of the Christian Democratic (DC, in 1993 still the largest Italian political party) members of Parliament and of those of other parties of the centre and right. The far left (Rifondazione Comunista) and the Northern League (mostly centrist, but relatively new) favoured a European force as a substitute for NATO.[29]

While the emphasis of the leftist parties on a European framework conveyed older reservations about NATO, it must be remembered that in 1993 there were also strong expectations about the possible growth of a common security policy at the European level, as envisaged by the Maastricht Treaty.[30] The position favouring a withdrawal from NATO and a neutralist position for Italy was supported in 1993 by a mere 10 per cent of those policymakers, while another 7 per cent favoured the withdrawal from all alliances (NATO and WEU) compensated by the strengthening of the United Nations.[31] NATO continues to be the preferred framework for Italian security policy, while two-thirds (65 per cent) of the members of the two Defence Committees support the development of a European Security Identity.

Public opinion surveys in 1994, while showing only a marginal change in the percentage of respondents identifying NATO as the most important security framework (69.2 as against 75.8 among the policymakers), indicated an Italian public considerably less interested than their leaders in building a European force within the Atlantic Alliance (32.9 per cent as against 51.7 per cent of the members of the Defence Committees). Interestingly, while not one politician on the far left looked at an unreformed NATO as the preferred security framework, over 35 per cent of the respondents among the public who identified themselves as belonging to the far left did look favourably on NATO. As among policymakers, only 7 per cent of the public showed an interest in a European force as an alternative to NATO. Among the Italian public, there was twice as much support for a neutralist position as there was among policymakers (20.5 per cent as against 10.3).[32] It was a sign of the reduced polarization among the public that the different options were backed in similar proportion by those of all political persuasions.

With specific regard to the institutional framework for military operations outside the NATO area, the public showed a marked preference for the UN over the Atlantic Alliance in early 1993. Participation in UN-led operations at that time found approval with 55–60 per cent of the public and about 90 per cent among the members of Parliament. In contrast, operations outside Europe in the NATO framework were favoured by 40 per cent of the public and two-thirds of policymakers. As for the type of operations, there was markedly stronger support for humanitarian operations in comparison with military ones.[33] Public support for possible Italian participation in the UN operations in Bosnia doubled when the second poll clarified that such a participation was conditional on the conclusion of a peace agreement (65 as against 30 per cent). Similarly, a considerable drop of support during the first half of 1995 was reversed after the conclusion of the Dayton accords.[34]

Part of the difference among policymakers and the public is explained by the fact that the public opinion survey we have cited was carried out one year later than that among policymakers – after a series of sobering experiences had contributed to make attitudes toward the security framework progressively converge. The lowering of expectations for a common European foreign policy and the poor showing of other organizations – of the WEU and the UN in particular – in interventions such as those in Somalia and in the former Yugoslavia, in combination with the demonstrated capabilities by NATO there, probably contributed a great deal in altering the positions held by different actors in the immediate post-Cold War and post-Gulf period.

Political Parties

The parliamentary elections of March 1994 were an important moment for the elaboration and definition of political parties' foreign and security policies. Somalia and Bosnia set the context in which those positions were defined. The far left (Riforndazione Comunista) attacked the growing role of NATO in the former Yugoslavia, maintaining that 'political negotiation, not more wars, is the key to peace'. They argued that the Atlantic Alliance was rendered obsolete by the end of the confrontation between two blocs. It followed, in the position taken by Rifondazione Comunista in 1994, that NATO should be 'prevented from using its forces "out of area", while all problems of security should be handed over to the UN'.[35]

The moderate left (PDS) insisted in 1994 that the function of the armed forces 'needs to be redefined on the basis of the commitments deriving from the Italian participation in political and security supranational institutions'. It is important, stated the PDS, that Italy 'does not devise foreign policies in isolation, but rather that it act more forcibly and consistently within the Western alliances and the main multilateral institutions, beginning with the European Union'. The PDS also asked for a reform of the United Nations (to enable it to 'carry out the function of political management of conflicts'), the devising of a policy of international stability that would prevent new wars, and the refining of rules and instruments for participation in peacekeeping and peacemaking operations.[36] Finally, the PDS urged that Italy promote a Conference for Security and Cooperation in the Mediterranean (CSCM), modelled on the CSCE, whose purpose should be to 'define a framework of rules [of conflict resolution] and the strengthening of the democratization process in the countries of the region'.[37]

The main successor party to the old Christian Democratic Party (DC), the Italian People's Party (PPI), for its part stressed that 'Europe, the UN, and the alliance with the US continue to be the framework within which Italy develops its foreign policy'. The PPI also strongly supports 'the universalist design of the UN, including humanitarian interference in those cases in which authoritarian governments deny individual and collective human rights'.[38]

The new centre-right political party in 1994, Forza Italia (FI, Go Italy, the party that gathered most votes in the March 1994 elections) stressed the need to base Italian foreign policy on 'an exact definition of Italy's national interests', pointing out that, with the end of the bloc system, Italy had again found 'the condition of a political actor capable of an independent foreign policy, even though in the context of the commitments undertaken with NATO and of those of European integration'. Forza Italia insisted in 1994 on the need to reform the UN and especially the Security Council in such a way as to increase 'the legitimacy of, and the support for the peace initiatives of the international community'. While supporting Italy's participation in the UN-led peace initiatives, FI recommended that participation be based on 'the feasibility of those operations, judged on the basis of their objectives, limits and character'. A strong emphasis was put in the electoral programme of FI on Italy's defence organization and capabilities, defined as an enterprise with 'the state as owner, the nation as client, and with security of the country as its product'. The level of defence spending (in 1994 only 1.6 per cent of the GDP) was judged as being much too low.[39]

The influential right-wing party National Alliance, in alliance with Forza Italia, in 1994 launched a slogan: 'More Italy, more Europe.' While on the one hand AN looked at the Atlantic Alliance as the 'basic pilaster' of Italy's defence policy, on the other it advocated a 'choice of independence in the alliances, that would constitute the foundation for the building of a confederation of European states. A Europe united and free, capable of dealing with determination with international crises.'[40]

Government Officials

Interviews with senior officials of the Foreign and Defence Ministries in late 1995 indicated a striking uniformity of analysis and prognosis, together with a marked emphasis on NATO as the only organization capable of dealing with the various aspects of security and international stability.[41] The tendency to focus on international organizations as the principal means for advancing national interests can be explained by the largely bureaucratized – or de-politicized – nature of foreign policymaking in this period. That tendency was especially pronounced in the programme presented by the new Minister of Defence, General Domenico Corcione, before the Defence Committee of the Chamber of Deputies in February 1995. Among other things, the Minister stressed the need for a political and military integration of Italy's capabilities with those of other countries, in the framework of the UN, NATO and the WEU, with the aim of acting together in areas of crisis both in Europe and outside the continent.[42]

NATO was unreservedly judged to be the most effective and relevant organization for peace-support operations. While some officials acknowledged that the Alliance has undergone a political crisis in recent years, they all pointed to its capabilities and effectiveness as an instrument of concerted action. Especially among the military, the solid trust in NATO contrasted with the negative opinion of UN capabilities as an instrument for dealing with international instability, crisis and conflict.

Consistent with that assessment of the relative effectiveness of NATO and the UN is an awareness of the new character and growing prominence of collective security functions in the post-Cold War environment, and an approach that makes little of the distinction between peacekeeping and peace-enforcement. The Gulf war and Somalia are cited as the most important learning experiences. In those operations, it is pointed out, Italy demonstrated an important ability to tolerate some loss of life. NATO was seen as a still vital organization – among other things for its deterrence and bridge-building capabilities – and none of the officials interviewed had any doubt that NATO should play the central role in peace support operations. Not much importance was attached to the delicate issue of legitimacy that interventions carried out by the Alliance can raise. Expectedly, such a critical approach was particularly pronounced among Defence Ministry officials.

If the recent experience in Bosnia highlighted the elements of competition and operational incompatibility between the UN and NATO, the official wisdom is to consider the two institutions as complementary elements of a single security architecture. In general, Italian officials judged the issue of inter-institutional rivalry irrelevant for Italy. The country uses all forums to maximize the influence it can exert with regard to conflict prevention, peace-enforcing or peacekeeping functions. Furthermore, while not in principle opposed to EU-based initiatives such as the French–German Eurocorps, Foreign Ministry officials explained their lack of enthusiasm for such initiatives by pointing out that they did not wish to send the wrong signal to the US about how much its continued engagement was desired by the West Europeans. That is a primary reason why successive Italian governments have declined to join. The same logic applies to the WEU. Although among the military there was awareness of the increased weight Italy would carry in a European-only security framework, the Defence Ministry does not differentiate itself from the general official position that favours a WEU unambiguously attached to NATO.

The WEU is seen as useful. Officials call attention to the Italian presidency of 1992–93 as a period of particularly serious initiatives intended to strengthen the WEU. The enforcement of the embargo in the Adriatic was first proposed by the WEU – later to be joined by

NATO. The same happened with regard to enforcement of the embargo along the Danube. The organization of a police force for Mostar under EU administration was another WEU initiative in this period. However, there is also awareness that expectations of the organization's potential in 1992–93 were not matched by actual accomplishment. The role played in the former Yugoslavia is considered, overall, to have been a minor one. The amalgamation of EU–WEU and the moving of the WEU headquarters to Brussels were judged as very positive developments. As a senior official explained, Italy values the WEU for its hypothetical future value – should the US decide to withdraw its forces from Europe. Realistically, the EU cannot pretend to build a common foreign and security policy, in the long run, without developing some military capabilities. Hence, these seem to be sufficient reasons for concluding that 'it would be irresponsible to abandon the WEU'.

Rome's position with regard to the WEU, in comparison with that of other European capitals, may seem reductive. Still, officials' defence of this attitude is grounded more on realism than on a philosophical rejection of a 'Europe first' approach. They do not object in principle to participation in European-only military structures. But Rome has been critical of the grand ambition implied by the character given the Eurocorps mechanized divisions: its continental function. In contrast, Rome has favoured the formation of more mobile forces (maximum strength one division), combining land and sea capabilities, and designed for operations other than Article 5 of the North Atlantic Treaty – peacekeeping, peace-enforcing, civilian evacuation, etc.

A realistic assessment of an organization's capabilities characterizes as well Rome's present approach to OSCE. Current thinking in Rome holds that there is an 'identity' and role problem for this organization in the light of the functions assumed by other more authoritative, more capable organizations – the UN, NATO and the EU. Overall, OSCE is viewed as unable to carry out even those decisions it does make in the realm of crisis-management. In 1994 the Italian presidency had the frustrating experience of being responsible for assembling the necessary forces for the peacekeeping operation in Nagorno-Karabakh conducted under OSCE auspices. It received a positive response only from Turkey. The OSCE's contribution to European stability is seen as lying elsewhere – as aiding in the political transition in Eastern Europe and in its serving as a forum for the integration of new states into a pan-continental security community. Generally speaking, the very limited capabilities of the OSCE have allowed the Western capitals to use it in politically expedient ways. Thus, the United States values it for its normative function in the field of human rights. France cares mostly about the organization's legal function. To Sweden, OSCE became a particularly relevant framework when the neutral group of European countries lost their diplomatic identity. Having given the organization the first Secretary-General, Bonn found in that another occasion for raising its international standing.

Italian officials stress the organization's conflict-prevention potential – especially within the CIS where it serves as a diplomatic anchorpoint for the fragile and vulnerable new states of Central Asia and the Caucasus. They pointed out how, from early on in the crisis, Russia accepted the sending of a OSCE mission to Grozny. For Moscow, those moves were viewed as possibly helping to establish the legitimacy of its military intervention there. Nevertheless, the OSCE's observer rule did enhance its status as the monitor of human rights, an extension of its main function after the signing of the Helsinki accords in 1975. Its good offices also have been used in Nagorno-Karabakh and Abkazia for multilateral efforts at mediating those conflicts. The OSCE proved less valuable for addressing conflicts in the former Yugoslavia. Thus, the Western powers chose to by-pass the organization in favour of the UN and/or their own institutional vehicles: the EU, the WEU and, ultimately, NATO. With the Dayton accords, the OSCE was called upon to organize and oversee the elections in Bosnia-Herzegovina as well as to monitor compliance with other civilian aspects of the agreement. The controversy over whether conditions for a free and fair election in fact had been met tarnished the OSCE's image while highlighting both its limited organizational resources and the reluctance of the Western powers to redeem that inadequacy. As the post-Dayton experience showed, some governments – including the Clinton administration – found the OSCE's weakness convenient.

Italy shared its allies' ambivalence about the OSCE's role in Bosnia. But, in general, it favours enhancement of the organization's authority and capabilities. Rome envisages a geographical division of labour among collective security bodies. It strongly backed the German–Dutch proposal for an 'OSCE first' approach – i.e. a crisis in the OSCE area should fall immediately within the organization's jurisdiction. There is awareness, though, of the resistance to that plan by the permanent members of the UN Security Council, its EU partners

France and Britain, as well as the United States. Rome hopes to reconcile those positions by emphasizing role specialization. In Rome's conception, the OSCE should be used mainly for (a) preventive diplomacy, (b) crisis management of a non-military type, and (c) overseeing peace accords. Summing up Rome's assessment, one official qualified the OSCE as having limited capabilities, but that 50 per cent of those existing capabilities were not being used.

Consistent with an approach that avoids choosing among security institutions, Rome places the OSCE in an architectural framework which leaves to NATO the main responsibility for military operations; WEU a subordinate role in supporting peacekeeping missions; and a complementary UN/OSCE role in legitimating and conducting classic efforts at mediation and monitoring compliance with conflict-termination and electoral agreement.

Rome officials point to the Italian loyalty to the institution and Italy's readiness to contribute to strengthening the organization. They cite the activism of the Italian presidency that used the existing mechanisms to their utmost (as in the case of the High Commissioner for Minorities) and worked to build new ones (as in the case of the Convention on Conciliation and Arbitration). Finally, there is undisguised coolness among Italian officials when considering the issue of NATO's enlargement to the East. While unwilling to openly challenge such a policy, they persistently raise the perceived problems and contradictions it creates.

CONCLUSIONS

Italian foreign policy's reliance on multilateral institutions grows out of a conviction that they serve both to stabilize the country's external environment and contain differences among its closest allies. Rome seeks to avoid being placed in a position where it must choose sides in inter-Alliance squabbles. That disposition, dictated by the logic of strategic circumstances, was reinforced by Italy's prolonged political crisis that militated against any deviation from this cautious and low-risk policy line: the non-selection to organizations conforms to this strategy. It is in marked contrast to France's pro-European institutions and anti-NATO stance in the early phase of the Yugoslav conflict; and to Washington's anti-UN and pro-NATO position. Rome sees little wisdom in posing questions of institutional preference in either-or terms and considerable danger in contests among allies for rank and status that use international organizations as surrogates. The stabilization of Italian politics promises no fundamental change. The parliamentary elections of Spring 1996 saw the amalgamation of political parties merge into two main coalitions: the centre-left Olive Tree coalition (inclusive of the PDS) and the centre-right Pole of Freedoms (with FI and AN as main components). Further integration in the EU and in NATO were the main tenets of the foreign policy platform of both coalitions. The PDS had by then entirely abandoned its earlier reservation against military operations abroad. As for the AN, its nationalist sensitivities about subordination to an integrated NATO have largely evaporated (along with its strident rhetoric about Italian irredentism in the former Yugoslavia). The decision of the Dini government to send troops to Bosnia as part of IFOR provoked serious debate. Among the public, 71 per cent approved of the decision in January 1996. Rome is more interested in enhancing the position in all international forums than in promoting one at the expense of another.[43]

In a 1996 debate in the Senate, then Minister of Foreign Affairs, Susanna Agnelli, explained the government's offer to participate in the ground operation in Bosnia because 'to be there means to be important'. Agnelli's insistence on Italy's admission into the Contact Group for Bosnia was characterized by a legislative critic as being in the Italian tradition of 'the policy of the seat' unconcerned, that is, with what initiatives Italy might take from its elevated position.[44] There is, though, growing sensitivity about Italy being taken for granted by more wilful allies. For that reason, Italy was particularly active in thwarting a reform of the UN Security Council that could reduce its possible influence within the organization. Italy tabled a proposal of Security Council reform that was presented as an alternative to the Council's enlargement to include Germany and Japan as permanent members. In the autumn of 1995 Italy succeeded in being elected itself to the Security Council, a goal toward which it invested considerable energy.

Enhancing Italy's international standing also has a political basis. In contrast to the slight influence that medium-size powers (and international organizations) could exert in the old bipolar system, today the important decisions more and more are taken within multilateral institutions. To gain a prominent position within them is to increase one's influence disproportionately to national power. The corollary is that it is imperative not to be cut off from where the major decisions are made.

Italy's policy of muted nationalism translates into a principled multilateralism. What it is prepared to commit to the resolution of any particular problem or what course it will support will be dictated by four considerations: the tenor and intensity of public opinion; Italy's role in the deliberation process; its concern for preserving the integrity of the international organization(s) involved; and what seems workable. In this, Italy may become the model for its Western partners.

NOTES

1. The reference here is to the lack of elaboration of long-term strategies, which is not to deny that Italian governments do fashion policies to advance self-defined national interests. Italian foreign policy is often accused of being 'occasional', 'amateurish' in its conduct. See, for instance, L. I. di Camerana, *La vittoria dell'Italia nella terza guerra mondiale* (Bari: Laterza, 1996).
2. V. Nigro and M. Smargiassi, 'La Agnelli dice no agli "Stealth" Usa', *La Repubblica* (Rome, 13 September 1995).
3. M. T. Lalli, 'Soldati italiani in Bosnia', *La Repubblica*, (22 September 1995).
4. See L. V. Ferraris, ed., *Manuale della politica estera italiana, 1947–1993* (Bari: Editori Laterza, 1996), Ch. 1.
5. See G. Pasquino, 'Pesi internazionali e contrappesi nazionali', in F. L. Cavazza and S. R. Graubard, ed., *Il caso italiano* (Milano: Garzanti, 1974); A. Panebianco, 'La politica estera italiana: un modello interpretativo', *Il Mulino*, No. 254 (1977); C. M. Santoro, 'L'Italia come "media potenza". La politica estera e il modello di difesa', in L. Caligaris and C. M. Santoro, *Obiettivo difesa. Straregia, direzione politica, comando operativo* (Bologna: Il Mulino, 1986).
6. Interview with E. Berlinguer in *Corriere della Sera*, 15 (June 1976).
7. W. Coralluzzo, 'Un bilancio di cinquant'anni', *Politica Internazionale*, No. 1/2 (1995).
8. See J. L. Rhi-Sausi, ed., *La crisi della cooperazione italiana: Rapporto CESPI sull'aiuto pubblico allo sviluppo* (Rome: Edizioni Associate, 1994), Ch. 1.
9. Interviews by the author with officials at the Ministries of Foreign Affairs and Defence.
10. C. dei Deputati, *Atti parlamentari della X Legislatura: Indagine conoscitiva sull'evoluzione dei problemi della sicurezza internazionale e sulla ridefinizione del modello nazionale di difesa* (Roma, 1991).
11. Capo di Stato Maggiore della Difesa, 'Presentazione del Nuovo Modello di Difesa' (Roma, 1992.) The NDM reduced to three (down from five in the Defence White Paper of 1985) the missions assigned the

Italian armed forces – one of those three being the defence of Italy's strategic interests abroad and the Italian contribution to international security, both through unilateral action and in the context of multilateral initiatives. All Defence Ministers who came after 1991 have presented their revised version of the NDM. However, Parliament has never brought it to a vote.
12. L. Caligaris, 'Il dibattito italiano sulla difesa', *Rivista Militare* (May–June 1991).
13. G. Bonvicini and S. Silvestri, 'The New "Arc of Crisis" and the European Community', *The International Spectator*, No. 2 (April–June 1992).
14. See P. Bellucci, *Politica militare e sistema politico: I partiti e il Nuovo modello di difesa* (Rome: Rivista Militare, 1994), especially pp. 65–70.
15. Data reported by F. Battistelli and P. Bellucci, 'Tra nazione e comunitá internazionale: il ruolo delle forze armate e le nuove missioni di *peacekeeping*', paper presented at the 1996 Conference of the Societá Italiana di Scienza Politica (Urbino, 15–16 June 1996).
16. P. Bellucci, *Politica militare e sistema politico*, *op. cit.*
17. G. Canino, 'Esercito e volontari: Analisi degli aspetti relativi alla costituzione di una componente operativa professionale', *Rivista Militare* No. 1 (1991) Supplement; S. Luigi, 'Riflessioni sul Nuovo modello di difesa', *Rivista Militare* No. 6 (1992).
18. General Lucio Innecco, 'Minaccia e modello di difesa', *Rivista Militare*, No. 6 (1990). For more on that debate and for a quick analysis of the military balance in the Mediterranean, see M. Simoncelli, 'La posizione strategica dell'Italia: Analisi delle Minacce', *Archivio Disarmo* (Rome, April 1994).
19. Partito Democratico della Sinistra, *Programma di governo del PDS* (Roma: l'Unita', 1994).
20. 'Sintesi del Modello di Difesa', CEMISS, *Informazioni della Difesa* (June 1992).
21. P. Bellucci, *Politica militare e sistema politico*, *op. cit.* (Interview No. 13), p. 56.
22. *Ibid.*, Interview No. 7.
23. *Ibid.*, Interviews No. 25 and 4.
24. F. Battistelli and P. Bellucci, 'Tra nazione e comunitá internazionale', *op. cit.*, p. 9.
25. P. Isernia, 'Opinione pubblica e politica internazionale in Italia', in C. M. Santoro (a cura di), *L'elmo di Scipio. Studi sul modello di difesa italiano* (Bologna: il Mulino, 1992), 250–1.
26. F. Battistelli and P. Bellucci, 'Tra nazione e comunitá internazionale,' *op. cit.*, p. 9.
27. P. Bellucci, *Politica militare e sistema politico*, *op. cit.*, p. 58.
28. N. Andreatta, 'Una politica estera per l'Italia', *Il Mulino* (September–October 1993), 881.
29. P. Bellucci, *op. cit.*, pp. 68–70.
30. The Treaty on European Union was signed on 11 December 1991 and came into force on 1 November 1993.

31. Opinion Research by CEMISS and Universitá del Molise, cited in P. Bellucci, *op. cit.*
32. *Ibid.*
33. 'L'opinione pubblica italiana e l'impiego delle Forze Armate per scopi di ordine pubblico', *Informazioni della Difesa* (Rome: Archivio Disarmo), Supplement to No. 1 (January–February 1993.)
34. F. Battistelli and P. Bellucci, 'Tra nazione e comunitá internazionale', *op. cit.*, pp. 12–13.
35. Riforndazione Comunista, *La forza dell'alternativa. Il programma di Riforndazione Comunista per le elezioni di marzo* (Roma, 1994), pp. 4–5.
36. Partito Democratico della Sinistra, *op. cit.*, pp. 26, 84–5, 88.
37. *Ibid.*, pp. 88–9.
38. Partito Popolare Italiano, Identitá e linee programmatiche del Partito Popolare (Rome, 1994), p. 3.
39. Forza Italia, *Programma elettorale. Cinque obiettivi per quarantacinque proposte* (Errebi, Falconara, 1994), pp. 5, 64–5.
40. Alleanza Nazionale (MSI-DN), *Destra di governo, finalmente per ricostruire l'Italia* (Roma, il Secolo, 1994).
41. The interviews were conducted in the Fall of 1995. The officials were mostly career officials, with only a few political appointees. The opinions expressed were understood to be not attributable.
42. Camera dei Deputati, XII Legislatura, *Atti Parlamentari*, Commissione IV, Seduta del (22 Febbraio 1995).
43. F. Battistelli and P. Bellucci, 'Tra nazione e comunitá internazionale', *op. cit.*, p. 12.
44. M. Tedeschini Lalli, 'Soldati italiani in Bosnia', *La Repubblica* (22 September 1995).

6 The United States
Michael Brenner

With the disappearance of the Soviet threat, the strategic imperative that vaulted the United States into a position of leadership in Europe no longer exists. Its allies' commitment to etch a more distinct personality of their own adds encouragement for Washington to yield some of its more outdated prerogatives of initiation and control. Moreover, a heavy agenda of domestic concerns has shifted Americans' attention away from foreign engagements and towards an introspective scrutiny of their internal affairs. This process of adjustment is neither smooth nor painless. It entails changes in the country's sense of international duty, in modes of interaction with allies, and in how the United States relates to collective security organizations that are regaining their vocation now freed from Cold War paralysis. Not surprisingly, ambivalence has become a hallmark of American foreign policy.

Foreign policy elites do share in a broad consensus that the US has four objectives in post-Communist Europe:

- bolstering the Allies' ability and will to take on major security responsibilities;
- maintaining a military commitment and an influential US voice in European affairs;
- preserving Washington's credibility, along with the respect for American power, at both ends of the European continent;
- and, not least, building a consensus in American public opinion for a policy of modulated engagement.

These objectives, properly viewed, are congruent. Enunciating purposes and principles has been easier, though, than formulating a strategy for realizing them. The translation of principle into precept now is being made all the more arduous by the upheaval in American domestic politics. For it has placed at the centre of the national foreign policy debate two basic questions that most thought resolved by the country's half-century of global leadership. One is the institutional issue, derived ultimately from a constitutional conflict until recently dormant, over where the locus of accountable authority for making US foreign policy decisions lies. The other is what America's rightful place in the world should be.

The latter, for Americans, goes well beyond a calculated determination of national interest in relation to other states and the international system they form. It includes a sombre reflection on the country's identity and calling as a nation. The United States' great successes, culminating in the victory over Soviet Communism, paradoxically left Americans vaguely disoriented and unsure of themselves. A sense of lost national virtue draws them inward; yet they cannot free themselves from demanding external involvements even as supreme power ebbs and certainties of purpose are blurred. Thus a relentless questioning of self has become thematic counterpoint to the reappraisal of America's place in the world engendered by the sea-changes since 1989. To save its political soul, should the United States lessen drastically its international engagements? To serve its interests, must not the US remain engaged? – if so, on American terms that suit the country's singularity and calling? This interrogation has been given point and prominence by the shift in political power to new forces, and new persons, in Congress. Compared to the Executive branch, Congress is always more sensitive to the popular mood and more inclined to take a populist view of foreign policy. This is particularly true of the House of Representatives where the turnover has been drastic and where 'nativist' sentiment is most pronounced. The parochial and mildly xenophobic emotions swirling through the American body politic thereby are conveyed directly into the policy arena by politicians who feel it is their constitutional duty, as well as partisan interest, to do so. 'America First' is their battle-cry.

A political generation has arrived in power without the sobering direct experience of what the exercise of American world leadership entailed in the postwar era. For those newly elected office-holders, many neophyte politicians, the Cold War has faded into the history books – leaving as its residue a keen desire to restore the purity of tarnished American values but little acquired wisdom as to the complexities of a world that cannot easily be bent to American standards. The fluid state of public opinion means that Congress will be an active broker between popular sentiment and the Executive, providing its own filter of institutional prerogatives and partisan politics. The strain between an inward-looking American public and a responsible Presidency thereby is being institutionalized.

INTERESTS

Maintaining a national consensus on US stakes in Europe is simpler than finding agreement on what the necessary American contribution is *or* on the appropriate modes of cooperation with allies. Few take exception to the propositions that the United States must be attentive to the shape and orientation of a federalizing European Union; and that it cannot be a passive observer of the historic attempt to implant liberal political and economic values in the former Communist lands. American interests in both enterprises are high. All acknowledge that their outcome largely will determine whether there will be a renewed military threat to the common welfare of the liberal democracies; whether a unified Europe will be a pillar of a wider world order based on principles of non-violence and peaceable engagement, as well as serve as custodian of continental peace; *and*, too, whether Washington's participation in the management of the continent's affairs will be welcomed, thereby ensuring that distinctly American interests and concerns in Europe's future evolution will be acknowledged.

What are these distinctly American interests? They entail a particular conception of the Western partners' *common* interests, and the essential importance of maintaining a shared vision of their future. There is little notion of American strategic interests, conventionally understood, being in conflict with those of its allies. That is to say, prevailing thinking in Washington (and in the country at large) rejects the idea that national interests of the Western partners are in contention or that there are objective grounds for their becoming so. For political elites, the gravest danger is that a lost sense of overriding common interest, as characterized Atlantic relations during the Cold War, will encourage the promotion of self-centred, parochial agendas. This outlook expresses the vitality of Americans' faith in the liberal model of international relations. The achievement of a Kantian civil community among the liberal democracies is viewed as confirming the validity of that vision while underscoring the crucial importance of preserving the community that embodies it as the cornerstone of a wider European order.

It is seen as endangered by two potential failings of political conviction and political will. One is to allow an erosion of the mutual confidence and unity of the Western partners by yielding to the impulses of national particularisms. A return to the traditional focus on relative gains in wealth, status or prestige, as opposed to the absolute gain for the West in advancing its security and prosperity, over time could loosen the unique bonds that give the Western community its staying-power and resilience. This is not to gainsay the existence of real differences in how to shape collective institutions or in the distribution of duties and prerogatives for directing them. Nor are Washington officials inattentive to how trade and commercial practices allocate economic wealth. After all, in our interest-based political systems those questions can make or break governments. The point stressed by American officials is that the ensuing rivalries and disputes must be kept in perspective. Otherwise, what is taken for granted may be lost. The risk is not in the renationalization of defence policy, or in the rekindling of ambition. Instead, it is in allowing shortsightedness and political convenience to dominate strategic considerations – a tendency to which the US itself is not immune, as anyone who has conducted US foreign policy these past few years is painfully aware.

A companion risk lies in the renationalization of strategic perspectives. For the United States, it is imperative that the Western partners not waver in their attachment to the neo-Wilsonian vision of a Europe 'whole, free and at peace with itself'. The goal should be a continental system that emulates the Atlantic community in progressively subsuming the national interest within a larger collective interest that is institutionalized in multilateral, cooperative organizations. To put it somewhat differently, American notions about the country's place in Europe's future are shaped by the belief that the West should dedicate itself to the rhetorical goal of creating a harmonious international society whose democratic member states take an enlightened approach toward their external relations. The United States, as the self-designated cynosure of liberal values and bearer of the Wilsonian faith, accords itself a unique role in bringing that vision to fruition. That conceit gives added importance to the question of what the terms of the United States engagement in European affairs will be. The leadership issue is central to American thinking about the continent's future political structure, therefore, not only because of a self-conscious desire to maintain American power for its own sake or to reap preferential advantages from such a position of moral leadership, but primarily because it is taken to be an essential ingredient of a stable European order.

Of course, American foreign policy at the end of the twentieth century no longer compulsively follows the maxims of Wilsonian idealism. Washington is no stranger to power politics. However, it rejects the traditional notion that, for the sake of stability, power – in all its forms – always must be balanced. *Whether* it needs to be balanced depends on the nature of a state's internal regime which, in turn, will strongly influence its external relations. *Raison d'état* is not an immutable precept of foreign policy. A liberal democratic polity, one dedicated to the welfare of its citizens *and* one which pursues its goals together with like-minded neighbours, needs no 'balancing'. Hence, American policymakers have given little if any credence to the notion, entertained in other allied capitals, that a united Germany could exercise such weighty influence in European affairs that it needs to be offset by a countervailing political force. They are made uneasy, too, by casual references to an emerging multipolar world system wherein the US and Western Europe, among others, constitute distinct poles. Each exercising independent judgement within a broadly shared strategic perspective is one thing; a reversion to separateness for its own sake is rather more serious. The American conviction still holds that a European system based upon common political principles (and practices) would be more peaceful and predictable than one based mainly on geostrategic ones. The United States has no permanent strategies, but a permanent belief in an ideal.

The apparent discrepancy between a public discourse that couches nearly all utterances about foreign policy in the language of Wilsonian idealism, and practical policies that display a large element of realism, is puzzling to many Europeans. The answer lies in the resilience of traditional American political thinking in the face of changes in the country's international position. Political discourse in the United States knows only one political vocabulary, shares in one common set of concepts. For domestic affairs, it is the lexicon of populism as enshrined in the country's peculiar civil religion. For external affairs, it is the lexicon of idealism derived from the enlightened, (generally) optimistic creed of classic liberalism.[1] They provide the filters through which worldly events are viewed, they set the reference marks against which achievement is measured, and they provide a moral compass for policymakers most of whom would feel ill-equipped to venture into the world without one. Even as American officials and politicians direct the country's foreign affairs with due regard for the logic of realism, their lodestar remains idealism. The result is an inescapable tension between the dictates of the environment in which they must operate and the philosophical premises that both justify action and are the basis for public understanding and support.

The attachment to the Wilsonian vision helps to explain why the US outlook concentrates so heavily on Russia. For if the outcome of liberal reform is not predetermined, then neither is the character of interstate relations in Europe. We can say with some confidence that the West's civil society will not embrace the entire continent unless liberal democracy prevails in most places, including the most important places. That is to say, a continent of diverse political systems and philosophies is a continent that lacks the essential requirement for realizing the comity and cooperation we have experienced among the Atlantic democracies. The belief that a world order based on moral commitments is more stable and enduring than one based on geostrategic logic is deeply ingrained in the American political psyche.

Signs that some West European partners are not so single-minded in their attachment to the Kantian/Wilsonian model evoke dismay in Washington. The sharp clashes over how to deal with the Yugoslav conflict are most important for putting in doubt the American assumption that the allies share a fundamental conception of Europe's post-Communist political order. It has little to do with the United States being contested for a position of influence in the Balkans. After all, pride of place was yielded to the European Community at the outset on the premise that such an arrangement conformed to the logic of alliance and environmental circumstances *and* that strategic aims and interests were identical. Rather, the main cause for consternation in Washington was the sense that two of the United States' major allies – Britain and France – were beginning to predicate their judgements and their actions on questionable conceptions of how relations among European states should be organized; they are the outdated and unwarranted conceptions of sphere-of-influence and balance-of-power. On Yugoslavia, they were scorned as sterile – and dangerous – formulations borne of fatigue and failure.

All of these faintly nineteenth-century notions with the stale smell of another epoch were viewed as counsels of despair. They are not rejected out of hand for dealing with all circumstances at all times. After all, the United States has acted in accordance with those logics for most of its tenure as the West's champion in the Cold War and as a global superpower. Nor are these ideas absent from the US drafted Dayton Accords on Yugoslavia and its implementation. They were judged tactically useful for salvaging what one could of Western ideals and credibility. The difference is significant for it points to a deviation from the norm (a norm unchallenged in the domestic debate) that leaves in place a conceptual frame of reference that continues to orient American policy. No exception could or should be made for the Balkans. The United States was not prepared to abandon lightly the goal of a Europe united and stabilized on the basis of common adhesion to democratic values.

Indications that conviction in the liberal hopes for post-Communist Europe is fraying badly in London and Paris (although still steadfastly held in Bonn) reinforce the United States' instinctive feeling that its continued, prominent presence in Europe serves a salutary purpose that goes beyond any particular interest of its own or its strictly practical contribution to Alliance diplomacy. American leadership is seen as existential reassurance against reversion to the fractious ways of Europe's past, while helping keep alive an optimistic vision of the continent's future – a double immunization against spectres arising from the past to bedevil the present and future. It is taken as an important complement to the tangible presence of US military forces and formal treaty obligations. In this sense, the form of the American contribution to management of Europe's political affairs, and methods for that collective management, are inseparable from the definition of US interests.

Collective Security?

The 'holistic' conception of European security coexists uneasily with the growing reticence about the United States' readiness to commit itself (in terms of men, money or political capital) to underwriting a pan-European system which conforms to such a conception. The resulting strain has been evident in the restless efforts to devise an intellectual framework for the country's place in post-Cold War Europe.

Collective security would appear to be the arrangement that best expresses the conviction that international conduct should conform to norms of a community of well-intentioned nations, one that is prepared to enforce them. Europe's liberal revolution promised to create the very conditions that might make the Wilsonian ideal realizable. For the first time in Europe's history there existed an ideological uniformity and near-universal adherence to a code of behaviour that proscribes the resort to force to achieve national purposes. Should it not follow that the United States dedicate itself to building a collective security system whose members form a legal order and accept a moral obligation, reinforcing enlightened national interests, to maintain it?

This facile logic conceals the dilemmas and paradoxes of operationalizing collective security that have counteracted the ideological affinity between American-style Wilsonianism and formulas for a European-wide collective security system.[2] If we could be assured changes ushered in by the events of 1989-90 would endure, there would be no reason for doubt or hesitation. But if we cannot assume a liberal teleology at work, then the question of what should be the mechanisms for maintaining the post-Communist peace are still open. Much of the ambivalence about collective security derives from the lack of clarity whether, to quote Richard Betts, 'since the collapse of communism... the invocation of collective security is meant to enforce peace or to celebrate it'.[3] Muted celebration of victory in the Cold War, in Washington as in other Western capitals, betrayed less optimism about the advent of a new age of peace than was conveyed in public rhetoric.

Qualified confidence about the future of liberal democracy in the former Communist lands (above all Russia) left American strategic planners face to face with the troubling truth that collective security works best where and when you need it least. That raised two basic dilemmas: (a) how to reconcile collective security mechanisms with the retention of mutual defence arrangements, and (b) whether it is necessary and cost-effective to intervene – whatever the means – in the political affairs of sovereign states so as to preserve/promote democratic forces.

The experience of the League of Nations, and then of the Cold War era United Nations, carried the lesson that dealing with violators of the peace could not be left to collective security organizations. A military alliance among states certain of their common interest was a necessary hedge against the potential danger posed by those of less certain orientation and interest. In this light, keeping NATO intact was seen as less a contradiction of the goal of a unified continental security system than a source of reassurance against the failure to make it work. As we shall see, enlarging NATO, a policy broached in 1993 and pressed the following year in tandem with Germany, was conceived as a way to extend that reassurance in tangible form to (some) Eastern European countries. 'Projecting stability' through enlargement thereby served the related purpose of intervening, indirectly, to influence the outcome of the historic project to implant democratic institutions.[4]

The enlargement initiative affirmed the United States' readiness to use its premier military alliance for a political objective – not only of providing external security but also of encouraging a preferred pattern of internal development. That line of thinking demonstrated two noteworthy aspects of how the United States has come to view the Atlantic Alliance: (1) it is now seen as an instrument for shaping the environment of the liberal democracies as much as a strict military alliance; (2) there is a belief that it behoves the West to support actively democratic regimes so as to ensure that states take an enlightened approach to their dealings with others. The policy premise is that active promotion of democracy serves Western security interests. This was the *leitmotif* of the Clinton administration's foreign policy. But does that logic hold across the board? The answer given in Washington is 'yes' in the sense that the West should do what *reasonably* it can to inflect the course of political evolution everywhere in former Communist Europe. However, discriminating judgements must be made as to where and how it is cost-effective to do so.

Yugoslavia and Russia have posed, in quite different respects, the issue of implementing such a strategy, whose analytical fulcrum is the presumed linkage between internal and external political behaviour.

THREATS

From the United States' vantage point, there are two serious threats to European peace and the well-being of the Western democracies. One is nationality conflicts, of the kind that has immolated the ex-Yugoslavia. The other is a recrudescent Russian nationalism dedicated to regaining control of its imperial *irredenta*. Each carries its own element of uncertainty.

Russia

Russia offers the great test for those instincts, intellectual predilections, and policy orientations we have ascribed to US policy-makers. Russia's threat remains conjectural, but the outlook clearly is worrisome. The country's political and economic turbulence poses a double puzzle: how can the West influence the path of Russia's political development? and how can any strategy so intended be executed while making contingent preparations to deal with the consequences of a possible Russian reversion to autocracy and aggrandizement?

The Russian puzzle overshadows US thinking about European security. Since the Soviet empire in Eastern Europe began to break apart, the United States – like its European allies – has struggled to fashion a strategy at once conciliatory and vigilant. The challenge has been made all the more daunting by the succession of changes in the status and political orientation of the leadership in Moscow. Within a short span of time, it has passed through four distinct phases. (1) From November 1989 until December 1991, when the beleaguered Mikhail Gorbachev yielded progressively to the freeing of the Soviet satellites while pursuing a course of rapprochement with the West and pragmatic domestic reform. (2) From December 1991 to December 1993, when the dissolution of the USSR left Boris Yeltsin as the head of a Russian government committed to liberal reforms and an accommodating, self-effacing foreign policy while groping for leverage on the multiple constitutional, economic, and territorial crises it faced. (3) The period ushered in by the revival of autocratic, ultra-nationalistic political forces, and the Yeltsin government's reversion from a philosophy of Westernization. It was characterized by a more assertive strategy aimed at establishing Russia's sway within the domain of the CIS, a more independent line in dealing with the West, and the retreat of democrats in the battle over who will shape the country's political and economic institutions. (4) The era of great-power restoration inaugurated, however tentatively, by the 1996 Presidential election campaign.

These last two (for the most part, unexpected) transformations in the political climate forced a reconsideration of three premises that have underlain US thinking about what was required to solidify a 'Wilsonian' Europe. The first was that a new chapter had opened in the history of Russia's place in European affairs. The country's affairs presumably were on a track parallel to, and in important respects convergent with, that of the West. Moscow's commitment to constitutional democracy and a market economy held the promise that a comity of outlook would be the natural expression of basic social realities; therefore, diplomatic cooperation could go beyond expedient calculations of transitory interest. Second, Russia's weakened position, as well as its new orientation, would lead it to prize good relations with the West. For the West alone could provide critically needed economic assistance while affording Russia the respected place in continental affairs that national self-esteem demanded. Consequently, Russia not only would cease to be a threat to the independence and interests of its neighbours, but would be a sympathetic participant – if not full partner – in the historic project of building a stable European order. Third, the Western nations could embark on that enterprise confident in the belief that their interests were secure as never before in history. Indeed, the values they espoused, and embodied, were being proclaimed across the continent. This feeling was especially strong in the US which historically has seen itself as the herald of a democratic age and whose victory in the Cold War was widely acclaimed as both fulfilling America's destiny and as opening a new peaceful age.

By 1994 each of these suppositions required amendment. Russia's political future looked more and more ominous. While the eventual form of the country's governmental institutions and leadership was an open question, anti-democratic forces harbouring nostalgic yearning for the defunct Soviet/Russian empire were clearly in the ascendancy. That trend, discernible a scant few years after the collapse of the Soviet regime, was a strong reminder of how inhospitable to democracy Russian soil is and how much Russian political identity is tied to the idea of empire. Internal upheavals had produced a noticeable shift in Moscow's approach to its foreign relations. Cordial relations with the West remained important, but that objective no longer overrode all other national interests. Those interests increasingly were defined in traditional terms: (1) restoring a Russian sphere of dominant presence in the territories that constitute the CIS – in Central Asia, the Caucasus, and the European republics of Ukraine, Belarus and Moldova; (2) establishing a position of protector for Russian communities in the 'near abroad' – including those in the Baltic states; (3) preventing Russia's segregation from the rest of Europe by the incorporation of its former East-Central European vassals into Western institutions of cooperation; and (4) securing for itself the recognized status of a continental great power whose self-defined national interest must be taken into account on all matters of European security, e.g the former Yugoslavia.

The Russian 'question' was ensconced at the top of Washington's foreign policy agenda. Through mid-1994, this was the one area where the Clinton administration had a clear, consistent line. It was composed of three elements: placing the highest priority on developing a constructive working relationship with Moscow; unqualified backing for Boris Yeltsin as the best hope for consolidating liberal reform internally and a Western-oriented foreign policy; and accommodating policy toward Ukraine, and the other Eastern Europeans, to this overriding goal. 'Russia first', as the strategy came to be known, was manifest in a number of areas: *inter alia* hesitancy in responding to pressures from the Visegrad 4 for NATO membership, and welcoming Russian partnership in efforts to bring an end to the Bosnian conflict.

Soon, however, the combination of events in Russia and the Republicans sweeping Congressional victory called into question the givens of the administration's approach to the Russian dimension of European security. Boris Yeltsin's new-found penchant for autocratic ways, his adoption of much of his rivals' nationalist platform, and his bloody power play in Chechnya, left the administration in a quandary. The Clinton administration sought to strike two delicate balances in Russian policy. One was between an agnostic appraisal, bordering on the pessimistic, of the chances for ultimately winning the bet on liberal reform in Russia and a continued effort to shift the odds in favour of the West. The other was to find a mix of policies that provide encouragement and incentive to Russian good behaviour while allowing for criticism of Russian actions deemed inimical to democracy at home and conciliation with the West.

Fashioning so subtle a strategy, and executing it with finesse, was hampered by the strident criticisms emanating from Capitol Hill. Freed from operational responsibility for American foreign policy, many in Congress yielded to stereotypical thinking and, for the Republican leadership, to the instinct for partisan attack. In truth, it should be noted that sentiment in Congress was only a more extreme version of prevailing conceptions within the Clinton administration. There, the early debate over NATO enlargement in 1993 had as its intellectual pivot the question of whether Russia should be viewed as a 'partner' or as an 'object'. A reasonable deduction was that Russia is behaving as an ordinary, traditional power whose definition of national interest – and, thereby its willingness to cooperate with the West – will turn on contingent judgements. The Clinton administration was reluctant to accept that conclusion. So much had been invested, and so much was at stake, in the historic enterprise of bringing Russia into the West's orbit for failure to be easily admitted. In addition, to do so was to face the prospect of an unremitting classic power struggle without an end-point. That was a distressing challenge to contemplate for a government whose attention was focused elsewhere and whose political instincts were hypersensitive to the domestic costs of embarking on a new containment strategy. In the absence of a well-articulated administration policy that avoided false dichotomies, and offered instruction as to the unavoidably wide confidence margins in predicting Russia's political evolution, Congressional hawks found it all the easier to condition popular opinion to its way of thinking in simplistic categories. Thus, both justification and a political base were being created for calling into question the avowed American faith in the possible rehabilitation of the old Cold War foe.

Russia and Collective Security

Adverse political developments in Russia have a bearing on important aspects of the ongoing effort to relate the transatlantic security relationship to European collective security while adapting NATO to novel problems and new tasks. First, there is a need to reconcile the process of devolving greater responsibilities on to the European allies, on the one hand, and the expanded security obligations (via NATO enlargement) that depend critically on a high US profile to establish their credibility, on the other. Second, Russia's growing readiness to use military force in the rimlands of its present domain and pressure tactics within the CIS underscore the connection between the West's terms of participation in peacemaking/keeping operations mandated by collective security organizations and the need to establish generalized rules-of-the-road applicable to Russia.

As to the former, significant progress has been made in overcoming the practical and political obstacles to constituting a European pillar within the Alliance. The June 1996 accord on giving concrete form to the Combined Joint Task Forces (CJTF) concept formally clears the way for the West Europeans to access American assets for operations, sanctioned by the Atlantic Council, that they might undertake on their own.[5] Unique tangible assets of the United States – C^3I, air- and sea-lift – can now be utilized even when the US does not participate directly. Intangible assets are equally, if not more important, though. It was American prestige, credibility and moral authority that enabled the Clinton administration to forge the Dayton Accords. There is no substitute for those attributes, and no way in which they can be borrowed. Indispensable on Bosnia, they will be less critical for the delicate tasks of contending with a prickly Russia while implementing plans for NATO enlargement.

As to the latter, the evident and increasing importance of constraining Russia's impulse toward unilateral action points to a policy of insisting on the imprimatur of the UN or OSCE for any armed intervention. But that logic was offset by the mounting disillusionment in Washington with the United Nations, and scepticism about relying on collective security methods to deal with regional conflicts.

The sour experience in Yugoslavia drained away the Clinton administration's enthusiasm for multilateralism of the UN variety while demonstrating the criticality of concerted Western action taken through NATO. IFOR's success (at least in performing its narrowly construed military mission, Operation Joint Endeavour) was heralded for several reasons: as confirmation of NATO's ability to act 'out-of-area'; as reinforcing American leadership claims; as a model for sub-contracting by the United Nations under Article 52 of the Charter; and as a precedent for enlisting Russia's participation in cooperation with the Western powers in a peacekeeping operation.[6] As to the last, the United States made much of how IFOR proved that there was no incompatibility between an expanded role for NATO and the cultivation of a constructive partnership with Russia.

Washington's rosy assessment of IFOR's lessons and implications was not shared in Moscow. The Yeltsin government's displeasure with being cast as a spear-carrier in a US-directed NATO production was made abundantly clear even before Yevgeny Primakov replaced the Western-oriented Andrei Kozyrev as Foreign Minister in the run-up to the 1996 Presidential election.[7] Russia rejected NATO's implicit claim to primacy in dealing with European security problems. Subordination to the UN (or OSCE) and strict control by a collective security body, Moscow argued, should be a condition for the delegation of operational responsibilities to any state or grouping of states. Moreover, Moscow continued to press for having the CIS designated as a regional security structure on an equal footing with NATO. It thereby would both be granted authority to maintain peace among its own members and be recognized as having the same right as NATO to initiate military action.

The Clinton administration preferred to evade this challenge. The United States was prepared neither to give the Russians a free hand in the CIS nor relinquish the prerogative to take action with its allies to protect Western interests where deemed necessary. It denied, though, that such a policy sought to relegate Russia to inferior status. American officials still sought to avoid having to admit either that NATO constituted a military bloc with a selective membership or that it should yield routinely to the authority of inclusive collective security organizations. Forthrightness in offering Russia an informal concert linked to both, as well as participation in the lofty G-7 summits, was the device envisaged as making this obviously uneven situation palatable to Moscow. The difficulty of doing so bedevilled American efforts to achieve success in its twin project of fashioning terms of

Alliance multilateralism and UN multilateralism that met the United States' strategic and political specifications.

Enlargement

NATO enlargement compounds rather than alleviates both problems. For it is a strategy that evades, rather than resolves the predicament of discouraging Russia from treating the West as a rival while encouraging the cause of liberal reform internally. To open NATO membership to Russia itself was unrealistic – both because the fate of its democratic experiment was unlikely to be determined by projections of stability from the West and because NATO's core *raison d'être* as safeguard against a contingent future could not be preserved while allowing entry of the one country that could present so serious a security threat.

The preferred American policy for smoothing Russian feathers ruffled by the enlargement initiative is to establish new forms of collaboration between NATO and Russia. The Clinton administration has sought every opportunity to demonstrate its respect for Russia's status as a great power with an essential contribution to make to continental stability. The White House's recognition of how hard it is to sell Congress and the American public on a strategy of modulated commitment to maintaining Europe's post-Cold War peace is one reason, among others, for striving to keep the relationship with Russia on a sure footing. For the various roles contemplated by the United States in multilateral alliance enterprises henceforth could become more or less credible and dangerous, depending on the Russian factor. It cuts both ways: an adversarial or even strained relationship with Russia would justify need to have American strength and prestige engaged; at the same time it raises the risks of doing so. Thus, there is a strong preference to continue policies designed to maintain a constructive working partnership with Moscow. NATO enlargement makes it all the more vital to offset Russian anxieties with conciliating measures.[8]

A forthright attempt to mollify Moscow by proposing *a formal treaty* between NATO and Russia appealed to many as the logical complement to enlargement. It would serve the dual purpose of acknowledging in principle Moscow's status as a major European power while making provision for regular consultation on matters of continental security. The charter eventually agreed upon has the same objectives. Reaching a *modus vivendi* with a suspicious Russia is of heightened importance since enlargement has occurred in Washington's politically charged atmosphere. However, establishing terms acceptable in both capitals became all the more difficult for the same reason that made an accord necessary. Moscow demanded more; Washington was ready and politically able to give less.[9]

Enhancing collective security organizations is a logical complement to formalizing a relationship between NATO and Russia. Bolstering the prestige and functions of OSCE has become a means for the West to partially compensate Russia for NATO's expansion into Eastern Europe. By proclaiming OSCE as the collective forum in which matters of continental peace and political stability should be addressed, the Western allies sought to issue reassurances to Moscow that NATO did not harbour the ambition of being Europe's security directorate. Schemes for upgrading OSCE were put forth as part of a package of proposals for mollifying a Russia unsettled by NATO's expansion plans. But Washington had no intention of endowing OSCE with the precedence and powers that would make it the centrepiece of a European security system. Rather, it was visualized as one piece in an arrangement of overlapping and intersecting institutions.

The agreements signed at the organization's Budapest summit in December 1994 represented a modest programme for the organization's revitalization. A number of steps were taken to enable OSCE to undertake an expanded range of collective security functions; *inter alia* mediating conflicts, protecting threatened minority communities, and providing peacekeepers (as was done in Georgia and Nagorno-Karabakh). Specifically, the Budapest communiqué foresees:

(1) the augmenting of capabilities to perform the conflict prevention and crisis-management functions accorded OSCE by the Convention on Conciliation and Arbitration;
(2) promulgation of a 'Code of Conduct on Politico-Military Aspects of Security'; and
(3) assuming responsibility for implementation of accords reached through the Pact on Stability.[10]

The United States fully supported the move to strengthen the OSCE's capabilities. Doing so served three interlocking purposes: constraining Russia to observe a clearly demarcated code of conduct in 'policing' the CIS, especially with regard to the use of force (presciently drawn to cover its use in suppressing civil unrest internally); offering Russia a place where it can cooperate with the West as an equal in addressing European security issues; and reifying the principles of the Paris Charter in the one pan-continental body. However, expanding the organization's mandate in this manner has the ancillary effect of posing on the continental level the same set of questions regarding the American contribution to collective security activities that have challenged it at the United Nations. They include funding, participation of US troops, designation of mandates, military command and political direction.

Upgrading the OSCE responded to a need for promoting a pan-continental security vehicle that went part of the way at least toward satisfying Russian aspirations, thereby blunting its opposition to NATO enlargement. While hoping to assuage Moscow, Washington was not about to put the OSCE at the apex of a new security system whose twin arms would be NATO and the CIS. As Assistant Secretary of State Richard Holbrooke pithily explained: 'It is time to upgrade the OSCE to turn it into a stronger organization but one that does not weaken or dilute NATO.'[11]

The constraints and limitations on US participation in peacekeeping operations apply equally to the UN and the OSCE. In the latter context, they are exacerbating the twin problems of reconciling the US claim to political leadership with a reticence about tangible contributions, and of reconciling divergent views among the allies as to what is a proper and workable formula for sharing or dividing responsibilities for dealing with the range of threats to the continent's peace and stability. Irresolution, or cognitive dissonance, in Washington means irresolution in the Alliance. An impaired, incomplete strategy for involving Russia in European collective security arrangements on acceptable terms to the West is at once a cause and a worrisome outcome of this condition. In Washington's evolving perspective, NATO provides the mutual defence element, the OSCE the collective security dimension, and both were complemented by *a concert of power* element.

The last has never been acknowledged as such, or given formal expression. But the constructive partnership Washington sought with Moscow could take no other form than a loose concert once the alternative of a full-blown collective security regime was rejected and NATO membership kept selective. In purpose and function, the special relationship between NATO and Russia that was conceded in the wake of the enlargement initiative served as the embryo of a concert. Including as it did a regular consultative mechanism, the arrangement pointed to a structured routinized dialogue between the Western powers and Russia.[12]

For the United States, this new mode of consultation could be seen as a continuation of great-power dialogue going back to the Cold War days. What is different is: (1) that Washington's European allies would participate in a collective dialogue; and (2) that the objective was to go beyond the prudent management of an antagonistic relationship to cover broader elements of cooperation. Both features signified a departure from the classic nineteenth-century model of a concert of power. The former substitutes an egalitarianism of membership (at least formally) for the hierarchical structure that subordinates the relatively weak to the elite strong. It also militates against the 'cabinet diplomacy' that was the original concert's *modus operandi* – a style that, in any case, is not compatible with the open politics of democratic societies. The latter feature, a hoped-for partnership in the consolidation of European peace, is a hope, if not expectation, made possible by the seeming ideological consensus, and Moscow's abandonment of its imperial designs – encouraged by its internal weakness and need for Western economic support. However uncertain the forecast for cooperation with Russia, and whether it was to be based on mainly mutuality of interest or reciprocity of interest, this implicit concert largely by-passed Europe's regional collective security organization, the OSCE. Its effects on the principle and procedures of collective security were mixed, though. On the one hand, the universalistic principle was compromised. But on the other, some tinge of collective security was being introduced into NATO by a process of progressive enlargement, along with the carving out of a place for Russia within NATO's political space.

Yugoslavia

The United States viewed the protracted wars of the ex-Yugoslavia as a grievous failure for the West that could endanger prospects for continental stability. Yet official thinking between 1991 and 1995 had been mixed in the assessment of precedents set, ideals tarnished, and Western credibility lost. Vacillating American policy on Yugoslavia owed something to the inability to gauge the US, and Western, interest in ending the violence and imposing terms of settlement. Separatist violence and ethnic disputes are troubling deviations from the desired norm. Yet, so long as they are geographically limited, and seemingly can be diplomatically contained, their wider implications are sufficiently unclear as to allow for multiple answers to the questions of what threat they pose to America's European interests. That was evident in the prevarications of two successive US administrations. Both Bush and Clinton found the lack of a clear stake to be politically convenient for coping with a moralistic yet risk-averse public, and with the strains of an allied diplomatic partnership Washington chose not to lead until forced to do so by the imminence of an American-led Balkan Dunkirk in the summer of 1995.[13]

Instinctively, though, official thinking inclined to view events in the ex-Yugoslavia through a glass darkly. There are a number of reasons for this. For one thing, Americans found it difficult to accommodate philosophically to the idea of a divisible peace, i.e. to a Europe where democracy and civilized behaviour is a sometimes, someplace thing. The dismissive comment, 'the Balkans are the Balkans', left Americans uneasy. It conveyed an unhealthy acquiescence in the rule of history and a too casual tolerance for its consequences. If the 'Balkans are the Balkans', is not 'Russia Russia' – i.e. autocratic and imperialistic? Is not the distinctive political mode in most of Central/Eastern Europe authoritarian and intolerantly nationalistic? Historical determinism is no more congenial to American political thinking than is *realpolitik* (taken as a dictum).

Another reason for the United States' rather dire view of the Yugoslav crisis lies in its own historically tinged image of Europe's past that is juxtaposed to its optimistic reading of recent progress and qualified hopes for the future. The nationalistic passions that bloodied Yugoslavia, together with the West Europeans' display of perceived ineptitude and lack of will, confirmed American prejudices about 'the Europeans': their proclivity for division and conflict; and the allies' dearth of political conviction and courage when facing dangerous challenges. Washington is not prepared to leave Europe's peace and stability dependent on its allies (i.e. Britain's and France's) skill at playing balance-of-power games. The corollary is that European security is too serious a matter to be left exclusively to the Europeans.

In a sense, the open question for American policymakers (and the foreign policy community in general) since the collapse of Communism has been whether it was dealing with a prolongation and expansion of the 'new' Europe *or* with a recrudescent 'old' Europe. Most recognized, intellectually, that realistically it would be composed of elements from both, even as the West strove to remake the entire continent in its image. Nonetheless, Washington is disconcerted in contemplating that amalgam, a sentiment that strengthens the impulse to realize fully the perceived historical opportunity: thus the renewed, ardent campaign for NATO enlargement. It is inspired in good part by a neo-Wilsonian belief in the power of good intentions – even when expressed in the extension of a military pact. Peter Tarnoff, Under-Secretary of State for Political Affairs, argued the case for NATO enlargement by stressing its mollifying influence on latent conflicts: 'a NATO which is reaching out to the east, which is trying to prevent...repetition of what has happened in the former Yugoslavia'.[14] Another tenet of Wilsonianism, the efficacy of intervention in the cause of democracy and peace, was severely tested in Yugoslavia.

The Yugoslav conflict implicitly posed the question of what the United States was prepared to venture in the cause of European liberalization and peace. Was intervention an obligation/requirement for preserving principles of acceptable political conduct? for establishing a collective security regime? for upholding the credibility of the West as guardian of international order? Intervention, when directed at the internal affairs of a state, as in Yugoslavia, complicates the issue by raising the question of its justification, and the desirability of breaching the wall of state sovereignty. The Yugoslav conflict, which combined elements of both aggression across internationally recognized borders and civil war (accompanied by widespread, gross abuses of human rights) forced the West to decide how deep was its commitment to enforcing avowedly universal norms of political behaviour. It had to decide as well whether it had reason to interfere in an internecine Balkan conflict in order to avoid setting a bad precedent by acting contrary to the belief in a linkage between democracy and continental peace that was supposition and goal.

The challenge of intervention was particularly acute for the United States given its Wilsonian traditions.[15] In the prevailing American conception, the judgement whether to intervene or not went beyond a *realpolitik* calculation of the cost/interest ratio. It also represented a test of the principle that support for civil liberties and a people's right to self-determination contributed to establishing a peaceful international order. Victory in the Cold War, moreover, had given new life to the conviction that there was a progressive logic at work in the world. If so, there are indeed universally valid and applicable norms of conduct that should be enforced. In these circumstances, the initiatives of those states who embody liberal democratic values to advance their enlightened creed conform simultaneously to their self-interest and to the greater good of the community of nations. In this sense, the West's defeat of anti-democratic forces in the Cold War makes the world safe for intervention and justifies it in the name of the collective interest.

This facile line of thinking proved difficult to sustain in the face of Yugoslavia's harsh realities and the American people's distinct lack of enthusiasm for observing politico-moral imperatives that cast the US in the role of global policeman. They were unready even to contemplate open-ended monitoring and enforcement of compliance with international rules, much less to take on the responsibility of imposing public morals on other societies. This widespread attitude led to policy conclusions that featured self-restraint rather than an activism driven by optimism, self-confidence and a keen sense of responsibility. For some, those conclusions were strengthened by the appealing (and convenient) notion that Europe's peace was 'divisible'.[16] That is to say, that a minor conflict among peripheral players need not be viewed as a serious threat to stable, non-antagonistic relations among the major powers.

There also were peculiar features of the Yugoslav situation that counteracted the classical Wilsonian view that intervention is a logical, and necessary, extension of the commitment to democracy and human rights. For one thing, making the determination as to whether direct intervention was warranted, and likely to be efficacious, was complicated by the uncomfortable reality that in Yugoslavia there was a clash among liberal principles: national self-determination, the sanctity of established boundaries, and the safeguarding of human rights. Reality did not present itself in a neat package that suited philosophical predilection (Wilsonianism) or political convenience (by pointing to a self-evident course of virtuous, necessary policy). Reality was too complicated for enlightened American opinion to bear.

Second, by its nature, the conflict in Yugoslavia promised to burden an intervening West/United States with the responsibility to engage in 'statebuilding', since the collapse of pre-existing structures was a cause of the conflict and the source of the humanitarian disaster. An American-led intervention in Bosnia was unlikely to be easy or short-lived. On what grounds could public consent be obtained? An appeal to humanitarian impulses would strike a resonant popular chord; but it was unlikely to elicit a response sufficiently strong to sustain a military mission. American idealism no longer readily translates itself into a sense of mission. A 'realist' understanding of how the national interest best could be served by engagement? Realist grounds for intervention suffered from the absence of a perceptible, compelling need or purpose. A citizenry more inclined to insulate itself from the world's turmoil than to involve itself in enterprises to resolve it is as unpersuaded by the demands of realism as it is resistant to claims on their moral obligation. Abdication by the White House of its duty to instruct the American people as to the country's continued stake in world affairs, and the requirements for securing it, allowed popular sentiments averse to foreign engagements to flourish. The consequent strengthening of parochial and prejudicial attitudes raises the cost for a President in pursuing, and justifying, an activist foreign policy.

Structural Ambivalence

The sum of American ambivalence about the magnitude and focus of its contribution to European security points to a fundamental dilemma of US foreign policy: how to devise policies that simultaneously meet the requirements of *legitimacy*, *political acceptability*, and *effectiveness*.

Ensuring *a legitimizing mandate* from a collective security body has grown in importance for two reasons: (1) the less threatening post-Cold War circumstances provide less compelling justification for acting unilaterally; and (2) the US – and the West generally – have an interest in laying down strict rules of interstate behaviour for a world freed from the discipline and controls that the rival blocs imposed. Building a stable new order on norms of peaceable intercourse among states needs an *institutionalized* code of conduct. The authority for establishing and enforcing such a code ultimately resides in the United Nations – and, derivatively, in the OSCE. Victory in the Cold War seemingly had cleared the way for multilateralism. Concomitantly, the United States could relax its heroic pose.

Washington's early optimism about an expanded role for United Nations 'peacekeeping' was based on a number of assumptions that flowed from the sense of having crossed an historic threshold. Peacekeeping, in its expanded definition that included non-traditional peace-enforcing activities, was viewed as a form of policing in a world in which 'criminal' behaviour was the easily recognizable deviation from the generally accepted norm. Presumed agreement on the underlying legitimacy of the *status quo* would allow for a progressive institutionalization of law-and-order functions. An international code of conduct, like any law regime, is conservative in effect since it restricts both the legitimate ends of political behaviour *and* the means for advancing one's interests. Only in a world where there is a broad comity of outlook, reinforced by shared values, would the requisite regulation of international behaviour be generally acceptable.

Those same conditions, if they were indeed crystallizing, would also be permissive of the United States' entry into the brave new world of nation-building (e.g. Somalia). They would remove great-power rivalry as an impediment to effective action by the UN; they would strengthen its authority as the agent of a world community united in adherence to liberal values; and, not least, they would ensure that the necessary resources would be forthcoming from member states to support more ambitious, and more numerous, peacekeeping missions. From this perspective *unilateralism and multilateralism* ceased to be exclusive chores.

Political acceptability takes two forms: acquiescence by a sceptical American public; and agreement from allies. The former reflects the narrowing of decisional autonomy granted US leaders by a populace that has psychologically retrenched from the forward positions and active engagements of the postwar period. A self-absorbed American public implicitly has withdrawn the broad mandate it accorded presidents to deploy national resources as they saw fit to contend with the Communist menace. The expanded sense of entitlement which is such a striking feature of contemporary American political culture extends to the right not to defer to the President in foreign policy.

The politics of foreign policy magnifies the importance of deepening public scepticism about overseas military commitments. Participation in United Nations directed missions is especially vulnerable to manipulation given the organization's pronounced negative image in the United States. Opinion surveys do reveal that a clear majority of Americans still believes that the country has a national interest in opposing aggression and in defending those countries that traditionally have been America's friends and allies.[17] Furthermore, in conflicts marked by genocide there was overwhelming agreement on an international responsibility to intervene. For this latter purpose, the United Nations was deemed the appropriate vehicle despite the poor grades it receives for effectiveness and competent leadership. One source of the discrepancy between support for peacekeeping in the abstract and a negative view of the UN is the skewed perception of what the United States contributes to UN missions. Most Americans believe that the United States provides at least 40 per cent of peacekeeping troops (against an actual 4 per cent) and the median estimate of the cost to the Federal Treasury of peacekeeping operations is an extraordinary 20 per cent of the military budget (the actual amount is less than 1 per cent).[18]

Neo-isolationist opponents of a US role in peacekeeping (especially on the Republican right as exemplified by Senator Jesse Helms, chairman of the Foreign Relations Committee) exploit these misperceptions to raise a political obstacle that must be hurdled by a President in order to send American soldiers to perform collective security missions under multilateral auspices. Clinton administration officials publicly bemoaned the difficulties caused them by growing domestic pressures centred in the Congress. Richard Holbrooke was most outspoken in declaring that Senators had 'told me flatly that the simple truth [that the United States has national interests requiring an engaged international security policy] is the one thing they can't sell to their constituents.... To the American body politic it's all crap.'[19] Discounting for hyperbole, the statement shows how heavily domestic political constraints weigh in the formulation of American strategy.

In the Gulf crisis, the UN had well served the interests of the American-led coalition in both marshalling wide international backing and legitimizing decisive action. The Bush administration drew the lesson from that experience that American purposes could be advanced by working through the world body. That tentative judgement became a foundation-stone of the Clinton administration's early foreign policy. In elaborated form, it prompted their early strategy of exploiting the United Nations' perceived capabilities. Their policy of 'assertive multilateralism' conformed nicely to a conception of a modified leadership role for the United States whereby influence could be maintained even while reducing tangible contributions and spreading risks. This multilateralism was proclaimed as the *leitmotif* of the United States' new strategy of restrained internationalism.[20]

These same arrangements, however, had the drawback of curtailing American control; control being correlated more and more with effectiveness – especially in the eyes of Congress and the public. Furthermore, multilateralism implies a method of diplomatic conduct that many, if not most, American officials find uncongenial. The necessity to win the consent of allies (and an even more diverse group of governments in the UN context) is recognized by foreign policy professionals as a function of the shift away from directive American leadership to consensual modes of conducting diplomacy by coalition. But the unavoidable implication that a common line of policy must be cultivated rather than dictated, and that the outcome might not match exactly American preferences, is harder for the inexperienced but self-assured amateurs who compose a growing portion of the Congress to swallow.

The need to cultivate a working partnership with allies is unavoidable – whatever its precise terms. But popular backing for the engagement of US military forces (especially the putting of soldiers in harm's way, as part of a collective enterprise) depends on a demonstration that allies are making their fair contribution. A close reading of opinion surveys reveals that it is not isolationist sentiment that is on the rise, but rather a desire to avoid taking on hazardous missions alone. The political acceptability criterion for American intervention therefore can only be met by winning both the agreement of the allies and the acquiescence of a sceptical, risk-averse American public. The former is a condition for the latter. For US foreign policymakers, therefore, encouraging the Western European allies to demonstrate their readiness to make commitments and to take risks serves the purposes of easing Uncle Sam's burdens and of bolstering support at home for residual US commitments.

This poses a double dilemma. Intra-alliance accord is at once more essential and more difficult to obtain given the allies' greater independence of judgement that Washington has encouraged by its retreat from a position of unqualified and unwavering leadership. At the same time, the terms acceptable to allies may be quite different from those acceptable to Congress and the American public. Reconciling the two is complicated by the strident, yet defensive nationalism now emanating from the Congress. This uncomfortable truth was evident during the troubled implementation of the Dayton Accords. European governments were not ready to follow the American prescription for how the political provisions of the agreement were to be interpreted and what the strategy should be for dealing with the local parties. The Clinton administration's influence was further weakened by its reluctance to accept the full political and financial costs of energetically asserting its leadership across the board. Aggressive implementation of Dayton's political provisions was precluded by the upcoming Presidential election. For domestic political reasons it was believed essential to avoid an IFOR 'mission creep' or disturb the carefully cultivated impression of a smooth operation.

Yet another contradiction presents itself. The increased importance of winning consent from allies, a function of the shift away from active comprehensive US leadership of the Alliance, carries the imperative to develop consensual modes of deliberation and decision attuned to a truly multilateral partnership. The sharing of duties and burdens foreseen by Washington, and its allies, carries with it the unavoidable implication that agreement must be cultivated. Moreover, it has been an expressed goal of the United States since 1989 that the West Europeans take more initiative and make the largest material contribution to building continental stability.

But the half-hearted strategy of shifting responsibilities on to the allies had unhappy results when tested in Yugoslavia. Allied performance was sub-par. Still, Washington hesitated at filling the breach for fear of arousing strong public criticism, while the display of vacillation cost the administration credibility among the attentive public at home and in capitals abroad.

The *effectiveness* measuring-rod stands in uneasy relationship with the other two. While bowing to the necessity of ensuring that actions are seen as legitimate, and are acceptable to both allies and the American public, US policymakers are chary of the constraints thereby imposed on them in deciding when and how they exert American power. The United Nations' collective judgement and organizational capabilities, which never inspired confidence, are derided in the wake of the Yugoslav débâcle; scepticism abounds about the ability of the Western Europeans either to take timely concerted action or to sustain serious commitments; while the fickleness of popular sentiment forces American leaders to keep one eye constantly fixed on the barometer of public opinion.[21] There remains, therefore, an instinct to hold on to the levers of control, and to safeguard the ability to take independent action – as safeguard against the dereliction or ill-judgement of others, despite or because of Washington's own equivocations as how to use that control. It is an instinct countered by the prudential need to bend to the constraining influences of the times.

Yugoslav Retrospective

The practical challenge of charting a strategy for the United States that meets the triple standard of legitimacy, political acceptability and effectiveness was vividly on display throughout the Yugoslav crisis. It was never satisfactorily met. Indeed, it can be fairly concluded that the allied experience has posed new obstacles to realizing the goal of a workable multilateralism. There, the objective of realizing a functional multilateralism among the Western allies converged with the complementary goal of resorting to the authoritative multilateralism of the United Nations. Neither was fulfilled. Indeed, their unplanned and erratic intermingling worked to the disadvantage of each.

The United States' dilemmas in trying to perfect multilateralism as the *modus operandi* best suited to serving American interests have been exacerbated by the experience of Yugoslavia. The difficulties and shortcomings of relying on burden-sharing allies and the authority of the United Nations were highlighted; moreover, few clues were offered as to how these arrangements could be made to serve United States' purposes. The conclusions drawn from the double experience of multilateralism in Yugoslavia were discouraging.

(1) *Legitimacy* and *effectiveness* too often pointed in divergent, if not opposite directions. This applies to concerted diplomatic strategies as well as to the actual or threatened use of military force. Similarly, gaining consensus in the Alliance and sustaining it meant a lessened ability to take timely, propitious and what appeared in American eyes as wise actions. That strain was compounded when Russia became a main player and the seemingly unavoidable need to maintain unity with Moscow (i.e. within the 'contact group') became an additional diplomatic consideration. Moscow's more independent-minded foreign policy also complicated the challenge of winning legitimizing UN Security Council resolutions for actions Washington deemed necessary.

(2) The outlines of a viable new division of labour within the Atlantic Alliance did not emerge from the experience in Yugoslavia. The European allies failed to demonstrate their competence (a meld of capabilities and will) to deal with a serious security challenge. Expectations that the EU Twelve could be relied upon to act as custodian of peace and stability on an undivided continent by dealing with less than strategic threats proved unrealistic. Individual Western European governments seemed unable to muster public support for interventions that carry some risk; while the EU's avowal of a Common Foreign and Security Policy masks the lack of a legitimate authority to forge, win support for, and execute a concerted strategy. Consequently, American interests and credibility were seen as held hostage to the fallible judgements, and increasingly self-serving actions of its West European partners. Germany's pivotal role in forcing the premature recognition of Slovenia and Croatia is seen in Washington as one monumental error – albeit as an example of misguided idealism. Britain and France's progressive slide toward a position of appeasement, through a series of acts dictated by a combination of political convenience and myopic strategic vision, is another.

The reversal of fortunes that culminated in the Dayton Accords is ascribed by Washington to the United States' imposing its control and ideas on its allies and on the United Nations. It confirmed the belief that for the West to meet any serious security threat in the future,

American experience and leadership skills must be engaged. American military assets (not necessarily, but probably, including manpower too) and some measure of American political impetus are crucial ingredients of a collective Western effort if one is to succeed. Even before the intervention of summer 1995, the indispensability of American resources became obvious at every point when the use of military force became an issue. They were critical for maintaining the embargo on Serbia in the Adriatic; for enforcing the 'no-fly' zone; for launching airstrikes; and to organize a NATO expeditionary force to extricate UNPROFOR – if that had proven necessary. That perceived reality places the Alliance on the horns of a dilemma – one felt with special acuity in Washington: American resources, American status and American credibility are invaluable assets for the Alliance as a whole. They should not be engaged cavalierly or in questionable causes where the stakes and/or chances of success do not warrant the risk. Conversely, to hold them in reserve, to seek to preserve them for the occasion when they are crucially needed, is to run two risks: (a) that they will lose a measure of their potency, and (b) that their absence from earlier, seemingly less significant encounters would have lowered the odds on the 'big one' actually materializing.

The dilemma was deepened by the American triumph at Dayton. That success glaringly exposed the enormous disparity between the United States' capacity for effective action and that of the Western Europeans. It embarrassed the latter and left the former poised unsteadily between its return to demonstrated mastery and its wariness about reassuming past roles and reacquiring past burdens. Allied embarrassment did not lead them to address candidly collective failings. Instead, in an unbecoming display of 'sour grapes', a barrage of criticism was levelled at the Clinton administration for a multitude of perceived sins: Richard Holbrooke's high-handed subordination of European participants in the talks; the unjustified taking of credit for ideas stolen from allies; Washington's monopolizing the glory of success; and an American sloughing of the financial burdens for rebuilding Bosnia on to others. This dyspeptic reaction to a signal accomplishment was partly foreseen. Accordingly, the Clinton administration readily agreed that the publicized formal signing of the accords should be held in Paris and other ceremonial events held in London (and Moscow). Moreover, it did not claim the dominant role in supervising implementation of the accords – although command of IFOR naturally fell to an American. Quite the opposite. A place was made for nearly everyone and every international organization.

Diversity was so much the watchword that functionality was a minor criterion in designating roles and tasks. The United States, hesitant about pushing itself forward for a combination of tactful diplomatic reasons and sensitivity to the domestic political risks of overextension, was willing to accept a measure of lessened effectiveness. The price in Bosnia was duly paid as the strategy for its political reconstitution died aborning. As for the hoped-for dividends in the form of a regenerated Alliance multilateralism, they never materialized. Only in the narrow military sense did the Allies work together effectively. That positive experience could not offset the residue of wounded pride and unhealthy dependence on a fickle American leadership that has hampered efforts to establish viable new terms of transatlantic partnership.

(3) One final lesson of Yugoslavia is indisputable. On future security problems, the United States needs to be present throughout, whatever the exact contribution it makes to the collective effort in a particular instance. That participation is a key to establishing its authority and exercising an emollient influence on its partners. Being present from the start has the companion benefit of avoiding a situation where the United States becomes an unengaged, or only indirectly engaged critic whose righteous advice is discounted accordingly, and whose offstage commentaries disrupt without improving the performance. For an American administration, continuity of involvement has a further advantage; it avoids the uneasy choice between abstention from messy situations where US interests are being affected or belatedly engaging in a perhaps futile and costly attempt at retrieving a losing cause under duress.

THE PREFERRED, THE NECESSARY, AND THE POSSIBLE

If the counsel of experience is that the United States should participate fully in Western efforts to manage sub-strategic security challenges in or near Europe, the ethic of restraint continues to exercise a strong influence. The latter is especially pronounced in two of Washington's power centres: the Congress and the Defense Department. The military establishment's aversion to any policy sympathetic to multilateral 'intervention', accompanied by a deep scepticism of 'limited' war or the calibrated use of force as an adjunct to a diplomatic strategy, stems from the ordeal of Vietnam. Those sentiments have crystallized into a doctrine of codified postulates regarding the use of force. It has roots in the Reagan administration, antedating the sea-changes of 1989–90.

The post-Cold War evolution in the US military establishment's thinking about modes and methods for the use of force proceeded independent of assessments regarding the issue of the country's role in collective security missions, peacekeeping in particular. They nonetheless have coloured official attitudes about peacekeeping. There is a line of continuity that runs from the doctrine on the 'Uses of Military Power' laid down by Secretary of Defense Caspar Weinberger in 1984 to the Clinton administration's guidelines on multilateral peacekeeping operations and the strictures of PDM-25. There are recurrent themes and points of contention as well. The latter reflect strains arising from the intersection of external pressures and domestic preoccupations that are yet to be resolved. The continuing struggle to resolve them can best be understood when placed in the context of the attempt to formulate a comprehensive military doctrine.

The initial Weinberger formulation contained elements that have shaped the debate about the purposes of military action and the requirements for its effective use, the intervening collapse of the USSR notwithstanding.[22] Its main characteristics can be summarized as follows:

(1) setting a standard that places the burden of argument on those seeking to justify the engagement of US military power.
(2) establishing a generous standard of sufficiency (in manpower and resources) for whatever combat action is under consideration.
(3) an imperative for 'transparency', i.e. a crystal-clear objective(s), a carefully plotted strategy for reaching it, and a fixed estimate of the operation's conclusion including performance measures, timetables, and 'exit strategies'.
(4) a readiness to rethink commitments when changing conditions suggest a shift in mission.
(5) a requirement that there be a broad base of popular support in the country – informed by a full and public explanation of aims and means – before US troops are committed to combat.
(6) Viewing the military option as the 'last resort'; to be taken only after other ways of dealing with the problem have been tried or, at least, thoroughly reviewed.

These principles have been stated and restated by US leaders through three presidential administrations, receiving their firmest and most inflexible formulation from the uniformed services. It has become very much the orthodoxy of the Joint Chiefs of Staff. General Colin Powell's oft-cited criteria for military intervention follow closely the Weinberger catechism. The Powell variation added a few accents and punctuation marks: the stress on 'overwhelming force'; the repeated cautions against trying to tailor military action to overly subtle, or complicated, diplomatic ends; and the imperative importance attached to keeping command control in American hands.[23] The strength of the Pentagon's conviction that this doctrine embodies the distilled wisdom of the United States' experiences since World War II was manifest in the reluctance that General Powell, and most of his fellow officers, demonstrated to transform Desert Shield into Desert Storm.[24] Neither the starkness of the threat, the seriousness of the interests at stake, nor the amenability of the conditions on the ground to US capabilities were able to overcome the deeply embedded cautionary instincts that are a part of the US military's present ethic. They were even more pronounced, and dominated the policy debate, over Yugoslavia.

Prevailing US military doctrine is more constraining of the use of force than it is enabling. Reinforced as it is by popular sentiment, it limits the utility of the military assets nominally at the disposal of the President. Consequently, measured use of force in support of a diplomatic strategy has become exceedingly difficult. The implications of rising neo-isolationist sentiment for the conduct of American foreign policy were recognized by the Bush administration as early as 1992, even as it basked in the afterglow of triumph in the Gulf. Its surprisingly positive attitude toward expansion of the United Nations' peacekeeping capacities was motivated in good part by the practical calculation that the United States was not suited to a policeman's duties. Addressing the United Nations General Assembly in September 1992, President Bush declared US support for creating a standing UN force and pledged various forms of direct and indirect support for such a force, including: transport, logistics, C^3I, and training facilities.[25] Thereby, the ground was prepared for the Clinton administration to formulate its own more ambitious ideas for augmenting UN capabilities with the political encouragement and tangible assistance of the United States.

Yet the Clinton Presidency was handicapped from the outset by contradictory elements that lay just below the surface of its earnest commitment to multilateralism. The US military establishment's planning for the post-Cold War security environment had two features of cardinal importance for the terms of cooperation with both allies and collective security bodies: (1) a force structure and contingency planning that stressed national capabilities; and (2) a canon on the use of force whose stipulations set strict inflexible conditions and rules for how and when American power should be applied. As to the former, the language of declaratory security policy and the concrete problems reshaping and reorienting the US military were divergent. The former spoke of burden-sharing, multilateralism, and striking a new transatlantic balance of duties and obligations. The latter proceeded with attention concentrated on what the United States would be able to do alone. This was especially pronounced with regard to prospective threats, of a kind (i.e. sub-strategic, regional conflicts) that were most likely to arise – and for US participation in United Nations peacekeeping and peace-enforcing operations.

Thus, the Clinton administration's much-touted 'Bottom-Up' defence review debated the recondite technical issues of preparing to fight two wars at once with only a passing reference to the contribution of allies. Yet, this exercise unfolded simultaneously with the administration's elaboration of doctrines for multilateralism – understood in the two senses of working through collective security bodies *and* acting in fuller partnership with the Western allies – that were proclaimed as emblematic of the United States' new strategy of restrained internationalism. Hence, a discrepancy existed between the doctrines being developed by the Defense Department for the engagement of American military forces and the requirements for operationalizing multilateralism.

The specific problems that the Clinton administration encountered in trying to realize its goal of enhancing the United Nations' competence as a useful, perhaps necessary supplement to American – and Western – security policies was the most acute manifestation of a wider dilemma created for US leaders by a military doctrine that set stringent conditions for exploiting the country's enormous military assets and a force planning built on a unilateralist logic. For that doctrine and those plans, in combination with risk-averse and disengaged public attitudes, excluded a considerable range of purposes for which the armed forces might be employed. To concentrate on warfighting alone, to stress compellence above all else, is to deny oneself the opportunity to use force in a variety of demonstrative ways: for intimidation, for deterrence, for reassurance. These drawbacks were recognized by Secretary of Defense Les Aspin who set as one of the goals of his short tenure as Secretary the reintroduction of flexibility into official thinking about the ways and means of exercising military power. In a series of public speeches, he took exception to important parts of the Weinberger/Powell liturgy, even while showing obligatory obeisance to the virtues of its underlying philosophy and the probity of its authors.

Aspin offered a number of significant modifications in received doctrine. He rejected the 'all-or-nothing' school of thought which he characterized as 'unwilling to accept the notion that military force can be used prudently short of all-out war'.[26] Limited objectives, based on a case-by-case determination of interests and appropriate means, were required if the United States were to bring its weight to bear on a wider variety of security problems than those encountered during the Cold War. Technological innovations favoured that approach. Precision guided weapons, in particular, were cited as versatile instruments for sending a timely message and imposing an intolerable cost on an aggressor within the bounds of reasonable risk for the United States, its partners and a United Nations in whose name and in support of whose authority it may be acting.

The Aspin assessment figured in the Clinton administration's early conception of muscular multilateralism. Even as enthusiasm waned in the White House for an expansive United Nations peacekeeping role, the idea that the United States' unique technological assets justified a special place for Washington in any operations that it might undertake. Indeed, the policy statement on 'Reforming Multilateral Peace Operations' of May 1994 offers a veritable technical assistance programme to upgrade and reconfigure the UN's Department of Peacekeeping Operations so as to enable the world organization to perform its growing load of peace operations more effectively.[27] It reiterated the judgement that the United States 'benefits from having to bear only a share of the burden. We also benefit by being able to invoke the voice of the community of nations on behalf of a cause we support.'

The attempt to develop a more flexible set of guidelines for exploiting American military resources in the maintenance of international order while observing the tenets of the new military doctrine received a boost from General John Shalikashvili who replaced Colin Powell as head of the Joint Chiefs of Staff in mid-1993. Unlike his predecessor, he was not a strict constructionist. Shalikashvili had a more flexible interpretation of the conditions for using US military power. He also had a more relaxed attitude about the possible dangers of 'losing control' of a military operation undertaken for avowedly limited purposes. Though conservative and cautious by temperament, he was not obsessed by the spectres of 'mission creep' or the need for 'exit strategies'. This attitude was evident in his willingness to consider a US military action in Bosnia, and the backing he would lend for a predominant American role in IFOR.

For Shalikashvili, there are conditions where a limited use of military force could be effective for achieving limited purposes. As he stated in Congressional testimony, 'whenever we have been resolute [in Bosnia] – NATO particularly – we have been able to have our way. Whenever that was so, the Serbs read it very correctly and acted accordingly. And I am frustrated that we are often prevented from doing it, and lately more so than not.'[28] A belief in the utility of military force selectively applied led Shalikashvili to the judgement that airpower should be employed in Bosnia to force Serb compliance with United Nations resolutions to make them politically more tractable, and to protect UNPROFOR. In this, he took exception to the policies of his British and French counterparts. In a more reflective mode, he averred that 'the President must have in his tool bag, in addition to the diplomatic tools,... also the tool of military power to protect American interests, even if those interests are not vital'.[29] Secretary Perry spoke in a similar vein:

> Because the war in Bosnia was against the national interest of the United States... we should have been prepared to use or to threaten to use military force from the beginning.
>
> I do not see any other way of doing that except through NATO and, therefore, from the beginning we should have been prepared to use NATO. That implies to me commitment of US forces.[30]

Secretary of State Madeleine Albright has been even blunter in rejecting the Powell Doctrine as setting conditions so strict for the use of military force as to obviate its utility as an instrument of American foreign policy. In her words,

> There was this doctrine that you'd be dealing with a crazy dictator with six months to prepare and the earth was flat and you'd use overwhelming force and somebody else would pay. But those circumstances don't come along very often.[31]

There is not a settled, inflexible set of beliefs about the use of American military forces – even within the Pentagon. That was manifest during the Bosnian endgame. In August, Shalikashvili gave his unequivocal support to the sustained air-assault that cleared the way to Dayton. He then lobbied Congress to approve the IFOR deployment which he defended as necessary and prudent. In so doing, Shalikashvili did not abandon totally the Powell philosophy. He pressed for a narrow interpretation of IFOR's mandate and role. American soldiers would not be drawn into 'state-building' exercises à la Somalia, police the 'civilian' parts of the accords, or hunt down indicted war criminals. That said, the overall approach taken by the Joint Chiefs under Shalikashvili toward Bosnia gave evidence that the Pentagon was not monolithically and unqualifiedly opposed to unconventional, limited military missions. Cautionary instincts would still prevail, for the most part, and strict terms of deployment would be observed. The military's bias against peacemaking/keeping interventions remained. But US presidents would not have their hands tied when considering committing the country to such actions by implacable opposition from across the Potomac. More influential would be perceived political constraints and a Chief Executive's lack of either interest or aptitude for conducting the country's foreign affairs. Both of the latter traits are more likely to be seen and less likely to be overcome by force of circumstances in the world that the United States now inhabits.

A NEW LOOK AT 'PEACEKEEPING'

In order to salvage UN-style multilateralism from the wreckage of recent failures, and to safeguard the United States' stake in its workability as an institution, two things were called for: greater selectivity in making commitments to peacekeeping missions, and greater effectiveness in performing those that are accepted. In President Clinton's words: 'If the American people are to say yes to peacekeeping, the United Nations must know when to say no.'[32] The same lessons were being drawn by Secretary-General Boutros-Ghali who himself had begun to preach the wisdom of more restraint in taking on obligations and more prudence in how they were funded and executed. Thus, discretion had become the watchword at both the White House and UN headquarters.

From the official United States perspective, discretion has meant balancing the political need to observe the strict conditions on the terms of American participation in UN peacekeeping with the recognized need to offer some measure of American participation in order for the potential value of the UN to be realized. The Clinton administration acknowledged publicly that the 'participation of US military personnel in UN operations can... serve US interests. First, US military participation may, at times, be necessary to persuade others to participate in operations that serve US interests. Second, US participation may be one way to exercise US influence over an important UN mission, without unilaterally bearing the burden. Third, the US may be called upon and choose to provide unique capabilities to important operations that other countries cannot.'[33] This formulation succinctly stated a viewpoint that shaped official US policy toward UN peacekeeping through two administrations. The exceptional value of US status and US capabilities for making UN operations diplomatically acceptable and operationally effective; the advantages of leveraging those assets through the world body; and the hoped-for magnification of American influence, thereby, are constant themes.[34]

What had changed over time was a growing recognition of the difficulties in giving practical expression to that strategy. Those difficulties were exacerbated by the political ascendancy of a Republican leadership in Congress. The electoral tide not only ushered in an era of Congressional activism as the legislature sought to regain influence over the country's foreign policy. More specifically, it amplified the voice of that section of public opinion that is deeply suspicious of the United Nations as an institution and keen to withdraw unrestricted US contributions for its activities. For them and for those legislators who vent their feelings, the very idea of working through the UN body was dubious, at best – not just the terms and conditions of the United States' participation in any particular operation.

The Congress is not bashful either about asserting America's right to act unilaterally – even while condemning the failure of the European partners to pull their weight in the Atlantic partnership or presuming to dictate policy to the UN. This cluster of attitudes typifies measures incorporated in the National Security Revitalization Act promoted by the Republican-dominated Congress in 1995 and 1996.[35] Although the bill did not survive intact, its rough passage through the roiled political waters between Capitol Hill and the White House (as well as its draconian provisions) testified to how inclement the foreign policy climate had become. Those provisions on sharing the costs of UN peacekeeping operations, and the severe restrictions it sought to impose on the President's authority to place American troops under the operational control of non-Americans (including NATO allies), evinced a combination of prickly nationalism and suspicion of foreign entanglements.[36] Its most onerous provisions were deleted from the legislation eventually passed. The net effect, though, is to reinforce the constraining forces that work against the engagement of the country's soldiers. The move to legislate a prohibition on placing American troops under the operational command of another country's officers is illustrative of the problem created by the deep ambivalence about foreign commitments and military actions. Upholding the principle of US command carries the unmistakable implication that the United States must provide the preponderant forces for any joint action in order to justify its claim. But that means easing the pressure on allies to take on their proper share of duties and risks. President Clinton encountered this problem as early as February 1993 when he committed the US to providing half the manpower for a postulated Bosnian peacekeeping force, if a settlement was in place. The size of the American contribution was dictated by the judgement that popular backing for so large an expeditionary force would be forthcoming only if US officers were in command. (A reinforcing argument was made within the administration: for the job to be done right, the US should take charge.) However, the 25 000-man commitment needed to reach the 50 per cent level was of such a magnitude as to provoke strong opposition – in the earlier Democratic-controlled Congress as well as in the country at large. That opposition posed a serious obstacle to the winning of Congressional acquiescence, two years later, in the mounting of a US-led IFOR. Only inhibition about undercutting a Presidential commitment to implementation of an accord successfully brokered by the US stayed Congress's hand. In the end, legislative majorities chose not to challenge the President's authority, while withholding approval of the deployment itself.

Henceforth, the White House's flexibility in arranging the terms of American participation in any multilateral operations will be narrow since the command consideration has become a formal stipulation of both Congress and the White House. That means greater difficulty in meeting the Alliance acceptability standard and in winning popular support to the extent that sentiment chary of large-scale interventions is independent of command preferences.

COLLECTIVE SECURITY FUNCTIONS

United States policy toward peacekeeping activities under the aegis of collective security organizations continues to be problematic. A number of factors point toward greater reliance on the UN and

OSCE: the requirement for legitimizing the use of force – in any form; the redistribution of power and the desirability of diffusing responsibility among the Western allies; the diversity of security challenges, many of them unamenable to simple responses whether they involve the direct use of military force or not; and the value of setting precedents that apply to Russia or any other would-be hegemon in regions outside Europe. At the same time, US foreign policymakers are acting under tightening domestic constraints, political and now legal, that narrowly delimit what the country is able to commit to collective security operations and what it is even in a position to support. Buffeted by these cross-pressures, American policy will prevaricate before any question of multilateral peacekeeping and vacillate in fulfilling any obligations it does assume.

On balance, Washington will opt for informal arrangements, preferably ones organized through an institutionally congenial NATO, rather than seek to work its will and reach its ends by taking the obstacle-strewn route that lies through the UN or OSCE. Instead of enunciating principles or promulgating doctrines, the United States will be inclined to treat the questions of military engagement on an issue-by-issue basis. Domestically, *ad hoc* coalition-building will take the place of well-cultivated, pre-existing consensus. Furthermore, multilateralism – within the Alliance and when acting through collective security organizations – will have to be on American terms. Applying what will be a rigorous standard of selectivity in practice will mean asking less of collective security bodies and doing less in whatever operations they undertake.

Implicitly, and by incremental steps, the United States has edged toward a policy of encouraging the UN to revert to classic forms of peacekeeping. Traditional United Nations activities in support of peace fall into three broad categories: (1) conflict prevention – diplomacy undertaken to prevent a latent or embryonic conflict from leading to violent conflict; (2) conflict resolution – the moderation of interstate disputes by purely pacific means, fact-finding, mediation at the behest of the principals, conciliation, etc.; and (3) peacekeeping as consolidation of settlements already agreed via the monitoring of ceasefires, the placing of blue-beret peacekeepers as an interpositional force maintaining a buffer zone, and overseeing elections. All of these may also entail the facilitating role of deploying observers in conflict or potential conflict situations with the mandate to provide impartial, reliable information that could serve as the basis for subsequent action.

Conflict Prevention and Crisis Management

No doctrinal position exists in Washington on when resort to the machinery of the United Nations (or the OSCE) is desirable for performing these functions. Rather, there are a number of rough benchmarks that will guide judgements made on a case-by-case basis. First, and most important, is the estimation of stake. The lower the perceived American national interest, the greater the willingness to cede initiative to a collective security body. During the Cold War, relatively few disputes did not have overtones for the East–West rivalry; therefore, there was a consequent reluctance to accept the diminution of influence that results from accepting the UN's jurisdiction. Today, by contrast, there no longer is a presumption of a major American national interest being engaged or indirectly affected; and, thus, the United States believes that it has greater latitude in deciding when it will defer to the UN (e.g. Cambodia, El Salvador, Angola). Other criteria then come to the fore.

Political convenience is one of these criteria. It is the second benchmark for estimating the value and need to resort to the UN or OSCE. There is now an in-built domestic incentive for American administrations to shed responsibilities. Shifting the burden to collective security bodies is one way of doing so. However, such arrangements cease to be politically convenient when three factors converge: the outcome of a UN-directed diplomatic effort is unsatisfactory, it is viewed as such by Congress and the American public, and the matter in question has crossed a certain threshold of attention and diplomatic concern. The last is not always foreseeable. Chechnya provides an illustration of how a problem's salience can change markedly in unpredictable ways, albeit this was not an instance where the United States had deferred to a collective security organization or had a direct stake. There, Moscow's ham-handed attempt to reimpose its control over the breakaway province at first was viewed with equanimity by a Clinton administration that saw no reason to make a *cause célèbre* out of what was deemed an internal matter. The brutality of the Russian onslaught, though, evoked a wave of criticism that jeopardized the administration's conciliatory approach to the Yeltsin government while accentuating pressures for an acceleration of NATO expansion. In an analogous situation, where the issue is one of yielding primacy to the United Nations (or the OSCE), the potential for political embarrassment if things go badly wrong will have to be weighed against the costs and inconvenience of acting outside the ambit of collective security institutions.

Where there is a question of intervening to impose a settlement to a dispute or to quell a conflict, the United States will strongly oppose acting under UN rules of engagement. UNPROFOR's performance in Yugoslavia is a negative reference-point. The traditions and philosophy of UN style peacekeeping are seen as inimical to the effective use of force – either by intimidation or by compellence. American military leaders reject the idea that dedicated US forces should be specially trained in peacekeeping. As General Shalikashvili has declared, 'The best peacekeeping force is made up of the most competent soldiers.... If you do it the other way around,' US lives are put at risk.[37] The experience of NATO in Yugoslavia will not be repeated so long as the United States is centrally involved in the planning and execution of NATO engagements. Neither the Pentagon's conception of peacekeeping (except in its minimalist expression) or sentiment in Congress will permit a President to involve American troops in operations where the terms of engagement conform to the model followed in Bosnia.

In the US view, observing the principles of impartiality and consent of the parties in conflict makes sense in the conduct of traditional peacekeeping missions. But it is viewed as dangerous and counterproductive to observe them in conditions where one local protagonist has been singled out as the aggressor and another as its victim. Operations mounted to enforce Security Council resolutions that identify one party as a threat to peace should not be confused either with operations designed to separate and to monitor belligerents who already have come to the conclusion that further fighting is not desirable, *or* to oversee an accord already reached. The Washington interpretation of what happened in Bosnia is that such confusion was not due to coincidental circumstances. Rather, it is seen as stemming from the intrinsic contradictions between the United Nations' institutional culture and the requirements for effective peacemaking or peace-enforcing. The US cites the series of aborted attempts at using airstrikes in a strategy of coercive diplomacy as cases in point. In the US view, the effectiveness of NATO air power was seriously degraded by command arrangements that placed UN officials – civilian or military – in the position of determining what was done and how. Disputes over targeting rules were symptomatic of more fundamental flaws in the organization's standard *modus operandi*. Peacekeeping *à la* the UN stressed scrupulous impartiality and neutrality (regardless of the local parties' conduct), shied away from confrontations, avoided passing judgement on the issues in contention, and was designed to maintain the widest consensus among United Nations member states based on a lowest common denominator of agreement.[38]

The role of Special Envoy Akashi in undermining the strategy of using airstrikes as an instrument of intimidation was most irksome to aggrieved American officials. Washington came to find it intolerable that the West's position in Bosnia, and the credibility of NATO as an organization, should be hostage to the dubious judgement and muddled thinking of a UN official seemingly accountable to no one but the Secretary-General. In American eyes, the hesitations and false compromises fashioned endlessly by the UN Special Representative, Yasushi Akashi, exposed the fundamental flaw in the United Nations approach.

Arrangements that subordinate NATO to a United Nations command are seen in Washington as suffering from another serious liability. They add substantially to the dangers of divisiveness among the allies undercutting the Alliance's ability to act decisively and in concert. An inchoate alliance multilateralism was aggravated by confused 'decision-sharing' arrangements with the United Nations. It had proven a formula for incoherence and ineffectiveness. Everyone's problem turned out to be nobody's problem. Just as the West's resort to military action had been just enough to irritate but not enough to intimidate, so did spasmodic American initiatives manage to accentuate pre-existing strains among the allies (and with the UN) without being sustained and strong enough to force a course correction. The Clinton administration's lack of internal consensus on a fine-grained interpretation of the country's stakes in the ex-Yugoslavia, or on an integrated strategy, contributed to the tentativeness of the initiatives that Washington did take. Conversely, shared responsibility among governments and international organizations who disagreed about the most important issues of analysis and prescription took the pressure off the Clinton administration to sort itself out. Those frustrating experiences deepened the conviction that were the United States to move decisively to lead Western policy, NATO would have to relieve the United Nations of effective control as a condition for success.

It follows that in the future the United States will favour arrangements whereby the United Nations 'contracts out' those operations that involve more than traditional peacekeeping, especially where the interests at stake justify American military involvement. Subcontracting for the UN (or OSCE) is not without its drawbacks, though. First, in order to get the desired seal of approval from a collective security body, Washington must be prepared to accept that the mandate will not necessarily be drawn to its exact specifications. In Europe, neither the UN nor the OSCE can be expected to give unrestricted authorization to NATO so long as Russia has anything to say about the matter. Moreover, the precedent is not one that Washington would like to see extended to Russia individually or to the CIS, which is moving toward some form of Russian-dominated security structure.

The need to receive a legitimizing mandate from the UN/OSCE has the further drawback of bringing into the larger forum any differences that might exist between the United States and its West European allies. There, opportunities and temptations will exist to exploit the sentiments of non-alliance states to resolve inter-allied disagreements on terms less rather than more congenial to the United States. Once again, the experience on Yugoslavia carries a cautionary lesson. Nonetheless, for Washington a 'contracting out' arrangement would be preferable to leaving direction in the hands of the UN/OSCE where the dilution of American influence would be greater and the difficulty of exercising operational control diminished.

At the same time, US policymakers remain chary of shouldering the main responsibility for complex, dangerous tasks of conflict management or peacekeeping. The resulting dilemma was on display during the implementation of the Dayton Accords for Bosnia; so, too, were the adverse consequences of a policy that evades rather than seeks to resolve that dilemma. The arrangements for carrying out the political provisions were notable for their prolixity – allocating tasks among the NATO, the EU, the OSCE, and sundry UN agencies; ensconcing Carl Bildt, as High Representative, in the position of superintendent; and customizing a bilateral link between the US and Russia. The procedures for consultation and decision were as convoluted as the structures through which they operated were complex.

Washington's willingness to accept a set-up that seriously compromised the chances for accomplishing the purposes stipulated in Dayton reflected the continued ambivalence about its preferred role in the performance of collective security functions in Europe. The US distrusts its allies' will and capabilities but feels bound to encourage them to take on a large slice of collective responsibilities (both because of their avowed desire to do so and because it is deemed beneficial for the good health of the Alliance). It inclines to the belief that joint ends are more likely to be met if the United States were to exert active leadership yet shies away from running risks that could turn American public opinion against intervention. It chafes at power sharing deals that make it harder for the United States to get its way while welcoming the availability of other parties and institutions that can justify inaction (where costly) and can share the blame when goals are unmet.

The large uncertainty factor in estimating the value of collective security organizations means that a United States decision to support giving the United Nations/OSCE jurisdiction over a particular dispute will not imply a *laissez-faire* attitude. This is especially true in Europe where fresh lessons have been given of how unreasonable it is to expect conflicts of any kind to be easily encapsulated – politically and diplomatically, if not geographically. The corollary for US policy-makers is that the US should participate actively in the framing of mandates for collective security bodies engaged in preventive diplomacy and/or conflict management, in supporting those efforts either individually or via NATO as a sub-contractor to UN/OSCE, and in monitoring results closely.

The United States, as noted earlier, has come to view OSCE more favourably. It is seen as a useful 'half-way' house where security matters of a non-strategic nature can be addressed on a pan-continental basis. The OSCE provides a somewhat more manageable setting than does the United Nations; furthermore, it is one where an appropriately prominent place can be accorded the Russians with less danger of either confrontation or paralysis. Its suitability for performing classical collective security functions such as providing 'early warning' of local conflicts and conducting strictly defined peacekeeping operations is recognized. However, even these carefully circumscribed functions are not without drawbacks for American policy. In post-Dayton Bosnia, the OSCE was given a key responsibility of determining whether conditions had been met for free and fair elections scheduled for September 1996. Authority for doing so lay with the Swiss Foreign Minister serving as Chairman in Office of the OSCE, Flavio Cotti. His principal deputy was a retired US diplomat, Robert Fenwick, who headed the OSCE's Sarajevo mission. They had clear and abundant evidence, presented by internal reports of the monitoring group (and by an independent group of senior diplomats), that conditions fell far short of the standard that could justify certification. Despite it, the Clinton administration insisted on going ahead with the September elections for a number of expedient reasons

– the most prominent being the political need to claim success in a Bosnian peace process which it had authored and took pride in. In administration calculations, concern for the OSCE's institutional integrity ran a poor second to American electoral considerations. Washington undertook a high-pressure campaign that shamelessly ran roughshod over equivocal allied governments, sought to intimidate Mr Cotti and to exploit the presence of an American in a critical OSCE post.

In this instance, ironically, the international organization's outlook and attitude was not one that endangered the effectiveness of policy but rather fell short of an American standard of political acceptability. The uncomfortable truth is that the United States government cannot live without collective security bodies, even if living with them does not make life easy for American diplomacy. This ambiguous situational logic has not shaken the bedrock conviction of US policymakers that a NATO-centred approach to European security problems (and, in most instances, those that arise on the continent's periphery) is to be preferred. Neither unilateralism nor a pure multilateralism through the UN/OSCE can better balance the criteria of legitimacy, political acceptability and effectiveness. Consequently, by indirection more than by design, Washington is recommitting itself to a strategy of reestablishing NATO as the prime instrument for protecting Western security interests and for exerting Western political influence eastward. This is the convergent conclusion of 'traditionalists' who never have abandoned their orthodox vision of European security, the promoters of NATO enlargement, and the 'devolutionists' who have encouraged the gradual shifting of responsibilities on to a competent European Union. For the first, this outlook puts the question of consolidating and revivifying the NATO core at the top of the policy agenda – where it should be. For 'enlargers', it conflates the issue of continental security architecture with that of Alliance adjustment to post-Cold War conditions. For the devolutionists, it is seen regrettably as the only alternative to Western Europe's drift into self-involvement and impotency.

The odd men out of this emerging consensus on a NATO-centred strategy are those who follow two other schools of thought. (1) The principled multilateralists who pushed the Clinton administration's early policy of promoting an expanded role for the UN will be the spokesmen within policy circles (when they have access) for observing the requirement for a legitimizing imprimatur from the UN/OSCE. They also will urge full utilization of those bodies' capabilities of

Table 6.1 The various schools of thought and political orientation towards the deployment of United States armed forces

	Threat Assessment		Division of Labour	Preferred Organization	Legitimation (Importance)
	Europe	Out-of-Area			
Multilateralist Internationalists	H	H	Equity	MIX	M/H
Liberal Isolationists	M/L	L	Devolution	UN/OSCE	H
Nationalist Isolationists	Rising	H (selective)	Unilateral or Abstain	NATO	L
Traditionalists	H	M	US Leadership of Alliance	NATO	M
Pentagon	L	L	Unilateral or US-led Alliance	NATO	L

performing traditional conflict prevention and peacekeeping functions. (2) The outright neo-isolationists divide into two sub-categories. The liberal camp will staunchly oppose both the retreat from multilateralism and the expanded role of a US-led and dependent NATO. This group's political influence is in sharp decline. However, conservative, or 'nationalist' neo-isolationists, are in a political ascendancy. As UN-bashers, they will be pleased by a policy of downplaying collective security organizations. But they will be hard put to reconcile their defensive unilateralism with deepening commitments in and around Europe. In this sense, their predicament is the country's – especially if a Republican enters the White House. Paradoxically reticence about military involvements could make Washington more assertive at the diplomatic plane – assuming an attentive and diplomatically adept Executive.

NATO EVOLUTION

NATO's slow, on-going transition from a straightforward mutual defence alliance to an alliance *cum* diplomatic formation, with a broader purpose and an extended geographical reach, is part and parcel of the adjustment in Alliance roles and functions. The process proceeds in each of the allied capitals and in Brussels among the allies collectively. The thresholds crossed in Yugoslavia have opened the way for NATO to act broadly as the West's security agent beyond mutual defence of its own territory. For, once the *functional* boundary limiting the organization to mutual defence was crossed, there was no obvious *geographical* or *political* line circumscribing its field of possible action. Consequently, three contentious aspects of the transatlantic security relationship now are intermingled: NATO's scope of action; its relationship to collective security organizations; and its sibling rivalry with the WEU.

NATO's self-declared successful 'out-of-function' foray in Bosnia reinforced the conviction in Washington about the organization's criticality for both maintaining political order and for the United States to bring its weight to bear on European security problems. A simple set of equations was made: the West = NATO, NATO = US leadership, US leadership = effective action. The self-administered compliment implies an American indispensability that sits uneasily on the American body politic. It confirms a key role for the United States in Europe's affairs; but it also carries the implication that Washington could not be selective in deciding when and how it would engage itself. Unqualified, open-ended commitments were as disconcerting for many Americans to contemplate in the aftermath of the successful Bosnian intervention as they were in the preceding four years of doubt and equivocation as to American interests at stake and the level of risk they warranted. That was made clear by the Clinton administration's dedication to a restricted role for IFOR and a strict observance of its time-bound deployment.

The two contradictory trends – functional enlargement and growing American insularity – were visible as early as 1991. The Rome Accords of November 1991 provided the legitimizing basis for widening NATO's purview, geographically and functionally. The 'New Strategic Concept' agreed at Rome cleared the way for Alliance missions out-of-area, out-of-function, and in concert with collective security bodies.[39] NACC and then Partnership for Peace were derivative of that enabling accord. Both programmes, however energetically pursued, still left obscure the United States' answer to the looming question of what obligations it was prepared to assume to deal with local conflicts and latent security threats in Eastern Europe or in places on Europe's periphery. Washington's vacillation in defining its roles on the Yugoslav crisis was both effect and cause of that uncertainty. As egregious failures there took their toll on the West's overall position, Washington's latent impulse to take charge resurfaced. Indeed, the Clinton administration's sudden move to press for NATO enlargement in Autumn 1994 was a declaration in principle of the United States' intention to reassert its leadership on all, or nearly all, issues of European security.

The push for NATO expansion was apiece with Washington's reinvigorated diplomacy directed at forcing a settlement to the simmering conflicts in the ex-Yugoslavia. Yet, at the same time there was no evident shift in US contingency planning for military operations, in intervention criteria, in the guidelines for participation in multilateral peacekeeping operations, or – most assuredly – in the American people's willingness to run risks and to make sacrifices. If anything, the psychological retrenchment, restricted vision, and scepticism about the efficacy of intervention all seemed to have been strengthened. The Clinton administration had embarked on a strategic course without preparing the ground domestically or with allies – or even having thought through its ramifications. They thus were forced to walk a tightrope, balancing a wider role entailing new commitments in Europe against internal constraints.

The Clinton administration's inability to fashion a conceptual framework suited to Europe's present realities, while offering guideposts for reaching the West's goals, was evident in the formulation and presentation of the NATO expansion initiative. Enlargement represented rather than settled the United States' irresolution. It was an irresolution at once conceptual, political and structural. Conceptually, it mixes but does not reconcile elements of mutual defence, collective security and concert of power (in its last ancillary institutionalization of a 'special relationship' with Russia). Politically, it leaves unanswered the cardinal question of what is the 'West' now that its mortal foe is vanquished? Is it a zone of political culture? a security community? a diplomatic formation? or a sum of the three? The question cannot be side-stepped because it has practical implications for maintaining the unity of NATO's core.

If we expect Europe to drift toward some amorphous assemblage of like-minded and like-motivated market democracies, then less priority need be given ensuring the diplomatic coherence and close collaboration of the Western powers. If the future is visualized in terms of a benign multipolarism (as President Chirac has declared – at times), then the idea and need of a disciplined Atlantic Alliance is *passé*. If, by contrast, the overriding feature of post-Cold War conditions is unipolarity – the predominance of Western values, institutions, and power – then realizing the goal of integrating the European continent on that basis depends crucially on finding methods for the West's collective tutelage to be sustained, constant and productive.

Two structural issues were left unresolved by the enlargement initiative. One was the form and function of a European pillar within the Alliance; the other how to meet the need for a collective political direction of joint enterprises where military force served diplomatic ends. The two intersected in so far as the degree of autonomy enjoyed by the West European allies, and their access to US-held military assets, would depend in part on the United States' willingness to relinquish its controlling influence that was institutionalized in NATO's integrated command structure *and* to shift powers on to the organization's inter-governmental organs for policy direction and oversight. In addition, to envisage operations led by the WEU was to raise the question of the relations between its governing authority (EU-linked or otherwise) and the North Atlantic Council. Finally, strengthening the Alliance's mechanisms of political direction was a logical requirement for both making the determination of when NATO would 'hand-off' operational responsibility to WEU and deciding what the terms of political-diplomatic coordination would be between a United States, whose abstention could not be equated with uninterest, and more independent-minded allies.

The arduous negotiations that led to the Berlin accord on giving practical meaning to the Combined Joint Task Forces concept highlighted two salient truths of NATO's post-Cold War identity: (1) the slowly emerging consensus on the desirability of building a European Security and Defence Identity, and (2) the difficulties of reshaping institutions dominated by US military commanders, US tangible military assets, and – not least – US leadership. The Berlin accords should be read as a good faith attempt at reconciling them, one that opens possibilities for realizing the goal of a better equilibrated transatlantic alliance while leaving large margins of uncertainty as to whether a stable new balance had been found and whether envisaged arrangements would prove effective when activated. Only experience could provide the answers.

The CJTF deliberations were at least as much about principles, and status, as they were about performance. This was especially true of the positions taken by the main protagonists – the United States and France. From Washington's perspective, the overriding concern was to find a way for the Clinton administration to reconcile its genuine wish to satisfy the Europeans' avowed desire to achieve a ESI, and the American interest in having allies able to shoulder a heavier share of Alliance burdens, on the one hand, with doing nothing that seriously compromises NATO's integrated command (deemed the essential ingredient for successful joint operations) or prevents the United States from making its voice heard on matters that involve American interests – even if they do not entail engaging American forces, on the other. The compromise eventually fashioned offers a formula that suffices to meet these different American interests even though it does not entirely quell uneasiness about what will happen when and if the agreed provisions are put to the test.

Qualms are especially pronounced among the uniformed services. The Pentagon's resistance to the final compromise reflected the military establishment's reluctance even to visualize letting go the levers of command and the low threshold of tolerance for ambiguity in either command arrangements or contingency plans. The Clinton administration's civilian policymakers had different apprehensions. The main one was the longstanding doubts that the European allies would prove up to the task were they to act independently of the United States. On this score, the Yugoslav experience fed deep-seated anxieties. Furthermore, there was thinly disguised feeling that the French vision of CJTF had less to do with effective military action than with advancing the Paris agenda of augmenting its influence over European affairs.

After five years of tug-o'-war with Paris over European security architecture, American officials were aware that French thinking was oriented more by an interest in using institutions to shape the diplomatic field of action than by an assessment of what arrangements were most likely to produce efficacious action. That is to say, functional utility was subordinated to considerations of national status and political influence. France's earlier strategy of seeking to achieve an ESI via the EU was seen as having been frustrated by a combination of factors: the resistance of some partners (above all, the British) to placing the WEU directly under EU direction; France's own hesitation to see security matters fall within the purview of truly federal structures (the German preference); the allies' manifest unwillingness to commit the resources needed to duplicate expensive NATO assets in intelligence gathering, transport, etc.; and a realization that since an American presence (via NATO) in European security was inescapable (and, for some purposes, desirable), it made sense to work through NATO rather within than against it or on its institutional fringes.

Given this reading of French policy, it was understandable that Washington should be reluctant to give a blank cheque to a political abstraction called a European Security Identity, and that it should be agnostic on the question of whether the Berlin accords inaugurated a golden new age of Atlantic partnership or, instead, introduced a new time of troubles.

One implication of the Berlin accords was clear: the political dimension of NATO's institutional identity would be of growing importance. France's demanding terms for reconciliation with NATO brought the matter to the surface. Paris had its own definite ideas on arrangements for giving the Alliance political direction. CJTF forced everyone to give the question their attention. France's objective, in a nutshell, was to enhance the authority of the North Atlantic Council; curb the independence of SACEUR along with a commensurate strengthening of the Military Committee; and create a plurality of possible command structures for the activation and deployment of all and any NATO military assets which did not involve the United States directly.

With the arrival of Jacques Chirac at the Elysée, the French position acquired sharper definition and its overtures greater credibility. His Minister of Defence, Charles Millon, outlined the French conception of a renovated NATO in a series of increasingly candid statements. The picture he drew had five notable features. (1) The North Atlantic Council (NAC), as the supreme body of the Alliance, should be the locus of all authoritative, collective decisionmaking. It should provide the framework for military as well as political consultation. (2) The reinforced authority of the NAC should embrace more frequent and active meetings of defence ministers, who would link the NAC's political authority to the operational functions of the Defence Planning Committee. The latter is deemed an essential, central body in the Alliance's decisionmaking structure. (3) The Military Committee should participate fully in the process of planning the Alliance's structures, in building the European pillar, and in assessing the practical consequences of enlargement. (4) The affirmation of a European security identity should occur *within* a more flexible Alliance structure. The NATO chain of command 'must be able to function in a "European mode"'. (5) Europeanization of the Alliance should be manifest in planning as well as operations, i.e. in the politico-military decision process overall.[40] The French agenda, so formulated, raises basic questions of the Alliance's diplomatic functions and its attendant political direction. (The links between France's policy of re-engagement with NATO and its ideas regarding organizational direction are examined systematically by Frédéric Bozo in Chapter 3.)

The United States, for its part, has been shy about a full and candid debate over NATO's political direction. In the past, American diplomacy calculatingly sought to avoid dealing with its allies *en masse,* preferring to treat with each one-on-one in the belief that so doing made it easier for Washington to work its will. That *modus operandi* is no longer as conveniently available. A European caucus, however occasional and undisciplined it might be, is becoming a feature of Alliance life. Moreover, acquiescence in American leadership, including manipulation of nominally multilateral policymaking procedures, is largely a thing of the past. Much of this is recognized in official Washington but leaves it discomfited. The lack of a strong initiative to make NATO structures and practices the mainsprings of concerted Western diplomacy expresses this apprehension – an attitude reinforced by an underlying ambivalence as to the importance of closely coordinated policies and the absence of a strategic design. Yet if serious challenges to that benign hegemony are posed by a reassertive Russia, local nationality conflicts and extra-European security threats, the need for a coordinated and well-orchestrated allied diplomacy – and the issue of how it might be structured – will not be easy to avoid.

Scepticism about making the NAC the central instrument for a truly multilateral process of deliberation and debate will not soon evaporate. At Berlin, the Clinton administration did bow to an irresistible situational logic. The text of the Berlin accords is studded with references to the responsibilities of the NAC and the Military Committee. Moreover, the allies announced the establishment of a Policy Coordination Group (PCG) which is intended 'to meet the need, especially in NATO's new missions (non-Article 5 operations), for closer coordination of political and military viewpoints'. The further reference to 'increased political-military cooperation in particular through the PCG, and effective exercise of political coordination by the North Atlantic Council through the Military Committee' is tied to the concept of 'one system capable of performing multiple functions'.[41]

The Berlin accords undoubtedly will result in some reinvigoration of the Alliance's mechanisms for collective consultation. It is less obvious that the allies have made firm pledges that will translate into diplomatic concertation that is both smooth and adequate. After all, the allies' failings in this regard so vividly on display through the long years of the Yugoslav conflict (and once again evident in the botched implementation of the Dayton Accords' political provisions) had less to do with structure than purpose and political will. NATO's suitability for serving as the instrument for a concerted Western diplomacy remains to be established. NATO structures and institutional culture express its nature as a military alliance. Mechanisms for political oversight and direction have always been a subordinate concern to Washington. One cannot dispute the critique of existing arrangements made by French officials on this score, however tendentious they might be. As one commentator on the French rapprochement with NATO has observed:

> First, Allied governments have used the Defence Planning Committee as a parallel council, effectively leaving NATO with two, coequal governing bodies. Under NATO's collective defence structure the DPC and the major NATO Commands (MNCs) have even exercised most of the real power within NATO, despite the NAC's status as the Alliance's supreme decision-making body and the MNCs' subordinate position to the Military Committee. If the NAC is to have the authority it was originally intended to have, it must meet with both foreign and defence ministers. Second, the separation between the NAC and the military implementing bodies of the Alliance deprives political decision-makers of adequate exposure to more technical military issues.[42]

Remedying NATO's political deficit requires more than tinkering with the organization chart. It is the institutional culture and habits entrenched by 40-odd years' experience that must be overcome. Arrangement for full consultation, candid debate and focused deliberation are not difficult to conceive. Breathing life into them is another matter. That depends on the conviction of major Western governments that a collective diplomacy is essential to achieving national and common purposes. One should think that the chastening experience in Yugoslavia and the looming challenge in Russia are sufficient to engender the necessary awareness and will. They have not yet been forthcoming, though. In this regard, the United States has been as neglectful of developing NATO's political capability as have the European allies. Some of the latter are uneasy about concentrating such a capability in a US-dominated organization at a time when the transatlantic balance is shifting and the project of European Union construction is a top priority. The thinking of many American officials, for their part, is still coloured by Cold War practices, as we have noted.

Objectively speaking, the challenges that are likely to compose the post-Cold War security agenda are ones that demand a subtle intertwining of the military and diplomatic. Preventive diplomacy, conflict management, and peacemaking/enforcing cannot be handled well on an *ad hoc*, piecemeal basis. They require that the West bring to bear their united weight acting as a political formation through a security organization that lends their diplomacy credibility. Diplomatic competence depends on maintaining NATO's military competence, and vice versa. The allies paid a stiff price for failing to recognize this truth in Yugoslavia. Their disjointed, mostly half-hearted attempts at intervention produced negative diplomatic synergy. Moreover, the Western powers' lack of conviction or concertation meant that Western interests were hostage to the skill, wisdom and influence of others. Deferring to the United Nations was convenient, but non-responsible. For three years, questions of Balkan war and peace were placed in the hands of a Japanese official in a United Nations post. His manifest lack of qualification for the job did not move any of the major Western powers to seek his removal. Some found him a useful ally or foil. Partial Western influence was exerted via French and British commanders of UNPROFOR. But they were occasional tools for advancing expedient, parochial agendas in Paris and London. The United States, too, yielded to the temptation to avoid tough issues by hiding behind the skirts of the United Nations. At times, Washington also displayed an unbecoming readiness to allow its military commanders, serving in NATO-*cum*-UN roles, an unhealthy degree of independence in deciding how to implement policy – once having declared off-limits action that could cause the White House political problems.

Admiral Leighton E. Smith, head of NATO's southern command, which conducted the airstrikes of May and then September 1995, and who later directed Operation Joint Endeavour, was tacitly given extraordinarily wide latitude. During the bombing campaigns, he made common cause with UNPROFOR commanders to weaken the terms of the NATO ultimata to the Bosnian Serbs and then to attenuate the airstrikes when undertaken. More important, and more revealing of the lack of adequate political oversight, Admiral Smith and General George A. Joulwan, commander of IFOR, were granted the licence to interpret the Dayton Accords in ways that served the Pentagon's purpose of minimizing risks to their men, but jeopardized achieving larger purposes. Their 'strict construction' of IFOR's role, of course, conveniently served President Clinton's political interests at home, and their avoidance strategy was not unwelcome by preoccupied Western European governments. That said, there is no gainsaying the fact that IFOR military commanders in effect implicitly assumed proconsular powers in the policy-void created by the distracted and divided Western governments.

High Representative Carl Bildt, for his part, bore an exalted title but had no backing or clear brief from his several masters. Major EU governments were chary of according him the authority that might set unwelcome precedents for a Common Foreign and Security Policy about which they all harboured doubts. The Clinton administration was neither comfortable with delegating serious powers to a non-accountable (non-controllable) European nor inclined for its own parochial reasons to confront hard decisions in Bosnia and divisive issues in the Alliance. Neither arrangement was a model of Alliance responsibility – collective or individual. Other mechanisms for political coordination, and the enhancement of existing ones are called for: so as to discourage NATO commanders from crossing the line between policymaking and implementation (whether acting on their own judgement or under instruction from a home government); and so as to place responsibility with appropriate accountable parties. Not to do so is to put conscientious military men in an untenable position where they are tempted to make decisions on matters outside their purview and competence, at most, or invited to allow the self-interest of their services to guide their actions, at least.

Moreover, to gloss over major policy differences among the allies, leaving its executants bereft of guidance or design, is merely to postpone the day of reckoning. Indeed, the consequently flawed implementation of a supposedly common strategy exacerbated the conditions in Bosnia that had to be mastered, while aggravating inter-allied frictions. This is the clear lesson of the West's failed multilateral effort in Yugoslavia. With four years to learn it, the post-Dayton lapse into incoherence does not lend confidence to prognoses for a renovated Alliance.

Reform à la Française

France's conditioned move back into the NATO fold seemed to refocus the related issues of command structure, political oversight, enlargement and the Alliance's 'Europeanization'. The scope of French aims for a 'global' reform of NATO, as a condition for its rejoining, caught Washington unawares. Clinton administration officials were familiar, of course, with France's exalted self-image. But the audaciousness of the Chirac government's claims came as a surprise. Even more unsettling was the backing given the French position by Germany. The United States underestimated the enormous weight that Chancellor Kohl attached to a close collaboration between

Bonn and Paris; the tactical calculations bound up with the momentous and hazardous Maastricht process; and the linkages that both allies made between the proposed 'Europeanization' of NATO and the strategy for its enlargement. Washington, accustomed to German support – if not deference – on fundamental Alliance issues, now found Bonn making common cause with France on the sensitive question of high-level commands. Germany saw itself as facilitator of a Franco-American conciliation by lending its support for a reform programme that amalgamated elements of each ally's position. A partial redistribution of posts accompanied by creation of a parallel European command structure conforming to the CJTF principle, it argued, maintained NATO's political unity and integrated command while accommodating European interest and French aspirations. As Volker Ruhe declared, a greater European presence in top leadership roles conformed to the goal of creating the possibility for Europe to act on its own as well as helping to bring France back into the Alliance fold – something that Bonn accorded the utmost importance.[43] Although the Clinton administration itself had expressed a readiness three years earlier to a shift in the transatlantic balance, it found forthright assertions that it was time to translate that principle into a tangible action on the sensitive command question unacceptable on both strategic and political grounds.

To relinquish NATO's southern command (AFSOUTH) was seriously to undermine the United States' ability to exercise predominant influence over the gamut of Mediterranean and Middle Eastern security problems. The concession of maintaining the Sixth Fleet's autonomy would do little to assuage American anxieties. For the stake was control of the field of diplomatic action. The fleet was a critical instrument for this control but not in itself the determining factor. The Clinton administration was not about to concede France the position of European surrogate acting on a co-equal basis with the United States in dealing with the Middle East peace process, the Gulf, or elsewhere.

Resistance to French ambitions was reinforced by the recognition that the President would pay a heavy political price were he to be seen as giving up traditional US leadership. The Pentagon adamantly rejected the idea of relinquishing the southern command, the Navy understandably being most upset at losing one of its prestigious posts. The White House would not sacrifice four years' work in repairing relations with the brass by doing something guaranteed to provoke a row. In addition, the barrage of criticism that would await him in Congress could severely damage prospects of healing the rifts on foreign policy which had bedevilled the first Clinton administration. While Clinton harboured no ambition to carve out his place in history through signal achievements abroad, he needed a smooth working relationship on Capitol Hill to help ensure that foreign policy issues did not upset his domestic agenda. Becoming the focus of a nasty debate over who 'lost the Sixth Fleet' was a dread prospect.

As for the notion that a 'Europeanized' NATO would make its enlargement more palatable to the Russians, Washington had ambivalent feelings. The Clinton administration was searching avidly for any formula or formulation that could help square the circle on enlargement. If projects like CJTF would assuage Russian anxieties, that was a welcome bonus. However, to use the concept to justify conceding to ambitious French demands intended to curtail American influence in the Alliance would give internal NATO reform a meaning and direction that had mischievous implications. Furthermore, some American officials were uneasy about the connotation that there were differences in kind between how 'soft' Europeans and 'hard' Americans would – and should – deal with a Russia that might veer from the path of conciliation. Although that may be only an academic question at the moment, few in Washington are so sanguine as to assume that it will remain so.

The more overt, self-interested linkage that France made in conditioning its approval for enlargement on the satisfaction of French views on structural reform received a less equivocal response.[44] In the American view, it was out of order for a historic initiative with profound implications to be held hostage to the parochial interests of one Alliance member. Clinton administration officials in fact never expected the French to try seriously at imposing a veto since they knew that Paris could not afford to stand in the way of something that its German partner believed to be a strategic issue of the highest order. France, never happy about enlargement, might feel free to use the issue to promote its own agenda, but at the end of the day had resigned itself to what had become inevitable.[45]

France's comprehensive plan to press its post-Cold War agenda within the Alliance, rather than from a critical position outside it, also had a bearing on the arrangements to be made for bringing Russia into a formal institutional relationship with NATO. The Clinton administration signalled early on that it favoured extending to Moscow a package of compensatory measures to sweeten the bitter pill of enlargement. The prize element was to be some form of institutionalized place for Russia within the Alliance itself. Responding to Russian demands for a permanent consultative mechanism dating from 1994, Washington thinking moved progressively to the judgement that satisfying it was in the interest of all parties. The notion took hold that by doing so the groundwork could be done for a strategic partnership between the Western powers and Russia even as NATO expanded geographically.

At the NATO ministerial meeting in September 1996 in Norway, Secretary Perry revealed how far the United States was prepared to go in that direction. A set of far-reaching steps was proposed with the preface that 'NATO is building a circle of security in Europe...[and] I believe that Europe cannot be secure unless Russia is inside that circle.'[46] They included:

- To consult closely on any possible NATO-led force that might remain in Bosnia in 1997.
- To establish permanent liaison officers at NATO headquarters in Brussels.
- To have access to planning done by NATO rapid reaction elements under the umbrella of the Combined Joint Task Force.
- To be involved in future crisis-management.
- To attend regular meetings at all levels up to defence minister.
- To post officers to the International Military Staff.

Taken together, these proposals could amount to a sort of *de facto* membership, a 'voice but not a vote'. Indeed, US officials implied that Russia might eventually become a fully integrated member of NATO's political structure on a model similar to that used by France and Spain.

The Clinton administration, in truth, was less committed to such drastic concessions than Perry's forthright remarks suggested. He expressed the Clinton administration's sentiments and the outlines of a plan still under construction rather than the finished product. The United States would temporize in the intervening period before the conclusive agreements on European security were reached at the 1997 summit meeting.

The Clinton administration did find itself in accord on the issue of permanent consultative mechanisms for Russia with both Bonn and Paris. The former was expected since Chancellor Kohl's government, and the Chancellor personally, had been adamant that conciliation with Moscow must be given equal weight with the objective of reassuring and stabilizing its eastern European neighbours. France's position, though, raised some eyebrows in Washington.[47] On the face of things, it seemed incongruous that Paris would countenance possible weakening of NATO's integrity as a Western club at the very time when it was resuming full membership with an ambitious strategy for enhancing French influence within it. Scepticism gave way to suspicion in some quarters that by backing plans for a Russian role inside NATO the Chirac government was motivated by the twin desires of constricting further the United States' ability to dominate the organization and of strengthening its own influence in Moscow. Could it be that France contemplated bolstering Russia as a counterweight to the United States and Germany? That question could not be raised, nor even considered, so long as American policy *vis-à-vis* Russia paralleled that of Paris.

Strikingly, no Western capital fixed on what seemingly was the most serious issue raised by the prospect of an institutionalized Russian role in NATO: the danger of it being a disruptive influence on Alliance deliberation and policymaking. All the major governments disparaged the idea that the organization's integrity might be compromised. Confidence on this score was based on two judgements. One was that Russia, for the foreseeable future, would have neither the inclination nor ability to pursue an effective diplomacy – either because its political weakness foreclosed a clever strategy of manipulation and because it could not afford to run the risk of conflicts with the West. The other reassuring notion was that the Western powers would instinctively pull together, relying on informal working parties as well as the Alliance's formal machinery, in the unlikely event that they had to deal with a trouble-making or antagonistic Russia. This equanimity prevailed despite the evidence of 'Yugoslavia' that Western solidarity and concert could not be taken for granted. The preoccupation with the French challenge on command appointments, in association with the complications of enlargement, diverted attention from the challenge of preparing NATO for expanded functions, for a concerted strategic diplomacy, and for providing the requisite oversight.

OUT-OF-AREA

The foregoing review of the United States' evolving perspective on peacekeeping operations mandated by the UN or OSCE has concentrated on Europe. It examines three sets of issues: those relating to the terms of transatlantic cooperation; those relating to the interface between Western mutual defence organizations (NATO and WEU) and collective security organizations (UN/OSCE); and those relating to the United States' changing vision of its global interests and international role generally. All are pertinent to an assessment of official US policy towards its participation in collective security operations outside Europe.[48]

There are nonetheless noteworthy points of difference in how Washington thinks about non-European security issues, as opposed to European ones, that should be considered before extrapolating the analysis. Firstly, the principles of selectivity and discretion for determining whether and how the United States should commit itself to dealing directly with a problem will be observed more scrupulously. In its monitoring of European developments there is a presumption that a conflict situation or threat to political stability warrants close attention because the American stake in Europe as a whole is so high. Yugoslavia was an outstanding exception to this rule, one that is explainable in terms of a peculiar concatenation of circumstances related to the Maastricht process of European construction, domestic American politics, the Gulf distraction, and the historical discontinuity produced by the collapse of the Soviet Union. The foremost lesson that the US has drawn from that experience is that it cannot afford to absent from such conflicts without risking damage both to Europe's future welfare and to the US position in European affairs. The presumption of a major American interest does not hold in regions on Europe's periphery with two important exceptions: the Persian Gulf and Israel.

Second, it follows that as a matter of principle, there will be a greater disposition both to rely more on the United Nations and to encourage a larger contribution from allies in dealing with whatever challenges might emerge. This dictum holds for such crises as might occur in the Caucasus, in the Maghreb, or in more distant locations.

Third, in practice it will prove difficult for the United States to substitute either form of multilateralism for what has been its longstanding policy of safeguarding its prerogatives for unilateral action and keeping at arm's length the United Nations and allies alike – except when their involvement accorded with Washington's reading of how they might serve American purposes. In the Cold War past, official Washington reactions to allied parochialism alternated between fatalistic acceptance and sharp annoyance. Long periods of resigned tolerance for the 'free-riding' and self-indulgent behaviour of allies were punctuated by bouts of outrage when Washington thought its partners' behaviour was egregiously irresponsible. This behaviour has been seen by United States officials as companion to policies and actions that left it up to the United States to protect Western interests put at risk in regional conflicts. The list of grievances was a long one, covering, *inter alia*, some West European coddling of dangerous regimes for selfish reasons (lucrative commercial dealings, immunity from terrorist actions); the withholding of facilities for critical US missions during the 1973 Yom Kippur war and air raid against Libya; and being less than rigorous in the enforcement of controls on sensitive export items (Iran). For Americans, that is no longer an acceptable arrangement. But neither Washington, nor the Alliance together, has yet to come up with a viable alternative.

In the absence of a definitive strategy in Washington, and the lack of a common strategic design by the West as a whole, American attitudes toward 'out-of-area' security engagements will be made in reference to a number of rough benchmarks.

(1) The more seriously the threat is perceived (a compound of stake and risk), as in Europe too, the stronger will be the American inclination to limit dependence on the UN restrictive mandates that deny the United States, and the West, the freedom to act in accordance with their judgement as to what is required.

(2) An informal coalition relying on NATO assets, if not NATO itself, will be the preferred instrument for dealing with any threat that might require military action. In this regard, the Yugoslav experience had the salutary effect of setting welcome precedents. The issue regarding the Washington Treaty's applicability to the Yugoslav situation had less to do with geography than mandated responsibility. At issue was not whether Yugoslavia was 'out-of-area', but rather whether NATO had the authority to act where and when there was no direct threat to one of its members. That logic extends beyond Europe. The planning for NATO-managed and -directed military operations in Yugoslavia was a declaration that the Alliance now saw its functions as reaching beyond self-defence alone. In this one respect, the changes in post-Cold War Europe have made it easier for the United States and its NATO partners to cooperate. The United States as a global power with global interests has almost invariably been more interested in facing up to out-of-area security issues, and in drawing the European allies into them, than has its NATO partners. With the purely defence tasks now so much less urgent and serious, and with out-of-area issues

on NATO's doorstep where they pose more immediate and practical problems for the European allies than for North America, those issues no longer split the US so distinctly off from its European partners in NATO.

(3) Since 'out-of-area' operations – such as those in Bosnia – that derive from the more informal procedures specified in Article 4 of the Washington Treaty rather than the more formal, automatic mechanisms provided by Article 5, they offer a welcome measure of flexibility in how an operation is designated, the forces organized and the command structure arranged. The modifications in NATO plans and force structures since 1991 encourage *ad hoc* arrangements by providing a versatile range of capabilities. Versatility is a particular asset in preparing for operations where the level of force required may change over time. The availability of forces that can perform missions ranging from traditional forms of peacekeeping through peace enforcement to significant war-fighting is an obvious advantage. Although US policymakers will do everything within their power to avoid committing themselves to situations where an unforeseen escalation of mission purpose can occur, it may not be possible to reduce that risk to zero. Therefore, having the capacity to escalate is a welcome asset that only a NATO-managed operation provides. Putting NATO in the lead has the further advantage in American eyes of reducing the chances that mismanagement will result in such an unanticipated mission-jump.

Today, the United States government finds itself caught between its globalist approach to international affairs, as well as its instinctive activism, and a waning ability or inclination to assert itself in the accustomed manner. Raising the alarm about a troubling situation carries with it the implicit obligation to initiate preventive or remedial action – for which the country might no longer be prepared. In the case of Bosnia, those divergent impulses opened an embarrassing gap between a rhetoric that expressed an intellectual judgement about the significance of what was occurring (and the need for more forceful Western action) and a policy position that expressed the new constraints on American actions.

Where and how the United States strikes a balance between the belief in its own superior judgement and capability, on the one hand, and the desire to curtail its commitments and encourage load-sharing, on the other, will be done on a case-by-case basis. Whatever guidelines are promulgated, whatever principles enunciated and declarations made, they will be no surer a measure of American action in the specific instance than they have been for the past three years. Similar hesitancy in making policy choices in other Western capitals will increase the likelihood that no common Alliance view on how to address 'out-of-area' security problems will crystallize in the near or medium term.

BILATERAL RELATIONS

The firm transatlantic agreement on basic strategic purposes during the Cold War era obscured variations in the bilateral ties between the United States and its major West European allies (the turbulence in the Franco-American relationship standing apart). Now those variations are assuming greater significance as each Atlantic partner feels free to be distinctly itself. Less is predetermined in how more self-confident European partners relate to American leaders who themselves are no longer entirely comfortable in their mantle of leadership and unsure of how to put their dealings with allies on a more equitable footing.

In the past, Washington may have called the tune but in fact the interplay with each Western capital had its own distinctive music. The harmonies have changed, even if the melody is recognizable.

Washington/Bonn

German and American conceptions of post-Communist Europe resemble each other. They are essentially neo-Wilsonian. There is a dedication to the goal of cultivating a continental-wide civil society rooted in democratic liberalism, *and* a genuine belief that it is a realizable goal. The moralistic strain of both country's approach to international questions reflects this commitment to reforming politics internally and inter-state. Therefore, they believe it is both proper and necessary to judge the behaviour of states in terms of whether they conform to universalizable norms of good behaviour.

These similarities have been on display in Yugoslavia. Throughout the long, troubled years of fitful Western diplomacy, the United States and Germany were most consistent in their profession of principle (observance of international law; the obligation to act against aggression; vindication of its victims). Furthermore, they found expedient compromise of these principles more difficult to swallow than did their counterparts in London and Paris. Reluctance to accept 'solutions' that confirmed local power realities derived as well from a different interpretation of the conditions for continental stability. The Yugoslav conflict was seen as setting precedents for the rest of post-communist Europe; i.e. modelling behaviour, determining the West's credibility in committing itself to upholding rules of conduct, and testing the validity of the rhetorical proposition that both ends of the continent henceforth would observe one political ethic.

The convergence of German and American strategic perspectives manifests itself also in the great emphasis placed on fostering democracy in Russia. Both have been firm in the twin convictions that the outcome of Russia's experiment with democracy is the key to Europe's future, and that the chances of winning this bet warrants heavy investments – investments that, for Germany, were economic as well as political. There are differences, though, in how prepared the two countries are to deal with a reversion to autocracy in Moscow and any revival of its imperial mission. Washington already has shown that it would find it far easier to adjust its thinking and policy toward Russia than would Bonn. What for Americans has been a practical foreign policy judgement (albeit flavoured by residual Wilsonian optimism), was for Germans the expression of a conviction basic to the vision it has of itself in Europe. The German sense of need to be surrounded by countries that are philosophically congenial and friendly attaches tremendous importance to the struggle for democracy in Eastern Europe, and to the consolidation of cooperative ties with Russia as a foundation-stone of a peaceable European system. Failure in either or both enterprises would erode faith in the belief that implanted, enlightened political institutions can thrive. Deteriorating relations with a more nationalistic Russia could give point to instinctive differences in German and American attitudes toward conflict. Bonn's preference for a 'soft' approach is at odds with Washington's readiness to back carrots with sticks. German promotion of the idea of a 'Europeanized' NATO is one indication that connections are already being made between the transatlantic balance and strategies for reconciling an uneasy Russia with post-Cold War security realities.

For Germany, the stress of etching a more distinct European political personality has the added attraction of relieving it from the burden of charting an individual course. The most disconcerting prospect for Bonn is being placed in a position where Germany may have to accept the unwelcome obligation to define distinct national interests and to act to defend them in an unaccommodating setting. Germany's compulsion to lay to rest the ghosts of the past, spectres revived in some European minds by reunification, have led it to follow a foreign policy of reassurance in all directions. Two essential elements of that approach are (1) a principled commitment to submerge German sovereignty within a (West) European political entity; and (2) to ensconce multilateralism – in both senses – as the standard *modus operandi* for bringing its political or military weight to bear on international disputes. Here, too, one discerns a principled German commitment expressing a compelling situational logic that is in contrast with more pragmatic judgements in Washington.

American ambivalence about political construction in the European Union, especially its commitment to a European Security Identity as embodied in the WEU and the Eurocorps, created strains for Bonn. The latter is equally committed to a vital NATO and to European construction, thereby putting itself in the position of being cross-pressured by Washington and Paris. A pronounced cooling of the great debate over European security architecture has been especially welcomed in Bonn. However, tensions over which organization will have precedence, and what the inter-organizational division of labour should be, are likely to surface again when the next crisis arises. Irresolution in Washington, and the lack of common Western contingency plans that anticipate future security crises in Europe, would place Germany in a particularly difficult position. Therefore, Bonn has a strong incentive to avoid these inter-allied clashes (and the damaging consequences that could result) by taking preemptive initiatives to define the terms of NATO/WEU collaboration and to designate the mechanisms for concerted Western action. Those initiatives, though, will not necessarily conform to US preferences and diplomatic priorities. That became strikingly evident when the Kohl government surprised the Clinton administration by supporting France in its clash with the United States over the French claim to senior NATO commands.

Still, German leadership in Western Europe goes down well in Washington. Expectations have risen since reunification that Germany would be the West's standard-bearer in central and eastern Europe. Indeed, it has been proclaimed as the United States' main European partner. For most senior US policymakers, it has become axiomatic that Bonn and Washington must work in tandem to achieve the conditions of continental peace and democracy. President Clinton's enthusiastic reaction to the July 1994 ruling of the German constitutional court on the legality of deploying troops on missions beyond the NATO area is indicative of the American conviction that a more activist German role in world affairs serves the two countries' common interests. The Bundeswehr's participation in IFOR, its willingness to place troops in a combat role within the follow-on SFOR, and signs from Volker Ruhe that Germany may even contemplate joining peacekeeping missions outside Europe were all taken as steps towards a healthy normality in Germany's external relations. Indeed, by holding out the prospect of a German–American special relationship – especially in addressing the challenge of stabilizing Eastern Europe – the President implicitly has offered Chancellor Kohl (and any possible successor) a revision of their partnership on terms of near equality. As the President pointedly declared during his state visit in July 1994: 'The US and Germany have a more immediate and tangible concern with those issues, even than our friends in Europe.... Our common partnership... is unique because so many of our challenges are just to Germany's East.... I think anything that can be done to enable Germany to fulfill the leadership responsibilities that it is plainly capable of fulfilling is a positive thing.'[49]

Germany has assumed exceptional importance in the American strategic vision at the same time as Washington has ceased to distinguish it by reference to historical circumstance. The United States is applying a utilitarian standard in considering whether Germany is fulfilling what Washington postulates as reasonable duties and obligations. Bonn's emphasis on concerting its foreign policy with its EU partners will not affect these appraisals in any fundamental way. The Clinton administration expects Germany to lead – be it in the European Union or outside it.

Operationalizing the German–American partnership that President Clinton presses on Chancellor Kohl has not yet materialized, for three reasons. Above all, German leaders are reluctant to accept a leadership position that singularizes Germany. For a country that compulsively seeks to submerge its national diplomatic identity in multilateral institutions, the honour offered by Washington is as disconcerting as it is complimentary. Second, there remain distinct differences in the American and German approaches to foreign affairs. The United States has been inclined to take a more activist approach to issues identified as problems or threats. Washington has followed the axiom that it is wise to take preemptive measures where danger portends, to act decisively, and to apply whatever means – including military force – the threat requires. The German approach, however, has been characterized by caution rather than decisiveness. Premature action is something to be avoided, and accommodation, not confrontation, is judged the most productive way to handle disputes. Washington will continue to urge on Germans the notion that virtue and tough-mindedness are not exclusive.

Finally, there remains an uncomfortably wide gap between the narrow geographic range of German strategic thinking and the United States' globalism. The United States will continue to encourage Germany to raise its gaze from those European affairs that affect it most directly to encompass security and political issues farther abroad. Bonn's separation of commercial questions from political ones in treating with China is an irritating case in point for Washington. China's reckless nuclear and missile export policies are not seen as a peculiar American concern which its European partners are free to ignore. An evolving strategic partnership between Washington and Bonn must close the globalism gap.

These differing philosophies with regard to the use of military force contribute to divergent ways of thinking about peacekeeping operations under the aegis of collective security organizations. For Bonn, having the imprimatur of the UN or OSCE is a constitutional and political requirement for the participation of German troops. Moreover, the peacekeeping culture of the UN matches the distinctive German approach to conflict prevention and dispute resolution while it remains a very uncomfortable fit to American military practice and political instincts. In dealing with the Yugoslav crisis, the similarities between the American and German approaches stood out while their differences rarely surfaced. This was due in good part to two factors: (1) Germany was not so directly involved as to have to confront the possible contradictions between its ethically driven judgements about what was happening in Bosnia, on the one hand, and its aversion to the use of compellent force, on the other; and (2) the United States refrained from forcing the issue by seizing control of the situation and demanding that its allies follow its lead until the situation became desperate in the summer of 1995, at which point broad allied agreement on more decisive action took the sting out of pre-existing disputes.

The American focus on the expanded role it wants and expects for Germany, rather than on constraining circumstances, testifies to the unqualified judgement that Germany is now beyond its post-war 'probation' period. Hence, the Clinton administration encouraged Germany to accept an expanded conception of its international responsibilities commensurate with its weight, and to loosen the restraints that have shackled German foreign policy. At the same time, Chancellor Kohl was showing evident uneasiness at being promoted as the United States' main partner in Europe, much less as a routine participant in the UN's farflung peacekeeping operations, despite Germany's having crossed a threshold in sending Bundeswehr units to participate in IFOR in a support capacity. The two allies' future relationship will not be symmetrical, however much it differs from the past. Each will likely continue to exhibit traits that reflect important differences in both historical experience and their current status in the world. Moreover, the fluidity of present circumstances, and the absence of immediate threats, suggest that national perspectives and style will be influential in shaping foreign policy. Germany and the United States often will find themselves on divergent tracks – especially on issues and in areas that are on the margins of each government's central concerns yet are important enough to elicit an identifiable line of policy, e.g. dealing with Iran and other regional trouble-makers.

The danger is that Germany will begin to distance itself from American leadership not as a natural process of maturation but rather as an ally who finds close partnership less and less compatible with a more acute sense of its own interests. This would be all the more unfortunate were it to occur because of mutual apprehensions that remain unspoken – Bonn's as to American constancy in its overseas engagements, Washington's as to German strategic myopia and fearfulness about the use of force.

Washington/Paris

The Franco-American partnership is marred by chronic frictions and an undercurrent of rivalry. Yet there are obvious and important areas of compatibility. Starting at very different points of philosophical departure, their approach to international affairs is broadly similar. Each mixes elements of realism and idealism. The United States has learned pragmatism and the arts of power politics; the French have come to concede that there is value and validity in liberal institutionalism. Both recognize the continuing need to maintain robust military forces and to be prepared to use them. Both affirm a principled dedication to the cause of human rights. Both are also imbued with a sense of national superiority and reluctant to yield to the claims of leadership or greater wisdom put forward by others. Each provides the primary challenge to the other's self-decreed superiority.

The two countries' vision of Europe's present and future reveals a similar mix of agreements and differences. The United States' modulated Wilsonianism does not resonate intellectually in Paris. France's own genuine devotion to the cause of human rights does not carry with it with the conviction in liberal tenets of belief or the optimistic hope that the West's civil international society can be extended across the continent. Like the British, the French find themselves as comfortable, if not more so, with traditional notions of balance-of-power and spheres of influence, without ever quite reconciling their penchant for *raison d'état* with their idealism. The dilemma lies in believing that while men and societies are civilizable, their perfectibility requires that nature be overcome, not discovered and liberated. In the end, French scepticism tends to prevail – with practical effects on policy.

It affects thinking about Russia. Compared to Germany or the United States, France is likely to turn bearish on Russian reform sooner. Like everyone else, they equivocated in deciding on a response in part because the political future was unpredictable and the risks incalculable; in part because of an historically influenced confidence in the ability of Paris to work together with Moscow. But NATO expansion was not seen by Paris as the panacea, for several reasons: it limits flexibility in how to deal with an unpredictable Russia; it prematurely blurs what are seen as objective, unavoidable distinctions between Western and Eastern Europe; and, not least, it makes NATO the paladin of European security with an attendant perpetuation and extension of American leadership no longer warranted. On all these points, the prevailing view in Paris diverged from official US (and German) thinking. But France chose to take a low profile on the enlargement issue – in part out of deference to strong German convictions about the need to stabilize its eastern frontier, in part because of its own lack of credibility in Eastern Europe, in part to relieve the pressure for an unwanted EU expansion, and in part because it gave precedence to the delicate task of fashioning its own rapprochement with NATO. French thinking about the course of political development in Eastern Europe will follow the historical pattern of seeing it primarily as a means to other, more compelling strategic ends involving Russia and Germany. Nonetheless, as the subsequent dispute over 'Europeanizing' NATO command structures showed, it is overly optimistic to think that ready compromises could be made on any of the major items that figure on the Alliance agenda.

Assigning places in Europe's security system to NATO and EU/WEU, as part of a new transatlantic division of labour, has been the largest bone of contention between Washington and Paris since the end of the Cold War. An uneasy peace was reached thanks to the Clinton administration's strategic decision to give its seal of approval for the development of a CFSP, and by the exigencies of the Bosnian situation. That truce set the stage for the dramatic improvements in Franco-American security relations under President Jacques Chirac who succeeded François Mitterrand in May 1995. On Yugoslavia, discord gave way to collaboration in pushing together, albeit not in perfect union, for a more forceful Western policy. In December, France made its historic return to NATO's Military Committee – a move that prefigured the wider agreement on a fuller French role in the Alliance reached the following year. The promulgation of a detailed plan for giving practical meaning to the Combined Joint Task Forces concept marked a critical threshold. It laid the basis for reifying the idea of a European pillar; added a major dimension to NATO's flexibility and adaptability for addressing sub-strategic threats; and carried the seed of a resolution of the simmering conflict over constituting the WEU as an independent security organization accountable to the EU. Nonetheless, it is overly optimistic to conclude that a durable agreement has been reached on the designation of roles or on the overarching question of what American place in Europe's affairs is desirable and acceptable. So long as that irresolution continues, the two countries will often find themselves at loggerheads on specific issues of how to prepare for, and to address Europe's emerging security agenda.

These tensions will be exacerbated by the strains experienced individually in trying to fashion strategies that maximize national influence while availing oneself of the advantages offered by multilateralism – in both varieties. For France, the stakes are even higher and the challenge starker. European construction especially places France on the horns of a dilemma. Developing EU institutions is an imperative dictated by the overriding need to dilute the power of a reunited, sovereign Germany. Yet doing so also curbs France's freedom of action and diminishes its ability to leave its mark on the world. That circle can only be squared if European institutions can be arranged in a manner where French genius is magnified rather than diminished. Considerable ingenuity has gone into the effort to conceive of such arrangements and to breathe life into them. In the long run, this is likely to prove a vain exercise. But for some time French devotion to the goal of transforming Community institutions into a 'force multiplier' for France will add a complicating element to the

West's striving for a new transatlantic equilibrium. As Washington sees it, France's desire to transform 'Europe' into a great world power will ensure that the jurisdictional issue, NATO vs EU/WEU, will add a chronic element of irritation to that effort. In the US, a certain optimism now prevails, tinged with stoic fatalism. The US will work with France where it can; forbear when it must.

French attitudes toward UN-sponsored peacekeeping reflect Paris' preoccupations with maximizing its influence through the management of organizational venues. As a permanent member of the Security Council, it looks favourably on the UN as another potential 'influence multiplier'. It is especially appealing as a forum through which it can exercise restraint on the United States – directly through the shaping of mandates; indirectly, by supporting the concentration of superintending authority over collective security operations in the Secretary-General and the Secretariat. This last arrangement worked to France's advantage in Bosnia. Thus, a readiness to participate in UN-mandated missions conforms to the overall strategy of leveraging assets and amplifying the French voice on multilateral actions. This sympathetic view of the United Nations notwithstanding, the EU/WEU still ranks higher on their priority scale of security organizations. For the latter serves more general, longer-term purposes. They outweigh what is only a tepid interest in enhancing the UN system as such.

From the United States' vantage-point, Paris' preferred way of using the United Nations leaves a mixed impression. Positively, it points to a common institution for legitimate, multilateral action. Negatively, it means that Washington will have to contend with an independent-minded French government that has no compunctions in using the organization's rules and apparatus for its own ends. The US was able to thwart French attempts to do so in the Gulf. In very different conditions in Bosnia, American policies were for years undermined, circumvented or simply blocked by France's adroit diplomacy in New York and in Yugoslavia.

As to the choice between the UN and OSCE, Washington's ambivalence is matched by that of Paris. For both governments, the veto power makes the UN more congenial than is the formless, egalitarian OSCE. In addition, the latter has substantially fewer organizational resources and, therefore, is limited as to the scope of operations it reasonably can undertake. On the other side of the ledger, those same features give it a greater flexibility, permitting *ad hoc* arrangements that can be adjusted according to changing conditions and preferences. To the extent that either government views the OSCE as an instrument for reinforcing norms of European good conduct, especially *vis-à-vis* Russia, it will be inclined to look to Vienna. However, to the extent that Russian pressures mount to have the CIS accorded the status of a regional security organization on a par with NATO, the more structured UN might offer useful defences against acceding to Moscow's demand. Whether this parallelism in French and American thinking translates into coordinated policies is uncertain. It depends on the nature of problems that arise and the will of leadership in Paris and Washington.

Washington/London

Anglo-American differences in concept and in approach to the political challenges of postcommunist Europe are as great as their similarities. The special relationship between the two countries no longer has much practical meaning. These two propositions are not causally related (although differences over the Yugoslav crisis have served to loosen the bonds of trust and mutual respect to an extent, and at a rate, that otherwise would not have occurred). Rather, the most important point is that in the absence of that special relationship the dissimilarities in thinking and approach will manifest themselves more readily.

At the conceptual level, rhetorical agreement on the historic importance of winning the struggle for democracy and enlightened internationalism in the former Communist lands conceals a gap in conviction. Whereas Americans and Germans hold to the belief that the Wilsonian vision is realizable, Britain is seen as not just being sceptical about the outcome but dubious of the model's applicability to Russian conditions at all. This, at least, is the way British thinking is perceived in Washington. Moreover, Britain's attitudes toward all of Eastern Europe are seen as leaning toward an unhealthy, and unhelpful, diffidence – if not outright scepticism. In sum, ritual support for a Europe whole and free notwithstanding, Britain is perceived as disengaged, lukewarm in its support, and intellectually and psychologically comfortable – too comfortable – with a different sort of Europe. That would be a Europe composed of mixed regimes, of *de facto* spheres of influence, of balance-of-power diplomacy. It is also a continent where the European Union at its western end remains something considerably less than a competent political entity with the capacity and will to assume major responsibilities for political order.

This image of Britain has a number of sources. Yugoslavia stands out. It is there that otherwise marginal differences in vision, and in mode of approach to the post-Cold War security environment, came to the fore and crystallized. Indeed, in the American reading of British foreign policy, conditions in Yugoslavia revived and gave substance to notions from the past which, it had been thought, were relegated to the history books. They include a belief that conflict is simply endemic to some peoples and places, that the best that can be dône is to quarantine them, that developments in the 'remoter' parts of the continent need not affect primary interests or give rise to serious threats, that programmes to build international structures designed to institutionalize norms of good behaviour are doubtful enterprises liable to prove unavailing. With regard to Russia, London follows the same path as Washington but agonizes less about the fate of a democratic cause for which it never had much hope. That might make it easier to join in efforts to form a modulated strategy for dealing with a less accommodating Russian leadership in the eventuality that reforms fail. For some time, that British attitude was associated with a more generalized diffidence toward continental affairs that Washington views as a liability in addressing problems in the here and now, witness Yugoslavia. In the future, the British approach to dealings with a more traditionally self-assertive Russia is likely to lean toward a loose concert in classic form. That may also prove congenial to the United States. However, whether London and Washington can agree on the measuring rod to use for gauging particular Russian policies is less clear.

These perceptual differences notwithstanding, there remain fundamental compatibilities between the evolving British strategy toward Europe and American interests. London has come to look on its security environment in terms of overlapping spheres. The transatlantic sphere is a key link in the chain that includes Western European and pan-continental links. Enlargement of NATO, and the EU, are supported as steps that extend and strengthen all those connections. The former in particular serves the critical purpose of engaging the United States formally in security arrangements across the continent. In this perspective, British initiative in promoting a new transatlantic charter (with the Transatlantic Free Trade Area (TAFTA) its centrepiece) should be seen as conforming to a larger strategic conception. It is a conception that matches the American one in all major respects.

There are other important aspects of the two countries' foreign policies where strong affinities exist. One is in the cardinal importance attached to maintaining NATO's position as Europe's preeminent security body, and to adapting it to undertake a range of the traditional missions. The other is the belief in the efficacy of military action and a willingness to take it. In the immediate post-Cold War years, these basic agreements were on display in the Anglo-American partnership that resisted French schemes for the marginalization of NATO, and in the Gulf. Yet, even with regard to the former, divisions have appeared between the American and the British view of the world. That is due to shifting circumstances and priorities.

As to European security organizations, the gradual evolution of American thinking about the European Union's Common Foreign and Security Policy, and France's reconciliation with NATO, have had the effect of lowering the saliency of the NATO/WEU dispute while heightening for Washington the value of a robust EU able to take on larger responsibilities. Britain's estrangement from its principal European partners, and the attendant weakening of its influence within the organization, has cast Anglo-American relations with regard to Europe in a different light. For Britain now is seen as a possible impediment to the EU realizing its positive potential, while at the same time London has lost utility as an instrument through which the United States could hope to shape it into an outward-looking, American-friendly union.

Equally striking adjustments have been made in Washington's assessment of Britain's role as a companion-in-arms. On this score, there are fewer doubts about national will and capability; rather the doubts centre on their relevance for the most likely tasks that lie ahead. Were there to be another Gulf War, US policymakers still count on Britain being there. The quality of the British contribution to NATO's Rapid Reaction forces is recognized as crucial and judged as dependable in every sense. Where divergences have opened is with regard to 'peacekeeping' operations such as that in Bosnia. These differences are both conceptual and operational.

The most significant points of friction between Washington and London lay at the level of political assessment and diplomatic strategy, as noted above. Fewer differences were or are observable in the thinking and characteristic approaches of the armed services themselves. The Pentagon showed no more enthusiasm for getting into a shooting war in Bosnia than did their British counterparts. That said, the prevailing US view of how force should be used, once there is a military commitment, takes a different tack. American doctrine and contingency planning makes little room for the discrete employment of military force for making political statements or for the self-limiting purpose of reassurance. That is evident from the extreme discomfort of the American military in contemplating peacekeeping operations of the traditional kind. Admittedly the Pentagon has dutifully prepared abundant materials on how to do the whole panoply of UN-style peacekeeping tasks, and conscientiously has undertaken to train troops in its methods. In this respect, it is on the same wavelength as the British practices.

However, there are notable differences. A comparison of PDM-25 and the Dibble report reveals that, for the latter, traditional peacekeeping is the norm, for the former it is the exception. The United States forces are preparing to act in the standard UN manner, but only where all the stringent conditions are in place for doing so safely and with a reasonably good chance of success. Where those conditions are not met, it will revert to established US rules of engagement to make peace or to enforce it. It may be that these differences, magnified in Bosnia before being composed in the rules of engagement for IFOR, will not soon or fully replicate themselves. But if they do, the United States and Britain will find themselves uneasy partners in peacekeeping.

On the question of which multilateral, collective security organization is preferred, the UN is more attractive for London than for Washington. Britain's seat on the Security Council allows it 'to punch above its weight'. No such opportunity for magnified influence exists in the OSCE. In this respect, both of the United States' major partners in prospective military actions have reason to act through the UN. In principle, Britain shows a greater willingness to bypass the UN. At the same time, Bosnia demonstrated the advantages of working through the UN system for containing American influence where US paramountcy and directive leadership is unwelcome. Washington is acutely aware of this. It is one of the factors that has contributed to the deep scepticism, now formalized in statute and Executive order, about participation in UN-sponsored and managed peacekeeping operations. Otherwise close allies are now identified as among those whose support cannot be taken for granted; indeed, those who might actively work to thwart American will.

Washington/Rome

Italy does not figure prominently in Washington's strategic vision for Europe. Despite its growing economic importance, and a geographical position that places it close to trouble-spots in the Balkans and along the Mediterranean littoral, Italy is not yet seen as playing a distinctive role in the Alliance's collective affairs. It lacks the foreign policy activism, the tradition of true partnership with the US in the great tests of the past 55 years, or the unique assets that ensure attention from American policymakers. Current attitudes also express the failure to develop finer methods for conducting its Alliance diplomacy. Cultivating consensus and building coalitions, in contrast to exercise of forceful leadership, would require Washington to be more sensitive to the preferences and contributions of its less powerful or assertive allies – Italy foremost among them.

Over time, it should become apparent that a more modulated approach of that sort is unavoidable. Until then, a discrepancy will exist between an implicit American judgement that Italy pretty much can be taken for granted and a mounting Italian campaign to have its status and concerns recognized by its partners in NATO and the EU. Signs that automatic deference to American judgement and wishes is ended were evident during the troubled Somalia operation. There, Italian officials – and unofficial opinion – were not shy about voicing their displeasure at being relegated to a secondary role in shaping and implementing the United Nations' programme. The nasty dispute over the alleged exclusion of Italian officers from influential positions was fed by a growing sense of grievance in Rome that its nationals have been denied their fair share of senior posts in multilateral organizations generally. Similarly, Italy's smouldering resentment at being excluded from the Bosnian 'Contact Group' triggered the petulant decision to deny the US the right to deploy F-111s at airbases which were the launching pad for the air campaign in September 1995. While US officials are cognizant of Italian sensibilities, Washington's slowly changing image of its dependable ally has not yet led to the conclusion that Italian *amour-propre* must be accorded the diplomatic respect that begrudgingly, and intermittently, it extends to France.

The practical value to the United States of bolstering Italy's status is potentially considerable. On the question of how to establish the division of labour between NATO and EU/WEU, Italy figures among those allies who are keen to reach a reconciliation that satisfies their own interests in the vitality of all three organizations. Indeed, as early as 1991, Italy joined with Britain in an initiative designed to counter the original Franco-German plan for building a European Defence Identity which, at the time, threatened to provoke a severe American reaction and perhaps an Alliance crisis. While Italy's internal troubles weaken its position within the EU on all manner of issues, it will become an increasingly self-willed player. A prudent Washington, anxious as to the orientation of an EU in flux, will eventually invest more in a working partnership with Rome.

With regard to collective security organizations, the lack of a permanent seat on the UN Security Council means that the world body has no obvious advantage for Italy compared to the OSCE. Overall, the value of a legitimizing mandate from one or the other is important to any Italian government as a condition for winning popular backing for participation in the whole panoply of peacekeeping missions. With the coming to power of the centre-left coalition, that consideration bulks larger. For this reason, as well as out of a desire to exercise a modicum of influence on their design and implementation, Italy most probably will be more inclined to go the formal collective security route than is the United States. When the two countries are joint participants in such an operation, there is a serious chance of friction arising from (1) exigent US command requirements, and (2) differing philosophies of 'peacekeeping' analogous to those that exist between the US and most of its other West European allies.

CONCLUSION

The United States' experience with multilateral peacekeeping in the 1990s leaves unresolved the basic questions of how the three criteria of legitimacy, political acceptability and effectiveness can be reconciled. American officials recognize, but have yet to accept the full implications of the obligation to obtain the imprimatur of the United Nations as a condition for using force. Whatever the exact form that anointing takes, whatever the exact degree of dependence on the world body's organizational structure it carries, this is now a fact of life – one established through the precedents of the Gulf War, Yugoslavia, Somalia, Haiti, and – one hopes – through the setting of strict rules of United Nations conditionality for Russian actions in the CIS. Congressional moves to deny the President the authority to involve US forces in UN peacekeeping operations, while foreclosing direct or indirect US support for any peacekeeping activities undertaken by the world body, cannot obviate this diplomatic truth. However they can complicate enormously this and later administrations' effort to cope with this reality.

American officials have a heightened awareness of how US prestige and moral authority can be valuable assets in preventing incipient conflicts from increasing or in resolving existing ones if employed skilfully and confidently. It is believed that it can best be done when unencumbered by the need to work under the operational control, if not the authority, of the collective security organizations of the UN or OSCE. Hence, premiums will be placed on acting early and decisively since the 'maturation' of a crisis will be accompanied by its 'institutionalization'. Enhanced capabilities of both are acknowledged and welcomed. At the United Nations, the establishment of a Department of Peacekeeping Affairs is judged a positive, long overdue development. On a technical level, significant improvements are seen as having been made in communications and control systems at UN headquarters. But the organization's overall ability to conduct complex operations in a conflict environment is still inadequate. Washington will continue to take a critical, sceptical approach to proposals for placing authority for dealing with high-stakes problems in the hands of the UN.

An overall American strategy for working through, and with the United Nations will emerge incrementally, if at all. The diplomatic and organizational issues are so daunting that only a US administration with a finer conception of its place in the post-Cold War world, and a more fully developed conceptual framework, will have a sure compass and maps for navigating this new terrain. Even so endowed, Washington faces the challenge posed by allies, and by Russia, all of whom are inclined to resort to the United Nations as a means of constraining or deflecting the thinking and conduct of the United States.

The net effects of the Clinton administration's multiple experiences with United Nations peacekeeping operations were to instill cautionary instincts about the participation of American troops and to induce deep scepticism about their effectiveness. PDM-25 is a stark reflection of these feelings. Its theme is the need to meet a strict set of conditions for US involvement in operations managed or overseen by the United Nations. Only passing attention is paid to modification of the world body's arrangements for conducting peacekeeping or for strengthening its capabilities. But this philosophy is likely to prove untenable in the long term, though, despite – or because of – tough new legislative strictures. The United States, diplomatically, cannot dispense with the legitimizing authority that comes with a UN mandate. Nor will it have the resources or domestic political support always to provide the disproportionate assets that would justify its assuming a commanding role – much less to act on its own outside the UN ambit.

Similarly, a more genuine multilateralism – as the standard *modus operandi* for undertaking a concerted diplomacy and concerted military actions with its European allies – will be a growing requirement for meeting most post-Cold War security challenges. To date, the lessons learned have been mainly negative ones. Moreover, the fundamental dilemma of seeking to reconcile the desire to retain many of the United States' past leadership prerogatives while progressively shifting burdens and duties on to its allies remains unresolved.

Finding ways of addressing the challenges posed by both forms of multilateralism will be a compelling task for US foreign policymakers (and thinkers) in the future. Reengagement with those issues, intellectually and diplomatically, is not a choice but a situationally determined necessity.

The one unavoidable imperative for American foreign policy is to follow a sustained diplomacy. It must simultaneously 'work' the UN system, routinize consultation with allies, and shape a modulated yet reasonably predictable relationship with Russia. It must be continual and not episodic. The United States' still unique global position, and wide array of assets, endow it with the potential for undertaking that challenge. However, it is less apparent that a distracted and introspective public, inclined to take a jaundiced view of overseas commitments – or an impulsive, parochial Congress – will allow a President the latitude to pursue so elaborate a diplomacy.

NOTES

1. The pervasiveness and resilience of the Wilsonian creed is such that anyone seeking to address the American public on matters of foreign relations must use its restricted vocabulary. It is not happenstance that Henry Kissinger titled his *magnum opus Diplomacy* (New York: Simon & Schuster, 1994). Although the philosophy that animates it is *realpolitik*, to give the book an honest title like 'Power Politics' would deny its author a receptive audience.
2. A critical examination of collective security as a possible paradigm for post-Cold War Europe is offered by R. K. Betts, 'Systems for Peace or Causes of War? Collective Security, Arms Control, and the New Europe', *International Security*, XVII (Summer 1992). See also C. A. and C. K. Kupchan, 'Concerts, Collective Security, and the Future of Europe', *International Security*, XVI (Summer 1991).
3. Betts, *op. cit.*, p. 23.

4. This justification for NATO's enlargement was succinctly presented by Deputy Secretary of State S. Talbott, 'Why NATO Should Grow', *New York Review of Books* (10 August 1995).
5. Communiqué, Ministerial Meeting of the North Atlantic Council in Berlin, 3 June 1996.
6. Secretary of Defense William Perry declared the agreement a landmark that 'will affect security relations in Europe between NATO and Russia for years to come'. Quoted in C. R. Whitney, 'Russia and NATO in Accord on Russian Troops in Bosnia', *New York Times* (27 November 1995). A. Lynch offers a cogent interpretation of Russia's policy on Yugoslavia in 'Russian Foreign Policy and the Wars in the Former Yugoslavia', in R. Lukie and A. Lynch, *Europe from the Balkans to the Urals* (Oxford: Oxford University Press, 1996).
7. In private discussions with Western officials, Primakov went out of his way to reject the idea that Bosnia was a constructive precedent.
8. The strategic and operational implications for NATO as a military alliance are critically examined in probing analyses by K.-H. Kamp, 'The Folly of NATO Expansion', *Foreign Policy*, no. 98 (Spring 1995); and M. E. Brown, 'The Flawed Logic of NATO Expansion', *Survival* (Spring, 1995).

The genesis of the Clinton administration's thinking about NATO expansion is recounted in detail in a series of articles that appeared in the *Washington Post* (5, 6 and 7 July 1995). 'Securing the New Europe', R. Atkinson and J. Pomfret. Among other revelations they disclose is that electoral sensitivity in the White House to the feelings of Polish-Americans figured in Clinton's decision to push NATO expansion.

The intellectual framework for the administration's enlargement strategy was laid out by three analysts from the Rand Corporation, who have been advising the State Department: R. Asmus, R. Kugler, and S. Larabee in 'NATO Expansion: The Next Steps', *Survival*, XXXVII (Spring 1995).
9. Concluding an accord with Russia that institutionalizes its relationship with NATO carries its own risks. There is a very fine line between acknowledging Moscow's right to be heard on the security issues that will figure prominently on the agenda of an enlarged NATO (a possible Ukraine crisis being the most serious prospective case) and giving it a *de facto* role in Alliance deliberations themselves. Safeguarding NATO's organizational integrity, and – still more important – the Western partners' solidarity, will prove a daunting challenge. One already has witnessed a disconcerting tendency to break ranks and to form tactical alliances with Russia when convenient (as over policy in Bosnia). Resisting the temptation to involve Russia in inter-allied debates, instead of observing self-discipline in seeking a common policy despite differences, would be harder were Russia accorded an official place within NATO's political space.

Moscow's insistence in June 1994 that its Partnership-for-Peace agreement entails an 'effective mechanism of consultation...on the whole range of European and world security matters' foreshadowed the demands it would make in exchange for acquiescence in NATO enlargement.

(Quoted in E. Sciolino, 'Russia Pledges to Join NATO Partnership', *New York Times* [10 June 1994].) Russian Defence Minister, Pavel S. Grachev, went further in demanding an exclusive 'full-blooded strategic relationship' with NATO that would go beyond partnerships. The West's lack of confidence in itself was expressed in the allies' own request that the agreement include a clause whereby Russia pledged not to interfere with the Alliance members' deliberations. Events since then confirm that there was good basis for those apprehensions.

10. Budapest Document 1994, *Towards a Genuine Partnership in a New Europe, CSCE* (21 December 1994). The OSCE's potential role in conflict prevention is considered by H. Vetschun in *The Art of Conflict Prevention*, ed. W. Baumans and L. Reychler (London: Brassey, 1994).
11. Quoted in S. Greenhouse, 'Clinton Outlines Plan to Bolster Europe-Wide Security', *New York Times* (15 November 1994).
12. See Communiqué issued by Ministerial Meeting of the North Atlantic Council, Brussels, 5 December 1995. Also, Address by Secretary of State Warren Christopher, Prague, 10 March 1996.
13. See my examination of the thinking that prodded this policy shift. *The United States Policy in Yugoslavia*, Ridgway Paper No. 6, University of Pittsburgh Center for International Studies, March 1996.
14. Quoted in B. Clark and G. Graham, 'Work Begins On New Wing', *Financial Times* (30 November 1994).
15. For an acute analysis of the intellectual and policy dilemmas that intervention poses for liberal approaches to international relations, see S. Hoffmann, 'The Crisis of Liberal Internationalism', *Foreign Policy*, no. 98 (Spring 1995). See also his article, 'The Politics and Ethics of International Intervention', *Survival* (Winter 1995–96); and *Beyond Westphalia? State Sovereignty and International Intervention*, ed. G. M. Lyons and M. Mastandumo (Baltimore: Johns Hopkins University Press, 1995), especially the essays by the editors and S. D. Krasner.
16. The term 'divisible peace' was coined by R. H. Ullman in *Securing Europe* (Princeton: Princeton University Press, 1991).
17. See Chicago Council on Foreign Relations, *American Public Opinion and U.S. Foreign Policy* (1995).
18. See poll conducted by the Program on International Policy Attitudes Center for International and Security Studies at the University of Maryland, April 1996. Two illuminating attempts to reconcile the results of public opinion surveys with the activism of Congressional neo-isolationist/unilateralists are S. Kull, 'What the Public Knows that Washington Doesn't', and J. D. Rosner, 'The Know-Nothings Know Something', *Foreign Policy*, no. 101 (Winter 1995–96). They reach divergent conclusions as to (1) how fixed is the seeming popular aversion to overseas military engagements, in general, and UN peacekeeping in particular, and (2) the latitude politicians have for exploiting the public's ambiguous attitudes in the interest of their own policy preferences. Together, the two articles underline the amorphousness of the country's thinking about its external relations in the absence of any salient threats.

19. Quoted by P. Worsnip, 'US Policymakers Fear New Isolationist Trend', *Reuters* (20 January 1995).
20. An exceptionally well-informed account of the Clinton administration's struggle to develop an overall foreign policy framework is E. Drew, *On the Edge: The Clinton Presidency* (New York: Simon & Schuster, 1995).
21. A perceptive assessment of the evolving United States's attitude toward UN-style peacekeeping is M. R. Berdal, 'Fateful Encounter: The United States and UN Peacekeeping', *Survival* (Spring 1994). A wider-ranging analysis that treats US policy as part of the larger NATO adaptation to peacekeeping is the well-informed and cogent work of F.-J. Meirs, *NATO's Peacekeeping Dilemma*, Deutschen Gesellschaft für Auswärtige Politik (Bonn, May 1996).
22. *The Uses of Military Power*. Remarks by Secretary of Defense Caspar W. Weinburger to the National Press Club, Washington, DC, 28 November 1984.
23. Powell's views were succinctly stated in 'US Forces: Challenges Ahead', *Foreign Affairs*, XXI (Winter 1992/93). They are elaborated as part of a broader philosophy in his autobiography, *My American Journey* (New York: Simon & Schuster, 1995).
24. Powell understandably plays down any differences with Bush administration colleagues, and General Schwarzkopf. They do emerge from the numerous published accounts of US decisionmaking. See Powell, *op. cit.*, Chapters 18–19; H. N. Schwarzkopf, *It Doesn't Take A Hero* (New York: Bantam, 1992), Chapters 16–17; B. Woodward, *The Commanders* (New York: Simon & Schuster, 1991); J. A. Baker III, *The Politics of Foreign Policy* (New York: G. P. Putnam's Sons, 1995); and L. Freedman and E. Karsh, *The Gulf Conflict 1990–1991* (Princeton: Princeton University Press, 1993), Chapter 9.
25. President George Bush, 'Remarks at the United States Military Academy', West Point, 5 January 1993.
26. L. Aspin, 'The Use and Usefulness of Military Forces in the Post-Cold War, Post-Soviet World'. Address by the Chairman of the House Armed Services Committee, Washington, DC, 21 September 1992.
27. *The Clinton Administration's Policy on Reforming Multilateral Peace Operations* (US Department of State, May 1994). This is the public version of Presidential Decision Memorandum-25.
28. Testimony before the Senate Foreign Relations Committee, 7 June 1995.
29. Quoted in *The New York Times* (29 July 1996).
30. *Ibid.*
31. Quoted in S. Erlander and D. Sanger, 'On World Stage, Many Lessons for Clinton', *The New York Times* (29 July 1996).
32. *Policy on Reforming Multilateral Peace Operations, op. cit.*
33. *Ibid.*
34. The efforts of successive US administrations to fashion a policy toward the use of power and post-Cold War intervention are recounted and critically reviewed by R. N. Haass, *Intervention* (Washington, DC: Carnegie Endowment, 1994).

35. Introduced in the House of Representatives as H.R. 7, 'a bill to revitalize the security of the United States'.
    The complementary piece of legislation in the Senate was the Peace Powers Act sponsored by Robert Dole. It would have amended the UN Participation Act of 1945 to give Congress a statutory role in setting the terms of US participation in UN activities and Dole's negative view of the United Nations, and international organizations in general, is strongly held. In his words, they often 'reflect a consensus that opposes American interests or does not reflect American principles an ideals'. Quoted in *New York Times* (11 June 1995).
    Anticipation that a Republican would soon be in the White House already had an effect on the Congressional leadership's attitude toward the War Powers Act. In June 1995, House Speaker Newt Gingrich led an attempt to repeal the controversial act which requires a President to bring home American troops within 60 days of their deployment in a combat zone unless Congress authorizes their continued presence. Enacted in the early 1970s by Democrat-controlled Congress at the height of the bitter debate over President Nixon's policy in Indochina, many Republicans had questioned over the years the constraints it imposed on the country's commander-in-chief. Gingrich declared the Act unworkable, if not unconstitutional, and exhorted the House in these words: 'I want to strengthen... the President on a non-partisan basis in foreign affairs and in national security. He does not deserve to be undermined and cluttered and weakened.' The move to revoke the act was rejected by eight votes; Republicans backing the move by a four to one margin, Democrats opposing it by a seven to one margin. The partisan split reflected primarily differences over how forceful a United States security role in world affairs is considered desirable and constitutional, and partisan consideration only secondarily (K. Q. Seelye, 'House Defeats Bid to Repeal War Powers', *New York Times* [8 June 1995]).
36. I assess the significance of Congress' new-found activism on foreign policy in 'Congress and US Policy in Europe', *International Politik und Gesellschaft* (Bonn) Autumn 1995.
37. Quoted by J. Martin, 'US Chief Less Cautious on Troops Abroad', *Financial Times* (11 December 1996).
38. The philosophy and forms of UN peacekeeping operations, and their suitability for a post-Cold War enlargement of the world organization's role, are treated in the authoritative work of M. Berdal, *Whither UN Peacekeeping*, Adelphi Paper No. 281 (London: IISS, 1993). See also E. B. Haas, 'How to Keep the United Nations from Sliding Down the Slippery Slope of Ineffectiveness', Testimony to the Committee on Foreign Affairs, US House of Representatives, 24 October 1994.
39. Berlin *Communiqué, op. cit.*
40. C. Millon, 'France and the Renewal of the Atlantic Alliance', *NATO Review*, no. 3 (May 1996). See also Minister of Defence, Charles Millon, 'Vers Une Nouvelle Alliance', *Le Monde* (11 June 1996).
41. Berlin *Communiqué, op. cit.*

42. R. P. Grant, 'France's New Relationship with NATO', *Survival* (Spring 1996).
43. See Ruhe's remarks in Berlin on 14 October, as reported in *The Week In Germany* (18 October 1996).
    The German position that a 'Europeanized' NATO would be more palatable to Moscow was first voiced in public by Karl Lamers, foreign policy spokesman for the CDU, a year earlier. Volker Ruhe picked up the theme in a London interview in February 1996; see Q. Peel, 'Ruhe's Mission to Europeanise NATO', *Financial Times* (23 February 1996).
44. France's position on linkage was stated unequivocally by Defence Minister Charles Millon; see C. R. Whitney, 'Paris Blames U.S. Position for Setback Over NATO,' *New York Times* (13 October 1996).
45. Matching preferences as to who should be in the first 'tranche' of inductees was another matter. France's promotion of Romania was in line with its penchant for the diplomacy of symbolism. By French logic, if the Visegrad three (or four) were accorded preference so as to satisfy Germany's interest in stabilizing an area of paramount concern to it, then reciprocity called for simultaneous admission of an eastern European country with which France felt some historical or cultural affinity (a Latin-rooted language) – thus Romania. The argument that this would avoid neglecting the Alliance's 'southern flank' was derided in Washington. It was accorded even less credit than other applications of the 'reciprocity principle': e.g. steps to satisfy Germany's special concern for the Baltics be matched by recognition of France's special concern for the Levant. Clinton administration officials only very slowly came to realize that these types of status games were now ensconced within the new politics of Europe and of the Alliance. They could not be ignored, however irritating they might be and whatever distraction from what the United States viewed as serious business they might create.
46. Quoted in B. Clark, 'NATO Debates How To Live With Russia', *Financial Times* (11 October 1996).
47. The French policy was affirmed by Millon on a visit to Moscow after the NATO meeting in Norway. See A. Frachon, 'La Russie se résigne de mauvaise grâce à accepter un èlargissement de l'OTAN', *Le Monde* (10 October 1996).
48. The organizational and operational aspects of Alliance action out-of-area are discussed by R. L. Kugler, *U.S.–West European Cooperation in Out-of-Area Military Operations* (Santa Monica, CA: RAND, 1994).
49. For an informed, insightful analysis of Germany's policy role in the Yugoslav situation, see H. W. Maull, 'Germany in the Yugoslav Crises', *Survival* (Winter 1995–96).

7 Strategic Outlook: Compatibilities and Incompatibilities
Hanns W. Maull

This project started from a simple premise: a capacity for multilateral action is imperative to the protection of the Western countries' security. National security, in turn, we see as dependent on a modicum of international order and stability. Our premise rests on the observation that international relations have become so complex, power so diffuse and interdependence so intense that, as a general rule, only a pooling of resources and the sharing of risks and responsibilities will be able to shape events or 'control outcomes' – as one key definition of power has it. An effective exercise of national power to enhance security and deflect threats will certainly require cooperation with other states, and, most probably, with international organizations. Moreover, with the evolution of international society has come a stronger sense of legitimacy. The exercise of national power therefore will often require legitimation through a collective security body: the United Nations or, in Europe, the OSCE.

We thus see multilateral action as an indispensable element of national security policy, but we are also therefore painfully aware of its problems. Our concern is with the efficiency and effectiveness of multilateral action. More specifically, on the basis of the country studies presented in this volume, we identify problem areas which may make multilateral action, while essential, also difficult. To do so, we analyse recent Western policy responses with regard to the following possible sources of disagreement and strain.

(1) Are there serious divergences in the perception of risks and the assessments of threats? Are there differing views about the organization of multilateral cooperation and its institutional framework?
(2) Are calculations of interests significantly different between the allies?
(3) Are there deficiencies in how collective action is conceived and should be implemented? In other words, are the potential fault-

lines at the level of policy implementation, rather than of interest definition or policy conception?

The following analysis tries to shed some light on those questions by comparing the strategic outlook of the five major Western countries with regard to their assessment of risks and threats, their attitude toward multilateral cooperation and their calculation of interests. It also looks at recent experiences with a view to evaluating the lessons they offer.

RISKS AND THREATS: THE ASSESSMENTS

A Broad Consensus about Risks and Threats

It is often argued that the Alliance is losing cohesion as a result of the loss of a clear-cut, simple threat – such as the one conveniently provided by Soviet military power. While there is no doubt some truth in this, there now exists a surprisingly broad consensus within the Alliance as to what risks it faces today and in the future. This shared risk assessment has found its expression in a number of official NATO documents, and our country studies show that this consensus is not just verbiage. All five countries consider themselves more secure than in the past – after all, the possibility of a large military confrontation involving NATO has become extremely remote. But all also share a sense of uneasiness about strategic uncertainty, instability in key geographic areas such as Russia and the CIS, South Eastern Europe, North Africa and the Middle East and, at farther geographical and political distance, East Asia. All five governments agree that a successful transition in Russia towards a market-oriented democracy is of paramount importance for the future security and stability of Europe. Moreover, all five consider the possible erosion, perhaps even disintegration of the Alliance as a major danger in its own right. Finally, they are all concerned about 'new threats' to their security and that of their people stemming from uncontrolled proliferation of nuclear weapons and other technologies of mass destruction, from international terrorism and organized crime, drugs, environmental degradation and mass migration.

Questions thus arise not so much over the degree of compatibility of risk and threat assessments as with regard to the exact nature and characteristics of those risks and threats. They are diffuse and very hard to evaluate. How should one assess, for example, the enormous destructive capabilities retained by the successor states of the former Soviet Union, specifically Russia? What does it mean that those capabilities are at best uncertain, perhaps under the limited political control of the government in Moscow, that they therefore may not be easily or readily wielded as instruments of power but still could wreak havoc if unleashed by accident – or by the design of political terrorists? Furthermore, the permutation of small risks into serious threats are hard to anticipate. Given the 'turbulent' nature of today's international relations,[1] seemingly small and distant events may set in motion a chain of events that causes large-scale repercussions close to home. As Lawrence Freedman has pointed out,[2] the dynamic escalation of violence in ethno-nationalist conflicts may lead to rising stakes, and also to mounting intervention costs, producing a dynamic process of 'self–deterrence'.[3] In such an instance, both the risks of non-intervention *and* of intervention escalate with the level of violence in the conflict itself, generating simultaneously pressures and fears about intervening at ever higher levels of danger. Those dynamics seem to have characterized much of the Western response to events in former Yugoslavia, which provides a fascinating example of how divergent perspectives complicated cooperation within the Alliance. Initially, America, France and the UK tried to keep Yugoslavia together, while the FRG had given up on this option by the summer of 1991, and was pressing for international recognition of the successor states. French and British approaches originally were coloured by balance-of-power considerations, while Germany assumed that a peaceful transformation of political relations in former Yugoslavia could be obtained. America and Germany early on were willing to consider military intervention (though Germany of course immediately excused itself from participation in any such mission), while France and the UK preferred a UN-led 'humanitarian intervention'.

But divergences narrowed over time, and eventually a broad consensus about the Alliance's objectives and strategies emerged. The need for a multilateral approach to the crisis was accepted, anyway, by all from the beginning – but there were differences about how desirable it was to have the United States involved. Again, those differences were eventually ironed out through a painful learning process. One key institutional mechanism for this was created specifically for the purpose – the Contract Group whose importance for crisis management in former Yugoslavia can hardly be overestimated. America's participation turned out to be absolutely indispensable.

It is also striking how much the assessment of stakes and risks varied not only between countries, but also within governments over time, illustrating the difficulties in defining national interests clearly.

A Shared Conviction about the Need for Multilateral Action

All five governments are fully aware of the need for multilateral action. Multilateral allied action is seen as an important, sometimes (as for Germany and Italy) even as an essential precondition for involvement and effectiveness. This holds true for both non-military and military dimensions of crisis management. Non-military steps will often require close cooperation and coordination to be effective (most obvious in the case of economic sanctions). In the military realm, with the exception of the United States, none of the members of NATO could sustain a substantial projection of military force over any appreciable time period or distance. Even the United States, while theoretically dedicated to maintaining a capability to fight and eventually win two major regional wars simultaneously, in practice would probably be dependent on allied support and contributions in almost all contingencies outside the Western hemisphere. Multilateral action thus holds attractions for all; for most allies, it will in most serious contingencies be the only conceivable form of intervention – certainly, for military intervention.

This awareness of the 'multilateral moment'[4] has evolved steadily since 1989. The Bush administration initially followed a rather unilateralist line (cf. the intervention in Panama). The Gulf crisis, however, was simply too big – in scope and consequence – to be handled in this way by Washington. Somalia to some extent represented a lapse. The first phase of the international humanitarian intervention was an exclusively American affair. Washington then handed Somalia over to the UN but continued to meddle heavily in an attempt to control action on the ground. The Clinton administration originally showed much enthusiasm for 'robust multilateralism', but after the disaster in Somalia reverted to a more ambivalent line that found its expression in Presidential Decision Directive (PDD) No. 25.[5] US intervention in Haiti was based on a legitimizing mandate by the UN Security Council and, through the participation of other countries, assumed something of a multilateral dimension. France went through a similar learning process towards a more multilateral approach in its interventions in Africa, with similarly ambivalent results. While France wanted, and received, a UN Security Council endorsement for its humanitarian intervention in Rwanda, it found few difficulties in other countries willing to supply troops for such an effort.[6] Britain traditionally looks to close cooperation with the US and also has some experience in military cooperation with France, revived through the generally harmonious but frustrating leadership of UNPROFOR in Bosnia. Germany and Italy supported multilateral action out of principle and almost reflexively.

The norm of multilateral action had been established rather firmly within the Alliance by 1996. Again, however, the crux may be not so much in broadly shared assumptions but in the small print. The key issues here concern the distribution of responsibilities, costs and risks and where leadership is to be found in multilateral enterprises.[7] A preference for multilateral action in itself does not promise solutions to those problems.

Non-Military vs Military Contingencies

The allies are in agreement, too, about the primacy of non-military methods for dealing with security challenges, and the limited utility of military action with regard to most conceivable contingencies. Many of the new threats are seen as, by their nature, not amenable to military responses. Rather, they call for preventive diplomacy, collective crisis-management or international peacekeeping measures of the traditional kind. At the same time, none of the five discards the use of military force altogether. All accept that there may be situations, even beyond individual and collective self-defence, in which force may provide the only effective option. Within that broad consensus, however, there clearly exist divergent attitudes towards military force. Britain and France at the one end of the spectrum, Germany at the other, and the US and Italy in between. The America position is closer to that of the UK and France, while Italy's position resembles that of Germany.

In Britain and France, the constraints on the use of military force by government are quite weak, for a variety of historical and institutional reasons, while they are very strong in Germany.[8] America falls in between: it has a tradition of unilateral military intervention and participation in major wars, but since the wrenching experience in Vietnam it also has developed considerable circumspection about putting American soldiers in harm's way. Thus, the 'Weinberger–Powell doctrine' that sets very restrictive conditions for the large-scale use of American military power abroad (as is discussed by Michael Brenner in Chapter 6). (Ironically, this restrictive doctrine was formulated by the Secretary of Defense who presided over the most lavish and extravagant build-up of American military power ever in peacetime.) Moreover, Congress, through the War Powers Act in particular and its growing foreign policy activism in general, has considerable influence over when and how American military power will be used. The legislature thereby provides a check on the Executive Branch which does not exist in either France[9] or the UK. These 'secondary' differences can in fact prove highly divisive, as witnessed in Bosnia. When coupled to the intrinsic difficulty of making confident risk/threat assessments, divergences about the utility of military force in a given contingency may severely hamper the ability to act together effectively. They may also colour judgements on issues of such importance as the relative utility and value of the Organization for Security and Cooperation in Europe (largely irrelevant in the context of traditional, 'military' security policies but potentially extremely important if contingencies are basically seen as rooted in socio-economic and political instabilities). There is also the uneasy balance of NATO enlargement and NATO reform, with enlargement as the main concern from a military security perspective, but NATO transformation and a constructive relationship with Russia as key issues if the problem is viewed through a non-military prism. Those differences will also surface in attitudes towards the ultimate objective of a Kantian 'democratic peace'. For the more realistically inclined, this vision has little chance to be implemented in the near future, and, therefore, has scant relevance for policy. For those governments with a stronger idealist element in their foreign policies, this Kantian vision is more than just a utopian dream, and they may try to integrate elements relating to Kant's dream into their policies. Anthony Lake's concept of 'democratic enlargement' is a case in point.

Collective Security, Collective Defence, Humanitarian Intervention and the Restoration of Failed States

With regard to contingencies where military means are perceived as relevant, all five governments share an awareness that in the new world of international relations, challenges to stability may go beyond traditional tasks of collective defence to include elements of collective security. It is important to note in this context that there is no fundamental contradiction between collective security and collective defence. Rather, meaningful collective security efforts will often include the ability to act in the collective defence. Thus, both the Gulf crisis of 1990/91 and NATO's intervention in Bosnia in 1995 involved both Article 51 of the UN Charter (stipulating the right of collective self-defence) and Chapter VII of the Charter, which defines a system of collective security. The ultimate objective of realizing a collective security system in and for Europe also informs NATO efforts at military cooperation with Russia (and other former Communist states) through the Partnership for Peace, NACC or *ad hoc* arrangements for Russian participation in IFOR. The Western allies' shared goal is the establishment of a collective security system – or, perhaps more accurately and modestly, a 'security community' covering the whole of Europe.

Apart from situations relating to individual and collective defence, military power has also been used with increasing frequency since 1989 in two other sets of circumstances: (1) in so-called humanitarian interventions wherein military means (including the use of force) are used to prevent a major human catastrophe resulting from, *inter alia*, action of a state against its own citizens (as in the case of Iraqi repression of the Kurds in Northern Iraq in 1991), ethno-nationalist conflicts within and between states (as in former Yugoslavia), or the decay of state authority into anarchy (as in Somalia or Haiti), and (2) in efforts to restore a modicum of domestic political stability and government authority in 'failed states', where anarchy has replaced order. In order to prevent the disintegration of one state's authority from becoming a threat to international security, it may become necessary to protect a stake in international order and national security stability through 'nation-building from without'. The UN operation in Cambodia (UNTAC), and the interventions in Somalia, Bosnia and Haiti, which fall into this category (with very different results), are thus likely to have successors.

The Dayton agreements to settle the conflicts in former Yugoslavia represent a fascinating case in point. The agreements could be seen as an effort to apply broader, pan-European policies to a microcosm – Bosnia. The effort contained elements of collective defence (NATO's intervention in the summer of 1995 against the Bosnian Serbs, assurances to Bosnia from Washington that its army will be armed and trained, Bosnian–Croat defence cooperation) and collective security (the notion that Bosnia could be reconstructed as one state, the political process pointing towards a settlement involving all parties to the conflict). Arguably, it even incorporated elements of humanitarian intervention in the role of IFOR and thus risked the same fate for IFOR which befell UNPROFOR. Furthermore, the Dayton agreements also assumed that a 'failed state' (or, more exactly, a state that never was), Bosnia, could be (re)constructed with external support. With their extensive political component, the agreements deployed a whole gamut of programmes and institutions (EU, OSCE, UNHCR) to achieve this aim.

Differences: Weight, Likelihood of Different Scenarios, Regional vs Global Preoccupations

We have stressed the point that broad agreement in risk/threat perceptions take the Alliance only so far. The complexity and diffuse nature of the most plausible risks/threats to Western security make it only too easy to disagree about whether there is a problem at all, its nature and seriousness, as well as the best ways to redress it. Moreover, as Michael Brenner has observed, judgements about those questions may not be entirely disinterested (i.e. individual governments are more inclined to let 'soft' interests in status and Alliance roles influence the policy debate), and multilateralism inherently may produce biases towards inaction.[10] Although the allies may share perceived interests, and agree on the rough outlines of a strategic design, they may nevertheless fall out when found to address a concrete problem situation. Those divergences may reflect substantive disagreements. Given the complexity of the problems under consideration, honest and intelligent national leaders might still come to quite different conclusions. They may stem from national biases and vested interests. But they could also reflect some more deep-seated features of the countries involved, namely differences in foreign policy cultures – a concept which we will pursue further below. Three such divergences in orientation seem to be of particular importance in this context: differences with regard to the geographical scope of security policies, policies towards Russia and China, and attitudes towards 'rogue states' (Iran, Libya, Sudan).

Regional vs Global Orientations
The United States' foreign policy still has the broadest geographic scope among the Western countries; it continues to be the only truly global power within the Alliance. The other four focus their attention much more on Europe and adjacent areas – aspirations towards the status of global players notwithstanding. To be sure, France and Britain still retain some residual post-colonial possessions and security

commitments outside Europe, and Germany's foreign policy recently also has emphasized global interests and reach (e.g. in its new emphasis on relations with Asia). But the realities of Europe's political and security involvement outside Europe and its vicinity are modest – leaving aside economics, where the European presence in other parts of the world is rather substantial.

This disparity in strategic orientations within the Alliance may cause the most serious problems with regard to East Asia, if developments in that region result in heightened great-power tensions and the United States finds it necessary to contain rising Chinese power. The Europeans are likely to put their economic interests in lucrative deals with China before their willingness to contribute to US-led efforts at the 'conditional engagement' of China[11] and thus help strengthen regional and global order. Given the tectonic shifts in international power and world economic gravity away from the Atlantic and towards East Asia presently taking place, this 'conditional engagement' of China may well be the major task for Western policymakers in the years and decades to come. The problem has many facets, ranging from the challenge of bringing China into the WTO (and inducing it to adhere to its rules and norms), to securing China's support for peace and regional stability in East Asia and for global nonproliferation regimes in weapons of mass destruction and missiles. Pointers to possible future tensions within the Alliance over East Asia already exist; thus, American officials have repeatedly complained about European reluctance to hold China to its obligations in the realm of international trade, specifically respect for intellectual property rights.

A second area of importance in this context is the Middle East. America and Europe differ in where they fix their attention in the region. Europeans – and in particular France and Italy – are more and more preoccupied with developments in North Africa, where the ramifications of political instability and Islamic fundamentalism could directly and severely affect the Northern Mediterranean countries. America, on the other hand, focuses primarily on the Israeli–Arab region and the Gulf. While both America and its European allies share concern over access to Middle Eastern oil, there have traditionally been differences about how best to ensure such access politically. As a consequence, there have been somewhat different attitudes towards Israel, whose policies Europeans tend to view more critically than do Americans. This has contributed to tensions within the Alliance in the past – e.g. during the first and second oil crises in the

1970s. More recently, there have been divergences between the US and France, in particular, about how best to move forward the stalled peace process between Israel and the Palestinians after the return of a Likud government to power in Jerusalem. President Chirac's trip to the Middle East in October 1996 put those differences into sharp relief. Finally, there is the inter-allied fracas over policy towards Iran, with Europeans favouring a 'critical dialogue' while America remains bent on isolating Iran politically and economically.

Policies towards Russia and China
As Michael Brenner argues in his analysis of American attitudes towards multilateralism, the Alliance may also risk drifting apart over the right policy approach towards Russia, with America opting for a tough line of what might be called 'neo-containment', while the Europeans follow a more accommodating stance. This may be so, although the risks of tensions within the Alliance over 'containment' versus 'accommodation' are probably greater with regard to China. At the time of writing (Fall 1996), Western policies towards Russia had broadly converged around a rather accommodationist stance, which found its most pertinent expression in the support which Washington and Bonn, in particular, extended to Boris Yeltsin's election-bid for the Russian presidency. In addition, both Washington and Bonn have made strenuous efforts to reconcile Russia to NATO enlargement by offering a package of measures designed to affirm its great-power status. Given Moscow's policies in Chechnya, the Chinese leadership had some cause to feel that America was applying double standards in its relations with Russia and China. In any case, Washington saw both an important interest and a realistic opportunity to bring Russia into the fold of an 'enlarged' community of democratic and market-oriented countries.

Attitudes towards 'Rogue States'
America's instinctive support for tough policies created tensions within the Alliance with regard to the 'rogue' or 'backlash' states – countries such as Libya, Iran, Sudan and Cuba – which Washington suspected of supporting international terrorism and trying to undermine international order. Having just decided that economic sanctions were inappropriate as a policy to prevent democracy and human rights violations by China, the government in Washington then proceeded to slap sanctions on Iran, Libya and Cuba. They were targeted not only against those countries but also against non-American com-

panies which refused to comply with the sanctions. Although President Clinton suspended sanctions against Cuba for six months, he did sign all the sanctions bills and thereby risked serious conflict with the European allies.

PERCEPTIONS OF SECURITY POLICY FRAMEWORKS: THE ROLE OF MULTILATERAL STRUCTURES

The first source of potential defects in multilateral cooperation we addressed were possible differences in risk and threat assessments. As we have seen, the problems there seem to be secondary and situation-specific, rather than generic. That does not suggest, however, that there is nothing serious to worry about. Still, agreement in principle will certainly increase the chance of working towards effective co-operation.

The source of potential trouble we now turn to concerns attitudes towards international security institutions. All five countries broadly agree on the need for multilateral approaches. However, they have had basically different views as to how to go about this. For example, if France categorically rules out the use of NATO in non-Article V contingencies and insists on going through the UN instead, while America, in turn, excludes any cooperation with the latter, efforts at multilateral crisis-management could quickly stalemate.

Broad Consensus about Institutional Arrangements

The present reality is, fortunately, rather more comforting. While our country analyses show that there were indeed serious disagreements over which institutions to entrust with multilateral use of force in the ex-Yugoslavia, they by and large were resolved in favour of the UN Security Council as the preferred source of legitimacy and NATO as the instrument of choice for implementation. The OSCE has also acquired a clearly defined (if somewhat neglected) political role as part of an agreed division of labour between international security institutions. But this broad agreement which by now has been reached again is only part of the story. There are two important caveats to add. First, the strategic consensus within the Alliance carries only so far. And second, it again conceals considerable potential for friction about the specifics of cooperation within and through institutions.

While generally supportive of UNSC mandates and NATO implementation, at least three of the five countries under consideration – namely, the US, the UK and (perhaps in a less clearcut fashion) France – prefer *ad hoc* cooperation over formal institutionalized arrangements. That is to say, their support for institutions is purely instrumental and allows little scope for institutional development *per se*. Even in the case of Germany, whose preference for multilateralism seems much more reflexive and principled, the limits to its commitment to institutional solutions have become apparent as Germany has come to confront the question '*mourir pour Sarajevo*'. Once the commitment to multilateralism came to entail risks to the lives and safety of German soldiers, the Bonn government, not international institutions, plainly could expect to be held responsible by their electorate.[12] Germany's reluctance to put its soldiers in combat situations once more was visible in the dénouement of the Yugoslav crisis. The debate about the role of German ECR and RECCE Phantoms in NATO's projection of force in Bosnia resulted in decisions which, despite the green light which the Constitutional Court had given Bonn to proceed, so tightly circumscribed the missions of the aircraft as to almost completely devalue their contribution to NATO's joint effort.[13] The reluctance to envisage institutionalized mechanisms – such as a standing UN force with some independent authority for the Secretary-General and/or the Security Council to deploy – is quite understandable. However, it also puts an additional onus on the efficacy and decisiveness of an Alliance decisionmaking process, at times of crisis, which has shown itself increasingly laborious as it has become truly multilateral.

The Fear of Entanglement and the Fear of Abandonment

The agreement in principle embodied in the Berlin accords conceals considerable potential for conflict when one considers specific instances. In essence, there are two fundamental, simultaneous but mutually obstructive forces at work. The first is fear of entanglement, the second fear of abandonment. Multilateralism carries the risk of entangling a country in a conflict against one's own prudential judgement and/or where it sees no direct stake. It can be dealt with either by opt-out provisions or by confirming a unit veto provision on the decision to deploy NATO forces. Thereby members of the Alliance would preserve sovereignty and autonomy in any major multilateral decision. The European Union's unhappy experience with trying to conduct a common foreign security policy while acting under a unanimity rule has heightened sensitivity to the constraints of multilateralism by consensus. NATO, too, is formally obliged to observe a unanimity rule.

The sort of complicated, delicate security problem faced in Yugoslavia invites the assertion of national prorogations that could lead to obstruction if not discord. Opt-out arrangements, by contrast, offer flexibility – albeit at the price of diminished solidarity. Rather than amend existing treaties to allow NATO or EU/WEU to act officially on the basis of qualified majorities (a course that would be time-consuming and problematic), the circumstantial logic points to a greater readiness to resort to *ad hoc* coalitions of the willing.

This antipodal anxiety of abandonment reflects uncertainty about the steadfastness of commitments by the partners to a multilateral venture: will they be willing to engage themselves on mutually acceptable terms? Will they stay the course if the going gets rough? The antidote against the fear of abandonment are tangible commitments, such as a presence of troops, and, more generally, a willingness to cede autonomy of decisionmaking to integrated structures, thereby accepting a dilution of elements of national sovereignty. Fear of abandonment (by the Europeans) is one reason why NATO has not been discarded completely in favor of *ad hoc* arrangements. Inversely, for America, support for NATO is an expression of commitment. But it also reflects concern about being left as the lonesome superpower in at least one sense: NATO holds the promise of America being able to play a dominant role in the international system at acceptable cost.

Again, the events around former Yugoslavia illustrate this point well. It seems as if the Dayton agreements were the result of an American *fuite en avant*. Confronted with the unpleasant prospect of having to intervene, in an election year, in Bosnia, either to rescue the UNPROFOR units of the Allies or try to impose a settlement, and facing increasingly strong political criticism from the Republican majority in Congress, the Clinton Administration decided to gamble on an imposed settlement, and got it right. The effort was not without its dose of 'fear of entanglement' – it represented a very determined, but also very tightly circumscribed effort to get the problem out of the way (cynics might argue, out of the way of the Presidential election). Even before, however, fears of entanglement (primarily by the US, but also by the UK) interacted with fears of abandonment. The latter held true for Germany first of all, but also for the European UNPROFOR participants.

Those two mutually obstructive fears of entanglement and abandonment also complicated other humanitarian interventions under UN auspices (such as Somalia), as well as relations between NATO and the WEU and the debate about NATO military reform. With humanitarian interventions, too, the issue was settled in favour of NATO, and against the UN. The bottom line was that any further 'robust' UN peacekeeping missions on the basis of Chapter VII of the UN Charter in Europe or involving the transatlantic partners seemed unlikely if they are not run by NATO, thus in effect reducing the UN to the role of legitimator.

With regard to NATO reform, and relations between NATO and WEU, the tension could not be resolved so easily. The European countries, led by France, demanded a capacity for European action because they feared abandonment by America and therefore they needed an alternative. America, in turn, was worried about the Europeans getting involved in conflicts either against US opposition, or with US acquiescence and failing to do the job, with the risk of eventually entangling the US in conflicts in which it had no core interests, did not wish to get involved and/or found the circumstances onerous. The compromise reached in Berlin in June 1996 did not, and could not, by itself resolve the issue. While the Alliance agreed to reforms in NATO's military organization that would create 'separable but not separate' Combined Joint Task Forces (CJTF) and command structures available for both NATO and European action, the reformed arrangement retained for the US the right to veto access to its assets in any conjectured European action undertaken without direct American participation, addressing the fear of entanglement. At the same time, it enables Europeans in principle to go ahead without direct US involvement but with US assets, reflecting European concern that America might not be willing to get involved in certain contingencies.

In the debate about NATO enlargement, the fear of abandonment of course resided in Central and Eastern Europe – and to some extent in Germany, which wanted to preserve the benefits of having moved out of the front line of the old East–West divide. Fears of entanglement, on the other hand, weighed heavily among European NATO members including, somewhat paradoxically, Germany which was loath to risk good relations with Russia over the issue of NATO enlargement. The US Congress, too, has its own fears of entanglement.

Politically, the process of NATO enlargement among the allies seems to have been driven by two major dynamics. The first came from 'old thinking'. It was held by those in the military and foreign policy establishments who distrusted Russia and felt that it would soon revert to a policy stance of opposing the West. The second, and in my view more important, dynamic originated in a sense of shared values between NATO and the young democracies in Central Europe and a feeling of obligation towards them. The dynamics in the opposite direction of keeping NATO intact were driven by concerns about the viability of an enlarged NATO and, perhaps more importantly, about the repercussions of enlargement on Western relations with Russia. The result was that the whole process was at the mercy of strong cross-currents, and consequently soon began to resemble efforts to square a circle (enlarging NATO, but at the same time developing a cordial strategic relationship with Russia).

This dialectic of apprehension has engendered efforts to reassure by regulating the Alliance's multilateral structures and procedures. Much of the bickering over the modalities of NATO's military reforms can be understood in those terms. There are, admittedly, additional factors at work: material interests (e.g. who gets which headquarters?); prestige (e.g. who gets what command?); leadership (e.g. how does one initiate multilateral action?); and the distribution of costs and risk (e.g. who carries which burden, and accepts which risks?). They complicate the challenging task of arriving at effective mechanisms for multilateral decisionmaking and decision-implementation. The core problem has been with the intermingled fears of abandonment and entanglement. It has been with the Alliance from its beginning. It certainly will not go away in the future.

CALCULATION OF INTERESTS AND SHARED VALUES

Much of the uncertainty and latent tensions within the Alliance are, as we have seen, of a secondary nature – i.e. they relate to problems that emerge within a renovated framework of agreements that have been hammered out in NATO since 1989. How risks and threats will be evaluated in a specific contingency, on exactly what terms the allies will decide to cooperate, and under what institutional aegis and according to what format their military assets will be employed, will only be determined in the event.

This uncertainty might be reduced, if not eliminated altogether, if there were clear, congruent and reasonably predictable calculations of national interests for foreseeable contingencies. Much of the recent criticism of Western policies – be they addressed to America,[14] Germany',[15] France or Britain – have taken the line that governments have neglected to identify their post-Cold War national interests and to pursue a consistent diplomacy. This type of criticism slights the difficulties of formulating a crisp threat assessment. Even more important, it also misunderstands the changed nature of foreign policy in democratic societies. In any open political system, the national interest is what the political process determines it to be. Foreign policy in the Cold War past was to some extent sheltered from this basic truth. This is now changing. The deepening impact of external events on domestic economic and social conditions, along with the prominent role of the media in shaping impressions, have tended to democratize and domesticate foreign policies. Beyond an obvious core of 'national' interests, for which public support is ensured, foreign policy objectives, strategies and even tactics, as in any other policy area, will be subject to the democratic political process.

National Sovereignty as National Interest

This process of policy equalization has not been complete, however. Some of the traditional insulation of foreign policy from the democratic process survives. There are several reasons for this. One is the particular character imparted to foreign policy by an international system still shaped by the surviving quasi-anarchic features of the Westphalia system. They impose certain constraints and obligations on national foreign policies. Another reason is provided by the logic of the 'two-level game'.[16] Since governments in international affairs often depend on concessions by others to secure their own objectives, they are in turn willing to impose certain compromises on their own people. A third reason lies in the persistence of foreign policy bureaucracies with a strong *esprit de corps*, considerable autonomy within the political-*cum*-policy process, and less intense scrutiny and control by elected legislatures (usually expressed through parliamentary supervision). This is especially the case in the European countries, in particular France and the UK, where the tradition of parliamentary involvement in foreign policy is weak.

One implication of this incomplete process of democratization and domestication of foreign policies has been the emphasis placed on safeguarding national sovereignty in the foreign policy postures of France and the United Kingdom, as well as that of the United States. Freedom of action, autonomy and ultimately, sovereignty have been defined as important national interests in their own right by London, most obviously, but also by Paris. This evocation of the national interest emotionally and in its symbolism harks back to the past. But at the same time it represents an entirely different phenomenon from nineteenth-century nationalism. Today's nationalism in Western Europe (and in America) essentially is defensive. It is rooted in two strong if dubious assumptions about the world we politically inhabit. The first assumption is that the nation-state is threatened by transnational and supranational forces. While this assumption correctly recognizes the changing nature of international relations and, consequently, also the lessened power of the nation-state, it fails to appreciate that politically there is simply no alternative to the nation-state in sight which could assume its still inescapable functions. The state will not simply be eroded by the undermining wave of market forces. Second, the renewed emphasis on protecting sovereignty assumes that states can still meaningfully and effectively act alone. This is in most instances illusory. There is considerable domestic resistance to the implications of this unpleasant reality in all our countries, however. It is often difficult for people to come to terms with the complex constraints and exigencies of interdependence. Modern forms of nationalism – i.e. those we encounter among rich countries – in this sense often express resistance to change.

Reluctance to accept transfers of sovereignty is often discussed in terms of a renationalization of foreign and security policies. This is somewhat misleading. International relations within the OECD world could hardly go back to old patterns of balance of power. It would perhaps be more appropriate to talk about the domestication and parochialization of foreign and security policies. Renationalization in this sense represents the preoccupation of societies with their own problems, their reluctance to change and to adjust to a new environment and to risk their very substantial achievements. The danger in this tendency towards parochialism is a loss of effectiveness of foreign policies and consequently a decay of international order.

The evolution of Western policies towards the former Yugoslavia illustrates this danger. Ultimately, they seemed to be driven by the interaction of events on the ground *as seen through the lenses of domestic public opinion*, on the one hand, and idiosyncratic and parochial tendencies in all major Western countries, on the other. The schizophrenic elements in Western policies (a desire to stay clear from the quagmire of the Balkans, coupled with 'humanitarian interventions' which turned out to be bloody, costly and hard to get out of) ultimately reflected the schizophrenia of electorates who wanted an effective Yugoslav policy to end the horrors at zero cost, with zero risk. Even the turn towards more forthright US leadership and the Dayton Agreement was essentially the result of domestic pressures (namely, the upcoming presidential elections) in the United States.

The UK's relations with Europe also illustrate the problems with insistence on national sovereignty and autonomy as core national interests. Britain's policy towards European integration has in effect marginalized the country within Europe, and has deprived it of much of the leverage and influence it might have exerted otherwise. France, by comparison, has been more effective. There is a subtle difference between the approaches of the two countries. The UK seems intent on securing independence and freedom of action from Europe, while France seeks independence and autonomy *within* the context of European integration. This has long been the logic of French policy towards Europe, and more recently also the logic of French policy towards NATO. By accepting the multilateral framework as such, and thus committing itself to working within it, a country will gain the capacity to shape and influence decisions and developments within the multilateral process. By building up some capacity for independent action and exploiting opportunities 'to be difficult', this leverage can be enhanced. This logic is well expressed in the old adage 'if you can't beat them, join them'. France has been following this line both in terms of European integration and, more recently, also with regard to NATO. Britain has never tried to 'beat' NATO, like France has, and thus arguably has suffered from being taken for granted. On Europe, Britain has never really 'joined', but just has gone along. As a result, its capacity to shape developments in and through both NATO and the EU has been considerably more circumscribed than that of France.

A similar comparison could be made between Germany and Italy. Italy, by and large, has been taken for granted both within NATO and within European integration. It has thus not been able to exercise much influence (perhaps it also did not see much reason for doing so, anyway). Germany, on the other hand, was determined from the beginning 'to join', i.e. to work in and through institutions. But it also could be difficult – explicitly, in situations such as the NATO double track decisions in 1979 and its aftermath in which the FRG helped to push Washington into serious arms control negotiations with Moscow, or implicitly simply because of its key position in the alliance. Germany therefore exercised considerable influence within NATO, without even having explicitly to invoke nationalist reservations about deepening integration.

In sum, 'national interest' has become a very elusive guideline in foreign policymaking. While the 'Soviet threat' in the past established a reasonably clear-cut, simple and plausible security interest which was broadly shared by NATO member countries, thereby disguising the problems of domestication and democratization of foreign and security policymaking, the new risks and threats are having a different effect. There may again be situations in which the threat is clear-cut and serious enough to make it easy to establish 'the national interest'. The Iraqi annexation of Kuwait was such a case. But it is more likely that future risks and threats will not be that obvious and easily recognizable. In those instances, the concept of 'national interests' will not be very helpful. Interests will have to be defined and worked out through the domestic political process on which is superimposed an increasingly complex process of multilateral institutional politics.

What remains of the national interest of the Alliance member states beyond the obvious but possibly not very relevant threats to territorial integrity, security of the people from large-scale military attacks, and their ability to determine their own way of life are two constants: the desire to preserve the Alliance itself (a defined interest shared by all five countries), and the insistence on preserving national sovereignty and freedom of action (shared by at least three of the five). The two are somewhat incompatible, and their reconciliation requires considerable collective effort and sophistication.

Both insistence on sovereignty and the desire to preserve the Alliance reflect historical experiences. One set of experiences goes back to the roots of the modern state, the other reflecting the very successful history of the Alliance since 1949. In the case of sovereignty, this historical justification is corroborated by contemporary domestic political constraints and calculations. The desire to preserve the Alliance expresses – along with memories of success – a sense of shared values.[17] The latter makes the Alliance into a 'community' and thus gives it additional cohesion and strength. Shared values also help to identify common or compatible interests. The open question is, however, how strongly felt this sense of shared values will be in any given situation, and to what extent it can prevail against domestic preoccupations and the temptations of 'parochialism'. The answers to those questions will determine the degree of Alliance solidarity in the future.

Divergent Foreign Policy Cultures: Power Politics vs Transformation of Interstate Relations

As we have argued, calculations of national interests do not take place in a domestic vacuum. They reflect specific domestic concerns and configurations of power and influence, as well as more enduring aspects of the politics of any given state which may be described as its 'political culture'. Political culture is defined here as 'a set of attitudes, beliefs, and sentiments which give order and meaning to the foreign policy process and which provide the underlying assumptions and rules that govern behavior'.[18] 'Foreign policy culture' refers to that segment of a political culture which relates to foreign relations, hence to behaviour in the international system. The concept of 'foreign policy culture' thus suggests that foreign policies reflect specific approaches and orientations which in turn are shaped by a country's history, geography and society.

If we accept the relevance of this concept of foreign policy culture, then we find a clear divergence in those terms among our five countries. Those divergences seem to turn on fundamentally different attitudes towards international relations. One set of attitudes assumes the perpetuity of international anarchy, balance of power and basically unconstrained national sovereignty. It thus sees international relations as essentially static, governed by their own laws and the quest for relative gains. The other set of attitudes assumes that international relations are undergoing fundamental and qualitative changes and can be transformed in ways which make them more and more like domestic politics; rules and institution-based, governed by peaceful resolution of conflicts and sanctions against those who break the laws. The focus here is on absolute gains.

We can place the five countries on an attitudinal continuum ranging from an unmitigated belief in balance of power politics and anarchy in international relations to the opposite end of belief in the transformation of international relations. On this continuum, we find the UK and France clustered near the *realpolitik* end, and Germany and Italy near the other. America occupies its own, special place in between. American foreign policy culture has been unique, and uniquely ambivalent, since the republic's earliest days. It has expressed both an optimistic belief that international politics can be transformed into an 'empire of liberty' (Jefferson) – and, indeed, that it was America's mission to achieve such a transformation; and an instinct to remain aloof, to avoid 'foreign entanglements'. In following these contradictory impulses, America has been willing to play by the rules of power politics as well as anyone, yet it has never been entirely converted to them. (This was, as Henry Kissinger has acknowledged, the principal reason for the failure of Richard Nixon's foreign policies).[19]

Differences in foreign policy cultures explain many differences in attitudes towards multilateralism, collective security and the institutions affiliated with it (the UN, the OSCE), and towards NATO enlargement. Those differences in foreign policy cultures are perhaps most relevant, however, with regard to the use of military force. Germany, in particular, has been guided by a distinct 'culture of restraint'.[20] The resulting potential for intra-Alliance frictions and decisionmaking paralysis is considerable. But there are two factors that work to facilitate their resolution. One is the key position of the United States, which not only is the most powerful among the five, but also occupies a middle position on the foreign policy culture continuum which in the past has allowed it to reconcile the differences between, say, Germany and the UK. Whether and how America uses its assets within the Alliance will therefore be critically important. The second positive development is a gradual rapprochement between the foreign policy cultures of France and Germany, with France shifting towards policies of national autonomy *within* the Alliance and Germany moving towards a certain 'normalization' of its foreign policy culture.[21] There thus exists the potential for a long-term convergence of European foreign policy cultures around a modified 'civilian power' posture. This posture would be European in its essence, and would provide the basis for an effective Common Foreign and Security Policy.

Differences in foreign policy culture also matter in the exercise of leadership. Only two of the five countries under consideration traditionally have tried to claim and exercise leadership – America and France. The UK has long been a follower – enthusiastically, within NATO, and reluctantly, within the European Union. Italy has been politically too weak to exercise leadership, while Germany has been reluctant to be seen leading, and has developed a peculiar style of 'leading from behind' through diligent attempts at consensus-building. (The one episode where Germany tried to lead forcefully and from the front – recognition of Slovenia and Croatia – backfired badly, rubbing in the lesson that Germany should never try to impose its will on reluctant partners.)[22] The exercise of leadership implies a willingness to mobilize resources and to run risks within a multilateral effort; and perhaps disproportionately. France recently has been willing to do so with the objective of ensuring greater political influence and European leadership. That was demonstrated by its participation in UNPROFOR in Bosnia with the largest national contingent (and the highest losses), its return to a 'reformed' NATO. America, on the other hand, has been trying to shift the burdens of risks and costs on to its European allies. By its acquiescence in NATO military reform it has succeeded so far in doing so without any significant loss of control. Issues of leadership (Who will be willing to take initiatives? How will competing claims to leadership between the US and France be reconciled? Can leadership be exercised collectively?) will continue to challenge Western statesmen.

IMPLICATIONS: YES, THERE ARE DIFFICULTIES IN ORGANIZING MULTILATERAL ACTION – BUT WILL THEY REALLY MATTER?

We have asked initially about possible sources of failure for multilateral cooperation – be it in its inception or implementation. Our findings are only partly reassuring. There has in fact evolved a remarkably broad consensus within the Alliance about future risks and threats to Western security, about the need for multilateral action and the indispensability of NATO, and about basic approaches towards security – namely, agreement to continue arrangements for collective defence while developing mechanisms of collective or 'cooperative' security. There has also been a broad convergence in another sense: key NATO members today share a considerable reluctance about military interventions, and they are all affected by foreign policy parochialism. Some experts have interpreted this convergence as the result of broadly comparable demographic changes and the material wealth in our societies.[23] Yet there clearly also exist important differences in strategic orientations. Those include differences in focus (regional vs global), potentially different policies towards Russia and China, and divergences in attitudes towards 'rogue' or 'backlash' states, as well as in basic approaches to international relations ('balance of power' vs 'transformation') and preference of instruments (reluctance to use force, in the case of Germany).

We have identified several causes for those differences. One important cause is divergent foreign policy cultures within the Alliance. This includes the tendency of at least three of the five states to seek national autonomy and freedom of action as a national interest in itself, and hence to prefer *ad hoc* arrangements of multilateral cooperation to institution-building. Against this, the preservation of NATO is now also generally seen as an important national interest, and there are signs not only for compatibility through the unique position of America as a mediator, but also through a convergence of foreign policy cultures within continental Europe. The Alliance also is a community of like-minded states with shared values, and thus carries potential for effective cooperation based on solidarity. While it would be naive to overestimate the weight of shared values in national and multilateral foreign policy, it would be analytically incorrect and misleading to exclude them completely.[24]

A second important explanation of divergences within the Alliance is the complexity and diffuseness of the challenges combined with pronounced parochial tendencies everywhere. As we have seen, the desire to keep one's options open is an expression of parochialism. Those leanings, in the case of the former Yugoslavia, worked against the forming of a common interpretation of the threat, and against timely, vigorous action. The failings there, in crisis-management and conflict prevention, set the stage for a hazardous encounter that produced a serious Alliance crisis. Governments still instinctively seek guidance from the concept of 'national interest', often touted as the one sure touchstone in this world of bewildering complexity. In reality it is unlikely to be of great help. Indeed, it may even further exacerbate the problem, if it is used (as it easily can) to justify non-involvement.[25]

There is thus a good chance that the Alliance will fail again in the future – as it repeatedly did in Yugoslavia. But will it matter? Does the disappointment with a sputtering Alliance multilateralism portend a crisis for Western security institutions?

A provocative line of argument runs roughly like this. The diffuse risks and challenges the Alliance is facing do not compel major security policy efforts. The reluctance to get involved is thus reasonable, given the limited stakes involved. To be sure, the future will not be a bed of roses. There will continue to be localized violent conflicts, with heavy casualties. We can expect further humanitarian disasters, perhaps with indirect repercussions for our own societies. But ethnonationalist conflicts eventually will burn themselves out. Mass migration may be their by-product, but they can be throttled by defensive reactions of host societies. Proliferation of means of mass destruction will result in nasty episodes, but will not threaten the West's fundamental security.

This view of the future assumes that things will go wrong, but not really in ways that jeopardize the security of the Western powers. Adverse effects could be handled through multilateral action by the Alliance. Individual nations may also develop their own, largely autonomous responses. Sometimes, political responses may even be coordinated between countries forming a coalition of the willing. Only when dangers mount and problems really threaten to get out of control, will democracies recognize the need for concerted effort and eventually muster the necessary will to activate it. In short, in this view the hour of multilateralism may not yet have come – things will have to become considerably worse than they are now before it does. Until then, 'satisficing' strategies will be the order of the day.

Let us illustrate this line of reasoning again with reference to former Yugoslavia. Imagine a scenario in which renewed Western military presence, SFOR, coupled with political efforts at restoring political stability to Bosnia-Herzegovina, falls short. Tensions between the ethnic entities would again rise, and SFOR would take casualties in isolated military incidents. Under such circumstances, growing domestic pressures in the US to avoid a quagmire and 'get the European allies to do their bit' might result in a withdrawal of all or much of the American element in SFOR. This could trigger a chain-reaction and lead to the dissolution of SFOR altogether. Bosnia would again slide into violence. There would be more displacements of civilians. Bosnia would turn towards militant Islam as a means to mobilize the population and as a source of external support. Militant nationalism would also prevail in Croatia and Serbia. Tensions would rise throughout the Balkans. NATO, having sidelined itself, would be concerned but inhibited to act.

How much would all this matter to Western security? The line of reasoning developed here suggests that the answer is, not enough to call forth a strong response. In this view, traditional international politics may have become irrelevant in shaping our civilian societies' view of their external relations. But the consequences would be hazardous for Western well-being. Can one be sure that the parameters of disorder will stay within the level of the uncomfortable but tolerable? Who can ensure that a sudden explosion in Kosovo, drawing neighbouring countries into the conflict, could be contained through *ad hoc* half-measures by a diffident West? What would be the impact on the moral integrity and self-respect of our democratic systems if our countries decided to abandon people in former Yugoslavia? The baneful effects of foreign policies governed by parochialism and 'domesticism' could breed a cynicism that extends to domestic politics. What would be the consequences of a cumulative erosion of the credibility of Western institutions for the ability to reconstitute the Alliance as a vehicle for extending its zone of peace, stability and prosperity?

To accept the abdication of international responsibilities, to abandon the enterprise of uniting Europeans on principles of democracy and peaceful engagement would be a reckless act of non-feasance. Yet, unfortunately, there is a real possibility this may happen. Nothing dramatic might occur for quite some time. The Alliance would still hang together, bound by a vague sense of shared values and the habits of cooperation. In the absence of the kind of challenge which could galvanize it back to life (such as a new threat from the East, which now seems highly unlikely), it would, however, more and more become an empty shell, or a 'masque'[26] – devoid of real substance, unable to shape events, its military infrastructure decaying because of fiscal retrenchment, and its political vitality drained away. NATO would still be around, it would perhaps even expand its membership – but it would become less and less relevant.

NOTES

1. J. N. Rosenau, *Turbulence in World Politics: A Theory of Continuity and Change* (New York: 1990).
2. L. Freedman, 'Warum der Westen scheiterte, Eckdaten des jugoslawischen Auflösungskrieges', *Blätter für deutsche und internationale Politik*, 40 (February 1995), 156–68.
3. S. Sloan, *NATO's Future: Toward a New Transatlantic Bargain* (Washington, DC: National Defense University Press, 1985).
4. M. Brenner, 'The Multilateral Moment', in M. Brenner, ed., *Multilateralism and Western Strategy* (London & New York: Macmillan/St.Martin's Press, 1995), pp. 1–41.
5. US Department of State, *The Clinton Administration's Policy on Reforming Multilateral Peacekeeping Operations* (Washington, DC: Department of State, 1993).
6. International Institute for Strategic Studies, 'France's African Adventure: Plus ça Change?', *Strategic Comments*, 2 (June 1996); N. Philippii, 'Frankreichs Rolle im ruandischen Bürgerkrieg – eine Wende in der französischen Afrikapolitik?', in H. W. Maull, M. Meimeth, and C. Neβöver, eds, *Die verhinderte Groβmacht, Frankreichs Sicherheitspolitik nach dem Ende des Ost–West-Konfliktes* (Opladen: Leske & Budrich, 1996) (forthcoming).

7. Brenner, *op. cit.*, pp.17ff.
8. H. W. Maull, 'Germany in the Yugoslav Crisis,' *Survival* 37 (Winter 1995/96), 99–130; F.-J. Meiers, 'NATO's Peacekeeping Dilemma', *Arbeitspapiere zur Internationalen Politik*, No. 94 (Bonn: Europa Union, 1996).
9. A. Kimmel, 'Die institutionellen und verfassungsrechtlichen Rahmenbedingungen der französischen Sicherheitspolitik', in Maull, Meimeth, and Nehöver, eds, *op. cit.* (forthcoming).
10. Brenner, *op. cit.*
11. Cf. J. Shinn, ed., *Weaving the Net: Conditional Engagement with China* (New York: Council on Foreign Relations, 1996).
12. J. Mathias, 'The Strategic Implications of European Integration', IISS Adelphi Paper No. 290 (London: 1994); R. Palin, 'Multinational Military Forces: Problems and Prospects', IISS Adelphi Paper No. 294 (London: 1994).
13. The ECR Phantoms could not be used to suppress the air defences of the Bosnian Serbs, although NATO's request for those aircraft had primarily been motivated by the superior capabilities of the German aircraft in such missions. Only the RECCE reconnaissance Phantoms of the Bundeswehr (protected, it is true, by the ECR Phantoms) with the photographs of Bosnian Serb positions contributed directly to NATO's military effort – in the first combat sorties of German aircraft since 1945, which did not, however, involve any use of weapons. See Meiers, *op.cit.*, 64ff.
14. R. D. Blackwill, 'A Taxonomy of Defining U.S. National Security Interests in the 1990s and Beyond', in W. Weidenfeld *et al.*, eds, pp. 110–19.
15. H.-P. Schwarz, *Die Zentralmacht Europas, Deutschlands Rückkehr auf die Weltbühne* (Berlin: Siedler, 1995).
16. R. D. Putnam, 'Diplomacy and Domestic Politics: the Logic of Two-Level Games', *International Organization*, 42 (Summer 1988), 427–60.
17. T. Risse-Kappen, 'Democratic Peace – Warlike Democracies? A Social Constructivist Interpretation of the Liberal Argument', *European Journal of International Relations*, 1 (1995), 491–517.
18. This definition closely follows that of L. Pye, 'Political Culture', *International Encyclopedia of the Social Sciences*, 12 (New York: 1968), 217.
19. H. A. Kissinger, *Diplomacy* (New York: Simon & Schuster, 1994), esp. Ch. 2.
20. This term has been used repeatedly by both Chancellor Kohl and Foreign Minister Kinkel to describe Germany's particular foreign policy orientation, reflecting its past and its geopolitical position at the centre of Europe.
21. M. Otte, 'A Rising Middle Power? German Foreign Policy in Transformation, 1988–1995', unpublished PhD manuscript, Woodrow Wilson School, Princeton University.
22. Cf. Meiers, *op. cit.*; H. W. Maull, 'Germany in the Yugoslav Crisis', *Survival*, 37 (Winter 1995–96), 99–130.
23. B. Buzan and G. Segal, 'The Rise of the "Lite Powers": A Strategy for the Postmodern State', *World Policy Journal*, 13 (Fall 1996), 1–10.

24. Risse-Kappen, *op. cit.* (1995).
25. The initial reaction in Washington to the crisis in Yugoslavia illustrates this well: Washington decided to leave the problem to the Europeans because there were 'no vital national interests involved'.
26. P. Zelikow, 'The Masque of Institutions', *Survival*, 38 (Spring 1996), 6–18.

8 Interface Between NATO/WEU and UN/OSCE
Jean Klein

Since the crumbling of the Communist regimes in Eastern and Central Europe and the reunification of Germany, the security institutions of the West have undergone significant changes. In spite of the vanishing of the Soviet military threat, after the dissolution of the Warsaw Pact Organization and the withdrawal of the Russian troops from the front lines they occupied during the Cold War, the North Atlantic Treaty Organization (NATO) remains the defence and security framework for the Western world. So much so that it seems that nobody wants to call into question the usefulness of an institution which is supposed to provide reassurance against a revival of a hegemonic power in the East; to stabilize and pacify the relations among the European countries, especially after the emergence of a united German state,[1] and to support peacekeeping and peacemaking missions under the aegis of the United Nations (UN) or the Organization for Security and Cooperation in Europe (OSCE). In this respect, the speculations of some analysts and observers who foresaw the dwindling of the Atlantic Alliance after the collapse of the bipolar order have not been confirmed by the history of the post-Cold War. It is likely that NATO will keep its *raison d'être* for a long time.

Simultaneously, the Europeans have expressed the will to play a bigger part on the world scene and to reduce their dependence on the United States as far as preventive diplomacy, crisis-management and peace-enforcement in the Euro-Atlantic area are concerned. The process of European integration took on a new momentum impelled by the unification of Germany and thanks to the close French–German partnership that led to the conclusion of the Maastricht treaty in December 1991. This treaty entered into force two years later. In the past, the emphasis was put on the promotion of a common market and common economic and social policies. In the future, the core of the EU will be the Economic and Monetary Union (EMU). The signatory states also agreed to cooperate in order to define and implement a Common Foreign and Security Policy (CFSP). Such a policy would cover all the questions related to the security of the

European Union, including 'the eventual framing of a common defence policy, which might in time lead to a common defence'.

According to the Maastricht treaty, the West European Union (WEU) is competent 'to elaborate and implement decisions and actions of the Union which have defence implications'. However it is ambiguous concerning the missions which the WEU is supposed to fulfil. As the defence component of the EU, the WEU is slated to develop its operative role so as to be able to act upon an autonomous basis; but it is also the 'means to strengthen the European pillar of the Atlantic Alliance'. In this latter respect, the WEU is mainly a means of linking the EU and NATO and, therefore, has to act in conformity with the positions adopted in the wider Alliance framework.

Hence it is not surprising that the building of a strictly European defence is a controversial issue or that the United States had been biased against such a venture. The initiatives first taken by France and Germany, in December 1990, to promote a 'European Defence Identity' faced strong objections from the Bush administration and from some NATO allies, e.g. the United Kingdom, the Netherlands and Portugal. The latter rejected the idea that WEU should become the 'armed wing' of the EU. For a time, Germany seemed to yield to these criticisms and retreated from its former stance. This seeming shift in attitude was reflected in the common declaration of the American and German Ministers of Foreign Affairs issued in May 1991. But it became apparent that if the Germans were underlining the primacy of NATO they had not renounced the aim of European defence. This trend was confirmed by the letter sent on 14 October 1991 to the Chairman of the European Council by President Mitterrand and Chancellor Kohl, in which they announced the creation of a Eurocorps, a multinational unit which would develop around a French-German core and might act as a catalyst for a closer cooperation among WEU member states.

This proposal was perceived in Washington as a direct challenge to American preponderance in NATO at a time when negotiations on NATO's new strategic concept were in progress. President Bush made sharp remarks in his speech delivered at the opening of the Rome summit in November 1991 where he warned the Europeans against the negative consequences of a free ride: if they wanted to go their way, the withdrawal of American troops deployed on the continent would be inevitable and disengagement would ensue. But it was a false alarm as nobody on the European side was willing to cut the transatlantic link and the Americans were aware that a military presence in

Europe served their global strategy. Most important, the aim of France and Germany was not to create a new European Defence Community on the model of the project which failed in the 1950s. The Eurocorps was conceived as a military tool which could be assigned to the common defence in the framework of the Alliance as well as to crisis-management and peacekeeping under the command or control of the WEU.

In February 1993, it was agreed that the Eurocorps would be put under the operative command of SACEUR in the case of an armed attack against any of the Alliance member (*casus foederis*). However, the contribution to the common defence according to Article 5 of the Washington and the modified Brussels treaties was not the only mission assigned to the European armed forces. One year earlier, the Foreign and Defence Ministers of the WEU member states had decided, in the Declaration of Petersberg in 1992, that they could be used for 'humanitarian and rescue actions, crisis management, peacekeeping and peacemaking'. Eventually, the transatlantic quarrels were settled and a compromise was reached. At the NATO summit in 1994, the United States accepted the principle of a 'European Defence Identity' in the framework of the Atlantic system and envisaged the prospect of putting military assets at the disposal of their European allies for the accomplishment of peace missions to which they did not wish to take part: the Combined Joint Task Forces (CJTF) concept.

In principle, it was decided that NATO can contribute on a case-by-case basis to peacekeeping and peacemaking operations but that its main function is collective defence. Conversely, the WEU – whose defence functions were transferred to NATO decades ago – might find a new *raison d'être* in developing its capacities for crisis management and peace-enforcement in missions mandated by the United Nations Organization (UNO) and/or the Organization for Security and Co-operation in Europe (OSCE). In this respect, the negotiations on the Combined Joint Task Forces would be the litmus test of whether and how far transatlantic relations could be reformed. If successful, there would be a new division of tasks between the United States and the European Union. The Americans would accept that their allies assume greater responsibilities in crisis-management without being subjected to the constraints of NATO's integrated military structures while the Europeans would shoulder a heavier burden of the common defence in the framework of a renewed Alliance. The United States would continue to be involved in European affairs and play the pacifying role which it had assumed since the conclusion of the Washington treaty in 1949.[2]

The central issues are, therefore, the place and function of NATO in the restructuring of the Western security system and the will of the Europeans to assert themselves as autonomous actors on the world scene. If NATO was conceived at the beginning as an alliance of the Western democracies against the Soviet military threat, it also played a stabilizing role in the relations between the member states. Thanks to the involvement of the United States in the promotion of European security after World War II, states which were bitter enemies in the past found the way to reconciliation and cooperation. This remark is particularly pertinent for Germany whose integration into the Western Alliance is generally considered as a security guarantee for its neighbours. Today, the strong requests of some Eastern and Central European states to become full members of NATO proceeds from the same perception. In their view, the enlargement of the Western Alliance towards the East would help the former Communist countries to overcome the difficulties they confront on their way towards pluralistic democracy and market economies and fill the 'security vacuum' implicitly created by the dissolution of the Warsaw Pact Organization.

The renovation of NATO proclaimed at the London summit of the Atlantic Council, in July 1990, and the links established soon after with the former Warsaw Pact states and the successor states of the Soviet Union through the North Atlantic Cooperation Council (NACC), reflected the drastic changes in security perspectives that occurred at the end of the Cold War. In the light of these trends, some analysts expressed the opinion that NATO was about to become a hybrid organization as two distinct security bodies coexisted under the same denomination: the one devoted to collective defence of its members in case of an armed attack and the other devoted to maintaining collective security on an undivided but not wholly pacific continent. In its latter incarnation, NATO was foreseen as performing functions of a peacemaking or peacekeeping nature normally the responsibility of the UN or OSCE.[3]

NATO'S COLLECTIVE SECURITY FUNCTIONS

NATO, by contrast to the WEU, has steadily improved its readiness to undertake collective security operations. While collective defence against an armed attack remains the highest priority of NATO, the organization adopted a more flexible approach with the changes begun in 1989. A landmark was reached at Oslo in June 1992 when the North Atlantic Council agreed to support, on a case-by-case basis, peacekeeping activities under the aegis of the CSCE. Six months later, NATO Foreign Ministers extended this commitment to possible support of UN peacekeeping missions, recognizing that NATO was ready to work with non-NATO states in the CSCE in supporting such operations. Almost immediately, the possibility of NATO supporting the peace efforts of another organization became a reality. In July, it decided to begin monitoring compliance with UN sanctions against the republics of the former Yugoslavia using the Standing Naval Force Mediterranean (STANAVFORMED). The advantage of this arrangement was that the naval forces were under operational command in peacetime and could be employed on new missions soon after the necessary political decisions are made. The effectiveness of the naval embargo operation was demonstrated by the fact that the last known attempted violations occurred in April 1993. The decision by the Clinton administration in November 1994 to end enforcement of the international arms embargo against Bosnia had no practical consequences. But it did undermine the solidarity of NATO members. For the allied governments it was a reminder of US readiness to impose its own views on a multilateral operation.

The original maritime mission was soon followed by the support given by NATO to the establishment of a command and control structure for the UNPROFOR. In September 1992, the NAC agreed to the provision of staff personnel and equipment from the headquarters of NATO's Northern Army Group (NORTHAG) to form the core of the headquarter of the newly formed Bosnia-Herzegovina Command (BHC). The impact of this arrangement, involving one-third of the staff and most of the equipment and vehicles, was judged very positive in ensuring the early effectiveness of the BHC.

In October 1992, the UN Security Council established a no-fly zone to prevent flights by military aircraft of the warring factions over Bosnia and Herzegovina and requested NATO support to monitor this air space. This task was entrusted to the NATO Airborne Warning Force (NAEWF) whose first mission was to provide early-warning coverage for the maritime monitoring operations in the Adriatic. In April 1993, the mission was expanded to provide for enforcement of the UN restriction against unauthorized military flights and a procedure was devised in close coordination with UNPROFOR, which allowed the NATO regional air command to order the attack of the violating aircraft without a formal request.

The UN Security Council also went a major step further by establishing safe areas around the Bosnian cities of Bihac, Sarajevo, Tuzla, Srebrenica and Goradze, and allowed UNPROFOR to rely on NATO-provided air power to defend their forces if they were attacked while performing their duties in the safe areas. The no-fly zone was generally successful in preventing air-to-ground attacks in Bosnia-Herzegovina but air strikes against Serb positions provoked the hostage-taking of UNPROFOR troops. This led to the adoption of a dual-key system which put tight limitations on the use of air power to protect the 'blue helmets' and the civilian population of the safe areas.

The first experience with NATO-conducted 'peace missions' was inconclusive. Since the conclusion of the Dayton agreement and the American participation to the implementation force (IFOR), though, the situation has changed in a radical way. As long as the United States will deploy ground forces in the region and contribute in a significant way to the peace mission in Bosnia-Herzegovina, the preponderance of NATO will not be challenged. The Supreme Allied Command in Europe (SACEUR) will keep the responsibility for the conduct of the military operations. Furthermore, flexible arrangements are available for the command of non-NATO forces participating in the peace mission, as demonstrated by the involvement of troops from Russia and other countries.[4] Nevertheless, considering the sensitivity of American foreign policy to domestic factors, as Michael Brenner has shown, one should not exclude a future reversion from peacekeeping and peacemaking operations, or at least the adoption of a very low profile of the United States in cases where European countries would be the main contributors to the implementation of a peace settlement. This raises at least two questions. Have the members of the European Union the political will to carry out peace missions in the framework of the WEU if the Americans stay aside? Assuming that the answer to this question is positive – and considering the lack or the inadequacy of European capacities mainly in the field of transportation, communication and satellite monitoring – would the United States put at the disposal of their allies the military assets necessary for the success of such a venture?

The accord reached on CJTF at the Berlin NATO summit in June 1996 is a milestone along the road towards a more symmetrically balanced Alliance. However, there are presently few signs that a united Europe will assert itself as a strategic actor in the foreseeable future. For most of the members of the EU are not prepared to devote adequate resources to the reinforcement of their military capacities, especially in the area of intelligence and space observation. Besides, the slow pace of the negotiations on the implementation of the CJTF concept invites scepticism on the building of the 'European pillar', despite the confirmation of the principle of a 'European defence identity' by the Atlantic Council in Berlin. It remains to be seen if the directives given to the military organs will lead to practical measures allowing a greater visibility and operational autonomy of the European component of NATO.

As far as the CJTF are concerned there are doubts about the fair implementation of the decisions adopted by the Atlantic Council in Berlin. The French government let it be known that its full participation in the military structures of the Alliance would depend on the fulfilment of a reform process pointing to the development of an enduring and visible European defence component. It also expected the strengthening of the WEU's operational capabilities so that it might play an effective military role with the logistical support of NATO.[5] The same scepticism prevails about the emergence of a common foreign and security policy of the EU, considering the divergent positions of the member states on important issues and the slight attention devoted to this subject at the intergovernmental conference launched in Turin in March 1996. On the one side, a former French ambassador to NATO, François de Rose, denounced the pusillanimity of the Europeans in missing the opportunity to assert themselves as an autonomous actor in Bosnia-Herzegovina when the prospect of an announced American withdrawal loomed. In his view, the Europeans should have demonstrated their will to assume the main responsibilities in the consolidation of the peace in the Balkans and tested the promise of the US to put NATO assets at their disposal in cases where they would not participate directly in military actions.[6] On the other side, the French Minister of Foreign Affairs, Hervé de Charette, complained about the absence of an 'external European policy' in the Middle East and the exclusion of the Europeans from the peace process despite their having vital interests in the region and contributing financially to the economic and social development of the Palestinian entity. On these issues, at the informal summit in Dublin in October, the EU was divided. The French and the Italians favoured a common initiative in the Middle East whereas the

Germans and the British pleaded for caution. They warned against the negative consequences for transatlantic relations of too-open support for the Palestinians. It is unlikely that these differences will be overcome in the foreseeable future and the *pax Americana* will be the only alternative in the region for the foreseeable future.

Does it mean that the self-assertion of Europe as a power on the world stage is out of reach and that the reform of NATO will seal the preponderance of the US in crisis-management and peace-enforcement in the Euro-Atlantic area? The answer to this question depends as much on the acceptance by the Americans of greater European responsibilities within the Alliance as on the readiness of EU members, or some of them, to act in concert in cases where their interests are distinct from the American ones. The quarrels over the reform of the military commands of NATO, the reluctance of the Americans to share their powers of initiation and control with their European allies, Germany's culture of restraint which limits the use of military force to support peacekeeping and peace-enforcement operations, and the huge obstacles to the definition and the implementation of a common foreign and security policy do not testify in favour of the future of a political Europe. Nevertheless, it is premature to presume the results of the negotiations on the on-going reform of NATO or of the French–German common initiative that seeks to produce a breakthrough in the adaptation of the European institutions to the new challenges.

The prevailing trend points to tactical, *ad hoc* alliances. Thus, the United States has proposed to Germany a 'partnership in leadership' for promoting stability and peace in the area located between the European Union and the Commonwealth of Independent States (CIS). The special relationship between Paris and Bonn, which has been the motor force behind the process of European integration since the 1950s, will continue to be the main element in the project of European integration. It serves, too, as the centrepiece of France's European strategy. But this partnership does not exclude special links for France with other countries like the United Kingdom, Spain, and Italy which do not have the same inhibitions as Germany about projecting their forces into crisis areas and/or are more concerned by the problems raised in the Mediterranean basin whereas Germany is inclined to develop its influence in Eastern and Central Europe.

In the same register, we should not ignore the fact that the defence of the national interest remains one of the main motivation of states. The risks of a renationalization of security policies are not purely academic nor should the danger be excluded out of hand. Presenting the CDU/CSU White Paper on European policy in September 1994, party foreign policy spokesman Karl Lamers warned precisely against the dangers of a return to the balance of power politics of the nineteenth century and pleaded for an acceleration of European integration that covers the field of security and defence policy. Although these apprehensions are shared by the majority of the German political elites, they do not seem to resonate strongly in other European countries where political leaders are content to consider defence matters mainly in terms of intergovernmental cooperation. For all, there is a contradiction between a federal Europe which would imply the 'deepening' of the European Union and the aim of 'widening' the Community. The latter is considered by the Germans, above all, as the right way to stabilize the situation of the Eastern and Central European States and to reinforce security on the continent. How this dilemma could be overcome was never clearly stated in the debates which took place on the other side of the Rhine as the Kohl government committed itself to an enlargement of both the EU (WEU) and NATO.

OPERATIONALIZING PEACE-ENFORCING/KEEPING

Peace missions conducted under the aegis of European regional organizations like NATO and the WEU, whose primary function is collective defence, raise a host of questions which have to be examined from various angles. The first concerns the nature of the mandate given by an international authority and the way that political control is exercised by the UN or OSCE. In the past, peacekeeping operations were conducted under the direct control of international organizations with the participation of 'impartial' countries and with the consent of the states in conflict. With the end of the Cold War, there was a multiplication of peacekeeping operations and a broadening of their missions. That placed a heavy burden on the world body which was organizationally and politically unprepared to undertake them. It was precisely to relieve the UN of this burden that the General Secretary pleaded for a larger involvement of regional organization and concomitantly sought to persuade the NATO and WEU countries to be more active in crisis-management and peace-enforcement in the Euro-Atlantic area. This request received a positive answer although there was reluctance to consider the WEU and NATO respectively as regional organizations according to Chapter VIII of the Charter of San Francisco.

As early as 1993, NATO naval and air forces were used for the implementation of Security Council resolutions concerning the arms embargo against the warring parties in former Yugoslavia and, as we noted, to enforce the no-fly zone in Bosnia-Herzegovina. The WEU, for its part, was associated to the policy of monitoring the arms embargo in the Adriatic as well as on the Danube, and contributed to keeping public order between Croats and Muslims in Mostar (a mission never fully achieved). These and other experiences in Europe deviated significantly from the norms of traditional peacekeeping which entailed, *inter alia*, collective financing by UN member states as an activity of the organization, the deployment of troops from countries with wide geographical spread, and the location of operational command in the Secretary-General and his secretariat. The UNPROFOR operation in Bosnia and Herzegovina, by contrast, was mainly financed by the participating states themselves; and was constituted overwhelmingly of troops from West European countries (the balance shifted in 1994 when a large number of troops from Muslim countries arrived). Traditionally, the absence of the great powers from UN peacekeeping operations was itself a sign of 'United Nationsness'. But in Europe this notion seems strained[7] since UNPROFOR relied on NATO for the enforcement of the Security Council resolutions, leading ultimately to the NATO-conducted air campaigns against the Bosnian Serbs. Though Security Council resolutions referred to NATO acting in support of UNPROFOR, it was obvious that NATO was not merely 'a subcontractor of the United Nations', as was demonstrated by initiatives like the creation of 'heavy weapons exclusion zones' around Bosnian towns, which gave UNPROFOR, new missions not explicitly authorized by the Security Council. Differences were exacerbated in Summer 1995 when the massive use of air power (Operation Deliberate Force), and the deployment of a Rapid Reaction Force by the French, the British and the Dutch created a new military environment that put into question the principle of UN primacy in the management of the peace mission in former Yugoslavia.

Another problem stems from the UN relations with the parties to the conflict. Characteristically, the peacekeepers worked with the consent and practical cooperation of all sides and tried to be impartial in judging the rights and the claims of the conflicting parties. The situation in former Yugoslavia was quite different, as there was no lasting agreement and UNPROFOR did not enjoy the cooperation of the parties for the accomplishment of its task. Moreover, it was under strong pressure from public opinion which challenged the idea of impartiality between 'aggressors' and their victims. It expected from the peacekeepers 'robust' action which went beyond their formal mandate and for which they were not armed. So, performing its routine duties, UNPROFOR was not acting without prejudice to the claims and the aspirations of the Bosnian Serbs; yet, at the same time, was unable to protect the Muslim population located in the so-called 'safe areas'. These circumstances brought into sharp focus the issue of peacekeeping versus peace-enforcement to which General Secretary Boutros Boutros-Ghali alluded in his 1992 *Agenda for Peace*.

In theory, peacekeepers are 'soldiers without enemies',[8] who use force only in self-defence and are deployed not to win a war but to help warring parties end it. The armament of UNPROFOR exceeded the needs of self-defence. Moreover, the threat of the use of force was central to the peacekeepers' ability to fulfil their responsibilities. In effect, they were engaged in 'coercive diplomacy'. In Bosnia-Herzegovina, the parties' recourse to certain military means was limited. Still, the policy was backed by the threat of military force provided by a regional security organization (NATO). The actual resort to air power underscored the uniqueness of peacekeeping in Bosnia. As the distinction between peacekeeping and peace-enforcement is blurred, some have suggested that conflict-mitigation in the former Yugoslavia belongs to a separate category from peacekeeping and that the principles of the latter do not apply. This argument is not entirely convincing as the task of peace-enforcement was given to peacekeepers as part of an operation whose viability ultimately still depended on close cooperation with all the local parties.

To sum up, the experiences with peacekeeping in Europe, be it in former Yugoslavia, in Cyprus or in Georgia, have questioned the primacy of the UN in the control, the financing and the composition of peacekeeping operations. Does it mean that the regional organizations have won the upper hand and in the future will take charge of peace missions that involve coercion whereas the UN would confine itself to traditional peacekeeping? What happened in Yugoslavia since the creation of a Rapid Reaction Force and the constitution of IFOR seems to announce such a transformation. It leaves many questions open, though. Will the states give to the UN adequate military and financial resources for either traditional peacekeeping and/or peace-enforcement? What is the likelihood that the Secretary-General will have at his disposal standby forces available to act in support of preventive diplomacy? Will the UNO renounce its operational responsibility for peace missions assumed by *ad hoc* coalitions of member states or regional organizations and confine itself to the role of a formal legitimizer? The answer to these questions, among others, requires a clarification of UN peacekeeping doctrine and restatement of its authority. Any attempts simply to restore traditional peacekeeping is meaningless considering the enlargement of the concept and the new forms of conflicts which have multiplied in the last years.[9]

UN Adjustments

To respond to the demands of peacekeeping in a changing world, the United Nations has to focus its attention on a series of interconnected challenges. Among them, three deserve special attention. The first relates to the capacity to deploy and manage peacekeeping operations in Europe or elsewhere to the satisfaction of the Security Council and the troop-contributing nations. In this respect, some improvements have been made in the functioning of the Secretariat, mainly by the creation of a Situation Centre to maintain constant communication to the field and by the merger of the former field operations division of the Department of Administration and Management into the Department of Peacekeeping Operations, which guarantees the unity of command from the headquarters to the field. Nevertheless, the sensitive issue of stand-by forces put at the disposal of the General Secretary for preventive crisis-management and peacekeeping has not been settled, in spite of the promises made by some governments. When an emergency occurred in Rwanda, all the states who had theoretically offered stand-by forces were not able or willing to provide them. The weakness of the United Nations at this level has been underlined in the 1996 report on peacekeeping issued by a group of 13 states under the chairmanship of Denmark. The members of the group have been invited to adhere to the report's conclusions and to approve its recommendation concerning the creation of a multinational rapid reaction brigade as part of a UN stand-by force. It remains to be seen whether these recommendations will be followed by the concerned states, but scepticism is in order.

The second point concerns the cooperation of the United Nations with regional organizations in order to ease the financial and resource burdens it bears. Secretary-General Boutros Boutros-Ghali underlined this point when he met heads of European states in Fall 1992. He elicited a positive response. Even in the Federal Republic of Germany the mood was in favour of participation in multinational peacekeeping missions in spite of the juridical controversies about the interpretation of the Basic Law (Grundgesetz) which was construed by some as prohibiting the intervention of the Bundeswehr 'out of area'. The European Union is a richly endowed grouping of states capable of playing a significant role in the implementation of peacekeeping mandates. They could serve as the instrument of *first* resort for the peaceful settlement of differences on the continent. Of course, the UNO has predominance over any regional organization but according to the principle of subsidiarity[10] it would be rational to give special responsibilities to European security institutions, provided that cooperation is in all cases conducted under the authority of the Security Council and in accordance with its resolutions.

Thus the OSCE can be seen as becoming the main framework for preventive diplomacy in the Euro-Atlantic area. Even the Russians have conceded an OSCE *droit de regard* on their manner of dealing with an *internal* conflict in Chechnya. It also played an important part in the implementation of the Dayton agreements. The acting chairman of the OSCE, the Foreign Minister of Switzerland, Flavio Cotti, and the Secretary-General of the UN, Boutros Boutros-Ghali, agreed to develop cooperation between the two organizations so as to improve their effectiveness in various regional conflicts.[11] They seized the opportunity presented by Bosnia-Herzegovina to demonstrate how smoothly they could work together. Thus, the OSCE monitored the implementation of confidence building measures and disarmament agreements, and was responsible for the organization of fair elections scheduled for September 1996, while the UN limited itself to humanitarian functions.

As far as NATO is concerned, the cooperation with the UN has been more problematic, because of differing organizational cultures and mission perceptions. The strains were particularly visible during the period which preceded the watershed crossed in the Bosnian conflict with the inauguration of airstrikes. Command arrangements made NATO actions dependent on authorization by the representative of the Secretary-General, Mr Akashi, who was reluctant to give the green light, fearing reprisals against UNPROFOR troops not mandated and ill-equipped to fight a war. Most of these difficulties were overcome with the conclusion of the Dayton agreement and the deployment of IFOR. The NATO-commanded force was not subordinated to the UN and had wide room of manoeuvre for accomplishing its mission.

Nevertheless, the division of labour between the UN and regional organizations carries the intrinsic risk that the latter might become the vehicle for a new hegemony, i.e. a dominant power exploiting a generous interpretation of Article 52, and its dominance of a regional bloc, to establish a hegemonic position. Russia is suspected by some of aiming at exactly that when it asks international blessing and financial support for actions conducted under the authority of the CIS in the Caucasus (irredentist moves in Georgia, conflict between Armenia and Azerbaidjan about Nagorno-Karabakh), and Central Asia. Arguing that nobody could replace Russia in making peace in the former Soviet Union, the authorities in Moscow tried to obtain a mandate from the international community for peacekeeping within the CIS. This approach received a relatively tolerant appreciation from some Western countries like France, Germany, Italy, the UK and the US.[12] But it was rejected outright by other states, mainly by the countries of the so-called 'near abroad' which were sensitive to the risks of slipping into a Russian sphere of influence and which interpreted the Russian move as a new form of covert colonialism. Russia was also suspected as an interested party in the outcome of local conflicts. Some UN officials pointed out that, as a matter of principle, peacekeepers should not be taken from adjacent countries as their impartiality is questionable. However, it is obvious that the world organization is not able to provide peacekeepers for conflicts on the territory of the former Soviet Union. Moreover, the prevailing mood in most Western countries is not in favour of sending troops to restore order or implement peace in areas where the Russians claim special responsibilities and interests. Thus, it would be sensible to give a clear international mandate to Russia in circumstances where there is no other alternative to no peace at all, and to define rules of conduct which should be applied in the implementation of peacekeeping operations. In this respect, cooperation between the United Nations and regional organizations might be a valuable tool for ensuring that international standards are met and that the larger interests of the world community take precedence over narrowly defined state interests.

The last controversial points concern (1) the command of the troops provided for peacekeeping operations and (2) the feasibility of using force by units that have never been mandated, equipped and deployed to apply coercion. The challenge of command is a complex matter.

The traditional assumption was that troops provided for peacekeeping operations were under the command and the control of the Secretary-General. In spite of the recent changes that have occurred in peacekeeping, this formula was maintained and reiterated in the text of a model agreement between the UN and troop-contributing countries submitted to the General Assembly in May 1991. Subsequently, a more lenient wording spoke of granting to the Secretary-General 'operational control' of the peacekeeping units.[13] Today the prevailing idea is that the business of commanding troops belongs not to the Secretariat but to the member states as peacekeeping operations have increased in complexity and risk. Contributing governments want a direct line of communication to their contingents in United Nations service. This trend was confirmed by the creation of the Implementation Force (IFOR) which was fully dependent on NATO: political control was exerted by the Atlantic Council and the military authority by SACEUR. According to Resolution 1031 by the Security Council, the responsibilities of UNPROFOR were transferred to IFOR and the role of the UN was only to give a political blessing to any military action deemed necessary for the full implementation of the peace agreement.

Finally, there is the dilemma of reconciling coercion and the performance of traditional functions. It was manifest dramatically in Bosnia-Herzegovina when UNPROFOR was blamed for failing to do things – involving force – it was not able to do. Those criticisms were founded on a false assumption. The mandate of the 'protection forces' was not to resist or repel 'aggression', nor to end the war in the Balkan peninsula. Because of the complex origins of the Yugoslav tragedy, the states involved in mitigation of its effects studiously refused to choose sides militarily in the conflict and adopted a more modest stance. Their objective was alleviating the consequences of the fighting for the civilian population, delivering humanitarian relief and creating conditions conducive to a peace settlement. Since an assertive use of coercive force by UNPROFOR might have jeopardized these achievements, it was sensible to adopt a low profile in order to demonstrate impartiality. Of course such behaviour was morally distressing, especially as the warring parties were not amenable to conciliation. Yet taking sides in the conflict would have been militarily irresponsible for UNPROFOR considering its vulnerability and its mandate to avoid fuelling the flames of war, but to help their extinction. That situation only changed when the French, the British and the Dutch decided to create a Rapid Reaction Force to protect the soldiers of UNPROFOR who had been humiliated by the Bosnian Serbs in Spring 1995. The Yugoslav experience shows that the UN can only intervene with success when the member states give it both mandate and means to carry out its stipulated tasks. With the reservation that peacekeeping is not a panacea for any international disorder, the Western powers have to decide what kind of UN they want, in which cases their responsibilities can be delegated to regional organizations, and which kind of action they are willing to approve, to support and to finance.

Comparative Institutions

The CSCE entered the brave new post-Cold War world without concepts, instruments or structures to deal with novel conditions. During the period of East–West confrontation, it served mainly as a channel of communication and a means to promote continental security based on confidence and security building measures (CSBM) and the respect of human rights. After 1989, it turned to preventive diplomacy, crisis management, and conflict resolution. In 1992, it ceased to be a discussion club and was formally transformed into a regional security arrangement as defined in Chapter VIII of the UN Charter. Two years later, it was rechristened a regional collective security organization (Organization for Security and Cooperation in Europe or OSCE) empowered to perform peacekeeping missions. With the UN, the OSCE's conflict-prevention and peacekeeping doctrine is based on cooperation, persuasion and search for consensus among the concerned parties. Eclipsed by the UN in Yugoslavia, the OSCE was not centrally involved in efforts at mitigating the conflicts in former Yugoslavia where it had only a residual function.[14] Nevertheless, it had the opportunity to experiment with various instruments of early warning and conflict prevention elsewhere. Among them the most promising has been the consultation system which permits the 'internationalization' of a problem in the framework of a 'new European concert', i.e. the regular meetings of the permanent council in Vienna. Furthermore, the discreet diplomacy of the High Commissioner on National Minorities and the intervention of the Office for Democratic Institutions and Human Rights have gone beyond early warning to the containment of armed conflicts and the consolidation of peace settlements. Finally, OSCE is involved in the implementation of the 'stability pacts' proposed by the French Prime Minister, Edouard Balladur, in May 1993, and adopted in Paris in March 1995.

The French initiative was motivated by the desire to prevent the outbreak of Yugoslav-like conflicts in Eastern and Central Europe and to create the conditions for an orderly enlargement of the European Union (EU) towards the East. It reflected the change in the meaning and the implications of security since the end of the East–West confrontation. With the disappearance of the military threat, the emphasis is now on the conditions which determine the internal security of a country: democratic consolidation, economic development, absence of domestic unrest, etc. Today, the common view is that the enlargement of the EU and/or NATO would facilitate the implementation of the social and economic reforms, thereby giving the 'new democracies' protection against outside pressures once they had been admitted to the Western 'security community'. It is thus logical that the EU and NATO have demanded, as one of the preconditions to be fulfilled by the applicant countries, the settlement of still-open conflicts between neighbouring states relating to the recognition of borders and the protection of ethnic minorities. The inaugural conference to promote the stability pacts, in Paris in May 1994, adopted a concluding document whose aim was precisely to define the objectives of stability.[15] One year later a treaty between Hungary and Slovakia on the rights of the Hungarian minority was signed on the eve of the Pact's adoption in Paris. The treaty between Budapest and Bucharest on the same subject was finalized in September 1996, ending at least in juridical terms the long dispute on the common border and the status of the Hungarian minority in Romania.

In spite of the controversies surrounding the French initiative when it was proposed in 1993, the usefulness of the process is no longer seriously challenged. The principle that border disputes and minority differences have to be solved by mutual agreement is becoming a prerequisite for joining the European or Atlantic security organizations. Furthermore, the 'stability pact' became one of the first expressions of an EU common foreign and security policy, while simultaneously leading to an extension of OSCE responsibilities since the latter is entrusted with monitoring the implementation of the Pact.[16]

Overall responsibility for applying crisis-management instruments rests with the OSCE's political bodies, in particular the chairman in office aided by the Senior Council and the Permanent Council. The Secretariat has been operational since September 1993. The Conflict Prevention Centre (CPC) deals mainly with OSCE peace missions and the implementation of CSBM. In dealing with actual or potential conflict situations (e.g. Baltic states, CIS and Yugoslavia), the OSCE tried to establish a permanent framework for conflict management and resolution and to assist the parties to conduct a dialogue. Three types of activities have been undertaken: the creation of steering groups to deal with specific conflicts, the sending of personal representatives of the CIO and OSCE peace missions to offer its good offices; and the legitimization of actions undertaken by other international organizations.

The Minsk group set up to mediate and settle the conflict in Nagorno-Karabakh is an example of the first type. By mid–1995, nine peace missions and an 'assistance group' (in Grozny) had been established. In former Yugoslavia, the OSCE took the lead with regard to observing human rights. Missions of long duration were established in Kosovo, Sanjak and Vojvodina with the purposes *inter alia* of monitoring the violations of human rights and to provide the local population with a kind of ombudsman service. Unfortunately, these missions had to be withdrawn less than one year after their deployment (August 1992–July 1993) at the request of the Belgrade government which resented the suspension of its participation in the Helsinki process. It was no longer inclined to accept a *droit de regard* of the CSCE on matters within its domestic jurisdiction. Conversely, the deterrent effect of the related monitor mission dispatched to Skopje in September 1992 worked well. The sanctions assistance missions have provided innovative operational experience in the field of preventive diplomacy. In this respect, CSCE legitimized actions undertaken by other international organizations such as the administration of Mostar by the European Community and the establishment of a military patrol operation on the Danube by the WEU to monitor sanctions compliance. Finally, this pragmatic approach to the management of conflicts contributed to the elaboration of a peacekeeping doctrine for the OSCE, the only body in Europe vested with the power to conduct this kind of operation.[17] The Helsinki summit in 1992 took decisions dealing with a number of detailed questions, including the arrangements with regional and transatlantic organizations to make their resources available in support of peacekeeping activities conducted under the control of the OSCE. Progress in this direction has been slow, as the OSCE has limited organizational capacity to embark on major endeavours. Moreover, most member states prefer limiting the organization to small-scale missions centred on conflict prevention to larger military operations which would require close cooperation with NATO or the WEU.

The Helsinki decisions regarding peacekeeping still await implementation. So far, what are commonly called OSCE peacekeeping operations are long-term missions established to maintain favourable conditions for preventing conflicts or facilitating negotiations. Nevertheless, the CSCE began feasibility studies for a deployment of a multinational peacekeeping mission in the Nagorno-Karabakh conflict for the monitoring of the ceasefire reached in May 1994. A High Level Planning Group (HLPG), established at the CSCE review conference and summit meeting of December in Budapest, made recommendations on the size and characteristics of such a force. But criticism was voiced as most of the participating states were not willing to defray the cost of such a large-scale operation, while NATO logistical, equipment and communication support was excluded for political reasons. In spite of these difficulties, the Minsk group[18] intensified its peace efforts and the OSCE was prepared to launch a more modest operation than it had initially planned. Nevertheless, political consent for the launching of the operation was not forthcoming. The auguries are not favourable. And the fate of this operation may well be the litmus test for the credibility of the peacekeeping function of the OSCE.

The most immediate and acute issues facing the OSCE concern its involvement in the settlement of conflicts on the territory of the former USSR. Since the dismantling of the Soviet Union, Russia has shown that it is willing to deploy its forces to ensure stability in its border areas, e.g. Georgia, Moldova and Tadjikistan. These military operations, conducted under the aegis of the CIS but mainly by Russian troops, are referred to by Moscow as 'peacekeeping operations' although they differ considerably from the classical model. For one thing, these engagements are not mandated by any international organization. The CIS has not yet been recognized by the UN as a regional security arrangement under Chapter VIII of the Charter – and could hardly be regarded as fully impartial considering the preponderant role of Russia. Nevertheless the Helsinki decisions of July 1992 mention explicitly the CIS as a 'peacekeeping mechanism' and since early 1993 Russia has indicated an interest in some form of OSCE political legitimation and financial support for its military operations in the 'near abroad'.

This request has provoked a keen debate. The Central and East European states are inclined to view this problem in the context of the globalization of Russia's national interests. They do not deny the necessity of keeping stability in the post-Soviet space or of putting the Russian-led peacekeeping operations under the control of international institutions to ensure that the principles of international law and OSCE norms of behaviour are respected. As no state other than Russia to date has shown a willingness to send troops to the troublespots of the territory of the former USSR, it can be seen as in the interest of the international community to cooperate with Russia in this matter. The participating states of the CSCE have recognized the merits in principle of such a move, deciding at the Rome Council meeting in December 1993 that 'on a case by case basis and under specific conditions, the CSCE may consider setting up a co-operative arrangement in order, *inter alia*, to ensure that the role and functions of the third-party military force in a conflict are consistent with CSCE principles and objectives'.[19] But the informal negotiations which ensued failed to produce agreement mainly because Russia rejected the need for any international legitimization of CIS peacekeeping operations and insisted on the 'proportionality' principle, i.e. the degree of involvement of OSCE monitoring missions having to be commensurate with their 'political, financial and other participation in the conduct of the third party operations'. In the wake of the Budapest review conference in December 1994, the controversies between Russia and the other OSCE states created an environment which prevented the conclusion of any agreement. Negotiations were suspended *de facto* as the concerns that the OSCE might be used by Russia as an instrument of its own policy were not dispelled.

OSCE's division of labour with NATO and the WEU is another sensitive issue. Given the OSCE's encompassing membership, in theory it should be the first organization to initiate preventive diplomacy and peacemaking in the Euro-Atlantic area. NATO and WEU may function as the instruments authorized to carry out specific tasks while the OSCE's role should be to mandate and politically supervise their peacekeeping actions or to subcontract to them. But NATO and the WEU need to develop more extensive operational links with OSCE bodies if they are to participate in OSCE peacekeeping operations. These links could be institutionalized by an exchange of letters similar to that between the CIO of the CSCE and the UN Secretary-General in May 1993.[20] Nevertheless there is a clear reluctance on the part of the Western powers to subordinate any peacekeeping or peace-enforcing operation conducted by NATO to the authority of the OSCE. In the course of the preparations for the 1994 CSCE review conference many proposals were offered to reinforce the role of the CSCE in the peaceful management of the local conflicts spawned by the Cold War's sudden end, and in the prevention of new divisions in Europe. The Russian Foreign Minister seized this opportunity to present an ambitious programme for enhancing the effectiveness of the CSCE. It was widely expected that the Budapest summit meeting in December 1994 would be decisive for shaping a European collective security structure. However, these high expectations proved unrealistic, engendering disappointment about the outcome, even though some of the measures adopted had positive potential which should not be underestimated.

At the opening session, Manfred Wörner representing NATO, underlined the significance of the CSCE in developing the European security of tomorrow and reaffirmed that the alliance was ready to respond to CSCE requests on peacekeeping or related operations on a case-by-case basis. He also stated NATO's willingness to develop a new pattern of cooperation with a number of Central and East European and Central Asian states in the framework of the Partnership for Peace and the North Atlantic Cooperation Council (NACC). In his view, 'such endeavors must be regarded as complementary to OSCE efforts and are in no way meant to duplicate or replace them'. The aim of the Russians was quite different despite the similarities of the language between the US and NATO proposals, and the Russian documents. Moscow strongly advocated affirming 'the central role of the CSCE', which would authorize and coordinate action by all other European security structures. In short, it should become the keystone of a regional collective security system.[21]

It was clear from the start, though, that 'any suggestion that other transatlantic or European organizations might be subordinated to CSCE' would be flatly rejected by the US and its allies. Eventually, a consensus emerged on the necessity to make a better use of the existing institutions rather than undertaking a major renovation since the CSCE problems 'are not structural, but political'. This point was underlined in connection with the NATO enlargement. In his statement at the Budapest summit, President Clinton took the NATO expansion for granted, saying that 'no nation will be excluded from the process and no country outside will be allowed to express its veto'. But he signalled that the reinforcement of the role of the OSCE would help to alleviate the frictions with Russia on this sensitive issue. In response, President Yeltsin expressed his opposition to the NATO expansion eastwards and warned against a move which might create new divisions instead of promoting European unity. This objection was brushed aside by the Polish President Lech Walesa, who denied that NATO enlargement was contrary to enhancing pan-continental institutions; the code of conduct adopted in the framework of the CSCE would guarantee the submission of any state to the norms regulating international coexistence. These three statements reflected the pragmatic character of the debate on the future security system in Europe and the common awareness that the emerging European security architecture should not seal the old divisions or create new ones. Existing institutions should not be seen as rivals but as complementary bodies serving the same ends. Giving tangible form to those shared sentiments is quite another matter.

Since the 1994 OSCE summit, the controversy over NATO enlargement has sharpened and the two organizations' relationship remains open. Whatever the merits of NATO as a stabilizing institution for the new democracies in Eastern and Central Europe, the Western powers have moved towards a compromise formula which tries to reconcile the aspirations of the applicant countries and the legitimate security interests of Russia. US Secretary of State Warren Christopher, in his landmark Stuttgart speech in September 1996, proposed to settle the problems raised by a NATO enlargement in the framework of a strategic partnership with Russia. He conveyed to Moscow a message of goodwill analogous to the encouraging words addressed by Secretary of State James Byrnes, to the Germans in the same city, 50 years ago. In this perspective, the OSCE might regain momentum as the logical framework for building the 'security model for Europe in the twenty-first century'. France and Germany for their part share the same views on the importance of the OSCE in shaping future 'European architecture', although there remain differences between Paris and Bonn on the merits of the NATO enlargement.[22]

Finally, it has been suggested that the OSCE could increase its peacekeeping effectiveness by establishing a clear division of labour with the UN. Having no mandate to conduct enforcement operations, the OSCE should concentrate on preventive measures in the early stages of intra-state conflicts while the UN would devote itself to the solution of interstate conflicts and use coercion if necessary. The comprehensive concept of security developed in the framework of the Helsinki process – linking the respect for human rights, military confidence building measures and political dialogue – offers a potentially unique model for the prevention and the resolution of conflicts. Until now, the OSCE has confined itself to 'soft' measures of crisis-management which it is best able to use effectively and flexibly. Nevertheless, its participation in 'hard' or large-scale peacekeeping with military involvement cannot be ruled out completely. Two conditions would have to be fulfilled, though: a close cooperation established with regional organizations whose resources are necessary for the success of any peacekeeping mission; and the enhancement of operational and decisionmaking capabilities that would allow it to act decisively without abolishing its cooperative nature based on consensus.

EU/WEU

As far as the European Community and the WEU are concerned, their contribution to the peacekeeping in the Balkan peninsula was modest. Of course, the Twelve tried to mediate between the warring parties in Summer 1991 and they succeeded to some extent in Slovenia where the fighting was quickly brought to an end. At that time, the United States had adopted a low profile in the Balkans. The Bush administration judged that the Yugoslavian crisis was primarily a European problem with its corollary that the Europeans should take the diplomatic lead. It soon became apparent, though, that they were divided on the way to approach the problems raised by the dismemberment of the Yugoslav federation, and were unable to produce a settlement that would put an end to the fighting. The impotence of the European Community led to the intervention of the United Nations. The WEU as such was not involved in the creation of a peacekeeping force; the six member states of the WEU that contributed troops to the UNPROFOR did so on a national basis. Thus, the WEU confined itself to the role of 'a regional partner of the United Nations'[23] in the monitoring of the arms embargo resolutions of the Security Council and, later, in the restoration of public order in the city of Mostar.

Operation 'Sharp Guard' in the Adriatic, as noted earlier, was formally a joint venture conducted under the combined command of NATO and the WEU. But in fact it was placed under the effective command of CINCSOUTH and its success depending on the communication and intelligence means of the Alliance which belong primarily to the Americans. Eventually, the 'competitive cooperation' between the two Western security organizations in the military management of the Yugoslav crisis led to the defeat of the WEU, which was relegated to a subsidiary role in 'civilian–military activities' as it was recognized by the WEU Council in the Noordwijk declaration in November 1994.[24] Although there are contradictory views on the results obtained, it would be unfair to consider the involvement of the WEU in Yugoslavia as useless. However, the performance of police and customs functions is a far cry from the ambitious goals assigned to the WEU in the Maastricht treaty. Despite the progress made in the development of operative capacities over the past few years (Eurocorps, Euroforce, Euromarfor, Franco-British Euro Air Group), the WEU had no part in the military operations related to the peace settlement in the Balkans. In this respect, it is noteworthy that the French initiative for the creation of a rapid reaction force was submitted to a NATO meeting in June 1995, not to the WEU, and that the WEU was not entrusted with a peace mission after the conclusion of the Dayton agreement. In these circumstances, it is not surprising that its record in former Yugoslavia has been harshly criticized and that doubts abound as to its potential for carrying out peacekeeping missions in the future.[25]

The situation in Bosnia-Herzegovina remained precarious, despite Dayton. Prudence pointed to maintaining troops in the area beyond the agreed deadline of the IFOR mandate (20 December 1996) if the aim was to establish a durable self-sustaining peace. The findings of a mission which went to Bosnia from the WEU Assembly in Spring 1996 made it clear that only NATO would be capable of assuming this new responsibility and that at least a symbolic American presence would be necessary.[26] This excluded the possibility of transferring the direction of a reduced peace force to the WEU. Its General Secretary, Mr Cutileiro, made this point firmly: 'The WEU will not replace NATO at the head of any peace force in Bosnia-Herzegovina if the United States decides to withdraw their troops before their European allies do the same.... If the WEU is the only European organization competent in defence matters, it is not yet equipped to carry out a task of such a magnitude.' Commenting on this statement, the Italian deputy Roseta expressed the opinion that the capacities mattered less than the psychological dimension, as the WEU lacks credibility to intervene in such a volatile and complex situation as Bosnia with purely European forces. But he suggested that the WEU might play a greater role in the future by utilizing CJTF arrangements.

CONCLUSION

Before the Dayton agreement and the broad mandate given to IFOR, the working relationship between the UN and NATO had been close.

But the development of the latter's new peacekeeping role was painstaking.

Four themes have emerged from their experience in Yugoslavia and from numerous high-level political and military consultations.[27] The first concerns political control and guidance. NATO accepts that the UN or the OSCE provides the international legitimacy of any peace operation but requires that it be treated on the basis of partnership and not merely as a subcontractor for the military aspect of a particular operation. Second, NATO authorities underline the need for a robust and flexible command structure to control large and complex peace operations for which they are inclined to use proven existing headquarters, as in the forming of the HQ BHC. Implementing the CJTF concept would provide separable headquarters and forces from within NATO for non-NATO contingency missions; this potential opens positive perspectives for future UN or OSCE peace operations alike. Third, it is necessary to tailor the force to the mission since peacekeepers may be called upon to implement a mandate quite different from the one for which they have been prepared. In intra-state conflicts, with frequent violations of ceasefire agreements and anarchic behaviour by renegade elements, the NATO states consider it important that the peacekeepers be physically and mentally prepared for the challenges they face. Finally, the rules of engagement have to be formulated in such a way that the use of force is authorized not only for self-defence but also to cover a broader range of contingencies. The success of peace operations in the new international environment depends on the flexibility in the application of these rules which means providing a wide range of options to military commanders so as to enable them to perform the critical tasks envisaged in their mandate.

With the successful American assertion of leadership that imposed a peace settlement on the warring parties in Bosnia-Herzegovina, followed by active participation in the NATO-managed IFOR to implement the Dayton agreement, NATO was confirmed as Europe's paramount collective security organization in Europe. The renewed mandate for SFOR reaffirmed the criticality of both the US role and NATO capabilities. Still, it must be asked to what extent this precedent of peace-enforcement with the full support of the United States can serve as a model for future interventions. Given the present configuration of the state-system on the continent, and the necessity to face new risks and challenges, the bigger NATO countries are building up their capabilities for what is now commonly called 'projection of forces' outside the area covered by the North Atlantic treaty. To this end, the Alliance has established Combined Joint Task Forces of which the IFOR, with the participation of non-NATO countries, is in some respects a forerunner. For the more active members of the EU, led by France, the adaptation of the structures of the Alliance should be combined with the development of a 'European defence identity' within NATO. In practice little progress has been registered despite the Berlin accords of 1996.

Two sensitive questions remain to be settled: the enlargement of NATO towards the East, and the relations among the NATO, WEU and EU components of future 'security architecture'. On the enlargement issue, a consensus emerged on the necessity to proceed cautiously and to take into account the security interests of Russia. As to the EU/WEU linkage, the United Kingdom and Germany hold opposing views. The latter pleads for the absorption of the WEU into the EU and the former for an autonomous role of the WEU as the European pillar of NATO. France is less trenchant than Germany on this issue but considers that the WEU should in due course be incorporated into the EU in accordance with the provisions of the Maastricht treaty. A European defence presupposed the intergovernmental conference's agreeing on at least the minimal purposes and means for the reinforcement of the CFSP: i.e. by the nomination of a high representative who could speak in the name of Europe; and a decisionmaking process which would allow the states that have the means and desire to act as a coalition of the willing on behalf of the EU. Here again, the Franco-German partnership is the key to EU development. Its ability to animate a CFSP will largely determine how unified, and forceful, will be a distinctly European voice within the Atlantic Alliance. That, in turn, is one of the key factors shaping NATO's adaptation to collective security functions and the terms of its relationship with both the OSCE and the UN.

NOTES

1. A German historian, Hans-Peter Schwarz, described the united German State as the 'central power in Europe' which may behave in a more assertive way as the former FRG, *Die Zentralmacht Europas. Rückkehr Deutschlands auf die Weltbühne* (Berlin: Siedler Verlag, 1994).

2. See J. Joffé, *The Limited Partnership. Europe, the United States and the Burdens of Alliance* (Cambridge: Ballinger, 1987); and A. DePorte, *NATO in the 1990s* (London: Pergamon Brasseys, 1989).
3. The former French ambassador to NATO, Gabriel Robin, expressed this opinion after the summit in Brussels in January 1994, 'OTAN: un sommet instructif', *Le Figaro* (31 January 1994).
4. General George A. Joulwan, Supreme Allied Commander Europe, expresses his satisfaction about the agreements concluded with general Shevtsov in the framework of IFOR in an article published by the *International Herald Tribune*, 'NATO and Russia are Working Together and Can Keep It Up' (30 April 1996). According to SACEUR, these agreements permitted the reconciliation of the principle of the unity of command and the Russian will not to be submitted to NATO military integration.
5. See the speech delivered on 29 August 1996 by the French President, Jacques Chirac, at the annual meeting of the ambassadors at the Elysée Palace, Documents d'Actualité internationale, 20 (15 October 1996) (La Documentation française).
6. See F. de Rose, 'Les balbutiements de l'Europe', *Le Figaro* (4 octobre 1996).
7. This point has been stressed by Shashi Tharoor, special assistant to the Under-Secretary-General for Peacekeeping Operations at the United Nations, in his article, 'United Peacekeeping in Europe', *Survival*, 37:2 (Summer 1995).
8. This qualification was coined by a research associate in the Foreign Policy Studies Program at the Brookings Institution. See L. L. Fabian, *Soldiers without Enemies: Preparing the United Nations for Peacekeeping* (Washington: Brookings Institution, 1971).
9. This way to settle the contemporary problems of peacekeeping in retreating into the past has been sharply criticized by S. Tharoor, 'Should UN Peacekeeping Go Back to Basics', *Survival*, 37:4 (Winter 1995–96).
10. This principle can be deduced from the Charter of San Francisco. See 'Towards a Subsidiary Model for Peacemaking and Preventive Diplomacy: Making Chapter VIII of the UN Charter Operational', *Third World Quarterly Journal of Emerging Areas*, 17:1 (March 1996).
11. Agreement concluded in Geneva, July 1996, *Neue Zürcher Zeitung* (2 July 1996).
12. See the contribution of Vladimir Baranovsky to the *SIPRI Yearbook 1994* (Oxford: Oxford University Press), 'Conflict Developments on the Territory of the Former Soviet Union', pp. 169–203.
13. See, for instance, 'Statement by the President of the Security Council' (S/PRST/1994/22).
14. See the contribution of Victor-Yves Ghébali, 'L'OSCE et la gestation du conflit yougoslave: évaluation d'un rôle résiduel (1991–1995)' to the collection of essays published by the Centre d'Etudes de Défense et de Sécurité Internationale' of the University Pierre-Mendès France at Grenoble, 'Les Institutions de sécurité face à la crise de l'ex-Yougoslavie' (sous la direction de Jean-François Guilhaudis), *Cahiers du*

CEDSI, No. 17, juin 1996 (hereafter quoted as:'Les Institutions de sécurité').

15. According to the concluding document, para 1.5, stability will be achieved 'through the promotion of good neighbourly relations, including questions related to frontiers and minorities, as well as regional cooperation and the strengthening of democratic institutions'. For a comprehensive view on this venture, see the study by A. D. Rotfeld, 'Europe: The Multilateral Security Process', *SIPRI Yearbook 1995*.

16. The 31st meeting of the OSCE permanent council (March 1995) specified concrete steps with which the Pact should be followed up. See A. D. Rotfeld, 'Europe: Towards New Security Arrangements', *SIPRI Yearbook 1996*, pp. 279–322.

17. For a clear presentation of the peacekeeping function of the OSCE and stimulating remarks on its potential, see J. M. Nowak, 'The Organization for Security and Cooperation in Europe', *Challenges for the New Peacekeepers*, T. Findlay, ed., SIPRI Research Report No. 12 (Oxford: Oxford University Press, 1996).

18. Set up in March 1992 to settle the conflict in Nagorno-Karabakh, it consisted originally of Armenia and Azerbaijan (the parties to the conflict), Czechoslovakia, Italy and Sweden (the three members of the troïka at this time), Belarus, France, Germany, Russia, Turkey and the US.

19. Decisions of the Rome Council meeting (1 December 1993), section II, para. 2, *SIPRI Yearbook 1994* (Oxford: Oxford University Press, 1994), p. 260.

20. Framework for cooperation and coordination between the United Nations Secretariat and the CSCE, constituting an attachment to the letters exchanged on 26 May 1993 between M. Boutros Boutros-Ghali and Mrs Margaretha af Ugglas from Sweden, quoted by J. M. Nowak, *op. cit.*, p. 139.

21. The Russian 'Program of Enhancing the Effectiveness of the CSCE' addressed to the CSCE on 23 June 1994 postulated, 'The transformation of NACC into a universal mechanism for military and political cooperation functioning in close contact with the CSCE', quoted by A. D. Rotfeld, 'Europe: The Multilateral Security Process', *SIPRI Yearbook 1995*, p. 298.

22. See the speeches delivered the same day (28 August 1996) by the Ministers for Foreign Affairs of Germany, Klaus Kinkel, and of France, Hervé de Charette, respectively in Alpbach (Austria) and in Paris, at the opening of the conference of French ambassadors.

23. The problems raised by the qualification of the WEU as a regional organization of Chapter VIII of the Charter have been analysed in a well-argued and -researched essay by L. Vierucci, 'L'UEO: un partenaire regional des Nations Unies?', Paris, *Cahiers de Chaillot*, No. 12 (décembre 1993).

24. The subordination of the WEU to NATO has been emphasized by M.-C. Plantin, 'Les Occidentaux aux prises avec la crise de l'ex-Yougoslavie: le rôle de l'UEO', in *Les Institutions de sécurité*. In describing

the monitoring operations in the Adriatic she uses the wording 'confiscation otanienne' to suggest the marginalization of the WEU.
25. See the debates at the Assembly of the WEU in 1996 and the essay by N. Gnesotto, 'Leçon de la Yougoslavie', Paris, *Cahiers de Chaillot*, No. 14 (March 1994). She reiterated her criticism in an article published just before the opening of the Intergovernmental Conference in Turin, 'La défense européenne au carrefour de la Bosnie et de la CIG', *Politique Etrangère*, No. 1 (1996).
26. See the report presented by Mr Roseta to the 41 session of the WEU Assembly, 'Le processus de paix dans les Balkans – La mise-en-oeuvre des accords de Dayton', Document 1526 (14 mai 1996).
27. On NATO's conceptual approach to peacekeeping, see the contribution by S. R. Rader, 'NATO' to the SIPRI research report quoted in note 12.

9 Reconciliation of Western Security Institutions
Mario Zucconi

Seven years after the fall of the Berlin Wall, the dissolution of the Warsaw Pact and the disintegration of the Soviet Union, the debate among the Western allies on the most suitable institutional arrangements for managing European security and political stability is still open. The process of renovation is a sign of institutional health for the Alliance, which has outlasted the end of the superpowers' rivalry. It has been a stressful process, punctuated by the conflict in Yugoslavia. Adjustment to new conditions and new threats has been aggravated by the upwelling of national particularisms.

The foreign policies of the Western allies have become more individualized even as NATO endures and adapts. Even though the Atlantic area remains the most institutionalized and most homogeneous one in the world, countries have acquired a more distinct profile. The Cold War gone, they became partially 'de-systemized'. The neat hierarchical arrangement of security issues and Alliance roles of the Cold War years has given way to a more fluid situation. The allies increasingly differed as to preferred instruments for sustaining common interests and for managing international stability. In part, that reflects the 'domestication' of foreign policy as described by Hanns Maull in Chapter 7. Reordered priority scales, parochial publics and, in places, opportunistic leaders, combine to erode the sense of collective solidarity and discipline.

Thus, the end of the East–West confrontation in Europe today affords London a more detached approach to continental affairs. By contrast, it opens for Bonn great opportunities and substantial responsibilities, but also unaccustomed burdens. To Paris, in turn, the diminished relevance of the US strategic guarantee offers the perceived possibility to reopen the debate on political arrangements – and on the role of France – at the head of Western security institutions. It also encourages France to more openly compete for influence in other regions, especially in the Middle East.[1] Italy, too, has its own angle of vision. While 'projecting stability' eastward by enlarging NATO necessarily has a strong appeal for Germans, who have lived for half-a-century on the border between two hostile systems, some Italian officials quietly point to the former Yugoslavia as indicative of how the nature and location of security threats has shifted. They urge priority be given the Mediterranean as the Western allies prepare to invest in broadening the zone of stability around their national territories.

The challenges of collective security heighten the importance of divergent thinking in Western capitals. Collective security organizations have been reconditioned by the new international environment. The UN and OSCE have been tasked with more ambitious responsibilities than they were during the Cold War. Their ability to fulfil expectations, which often push them beyond their traditional competences and mandates, depends on acquiring corresponding authoritativeness and practical support from members. Where the UN fails, as in the former Yugoslavia, it loses credibility and utility. As that episode demonstrates, multilateral organizations are pushed and pulled by the differing interests and wavering allegiance of states to multilateral institutions. The ambivalence of the Western powers has been of capital importance in first bolstering and then constraining the world body's management of international conflict.

They tend to pick their preferred forum by the self-serving criterion of where their influence goes furthest, and adjust their level of support accordingly. In Yugoslavia, much of the Western allies' ineffectiveness and lack of a substantial commitment before the turnabout in Summer 1995 derived from the way collective instruments were used – in competition and as possible alternatives to one another.[2] Their intrinsic capabilities and competences often seemed of secondary consideration. The competitive use of institutions as instruments of national policy, and as 'influence multipliers', is an important feature of the Western approach to multilateralism. At the institutional level, NATO has taken a series of steps to prepare itself legally and structurally to take on peacemaking and peacekeeping functions. A key decision, enabling NATO to intervene in crises outside the Treaty area, came at the Oslo Ministerial North Atlantic Council (NAC) of 4 June 1992. The conflict in the former Yugoslavia had then just moved to its second, bloodier phase – that of the Bosnian civil war. Although it was a fundamental formal step forward, the 1992 NAC decision did not amount to an unqualified allied commitment to peace support. At Oslo, the allies affirmed the authority and interest of the Alliance to act 'out of function'. They also stated that NATO actions would be carried out in a collective security framework where broader international legitimation was provided – by the OSCE or, as the NAC added in December, by the United Nations. However, peace support was to be decided on a case-by-case basis. Moreover, from the beginning there were different readings of the decision itself.

France was most outspoken in stating its unhappiness about the extension of NATO's mandate. France had been optimistic that, with the disappearance of the Soviet threat, the Europeans could achieve strategic autonomy. Accordingly, in the former Yugoslavia, it preferred the OSCE, EU and UN as frameworks for multilateral action, while opposing NATO's assumption of Article 4 tasks. Reflecting Paris' strong reservations, Secretary-General Manfred Wörner declared that the organization wanted to 'avoid any automatism'.[3] Washington's suggestion at the Oslo meeting that NATO could be used to enforce the UN-established security zone around Sarajevo and its airport was turned down by the European allies. Afterward, in the preparatory meetings for the Helsinki OSCE summit of early July, France continued to thwart what it considered attempts by the US to institutionalize a peacekeeping role for NATO.[4] Reluctantly, Paris would concede a progressively enlarged role for the Alliance for the want of credible alternatives and an evolving consensus that the West's premier security body could not remain detached from Europe's first major security crisis of the post-war era.

Over time, NATO took up one new task after another: from the monitoring and then enforcement of the embargo in the Adriatic (Operation Sharp Guard), to the enforcement of the no-fly zone over Bosnia; and the ultimata issued to the Bosnian Serbs intended to protect Sarajevo and Gorazde as 'safe areas'. Strong disagreements over strategy notwithstanding, NATO progressively became the key instrument of Western action. The successful resort to large-scale air-attacks in August/September 1995 was a watershed. NATO had earned its spurs as the agent of continental peace and stability. The constitution of IFOR cemented a consensus that the Alliance as the most capable and credible security body available had to have the central role in meeting the West's collective responsibilities and interests in the new Europe. It thus pushed into the background other operational options considered in an earlier phase of the conflict, e.g. a better-equipped, more fully empowered OSCE or the creation of a substantial standing force at the disposal of the UN Security Council. The determining influence exercised by the Yugoslav experience in the evolution of the Atlantic Alliance was registered through the transformation in the positions of the major allies with regard to the out-of-area and collective 'peace support' issues.

The United States' attitude, of course, was most crucial. As Michael Brenner explains, when Washington finally felt compelled to intervene, it recognized NATO was the multilateral instrument of choice. A disparaging attitude toward the UN, which was already widespread among American policymakers and the public, was reinforced by experiences in Somalia and former Yugoslavia. The accompanying reluctance to deploy US troops on the ground in collective operations under command other than NATO took on the force of sacred canon. It is now a given of both military doctrine and political sentiment. Specifically in the case of Yugoslavia, whenever the issue arose of a possible US participation in operations on the ground in Bosnia (to extract UNPROFOR, or to enforce a peace plan), Washington immediately made known its insistence that the UN be excluded from the chain of command. That demand, along with allied differences over the use of coercive force, had worked against the forming of a Western consensus on the Alliance's responsibilities in the conflict. Consequently, a temporizing NATO had to share the blame for the ineffectiveness of the international intervention. In the end, Washington ultimately felt vindicated in its approach when the unimpeded use of NATO air power compelled the Bosnian Serbs to accept a ceasefire and moved all the warring factions toward the conclusion of the Dayton peace agreement.

As for Paris, as Frédéric Bozo explains in Chapter 3, it was the gradual recognition of NATO's unique capabilities during the Balkan conflict that was a principal factor in bringing France back into the military structure of the Alliance. France had been most explicit in resisting a paramount role for NATO in performing collective security functions. Instead, it attempted to build up the competences of other institutions. The inadequacy of those institutions, including the European Union, was manifest. When it announced its desire to re-enter NATO's political-military bodies in the autumn of 1995, Paris had long ceased resisting the transformation of NATO into a structure capable of performing collective security functions. That move, indeed, had been foreshadowed for some time. As early as April 1993, it had directed its representatives to participate in the deliberations of the NATO Military Committee on non-Article 5 operations. The French rapprochement with NATO was not without qualifications: its ongoing search for European freedom of diplomatic manoeuvre; its self-promotion as Europe's surrogate in an equal partnership with the United States; and its concern that enlargement should not unbalance the Alliance's geographical orientation in Germany's favour. That, however, does not diminish the importance of the fundamental change in the French policy – namely, the recognition of NATO as the primary framework in which to pursue its policy interests. Coupled with the fading of a strategy based on European-only capabilities, that judgement meant (as concerns specifically out-of-area operations), that only NATO was competent – for the foreseeable future.

In Bonn, NATO's decisive action in the summer of 1995 further strengthened the conviction of the Kohl government, in particular Defence Minister Volker Rühe, who appraised the Alliance as the only effective military instrument for crisis-management. The Alliance's decisive intervention in Bosnia helped overcome its residual inhibitions. Reservations remained among the German public with regard to a combat role for the Bundeswehr. In contrast with the strong support for humanitarian interventions, backing for peace enforcement operations remained lukewarm, despite the lack of opposition to participation in SFOR on an equal footing with its allies. But clearly the political tide had turned. Great Britain, sustained by a political culture largely free of inhibitions regarding military operations abroad, has no problem with the extension of NATO's mandate – one deemed central to all post-Cold War allied cooperation. Still, in Bosnia, London often found itself at odds with Washington. The clash stemmed from divergent assessments of Western interests in what for Britain was a 'distant' conflict. In the end, pragmatism and events on the ground led to a rapprochement. One welcome outcome for London was the discrediting of plans to foster purely European security bodies. In Italy, the most recent experiences of peace-support operations have greatly reduced the political and legal objections to the use of the armed forces outside the national territory. Both policymakers and the public have increased their support for NATO as it is (with a diminished enthusiasm for strengthening of the Alliance's European component). Bosnia has produced a uniform assessment, among officials, of NATO as the most relevant and most effective organization for performing peace-making and peacekeeping functions. Especially among the military, that favourable view of NATO is matched by a strongly negative opinion of the UN's utility as an instrument for managing regional conflicts.

EUROPEAN SECURITY ARCHITECTURE

The NATO consensus formed in the last phase of the Bosnian conflict clearly established it as the preferred Western instrument for both collective defence and collective security. The post-Cold War debate on the European security architecture abated, as a consequence. The Berlin accords of June 1996 on CJTF formalized a compromise that resolved, within the NATO fold, some of the main issues that had bedevilled the Alliance. CJTF was not just an exercise in institutional engineering. That agreement should be understood in relation to other achievements: the demonstrated process of IFOR in Bosnia; the return of France – however incomplete – to the integrated military structure of the Alliance (and the decision of Spain to do the same); and the availability of Germany for non-Article 5 operations. The division between a 'Europeanist' and an 'Atlanticist' approach to European security of the early post-Cold War years is blurring – even if some of the differences are not yet fully overcome. In 1991, Paris and Bonn took the lead in setting a Common Foreign and Security Policy (CFSP) as a central goal of the Treaty on the European Union (Maastricht). Despite the scepticism of some, above all the British, the Treaty did commit the members to a CFSP that would cover 'all questions related to the security of the union, including the eventual framing of a common defence policy, which may in time lead to a common defence'.[5]

Washington's reaction was ambivalent. While inclined to devolve on to the European allies much of the responsibility for stability in the continent (most clearly in the early phase of the armed conflict in the former Yugoslavia), US leaders were at the same time uneasy at the prospect of the Europeans coalescing as a strong caucus within the Alliance. Five years and a bloody Balkan war later, a European CFSP is an abstract distant goal. For the time being, any European security personality will evolve within the 'Atlanticist' framework. For France, the primary force behind a European security identity, that is a disappointment. The conflict in the Balkans put French conceptions through a severe trial. As Frédéric Bozo shows, the weakness of the European concert and the ultimate resort to a US-led NATO was crucial to the evolution of French thinking about European security architecture that refocused on a reformed NATO.

The US moved to meet the French halfway at the Berlin NAC meeting.[6] The accord on CJTF suspended indefinitely plans to upgrade the WEU into a competent military organization. The Berlin communiqué specifies that the Alliance needs a 'single multinational command structure' to undertake both Article 5 and non-Article 5 contingency operations.[7] The concessions the Clinton administration made to the European desire for a ESDI do not reflect confidence that the Europeans can act effectively without American participation. Few in Washington had any doubt on that score in the light of the sour experience in Yugoslavia. 'The fundamental mistake in 1991–92, during the early phase of the Yugoslav crisis, was the decision to let the European Union handle it *rather than NATO*' – thus Richard Holbrooke, the architect of the Dayton accords, recently assessed four years of problematic Western response to the conflict, while lauding President Clinton for eventually unleashing NATO.[8]

As for the Alliance's future evolution, NATO's eastward enlargement will have the dominant influence in shaping continental security architecture. The enlargement strategy emerged slowly as the Alliance's formula for Europe's post-Cold War security conditions. It became official Alliance policy only when the Clinton administration fixed upon it as a policy for maintaining a high US profile in European affairs via its most congenial organization, and when Bonn adopted enlargement as the central element in its strategy of regional stabilization. That said, the idea of enlargement gained prominence because of unceasing entreaties from Warsaw, Prague and Budapest. As early as Spring 1991, the 'Visegrad 4' had clearly defined their goal, and coordinated their policies towards some form of integration into NATO.[9]

The Western allies, whose overriding concern was sustaining a cooperative relationship with Moscow, did not respond with open arms. Grudgingly, they offered a looser form of affiliation – on a non-exclusionary basis. Thus, the Alliance established a limited agenda for cooperation within the North Atlantic Cooperation Council (NACC) promulgated at the Rome summit of November 1991. Even this modest step met opposition in France. Paris saw NACC as part of a new US strategy for maintaining political dominance in European affairs. Paris hoped NATO could be limited to providing a strategic insurance policy that would allow for the enhancement of Western European influence via the European Community and WEU while OSCE satisfied the need for a comprehensive collective security. The NACC was suspect because it overlapped with the competence of the OSCE.

By contrast, London, like Washington and Bonn, found the NACC useful as a way of forestalling the Eastern European demands for NATO membership. British officials later looked at the Partnership for Peace (PfP), approved in January 1994, in the same light.

Enlargement changed the picture dramatically. In Washington, the sudden conversion to a pro-enlargement position in the fall of 1994 came in the context of the Clinton administration's restructuring of its European policy. The failure of the Western intervention in the Yugoslav conflict motivated the US to restore the Alliance's status and cohesion as well as its own prominent position in European affairs. Furthermore, the White House had become the easy target of partisan Republican attacks who championed the cause of the Eastern Europeans. An unqualified 'Russia first' policy was no longer tenable on either strategic or political grounds. While not oblivious to Moscow's anxieties, and President Yeltsin's political vulnerability, Washington stood steadfast behind its commitment to enlargement even as it preferred a package of compensatory measures designed to satisfy Russia's demand for recognition as a central player in all European security arenas.

NATO – in contrast to the discrediting performances by other institutions and arrangements – offered Washington a ready-made instrument for exerting Western political influence eastward. However, as Michael Brenner points out, that ready-made option did not solve, indeed bypassed, the fundamental issue of Europe's post-Cold War security structure and the American place in it: i.e. the reconciliation of Western defence bodies with pan-European security arrangements that accorded high status and prominent place to Russia.

In Bonn, the appeal of NATO enlargement goes beyond strategic calculations. It emerges from the political culture of a country which has been, for half a century, on the front line between two hostile systems. It yearns for stability on its eastern borders parallel, if not matching, the institutionalized stability of its multiple Western affiliations. After unification, German leaders looked at the OSCE as the best framework for ensuring stability in post-Cold War Europe. Foreign Minister Hans-Dietrich Genscher was a strong advocate of bolstering the OSCE as an inclusive, continent-wide security body. However, that institution could not easily be developed into what Bonn desired. By 1994, NATO enlargement had replaced the OSCE in the minds of the Kohl government as the main instrument for establishing stability in the political space to Germany's east. Still, the fear that an isolated Russia could endanger post-Cold War

European peace and conciliation was ever present as Bonn – and the Alliance – moved gingerly along the enlargement path.

Defence Minister Rühe was the strongest advocate of the inclusion into NATO of the Visegrad 4. He argued from the first that the continued Western orientation of those countries was at stake. Sensitive to Moscow's anxieties, Rühe also was an early proponent of a formal treaty of partnership between Russia and NATO. Consistent with that concern, Rühe was inclined to limit enlargement, while repeatedly singling out Poland for early admission. Those propositions became the basis for a government consensus in Bonn with Chancellor Kohl as its anchor-point.

The commitment to enlargement, along with the CJTF accord and the IFOR deployment, brought a clarification of the actual capabilities, potentialities and competences of NATO relative to other security organizations. That assumption of broad responsibilities by the Alliance became possible when the outlook and preferences of the major allies came into close convergence. In addition, NATO's demonstrated effectiveness pushed into the background its putative European challenger – the WEU, as well as collective security bodies. However, the present consensus should not be confused with a conclusive settlement of allied differences. All national objectives were not achieved in the compromises reached. France, for one, cheered the Berlin decisions as 'the first time in the history of the Atlantic Alliance [in which] Europe can express its defense identity.'[10] But in fact Paris' desire for a tangible, acknowledged European entity within NATO was not met at the 1996 Berlin NAC. Others, too, have status ambitions that will complicate on-going efforts to enhance the Alliance's flexibility and operational effectiveness while expanding its geographic and functional reach.

NATO holds centre stage. It remains to be seen, though, if the cast can master the roles in an unfolding political drama without a closing act.

NOTES

1. See 'French, Upset, Hint at Politics in Africa Visit by Christopher', *International Herald Tribune* (10 October 1996) 10; and C. R. Whitney, 'French Peeved at Life, and at Washington', *International Herald Tribune* (11 November 1996) 1.

2. For analyses of the mobilization of collective organizations in the response to the Yugoslav crisis, see M. Zucconi, ed., *The International Responses to the Conflict in the Former Yugoslavia: Reorganizing Multilateralism after the Cold War* (New York: St. Martin's, forthcoming); and R. H. Ullman, *The World and Yugoslavia's Wars* (New York: Council on Foreign Relations, 1996).
3. *Nouvelles Atlantiques*, XXVI, no. 2430 (6 June 1991) 2–3.
4. *Nouvelle Atlantiques*, XXVI, no. 2433 (17 June 1992) 1.
5. Treaty of the European Union, Article J.4.1.
6. See P. Cornish, 'European Security: The End of Architecture and the New NATO', *International Affairs*, LXXII, no. 4 (1996).
7. See the Berlin Communiqué in *NATO Review*, XLIV, no. 4 (July 1996).
8. 'How Peace Is Doing', *Time* (16 September 1996) 26. Emphasis added.
9. The three governments were reported to have asked individually for some security guarantees from NATO already in 1990. See *Economist* (17 November 1990) 30.
10. Foreign Minister Hervé de Charette quoted in 'Defence Deal Keeps All the Parties Happy', *The Independent* (4 June 1996).

Conclusion
Michael Brenner

The Western allies have struggled since 1989 to reorient their strategic thinking and to renovate their security structures to account for the radically changed environment they now inhabit. The difficulties they have encountered bespeak the unique complexities of the situation they face, rather than the severity of the problems it presents. Their Cold War victory meant leaving a world at once readily comprehensible and diplomatically unidimensional. They enter one that eludes easy formulation and defies the charting of clear lines of policy. The collective discipline and concentration required to navigate in it have proved hard to muster. There is no stark threat to galvanize attention; rather, amorphous conditions that carry only latent dangers of uncertain shape or magnitude. Decompression from the rigours of the protracted East–West confrontation diffuses political energies, while there is slackening public interest and willingness to defer to the designs of leaders.

For NATO as a military alliance the challenge of strategic uncertainty has been especially acute. It is always a daunting feat to plan without a preferred enemy in mind. Today's exceptional conditions compound the problem. For the very concept of security has become elastic. It encompasses not just the external policies of European states and the correlates of power; but also the nature of domestic political and economic systems. In addition to making prudent arrangement for contending with contingent threats at some unforeseeable time in the future, the Western allies have set themselves the more ambitious, and hopeful, goal of nurturing facsimile liberal democracies to the East whose internal dynamics would point them to partnership with the West rather than to rivalry or conflict. In this frame of reference, NATO is one institutional vehicle among others that can contribute to a knitting together of polities and societies at the two ends of the continent.

The process of continental reconciliation was visualized, for a time, as something that might occur 'organically', if not spontaneously. That is to say, the liberal teleology some discerned at work in the post-Communist world could sustain a relatively painless process leading to a fundamental compatibility, a compatibility that would ensure security among congenial neighbours. The halcyon days ushered in by the liberal revolutions in most of the former Communist world encouraged optimistic visions of a homogeneous Europe – a fleeting time remembered as a feast of brief hopes.

As that sanguine mood has faded, the full dimensions of the Western allies' post-Cold War adaptation soon emerged. The Alliance's agenda encompassed four projects.

(1) Renovation of NATO's military structures and plans to accord with an altered threat perception, the scaling back of defence budgets, a shift in anticipated missions, and the revival of collective security institutions.
(2) Designing a strategy for serving the West's broad interests by extending the range of the Alliance's emollient influence eastwards without degrading itself in the process or loosening the ties that bind the Western partners.
(3) Finding means to compensate for a United States leadership that was becoming more attenuated, selective, and moderated by the greater inclination of the West Europeans to assume a larger role in managing continental affairs.
(4) Making it into a competent instrument for a concerted Western diplomacy aimed at consolidating a pan-European security system built on norms of peaceable intercourse.

The record is mixed. The Alliance has done well in reforming organizational structures, less well with policy innovation. Strictly military matters have been handled more effectively than political affairs. Conviction and direction have been most evident in declaration, but erratic in action. In the military sphere, NATO's most solid accomplishments are in the revamping of force structures. Starting in 1990, a series of progressive steps have been taken to make Alliance forces lighter, more mobile, and, consequently, more flexible. Parallel adjustments have been made in command arrangements. The CJTF agreement initialled in June 1996 is the most far-reaching achievement, its problematic elements notwithstanding. It goes beyond the modularization of military assets to laying the basis for military operations undertaken by the Western European allies without direct American participation. CJTF commits NATO to making provision for constituting a standing European command for the accessing of US-held assets. In concept, it resolves the contentious issues raised by the overlapping jurisdictions of NATO and WEU, at least for the time being, and clears away impediments to genuine burden-sharing.

Implicitly, it also better prepares the allies to perform unconventional, 'out-of-function' missions that go beyond defence of their national territory.

When one turns toward questions of strategic design and diplomacy the picture is cloudier. As for joint efforts at conflict management, the experience in the former Yugoslavia raises troubling questions about the Alliance's readiness and aptitude for coping with 'new age' security problems.

A Strategic Void?

At the strategic level, the Alliance has not been inert. In fact, it has been hyperactive. Inauguration of the North Atlantic Consultative Council (NACC) was swiftly followed by the launching of the Partnership-for-Peace (PfP) program. PfP had barely left the drawing board before the more ambitious and daring plan for NATO enlargement was promulgated. Simultaneously, the WEU took steps to bring the East Europeans into its ambit – offering an array of associate and observer memberships. OSCE, too, was endowed with fresh mandates, an expanded organizational apparatus and a plethora of collective security functions. Europe became host to an *omnium gatherum* of security bodies. Each initiative was presented with a reasonable justification and plausible objective, the far-reaching, potentially divisive enlargement plan being the exception. That historic project was notable for having been decided in principle before a full review of its implications was conducted; statements of its purposes varied from capital to capital and shifted with the changing diplomatic winds; and it was subject to a series of *ad hoc* emendations and annexes as the allies dealt with acrid reactions in Moscow and uneasiness among those East European countries not slated to be among the first tranche of entrants. Enlargement has gone through a ceaseless process of self-definition even as the plan was being implemented.

The Western powers' acronym-loaded toolbox has yet to construct a comprehensive, coherent strategy. The pieces on the workbench have not been fitted together into a coherent whole. The strenuous attempts made to represent them as such evokes the image of Rubik's cube; in this instance, a committee trying earnestly but vainly to match all the faces of the puzzle.[1] Claims of success are routinely made but no definitive exposition of the strategy exists. Instead, different faces of the cube are displayed depending on which aspect of European security is raised.

Polish security anxieties? NATO enlargement. Baltic security anxieties? A 'super' PfP and NACC supplemented by 'associate partnership' with WEU. Russian hostility and estrangement? A Charter of concord and cooperation along with permanent consultative mechanisms within NATO that gives Russia a 'privileged' relationship with the Alliance. For both Baltics and Russians an Atlantic Partnership Council (APC). A European Security Identity? A Petersberg Declaration buttressed by an elaboration of WEU infrastructure. A European pillar within NATO? CJTF with a medley of command choices. Keeping the United States fully engaged in European security? NATO expansion; PfP; NACC; OSCE. Establishing a more balanced transatlantic division of labour? CFSP, CJTF, and WEU development. A Common Foreign and Security Policy for the European Union? Strengthening the secretariat of the Commission, the secretariat backstopping the Council of Ministers, and schemes for some measure of majority voting at some point down the road. Preventing nationality conflicts? The Stability Pacts to be negotiated, sealed, and monitored under the auspices of the OSCE. Conflict prevention and crisis management? One or a combination of the above depending on circumstances. Peacekeeping? Some combination of the above, plus – maybe – the United Nations, depending on the circumstances.

In the amorphous threat-free post-Cold War security setting, mere words are given exaggerated meaning. The risk is that in the forest of insignia and symbols one loses sight of the practical and purposeful.

The amalgamation of these bits and pieces of policy does not amount to an adequate Alliance strategy. The lack of one is matched by a similar lack of broad policy designs in member capitals. None of the major allies has succeeded in articulating a comprehensive strategy that integrates the various organizational components or addresses the several facets of European security. That conclusion stands out from the country portraits presented in this volume. One consequence is that the disjointedness of collective Western policy is not tested against the bracing challenge of a government (or governments) with its own decided view of what a common design should look like. Alliance irresolution is not caused by the clash of incompatible strategic ideas. Rather, we have seen an additive process whereby individual pieces of Alliance policy are debated – sometimes seriously and deliberately; sometimes in a fitful, unfocused manner – but without sustained attention to how they are to be combined into a coherent whole. That process generates little pressure for a rigorous examination of inner strains and points of contradictions (e.g. the enlargement initiative coupled with far-reaching compensatory measures for Russia) or for the precedent-setting effects of expedient actions (IFOR's contrived, ineffectual partnership with OSCE-based civilian operations).

The absence of frank and full debate has the further deleterious consequence of leaving unattended latent differences of opinion on particular aspects of security structure and purpose. France's deep but muted apprehensions about alienating Russia by pressing forward with enlargement was one example. Germany's belief that a 'Europeanized' NATO would assuage Russian anger at enlargement is another. Failure to admit openly that disagreements exist, and to thrash them out, allows them to surface in disruptive, disconnected ways. Thus, the French for a time had no compunction in holding their approval of the conclusive decision on admitting new members hostage to its partners' meeting its demands for constituting a parallel European command structure conforming to Paris' conception of CJTF. Paris made a simultaneous linkage to its further demand that a French officer replace an American as head of NATO's southern command. Germany's tactical decision to back French claims, motivated by its own judgement that Europeanizing NATO could better cope with the conundrum of enlargement and by a renewed desire to cement French–German collaboration, led Bonn to rebuff Washington in ways that surprised uncomprehending American officials.

Self-indulgence in subordinating judgement on matters of truly historic dimension to a parochial national interest testifies not just to narrow-mindedness by one individual allied government or another. Rather, it illustrates the price the Alliance as a whole pays for a practice of evading rather than honestly confronting fundamental strategic choices and divergent views on them. An open debate on enlargement, one conducted before the declaration in principle that NATO would expand, either would have produced a consensus position to which all member governments were bound or would bring clashing positions out into the open where they could be addressed. Whatever the outcome, a more clearly enunciated Alliance policy would have emerged, one that could not easily be bent or broken through linkage with secondary issues.

By contrast, the Alliance's position favourable to enlargement evolved by fits and starts over two-and-a-half years. As Hanns Maull notes in Chapter 7, the seeming consensus in support of it was a soft consensus. That conforms to a discernible pattern. The allies have found it relatively easy to establish and maintain a common position on broadly stated post-Cold War security objectives as long as they are cast at an abstract level. Rhetorical declarations, however, conceal significant differences over operative assumptions; priority scales for valuing multiple objectives; the implications foreseen were developments to take an adverse turn; and plans for dealing with them. The dangers of hazy strategic thinking at the conceptual level are potentially serious – but those dangers are conjectural. In dealing with a concrete problem, they become real and readily visible. When it comes to action (or inaction), the gap between NATO's soft consensus and the requirements for effective joint effort is a yawning one. Witness the disarray and near débâcle in Yugoslavia. That performance should not be treated as an encapsulated phenomenon of no wider or lasting consequence.

Yugoslavia in Retrospect

Over the five years during which the Western powers wrestled with the conflicts of the former Yugoslavia, they never succeeded in agreeing on an estimation of stake; in fashioning a common strategy that went beyond a lowest common denominator of agreement; on a risk calculus; on Russia's proper interests and the correct terms of cooperation with Moscow; in evaluating the United Nations' mission; or in determining the appropriate division of labour between NATO and the world body. Expediency and tactical considerations ruled their behaviour throughout. The seeming success of IFOR, in its restricted military role, has cast a rosy glow over the West's tragic failures in Yugoslavia.

A fair assessment of the allies' performance, however, should admit the dire straits in which they found themselves in the summer of 1995. NATO was poised to dispatch an extrication force to punctuate a humiliating Balkan Dunkirk. Western cooperation was unravelling rapidly in an atmosphere of recrimination and mutual distrust. The effects of a forced evacuation would have been a stunning loss of credibility in the eyes of others, of self-respect, and a possible rupture of the transatlantic tie. Only a set of fortuitous developments, followed by a spasm of vigorous American leadership, saved the allies from ignominy. Even on the brink of disaster, the allies were unable to pull truly in unison or to orchestrate a common plan. Sleep-walking toward catastrophe in July, they untangled themselves long enough to allow the Dayton accords to be signed. A reversion to fractious ways, if not public discord, marked the fretful, half-hearted and badly flawed implementation effort. Learning from mistakes was shallow and fleeting.

The Western powers' diplomatic record in Yugoslavia is one of anemic multilateralism and reflexive unilateralism. Throughout, consultation was a sometime thing – more forthcoming after the event than before it. At odds with each other, they were as inclined to find backers outside the Alliance – Russia, the UN, local parties – as to hammer out differences among themselves. Tactical alliances with Russia to advance a preferred policy-line at the expense of Alliance partners were common. Disunity also warped the relationship with the United Nations. Inter-organizational collaboration suffered from the lack of a firm, clear Western position and coordinated diplomacy. Effectiveness as a measuring-rod was replaced by more flexible measures of convenience and expediency. The United Nations thus came to serve alternately as a device for evading hard choices, for deflecting pressures to act decisively, and as an instrument for doing things that governments dare not publicly do themselves (e.g. trade Serb-held hostages for pledges to abstain from airstrikes).

Collective security was the operative principle in Yugoslavia. In practice, it did not work. The reasons are to be found more in the derelictions of the Western powers than in the undeniable weaknesses and shortcomings of the UN as an organization with a distinctive philosophy and *modus operandi*. The allies had the opportunity to impart will and direction to a UN mission they dominated – especially in the period of 1991–93 before Russia became a self-willed and active player. The inescapable conclusion is that collective security is not a substitute for Alliance commitment and effort. The latter are the conditions for success for any security enterprise in, or around Europe, whatever the institutional arrangements may be.

Is Yugoslavia a valid basis for judging the West's aptitude and readiness to handle Europe's post-Cold War security problems? Many answer 'no' – pointing to the singular complexities of the situation, the ambiguous nature of the conflict, the country's dark and troubled history, the multiplicity of local and external parties involved, etc. It is a viewpoint widespread in official quarters. Indeed, some argue that there are grounds for self-satisfaction in having contained the conflict and avoiding the embroiling of other states. It is not persuasive. Admittedly 'Yugoslavia' posed a formidable challenge. But would a conjectured future crisis in the Baltics or Ukraine (not to speak of new acts of aggression in the Middle East, also in the Alliance's area of strategic interest) be any easier to manage? In those places, unlike Yugoslavia, the intrinsic stakes would be higher, Russia's security interests would be directly engaged, and the Alliance would not enjoy either the luxury of a deliberate, desultory response or the freedom of action that it squandered in 'Yugoslavia'.

It is sobering to reflect that the West's egregious failings occurred in the immediate aftermath of their triumph in the Gulf. That demonstration of resolve, might and unity brought the allies' prestige and power to new heights. The United States' paramountcy in particular was confirmed in vivid fashion. Such signal success normally amasses a reserve of political capital sufficient to underwrite diplomacy for a generation. Yet within a few short years much of that prestige had dissipated, American leadership was impaired, and Western cohesion was compromised. That reversal of fortune behoves us to consider the causes of the West's incongruent record.

The failings in Yugoslavia derived from institutional flaws in the Alliance that go deeper than individual misjudgements or lapses in attention and cooperation. The allies have avoided confronting the questions of discipline and purpose that bedevilled the allies' diplomacy throughout the long frustrating years of the crisis. Rippling just below the surface for the most part, they came to head on a number of occasions: over the recognition issue in December 1991; and in the airstrike episodes of November/December 1994 and May/June 1995. Two flaws are most noteworthy.

Inner Faultlines

One is the chronic strain between the requirements of solidarity and the propensity for unilateralism. On the one hand, the Western allies commit themselves to an expansive array of multilateral security responsibilities: an enlarged NATO; for a United Nations embarked on a growing range of peacekeeping missions – its chastening experiences in Bosnia and elsewhere notwithstanding; to backing the collective security functions of a maturing OSCE; and – for the West Europeans – the formal obligations of a Common Foreign and Security Policy. Yet, on the other hand, national governments are inclined to let their *amour-propre* stand in the way of collective decision and joint action. The resulting tension is less between the particular and general Alliance interest than it is between the parochial conceptions of the general interest and the requirements for successful concerted action.

All the Western powers recognize that they share broad strategic interests. In principle, they are aware as well that sustaining their unity is essential both to ensure against a reversion to past rivalries and to exercise a positive influence over developments to the east. Yet, the slackening of external pressures to keep in tight formation has created space for parochialism. Parochialism leads to behaviour quite different from old-fashioned impulses toward aggrandizement or domination. It has to do with status more than with power; it is selfish rather than ambitious; it evokes tame pride rather than passion; it serves convenience rather than demands sacrifice.[2]

We have seen little sign of a renationalization of defence policy or the pursuit of a dominant power position. Quite the contrary. Rather we have seen a tendency to subordinate concern for any type of tangible achievement to the maximizing of symbolic gratifications – while minimizing obligations. Gratification comes from protecting positions of rank and command or acquiring them; by securing a division of labour within the Alliance (and drawing the jurisdictional boundaries among security bodies) so as to enhance a country's ability to put its imprimatur on policies and programmes. The consequent emphasis on form rather than on performance was on display throughout the protracted Yugoslav conflict. Status preoccupations also have pervaded the Alliance debates over links to the WEU, over CJTF, and – in a minor key – in the on-going effort to shape a strategic relationship with Russia.

The renewed importance that governments attach to their national particularity weakens any disposition to defer (to an Alliance leader, to a predominant collective point of view) or to submerge one's identity in common enterprises. The result is a certain prickliness about infringements on the autonomous right to judge and decide for oneself. This attitude is manifest in Italy's straining to ensure that it no longer should be taken for granted – whether in the conduct of the mission in Somalia or in military operations in Bosnia. France, for its part, has pursued an across-the-board campaign to establish its rank, status and position in the rearrangements of Alliance structures and functions – its leading role in the integrationist Maastricht process, and its rejoining NATO's military organization notwithstanding. The United States has relinquished or shared its leadership prerogatives only reluctantly and tinged with a lingering uneasiness at having done so. Washington has demonstrated that when the stakes are high enough, and its doubts about the agreement or cooperativeness of its allies strong enough, it will act alone. It remains hypersensitive about command arrangements that compromise its freedom of action – whether they be under United Nations auspices or within the Alliance. Practical considerations enter into this thinking. So too, though, does an ingrained aversion to constraints and a keen sense of American exceptionalism. Nor are the perceived exigencies of domestic politics absent. The Clinton administration at times acted as if all planning for IFOR and its successor had to observe obediently the partisan requirements of the American electoral calendar.

As for Germany, its dedication to being the good multilateral citizen has muted any impulse to self-promotion. However, as its self-confidence grows and inhibitions are shed, it too will expect recognition and authority commensurate with its strength. This is likely to be especially true with regard to matters affecting Eastern Europe and Russia where its stakes are highest. A benign form of status-nationalism already is discernible in the claim to leadership posts in IFOR. As for Britain, it has been relatively unassertive largely because the *status quo* accorded it a substantial number of influential positions. With the heightened competition for commands sparked by France's return to the Alliance fold, along with the inauguration of new members and new commitments, we can expect a sharpening of efforts to protect its status within the Alliance. For a country eager to 'punch above its weight' in international affairs, a prominent place in the West's premier security organization is essential.

The indulgence of parochialism magnifies the difficulties of managing an alliance faced with security threats that are contingent and handicapped by uncertain leadership. Hard choices are finessed, dissonance over detail mounts while serious strategic differences are stifled for the sake of apparent unity, and the allies contrive to keep sensitive security questions out of domestic political debates. The last is a noteworthy feature of Alliance life. One strikingly successful area of collaboration among government leaders is the mutual assistance provided to cope with sceptical and undeferential publics. The risk of arousing popular disfavour is often the most convincing basis on which a leader can ask and expect accommodation from his peers. Most of the time, that accommodation takes the form of delaying a potentially contentious action, postponing a painful decision or making a symbolic bow to national sensibilities. Yugoslavia once again offers us bountiful examples.

Such reciprocal back-scratching is not necessarily a bad thing. It can lubricate the wheels of intra-alliance diplomacy. The danger lies in making the practice of accommodation habitual. Then, it stymies or skews collective action. Today, that is the greater obstacle to effective cooperation than deadlock produced by unyielding, opposing views. All this is quite normal for a peacetime alliance. NATO's identity and purpose, though, are exceptional. There is the rub.

Pervasive parochialism is both cause and effect of a second stress-point in the alliance's present situation: the uneasy relationship between leaders and their publics. Decisiveness – intellectual and political – is needed for the West to capitalize on the opportunities created by the demise of Communism; to requilibriate the Atlantic partnership; and to extend the Alliance's reach in function and membership. These are historic undertakings. But they leave undisturbed the placidity of Western societies and their citizenry uninspired. Momentous as these times may be, they are experienced quite differently by publics preoccupied with their own mundane affairs. Western leaders bear much of the responsibility for this insularity. The Cold War triumph was never punctuated by explanation of its full significance or instruction as to its implications, including new sorts of challenges. They surely would be less dangerous than those just met but equally demanding of collective effort and enlightened thinking. The hesitation of elected officials to address their publics frankly has put them in the awkward position of attempting to organize great enterprises, on a multinational basis, without taking their peoples into their full confidence as to what their justification and requirements were. Great projects were proclaimed and then implemented more by stealth than by mustering the backing of the citizenry they were meant to serve.

The allies' approach to NATO expansion bears disconcerting similarities to the Maastricht process. A commitment to an enterprise of historic dimensions is made without prior public debate; the course of inter-governmental deliberations and their content is opaque; and the plan that is brought forth is unrealistically presented as an antiseptic exercise in political engineering. Matters of great moment are cited as the reason for the initiative, but the full implications for attempting to deal with them in the prescribed manner are not candidly discussed. Thus, serious risks are run of an adverse popular reaction that could create new problems while jeopardizing the proposed strategy's chances of meeting its stated objectives. When the inevitable wave of scepticism breaks, the urgent appeals to stay the course emphasize more the hazards of upsetting plans in which so much has been invested than their intrinsic merits.

The discomfort that Western leaders feel about taking their publics fully into their confidence has a number of sources. They lie in the distinctive political culture of our prosperous, prosaic and self-absorbed democracies. The characteristic defect of these secular, 'civilian' societies is their indifference to collective needs and obligations. As we have argued, parochialism writ small is their abiding sin, not the clash of ambitions. Relations *among* them is a macrocosm of each's internal politics. The tolerant if inward-looking polities we inhabit have developed their distinctive personality as much by the subtraction of certain disruptive elements (aggressive nationalism, ideological passion) as by the addition, or accentuation, of a civil ethic of community and responsibility. A hollowed-out democracy does not easily sustain a competent state. That is to say, a state competent to ensure a safe, congenial external environment, and competent to act jointly with other like-minded states to exert the influence of which they are capable to consolidate liberal institutions in Eastern Europe and Russia or to deal with their failures.

It is understandably tempting for leaders to be partisans of the course of least resistance. To send messages that minimize the costs, risks and disruptions of dangerous (intervention in Bosnia) or far-reaching (NATO enlargement) security policies seems to them to be the politically low-risk option. Whether that is wise, or even prudent, depends on what value one attaches to the objective, how one defines the objective ('peace' or 'justice' in Bosnia?; with regard to NATO enlargement, 'projecting stability' or issuing security guarantees?); and the likelihood that a stealth strategy can be brought to completion without undue turbulence. A strategy predicated on the silent judgement that the resources to deal with the challenges of instability and nationality conflict to the east can be mustered, and deployed, without a heightened awareness of citizens' self-interest, and conscious support for a policy of activism, is a gamble. Perhaps an unavoidable one, but a gamble nevertheless.

The irony of this situation is that domestic constraints on external action arise from the very conditions that make the rich and free liberal democracies the dominant political model for the entire European continent – and much of the world beyond.

The passionless do not make history – so it is said.[3] Yet it is the dispassionate societies of the Western democracies who have altered international life – among themselves – more radically than has ever occurred before. Their transcendence of traditional types of conflict is a sharp break from the standard of inter-state behaviour. Moreover, their singular achievement now has put them in a position to shape their environment in a similar mode. The exertions needed to succeed, though, strain the political imagination and interfere with the self-centred pursuits that dominate the lives of a complacent populace and the thinking of elected leaders who depend on their sufferance.

Cold War Inheritance

Western publics' diminished sense of the collective interest, along with a strong aversion to risk or sacrifice, has two effects that restrict the ability of governments to act effectively on Europe's new strategic agenda. First, attention fixes on external relations only at moments of unmistakable crisis or threat. Second, severe domestic constraints militate against the use, or threatened use, of military force. Both, in different ways, stem from the extraordinary nature of the international relations that Western nations have experienced over the past half-century – in the Cold War with the USSR and among themselves. It was a period that saw very little of any 'ordinary' inter-state politics in Europe. The East–West confrontation and the developing Kantian community had one remarkable feature in common: the absence of opportunity or inclination to play the classic games of diplomatic manoeuvre and power politics. The one occupied a political space too tightly configured and dangerous; the other rendered it obsolete.

The threat-perception in the one direction was dire: a military and ideological menace that jeopardized the democracies' very survival (one that succeeded the equally dire threat from Nazi Germany). In the other, the harmony produced by ever-closer cooperative ties prevailed. Thus, in a literal sense the threats to national interests were all or nothing at all. Their conditioning effect leaves popular opinion unprepared to recognize and to make sense of security threats to less than vital national interests – especially if they are indirect or potential.

The diminished threat-perception is accompanied by a narrow conception of what national interests deserve the investment of physical resources and political capital. In the decompression from the Cold War – when survival was at stake – other national interests can too readily be undervalued. A congenial external milieu – one where liberal democratic values predominate and peaceable rules of inter-state behaviour are observed, may well look like luxuries when compared to the essentials that were steadfastly defended in the earlier period. Hence, the generally untroubled attitude that marked both popular (and, even more so, governmental) reaction to mayhem in the Balkans. A similar diffidence is observable in the equanimity with which a more nationalistically assertive and less cooperative Russia is met.

Unattentive, disengaged publics, in theory, could create space for national leaders to carry on quiet diplomacy free from the critical gaze and importuning voices of their constituents. As a practical matter, though, room for discretionary action is rather tightly circumscribed. Wherever concrete action is considered, domestic support is required – whether it is for substantial economic assistance, security commitments or, most certainly, the deployment of military forces. It is not surprising that Western leaders are most forthright and venturesome in symbolic acts, declaratory policy, and the drafting of architectural plans. Extreme caution prevails, by contrast, when it is a question of doing something definite and specific. We should recall that four years of prevarication and timidity in Yugoslavia coincided with a building-boom in European security architecture that saw a proliferation of plans, blueprints, charters and ceremonial inaugurations. The intellectual confusion in much of Western Europe when confronted with Saddam Hussein's naked aggression was illustrative of the disorientation produced by what have come to be seen as 'alien' types of behaviour. The even greater disarray – intellectual and diplomatic – on display during the long-running Yugoslav crisis reveals both the extent and tenacious grip of attitudes antithetical to power politics, and how much of a liability they are for contending with a still-unruly external environment.

The tendency to downplay war's value and/or naturalness as an ingredient of international life coincides with the attention properly paid the remarkable post-war achievement in building structures of peaceful engagement among the politically secure and prosperous societies of the liberal democratic world. They have been dubbed 'civilian societies'. The term describes an outlook that sees peaceable social intercourse as a model for interstate relations as well as for the conduct of domestic affairs. Reflecting the experience of conciliatory domestic political cultures, it stresses reconciliation as opposed to confrontation, whatever the cause; is uncomfortable with stark depictions of clashes in terms of right and wrong, virtue and evil; and fights shy of making choices that carry risk of jeopardizing civil peace and order.

These civilian societies, and the decidedly unwarlike quality of relations among them, stand out all the more clearly for their contradistinction to both the traditional norms of interstate politics and the implacable hostility between the power blocs which was the mainspring of the Cold War. However, both salient dimensions of the postwar world may contribute to the widespread disposition to question the older tenet that sees the ubiquity of conflict situations as the hallmark of the international system and war as an inescapable, if contingent, fact of international life. Much of Western European (and a smaller share of American) public opinion, and a significant number of elected officials, now appear to see peaceful engagement as the norm rather than the exception.

Intervention

This mesh of inhibitions and popular political constraints affects security policy most when the issue is one that raises the prospect of military action. The resort to force, in turn, is most problematic when it takes the form of possible intervention in the name of collective security. This is so in two respects. Alliance multilateralism, or coalitions of the like – interested and willing – are preferred when major national interests are at stake, when one can readily recognize a need to act and, therefore, there is a greater inclination to accept risk and danger, relatively speaking. Resort to collective security organizations, by comparison, correlates with peripheral threats to second-order interests – a situation that evokes greater scepticism and reticence from the populace, thereby raising the bar for leaders struggling to justify participation in military mission – if they themselves judge it necessary.

Intervention therefore poses most acutely the dilemma that the Western democracies have faced in operationalizing their commitment to collective security. It also is the central dilemma of liberal internationalism – whether of the American neo-Wilsonian variety or the German 'non-belligerent' variety. It is a dilemma as well for those countries whose dedication to the propagation of essentially liberal values is alloyed by dollops of realism in both public discourse and the calculations of leaders (as in Britain and France). Even the latter must wrestle with the twin questions of when intervention is necessary and desirable; and how to persuade citizens to run the risks of intervention without a compelling national interest at stake.

The West's predicament has a number of facets.

(1) Which liberal norms should serve as the benchmarks for determining when intervention is called for: protection/advancement of democratic institutions?; national self-determination?; securing human rights?; or defending the principle that established political boundaries should not be altered by force? The contradictory conclusions one might reach depending on which of these criteria is given precedence, and the difficulty of composing them into a persuasive set of policy guidelines, was all too evident in Yugoslavia where it contributed significantly to the West's fumbling, discordant and halfhearted intervention.[4]

Reality does not present itself in neat packages that suit our philosophical predilections or political convenience.

(2) Does the West have the responsibility, and interest, to engage in 'state-building' where the collapse of public order leads to a humanitarian disaster and endemic conflict, e.g. in Bosnia? A strategy of activism in that situation unavoidably entails physical intervention. What is the basis for doing so: to uphold principles of human rights and standards of decent political conduct? To prevent disorder or, worse, the rise of an alien political regime in a place of intrinsic political or economic importance? To avoid a bad precedent being set (including the violation of international norms and the indifference of the Western powers) which could harm efforts to deal with more dangerous parties in more strategic places – Russia; or China; or in the Persian Gulf?

(3) If the answers to the first two sets of questions point to an interventionist policy, how to gain the approval of a risk-averse, distracted citizenry? A plea to instinctive idealism is one approach, especially where there have been gross atrocities or naked aggression. Another is to foster an understanding of how the enlightened national interest will best be served by engagement. The chances of 'selling' go down either when the situation in question has emerged slowly, exhibits ambiguous elements, and is not obviously amenable to a simple, simply understood course of action. The Yugoslav conflicts, of course, were of this nature. Their peculiar traits notwithstanding, future security challenges (over Ukraine, perhaps) are more likely to resemble Yugoslavia than the classical model of military threats and confrontation.

A call to conscience and principle is strengthened by tangible evidence of human rights violations. But the prospect of the West's resort to force to deal with them evokes mixed reactions, as was the case in Bosnia despite a clear-cut pattern of abuses. There is a substantial segment of the public in all the Western democracies (predominant in Germany and Italy) that instinctively questions the rightness of resorting to violence – whatever the circumstances, however laudable the goals. Passivity is justified in a number of ways. One is to pose the dilemma of choosing between peace and justice. A case can always be made that to intervene with the aim of righting a wrong can add to the chaos and add to the sum of suffering, rather than end or alleviate it. One heard this argument from many quarters whenever military action in Bosnia was under consideration. Another is to cast doubt on the purity of the West's (or a particular government's) motives and moral standards. The suggestion that only the righteous, able to meet an exacting standard of ethical behaviour, may act to enforce good conduct is a convenient excuse for inaction – however illogical the premise. Some use it calculatingly to rationalize a lack of appetite for courting danger or incurring costs. Realists also use it as they grasp for an 'ethical' reason to subordinate moral concerns to the dictates of what is supposedly *realpolitik*.

It is noteworthy that on every occasion when the Western powers have used military force in recent years, the question of civilian casualties comes to the fore. Attention in the media quickly focused on whether innocents were being hurt and how many. There are national variations. Public hand-wringing of this type is most common in the United States, Germany and Italy. In the former, a mawkish hunt for presumed derelictions by the government is a feature of news coverage – a hangover from Vietnam days that is reinforced by the peculiar gratification many Americans get by affirming their individual superiority to those who presume to direct them. Exaggerated sensitivity to the harm one might be doing through intervention is related to pervasive squeamishness about violence in general. It encourages the search for arguments as to why military action is counter-productive – not just unnecessary or unavailing.

An exaggeration of the conjectural enemy's grim resistance to coercion and its lethal ruthlessness serves this attitude nicely. On the Gulf, the disciplined toughness of Saddam's supposedly implacable legions was routinely conjured to buttress arguments against Desert Storm. On Yugoslavia, the analogous image of the Serb nation rising up as one to oppose any outside intervention was a staple of the political debate. A modern-day equivalent of the partisan army that 'pinned down 30 German divisions' was always a red herring, but no less potent an image for being utterly at odds with the less fearsome truth. Whenever similar confrontations present themselves in the future, we must anticipate that the twin sentiments of fearfulness and sanctimoniousness will be much in evidence.

If the moral basis for armed intervention has its limitations and possible pitfalls, 'realist' arguments are liable to prove unpersuasive. For 'realistic' thinking to prevail there must be a level of comprehension and capacity for critical reasoning that eludes a citizenry of societies where public discourse tends scrupulously to avoid deliberation of the public interest, its wider setting, and the threats posed to it. This will remain so unless Western leaders are ready and able to instruct their populaces as to how their peace and prosperity is affected by developments across Europe and in places on its periphery. For leaders to do so, they must first sort out their own thinking. In the absence of a coherent conception, the basis for individual initiatives will appear obscure and the arguments offered in support of them unintelligible. The process of building comprehension has to include the fashioning of a strategic consensus among the Atlantic partners. For no national strategy can make much sense without taking account of the collective purpose. The multilateral road may seem the hard road – given national differences in interpretation of problems, diverse preferences for how a reformed Alliance should work, and national vanities. In fact, greater difficulty will be encountered by holding to the pretence of national prerogative, and by trying to prepare for joint action through pantomime rather than through candid encounter.

In the seven years of the post-Cold War, post-Communist era, the Alliance has sought to 'get right' three relationships crucial to its future. They are: (1) between their own security community and pan-continental collective security institutions; (2) the transatlantic balance of responsibility and leadership; and (3) among the Western Europeans as a self-conscious grouping within the Alliance and in their own neighbouring organizations. The three dimensions are interrelated – as this set of essays has shown. Great effort has been expended on initiatives in each sphere, and some noteworthy results recorded. Segmental approaches, however, produce self-limiting accomplishment. Their sum does not yet add up to an adequate strategy for the not-so-brave world the Western allies now find themselves in.

That world defies easy conceptualization as much as it is unyielding to piecemeal strategy. A Europe that is part Kantian civil community (however attenuated) and part something else (i.e. more traditionally statist and conflictual); that mixes elements of cooperation and conflict; where there are marked disparities in current wealth and in prospects for future prosperity; where fully developed democratic polities co-exist with regimes democratic only in form – if not manifestly autocratic; where post-modernist societies share the same continent with societies prey to nationalist passion; that Europe will be as difficult to make conceptual sense of as it will be to cope with. This quasi-system will demand in large amounts exactly those critical aptitudes that are in short supply in the West. The inward-looking, self-absorbed nature of democratic publics; the fearful instincts of the 'civilian society'; a leadership driven by the compulsion to cater to their electorates; and the inherent liabilities of a leaderless grouping of nations – together work against forging a finely-wrought strategy and its orchestrated execution.

The still open question is how societies so constituted will be able to contend with a Europe of disparate polities. The goals the Western allies have set themselves look all the more audacious for the evident reluctance of Western countries to extend themselves to reach them. Open, non-exclusive and conciliatory in principle, they at the same time are habitually parochial and shortsighted. So constituted, they have been able to develop their Kantian civil order and abandon the quest for glory and aggrandizement. So constituted, they are in danger of not being up to the tests now awaiting them.

NOTES

1. Philip Zelikow uses the metaphor of the performance masque to make a similar point about the propensity to manipulate institutional arrangements as a substitute for delivering substantive messages and making real commitments. See 'The Masque of Institutions', *Survival*, Spring 1996.
2. The pacific impulses of the West's 'domesticated' civilian societies requires us to reconsider the classic realist proposition that the nation-state is distinguished from other international actors by the readiness of its citizens to meet the test of loyalty and self-sacrifice. The very terms have nearly disappeared from political rhetoric, while acts of self-sacrifice are becoming rare to the point of extinction.
3. This line is from Czeslaw Milosz's poem 'A Confession', *The Collected Poems, 1931–1987* (Hopewell, NJ: The Ecco Press, 1988).
4. Stanley Hoffmann provides an illuminating examination of liberalism's intellectual and policy predicament in 'The Crisis of Liberal Internationalism', *Foreign Policy*, No. 98 (Spring 1995).

Index

Achille Lauro terrorists 119
Adriatic 253
 arms embargo 258
Africa 120, 223, 225, 230
The Agenda for Peace (1992) 27, 159
Agnelli, Susanna 117, 135
Akashi, Yasushi 179, 261
Albright, Madeleine 172
Allensbach Institute 103
Andreatta, Nino 127
Andreotti, Giulio 120
Arab–Israeli disputes/region 122, 230
Asia, East 223, 230
Aspin, Les 170–1
Atlantic
 Alliance 1–2, 6, 64–5
 Council 52–3, 151, 252, 255, 263
 Pact 118
 Partnership Council (APC) 291

Bahr, Egon 94
Baker, James 41, 90
Baker–Genscher initiative 90
Balkans 3
Balladur, Prime Minister 49, 54, 264
Baltic security 291
Belgium 35
Berlin
 accords (1996) 23, 99, 186–9, 233, 235, 274
 Atlantic Council 255
 NATO summit meeting (June 1996) 70–3, 151, 254–5
 Wall 40, 278
Berlinguer, Enrico 119
Berlusconi, Prime Minister Silvio, government 120
Betts, Richard 146
Bildt, Carl 180, 192
Bosnia 9, 12, 14, 24, 29–32, 34, 46, 50, 56, 59, 103, 105–6, 126, 128, 166–7, 178, 184, 192, 199, 253

Contact Group 117, 135, 213, 224
Dayton Accords 151, 180–1
elections 107
follow-on-force (SFOR) 102, 107, 273–4, 282
IFOR 283
military operations 296, 304
NATO 228
Operation Joint Endeavour 27, 34, 106, 191
OSCE 133
peacekeeping force 175, 259
UNPROFOR 22, 226, 234, 243, 281
Bosnia-Herzegovina 255, 259, 261, 272–3
 Command (BHC) 253, 273
 no-fly zone 253, 258
Boutros-Ghali, Boutros 173, 259–61, 263
Bozo, Frédéric 98, 188, 281, 283
Brenner, Michael 229, 231, 254, 281, 285
Britain 6–38
 collective security organizations 25–8
 Defence 35; Ministry 11, 23, 29; White Papers 20, 52
 Europe relations 239
 European security, attitudes to 17–19, 33
 European Union legislation 15
 external security operations 11
 Foreign and Commonwealth Office 29
 foreign policy 7, 35, 210
 military
  force 15, 226
  organizations 33
 multilateral peace support operations 28–32, 34
 mutual defence, comparative estimation 25–8

307

Britain (*Cont.*)
  NATO 239
  peacekeeping operations 13
  post-colonial security
    commitments 229–30
  Royal Navy 24
  Russia relations 14
  Security environment 6–15
  UN Security Council 212
  United States relations 6, 12, 15,
    209–12
  Western cooperation 19–25
  Yugoslavia (former) 210
Brussels
  NATO summit meetings:
    (December 1992) 42–3;
    (January 1994) 19, 22–3,
    49–51, 53, 63, 70–1, 251;
    (December 1994) 154,
    267–9; (Summer 1996) 70–1
  Treaty 21, 96, 251
Bush, President 42, 44, 169, 250
  administration 41, 162, 169, 225,
    250, 271
Byrnes, James 270

Callaghan, James, and Carter,
  President 10, 16
Cambodia 228
Canino, General Goffredo 123
Caucasian republics 86
Central Asia 269
Central and Eastern Europe (C &
  EE) 14–15, 20, 83, 90, 235,
  249, 256–7, 265, 267–70
CFE (Conventional Forces in
  Europe) Treaty (1990) 14, 44,
  86
Chechnya 93, 150, 177, 261
China 204, 229–31, 243
Chirac, President Jacques 39, 50–1,
  53–4, 64, 66, 73, 77, 99, 185, 188,
  207
  administration 192, 196
  Middle East trip 231
  NATO 58–66, 73
Christopher, Warren 50, 71, 270
Churchill, Winston 10, 14
CINCSOUTH 73, 271

CIS (Commonwealth of Independent
  States) 86, 133, 149, 151–2,
  155, 180, 209, 214, 223, 256, 262,
  267–8
CJTF *see* Combined Joint Task
  Forces (CJTF)
Clinton, President 98, 173, 175,
  191, 194, 202–3, 269, 284
  administration 50, 54–5, 133,
    147, 149–53, 162–3, 166,
    168–71, 173–4, 177, 179,
    181–7, 189, 192–5, 202, 204–5,
    207, 215, 234, 253, 284–5, 297
  Cuba sanctions 232
  guidelines on multilateral
    peacekeeping operations 168
  Presidential Decision Direction
    (PDD) 225
Cold War 1, 6–10
  see also post-Cold War
Colombo Plan 119
Combined Joint Task Forces
  (CJTF) 10, 22–5, 34, 53, 70–2,
  97, 151, 186, 193–4, 207, 254–5,
  274, 283, 291
  agreement (June 1996) 289
  arrangements 272–3, 286
  France 187–8, 292
  United States 251
Conference on Security and
  Cooperation in Europe
  (CSCE) 8, 42–4, 47–8, 89–90,
  264
  Budapest (December 1994) 154,
    267–9
  CIO 268
  Rome Council meeting (December
    1993) 268
  see also OSCE
Conference for Security and
  Cooperation in the
  Mediterranean (CSCM) 129
confidence and security building
  measures (CSBM) 264–5
Conflict Prevention 177–83, 291
  Centre (CPC) 265–6
Contact Group for Bosnia 117,
  135, 213, 224
Corcione, General Domenico 130

Index

Cotti, Flavio 181–2, 261
crisis management 45, 47, 89, 177–83, 225
Croatia 34, 46, 48, 54, 56, 87, 99, 165, 242
CSCE *see* Conference on Security and Cooperation in Europe (CSCE)
Cutileiro, José (WEU General Secretary) 272
Cyprus, peacekeeping 259

Dayton Accords 27, 67, 163, 165–6, 172–3, 189, 293
  for Bosnia 32, 52, 128, 151, 180–1
  Bosnia-Herzegovina 133
  Germany 103
  Holbrooke, Richard 284; *see also* Holbrooke, Richard
  IFOR 191, 229, 272–3
  OSCE 261
  post-Dayton climate 72
  US 239
  on Yugoslavia (former) 98, 144, 228, 234
de Charette, Hervé 98, 107, 255
de Gaulle, General Charles 39–40, 43, 47, 49, 55, 57, 73, 76–7
  NATO policy 59–60, 62–3, 66
de Michelis, Gianni 120
de Rose, François 255
defence alliances 50
  see also NATO; WEU
Defence Planning Committee (DPC) 71
Der Spiegel 94
Desert Shield/Desert Storm 45, 304
Dibble report 212
Dublin, NATO summit meeting (October 1996) 255
Dumas, Roland 95, 99

East–West confrontation 1, 288
Eastern and Central European States *see* Central and Eastern Europe (C & EE)
Elysée Treaty 40
ESDI *see* European Security and Defence Identity (ESDI)
EU (European Union) 8, 28
  Commission 291
  Common Defence policy 34–5, 43
  Common Foreign and Security Policy (CFSP) 43, 61, 83, 95, 98–9, 128, 165, 192, 211, 242, 249, 255, 265, 274, 283, 291, 295
  Council of Ministers 291
  Economic and Monetary Union (EMU) 249
  enlargement 93, 206, 210, 265
  post-cold War security 3
  security role 33, 74
  United States 141
  WEU 12; enlargement 257; peacekeeping operations 25–8, 271–2
  Yugoslavia (former) 47–8
Eurocorps 96–7, 107–9, 131–2, 202, 250–1
Europe
  collective security and defence 81, 96, 145–7, 151–3, 175–83, 227–9, 269, 279
  collective organizations 25–8, 50, 52, 146, 181, 278–87; *see also* CSCE; UN
  command 289, 292
  crises foreseen 13
  Eastern 1, 85, 87, 94, 290
  external policies 288
  leadership 243
  multinational forces 22
  mutual defence organizations 197; *see also* NATO; WEU
  Northern 6
  peacekeeping 259
  political and security involvement outside Europe 230
  post-Cold War 88
  regional organizations, peace missions 257
  security 9, 290
  security architecture 7, 187, 202, 274, 283–6, 301
  security organizations 8, 25–8, 206–8, 261, 278–87; *see also*

Europe (*Cont.*)
  EU; NATO; OSCE; UN; WEU
  South East 223
Europe–The Future 7
European
  Coal and Steel Community 118
  Community, Southern edge 123
  Confederation 44
  Council 54, 334–5
  Economic Community 118
  Security and Defence Identity (ESDI) 7, 10, 24, 43, 54, 186–7, 202, 213, 250–1, 255, 274, 284, 291

failed states, restoration of 227–9
Falklands War 10, 15
Fenwick, Robert 181
Fontainebleau summit meeting 7
Fouchet plan 40
France 39–80
  analytical framework 54–8
  Berlin accords (1996) 70–3, 286
  Bosnia 208
  Chirac, Jacques, NATO 58–66, 73
  CJTF 187–8, 292
  defence and foreign policy 35, 42
  European integration 239, 274
  European strategy 60–2, 256
  external security operations 11
  future options 73–7
  Germany: relationship 60, 75, 256, 274, 292, *see also* Eurocorps; 'Strategic Concept' 75
  Gulf War 45
  influence and status, restoring 59–60
  military force 226
  multilateral interventions 225–6
  NATO 211, 292;
    enlargement 194, 280;
    future 66–77, 196;
    reform 43, 62–6;
    relations 39–58, 188, 190, 202; return 53, 281, 297
  policy, assumptions and limits 47–9

post-Cold War agenda 48–9, 194
post-colonial security commitments 229–30
Secrétariat Général de la Défense Nationale (SGDN) 53
security environment 45–7
stability pacts initiative 264–5, 272, 291
strategic vision 43–4
traditional framework (1989–92) 39–47
United States, partnership 60, 187–8, 193, 200, 205–9, 231
weight of the past 40–3
Western security institutions 278
Yugoslavia (former) 45–7, 50–4, 59–60, 67–70
Franco-British Rapid Reaction Force *see* Rapid Reaction Force
Freedman, Lawrence 224

G-7 summit meetings 152
Genscher, Hans-Dietrich 87, 89–90, 93, 95, 119, 285
Georgia 259
Germany 81–115
  armed forces 81, 85, 100, 104, 226, 233
  Bundesnachrichtendienst (BND) 88
  Bundestag 87
  Bundesverfassungsgericht 81
  Bundeswehr 81–3, 100–5, 107–8, 282
  CDU/CSU, White Paper on European policy (September 1994) 257
  Constitution 81
  crisis-management 95–9
  culture of restraint 242, 256
  defence and foreign policy 35, 81–2, 88, 108
  Defence Policy Guidelines (VPR) (1992) 83–5, 104–5
  European integration 239
  foreign policy 88, 90, 95, 97, 105, 204, 230
  Heeresführungskommando 100

IFOR 203, 205, 297
Intelligence Agency 88
international responsibility 81
military risk 85
multilateral security and defence cooperation 108, 226
multilateralism 233
multinational peacekeeping missions 261
NATO 106, 239–40, 282, 285, 292
OSCE 285
post-cold war, security 83–108
responsibilities 278
security strategy 88
United States relations 200–5
White Paper on Defence (April 1994) 83–4, 103
Gorbachev, Mikhail 44, 148
Gulf crisis (1990–91) 10, 45, 120–2, 124, 131, 162, 225, 228, 230
Gulf War *see* Gulf crisis

Haiti 225, 228
Harmel Report (December 1967) 40–1
Heath, Edward 16
Helms, Jesse 162
Helsinki
 OSCE summit meeting (July 1992) 89, 266–7, 280
 process 43–4, 270
High Level Planning Group (HLPG) 267
Holbrooke, Richard 155, 162, 166, 284
humanitarian interventions 225, 227–9, 235
Hussein, Saddam 301, 304

IFOR (Implementation Force) 67–8, 72, 75, 87, 103, 106–8, 126, 152, 163, 166, 184, 229, 254, 261, 263, 286
 Bosnia 283
 constitution 259, 280
 mandate (20 December 1996) 272
 military commanders 191
 operation 27
 peacekeeping 65

role 191
Russia 228
United States 172–3, 175
Inter-Governmental Conferences (IGC) 26, 28, 76; (1991) 17, 41; (March 1996) Turin 11–12, 17, 99, 255
inter-organizational collaboration 294
international humanitarian intervention 225, 227–9
international law 268
Iran, exports to 198
Iraq 228, 240
Islamic fundamentalism 123, 230
Israel
 Likud government 231
 Palestine peace process 120, 231
Israeli–Arab disputes/region 122, 230
Italy 116–38, 239, 278
 African policy 119
 armed forces 125, 256
 Atlantic Pact 118
 Bosnia 135, 213
 Communist Party (PCI) 118–19
 Constitution 124–6
 defence and foreign policy 35
 Dini government 135
 European Coal and Steel Community 118
 European Economic Community 118, 121
 foreign policy 119–22, 134
 government officials 130–4
 Gulf War 120–2, 131
 internal setting 124–6
 Mediterranean policy 119–20
 multilateral disposition 116–21, 136, 226
 NATO membership 121, 124–32
 New Defense Model (NDM) 122, 124–5
 peace-support operations 282
 policymakers and public 126–8
 political parties 123–30, 135
 post-Cold War Europe 119–20, 122
 Rifondazione Comunista 129

Italy (*Cont.*)
  security 122–4, 127
  survey of policymakers' opinions
    (1993) 123, 126–7
  UN 128–35, 214
  United States relations 212–14
  Western cooperation 122, 125–34
  WEU 130–3

Jefferson, Thomas 241
Joulwan, General George A. 105, 191
Juppé, Prime Minister Alain 53, 57

Kant, Immanuel 1, 141, 227, 300, 305–6
Kantian/Wilsonian model 144
Kennedy, President Jack 10
Key Largo meeting (1990) 42
Kinkel, Klaus 87, 91–5, 105
Kissinger, Henry 74, 242
Kohl, Chancellor 84, 87, 92–3, 96, 101, 108, 192–3, 203, 205, 250, 286
  government 92, 101–2, 106, 195–6, 257, 282, 285
Kozyrev, Andrei 152

Lafontaine, Oskar 94
Lake, Anthony 227
Lamers, Karl 104, 257
Lanxade, Admiral Jacques 50, 53
leadership 242–3
League of Nations 146
Lebanon 119, 122
Léotard, François 52, 107
Libya 198, 231–2
Lisbon, European Council meeting (1992) 54
London, Atlantic Council summit meeting (July 1990) 41–2, 252
Luxembourg 35

Maastricht Treaty 8, 21, 43, 48, 54–5, 99, 101, 121, 127, 193, 197, 249–50, 272, 283, 296, 298
Macedonia 34
Macmillan, Harold 10
Mahncke, Dr Dieter 96

Major, John, government 17–18
Malta 119
  Bush–Gorbachev meeting (December 1989) 44
Maull, Hanns, W. 278, 292
Mediterranean 6, 8, 13, 119–20, 230, 279
  Conference for Security and Cooperation (CSCM) 129
  Standing Naval Force (STANAVFORMED) 253
Messmer, Prime Minister Pierre 73
Middle East 122–3, 193, 223, 229–31, 255, 278
Millon, Charles 188
Minsk group 266–7
Mitterrand, President François 7, 42–3, 48, 108, 207, 250
  European Confederation 44
  Kohl, Chancellor policy initiative (1991) 42
  Sarajevo visit 54
multilateral
  actions 225–6, 243–6
  institutions 47
  security responsibilities 295
Mussolini, Benito, years 117

national sovereignty 237–40
NATO 13, 20, 146, 179, 298
  air power 178, 281
  Airborne Warning force (NAEWF) 253
  Bosnia 228
  collective security 64, 68, 252–7, 274
  Commands (MNCs) 190
  comparative institutions, peacekeeping operations 264–71
  crisis management 51, 257–8
  Defence Planning Committee 188, 190
  East-West partnership 288
  enlargement 19–20, 65, 70, 90–4, 151, 153–8, 177, 184–5, 210, 227, 235, 257, 265, 269–70, 274, 279, 290–2, 298–9
  European security 8, 25–8, 273

evolution 183–96
forces 21, 233, 261–2
foreign policy cultures 241–3
future 94, 246
inner faultlines 295–300
instable geographic areas 223
institutions 53
Integrated Military Structure (IMS) 23–4, 63–4
interstate relations 241–3
intervention 302–6
Italy 121
military 74, 191, 235–6, 243, 289; commands 23–4, 186, 192, 255–6: chain of 64, 188; southern (AFSOUTH) 193, 292
Military Authorities 72
Military Committee 52, 188–90, 207, 281
mutual defence 155
naval and air forces 258
Northern Army Group (NORTHAG) 253
operations 67, 75
 Deliberate Force 52, 258
 Deny Flight 50, 69
 Sharp Guard 50, 69, 271, 280
OSCE 274
peace missions 254
peacekeeping role 51, 69, 273
plans: MC 40103 'Disciplined Guard' 51, 69; MC 40104 'Determined Effort' 51, 69
Policy Coordination Group (PCG) 189
post-Cold War identity 186
Rapid Reaction Force *see* Rapid Reaction Force
reform 1, 8, 25, 43, 62–6, 70–2, 75, 98, 151–2, 192–6, 227, 235, 243, 256
Russia 153–5, 194–6, 206, 231, 286, 291–2, 296
summit meetings: (1990) 42–3; (November 1991) Rome 42, 184, 250, 284–5; (June 1992) Oslo 42, 279–80; (December 1992) Brussels 42–3; (January 1994) Brussels 19, 22–3, 49–51, 53, 63, 70–1; (September 1994) Seville 52; (December 1994) Budapest 154, 251, 267–9; (June 1995) 272; (June 1996) Berlin 70–3, 151, 254–5; (Summer 1996) Brussels 70–1; (September 1996) Norway 195; (October 1996) Dublin 255; (1997) 195
supporting purposes 4
UN 261, 272, 274
WEU 50, 235, 249–77, 289–90, 296
Yugoslavia (former) 178, 198, 224
Naumann, General Klaus 53, 85, 96, 102, 104
report (January 1992) 83–4
Nerlich, Uwe 82
Nixon, Richard 16, 242
North Atlantic
 Consultative Council 290
 Cooperation Council (NACC) 19, 44, 90–1, 184, 228, 252, 269, 284–5, 291
 Council (NAC) 24, 66, 71, 97, 188–90, 189, 253; Oslo meeting (June 1992) 42, 279–80
 Treaty 124, 132, 274
Norway, NATO, summit meeting, (September 1996) 195
Nuremberg (December 1996), 'Strategic Concept' 75

OECD 238
Office for Democratic Institutions and Human Rights 264
Organization for Security and Cooperation in Europe (OSCE) 2, 8, 25–8, 89, 92–4, 132–4, 151–2, 154–6, 176–7, 180–2, 196–7, 204, 208–9, 212, 227, 232, 261, 290–1
division of labour 268
monitoring missions 268
peacekeeping operations 268, 273
responsibilities 265–6, 279
role 269–70

Organization for Security (*Cont.*)
  summit meetings, (1994) 270
  summits, (1992) Helsinki 89, 266–7, 280
OSCE *see* Organization for Security and Cooperation in Europe (OSCE)
Oslo, NATO ministerial meeting (June 1992) 42, 279–80

Palestine 120, 255–6
Paris
  accords 166
  Charter 56, 155
  stability pacts conference (May 1994) 265
  summit meeting (November 1990) 42–3
Partnership for Peace (PfP) 19–20, 22, 24, 184, 228, 269, 285, 290
PDM-25 212, 215
peace-enforcing/keeping, operations 82, 257–71; *see also* NATO; UN; US
Perry, Secretary William 172, 195
Petersberg Declaration (June 1992) 20–1, 26, 96, 251, 291
Poland 91, 93, 286, 291
Policy Coordination Group (PCG) 71
Ponsonby Rule (1924) 15
Portugal 250
post-Cold War Europe 48–9, 88, 119–20, 194, 300–2, 305
  security structure 2–3, 83–108, 190–1, 291, 294
post-Communist world 288–9
Powell, General Colin 169, 171, 173
power politics vs transformation of interstate relations 241–3

Rapid Reaction Force 22, 34, 41, 51, 106–7, 211, 258–9, 263–4
Reagan, President Ronald, administration 168
risks and threats 223–32
Rognoni, Virgilio 122
Rogue States (Libya, Iran, Sudan and Cuba) 198, 229, 231–2

Rome, NATO summit meeting (November 1991) 42, 184, 250, 284–5
Roosevelt, President Franklin D. 10
Rose, General Sir Michael 31
Roseta (Italian) 272
Rühe, Volker 83–4, 90–1, 93–5, 98, 100–2, 105, 107, 109, 193, 203, 282, 286
  Prague speech (1993) 95
Rühl, Lothar 85
Rühle, Hans 85
Russia 85–6, 210, 215, 223, 227, 229, 231, 236, 243, 262, 269
  arms control negotiations 239
  CIS partners 86; *see also* CIS (Commonwealth of Independent States)
  foreign policy 87, 90
  Germany relations 92
  IFOR 228
  NATO 153–5, 194–6, 206, 231, 286, 291–2
  peacekeeping operations 268
  Yugoslavia (former) 293–4
Russian Federation 8, 13–14
Rwanda 107, 226, 260

SACEUR (Supreme Allied Command in Europe) (NATO) 23–4, 63–4, 251, 254, 263
SACLANT (Supreme Allied Commander Atlantic) 24
Salatiello, General Luigi 123
San Francisco, Charter 258
Scandinavia 6
Scharping, Rudolf 94
Schäuble, Wolfgang 97
Scholz, Rupert 86
security policy frameworks 232–6
Serbia 48, 166
Seville, NATO summit meeting (September 1994) 52
Shalikasvili, General John 50–1, 53, 171–3, 178
SHAPE (Supreme Headquarters Allied Powers Europe) 23, 65–6
Sigonella, incident (1985) 119

Sinai 119
Slovenia 46, 56, 87, 99, 165, 242
Smith, Admiral Leighton E. 191
Somalia 95, 120, 122, 128, 131, 225, 228, 281
Soviet Union 89, 197, 223
  threat 49, 55, 147–53, 249, 252
  see also Russia
Spain 256
Stability Pacts 264–5, 272, 291
Standing Naval Force Mediterranean (STANAVFORMED) 253
Stercken, Hans 87
strategic outlook 222–48
  China and Russia, policies towards 231
  differences: weight, likelihood of different scenarios 229–32
  entanglement and abandonment 233–6
  institutional arrangements 232–4
  interests and shared values 236–43
  non-military vs military contingencies 226–7
  regional vs global orientations 229–32
  restoration of failed states 227–9
strategic void 290–3, *see also* strategic outlook
Stuttgart, Christopher, Warren (September 1996) 270

Tarnoff, Peter 158
Tashkent, Treaty of (15 May 1992) 86
Thatcher, Margaret
  Bruges speech (1987) 17
  Reagan–Bush relationship 10, 16
Transatlantic Free Trade Area (TAFTA) 210
Turin, intergovernmental conference (March 1996) 11–12, 17, 99, 255
Turkey 102–3, 132

UN (United Nations) 2, 146, 178, 279, 294
  adjustments to peacekeeping operations 260–4
  Administration and Management Department 260
  Cambodia (UNTAC) 228
  Charter 27, 89, 100, 152, 228, 235, 264
  conflict prevention and crisis management 177
  General Assemblies: (May 1991) 263; (September 1992) 169
  General-Secretary 257–8
  Gulf crisis 162
  Italy 135, 214
  mandates 198
  NATO relations 65, 272
  OSCE interface 181–2, 249–77
  peacekeeping 3, 160, 169, 171, 260, 291; Affairs Department 215; missions 178, 235, 253, 295; Operations 214–15, 258; Department of 171, 260; report (1996) 260; troops 105
  Secretary-General 268
  Security Council 11, 34–5, 47, 89, 95, 133, 178, 208, 232; arms embargo resolutions 271; Britain 212; mandates 225, 233; no-fly zone 253, 258; reform 135; resolutions 65, 165, 258, 261, 263; safe areas 254; standing force 280; Yugoslavia (former) 3, 46–7, 264
United States 139–221
  armed forces 183
  bilateral relations 200–14
  Bosnia 9, 159, 172–3, 175, 211–12
  Britain relations 6, 209–12
  collective security 139, 145–7, 175–83, 215
  Combined Joint Task Forces (CJTF) 251
  conflict prevention and crisis-management 177–83, 255–6

European security 9–10, 160–4, 283, 291
United States (*Cont.*)
European Union 141
foreign policy 139–40, 142–3, 149–50, 160–1, 169, 176, 216, 229, 241
France relations 187–8, 193, 205–9, 231
Germany relations 193, 200–5
IFOR 172–3, 175, 273
interests 141–7
Italy relations 212–14
leadership 99, 239, 273, 289, 293, 295–6
military 163, 168, 170–2, 178–9, 226–7
multilateral peace operations 168, 171, 173, 197, 214–16
National Security Revitalization Act (1995) 174
NATO 149–50, 153–6, 183–96
out-of-area 196–200
post-Cold War security agenda 190–1
preferred, necessary and possible 167–73
'Reforming Multilateral Peace Operations' (May 1994) 171
structural ambivalence 160–4
threats 147–67
UN 170; peacekeeping operations 173–5, 214
War Powers Act 227
Yugoslavia (former) 50, 144, 147, 156–60, 164–7
UNPROFOR 27, 51, 53, 67, 69, 105–6, 166, 172, 178, 191, 229, 253–4
Bosnia 22, 226, 234, 243, 281
Bosnia-Herzegovina 258, 263
European participants 234
IFOR transfer 263
troops 261, 271

Vance, Cyrus, Owen, David plan 51
Vietnam 167

Visegrad Group 19–20, 90, 92, 149, 284
Voigt, Karsten 94

Walesa, Lech 269–70
Warsaw Pact 25, 65, 89, 249, 252, 278
Washington Treaty 21, 55–6, 81, 96, 198–9, 251–2
Weinberger, Caspar 168–9
Powell, General Colin, doctrine 171–2, 226–7
'Uses of Military Power' 168–9
Western, cooperation 19–25, 122, 125–34; *see also* Organization for Security and Cooperation in Europe (OSCE)
WEU (Western European Union) 7, 23–8, 74, 90, 95–6, 99–100, 186
Adriatic arms embargo 258
chain of command 73
Council 72, 271
crisis-management and peace-enforcement 257–8
future of 20–1
infrastructure 291
NATO double-hatting system 64
Noordwijk declaration (November 1994) 271
operational capabilities 61
post-Berlin accords on Combined Joint Task Offices 7, 71
summit meetings 35
Yugoslavia (former) 272
Wider Peacekeeping document 30
Wilson, Harold, Johnson, Lyndon 16
Wilson, Thomas Woodrow, idealism 142–6, 158–9, 200, 206, 209, 302
Wörner, Manfred 41, 269, 280

Yeltsin, Boris 148–50, 231, 269, 285
government 152, 177
Yom Kippur war (1973) 198
Young, Thomas-Durell 84
Yugoslavia (former) 1, 3, 9, 15, 28–9, 47, 65, 67–8, 87, 89, 95,

98–9, 105–8, 116, 120, 122–3, 128, 184, 189, 191–2, 198, 244–5, 278–9
collective security 294
crisis 45–6
France 45–7, 50–4, 59–60, 67–70
IFOR 10, 12
NATO 178, 198, 224
peacekeeping 259
in retrospect 164–7, 293–5
Russia 293–4
security problem 234
UN 3
United States 50, 144, 147, 156–60
UNPROFOR 10, 12
Western policies towards 238–9